J.K. LASSER'S™
PERSONAL FINANCIAL PLANNER

1 9 8 8

J.K. LASSER'S™

PERSONAL FINANCIAL PLANNER

1 9 8 8

by
Judith Headington McGee CFP

with the assistance of:
Donald Adair; Ronald Brock, JD; Jerrold
Dickson; and Robert Irwin
Edited by Jack E. Jennings and Jay Wurts, MBA

J. K. LASSER
TAX INSTITUTE
New York

ACKNOWLEDGMENTS

We wish to thank the following friends and colleagues for helping to make this book possible:

Marv Tuttle	Steve Davis
Michael Vitkauskas	Phil Wilson
Venita Van Caspel	Colin (Ben) Coombs
Allan Feldman	George C. Huff
Jeremy Black	Allen Peterson, II
Loren Dutton	Mitchell T. Curtis
Andy Rich	Diane P. Blakeslee
Judith Cowan Zabalaoui	George Cranmer
Brenda S. Payne	Charles Brandes
Robert E. Cole	Claire S. Longdon
Luke V. McCarthy	Ronald Kaiser
John A. Watson	Avery Neumark
Nic Pilger	

J. H. M.

 J. K. LASSER TAX INSTITUTE

Simon & Schuster, Inc.
Gulf+Western Building
One Gulf+Western Plaza
New York, NY 10023

Interior designed by BMR, Mill Valley, California
Illustrated by David Gross
Produced by BMR, Mill Valley, California

J. K. Lasser and the J. K. Lasser Tax Institute
are trademarks of Simon & Schuster, Inc.

DISTRIBUTED BY PRENTICE HALL TRADE

Manufactured in the United States of America

1 2 3 4 5 6 7 8 9 10

ISBN 0-13-510504-8

Publisher's Note: *J.K. Lasser's Personal Financial Planner* is published in recognition of the great need for clarification of personal financial and tax matters for millions of men and women. We believe the research and interpretation by the authors and the J.K. Lasser Tax Institute to be authoritative and will be of general help to readers. Readers are cautioned, however, that this book is sold with the understanding that, although every care has been taken in the preparation of the text, the Publisher is not engaged in rendering legal, accounting, financial, or other professional service. Readers with specific problems are urged to seek the professional advice of a certified financial planner, an accountant, or lawyer.

CONTENTS

PREFACE

Today, financial planning presents not a choice but a necessity. People cannot function with market volatility as we experienced on October 19, 1987, when the Dow culminated its fall of over one thousand points, tumbling from the high of 2,722 reached during the previous month. The total value of stocks on the market fell from a peak of $3.3 trillion in September to a low of $2.3 trillion in late October. Over one third of this country's wealth was lost during the Black Monday crisis.

Financial planning becomes more important than ever in these uncertain times. Although a recession, a depression, or another Black Monday is inescapable at some point in the future, by following the principles explained in this book, individuals can avoid being excessively harmed or distressed during an economic crisis. To protect you and your assets as you make them grow is one of the main reasons we have written this book.

It is important, too, of course, that we have strong leadership in government—one that will assume fiscal responsibility and exercise more prudent control of the economy. The fall of the Dow sent a strong signal to Washington: More conservative policies on budget deficits and trade deficits are vital. Faith in the dollar must be restored to put confidence back into our economic system. In this regard, individuals do not have much control, other than by voicing an opinion and voting for what government policy should be.

In the past, financial planning was played much like a football game: The coach could take time to sit back and watch the plays, talk to his men, and decide what to do between offensive and defensive plays. But in today's financial world, to continue the sports analogy, we play a kind of fast-paced dynamic basketball in constant motion.

I believe that what we have experienced in late 1987 will bring about a consciousness that will reach a new intensity. When reading the chapters in this book which discuss emotionalism and how people deal with investments, I am sure that many events, including the shooting of the Merrill Lynch stockbroker, will come into focus. Once fear is instilled in the public, this fear can be built up by the media—a form of "media mania" during a time of crisis. People lose their sense of logic and panic—an example of the "herd instinct." If people do not have the right asset allocations in place and do not seek advice from financial planners, they most likely will panic, moving investments at the wrong time.

More individuals in this country need to become fiscally responsible by using financial planning tools and by accepting the fact that they have a responsibility for their own security. Today, most people know what a trade deficit is, understand the markets, and understand that when the market gets undisciplined it can become tragic.

But, the individual savings rate in this country remains a basic problem, and it puts pressure on the liquidity that we face in government. We have become too much of a consumer society. Consumerism has to be kept in balance. To strengthen our national economy, and to build individual wealth, it is imperative that we bring our savings and investments back to more normal levels.

When making investment decisions, one creates a point of departure: One's money is being directed to do something specific; one is not speculating. From this point on, one is also cautiously measuring his or her risk tolerance in case of a sudden crisis.

The term "asset allocation" is more important today than ever before. Putting all of one's money into one investment, whether in oil and gas as in the early 80s, or in the stock market as in the mid-late 80s, makes one vulnerable to an economic shakedown in that particular market sector. Remember, it is extremely important to allocate assets among different types of investment categories—such as money market instruments, stocks and mutual funds, commodities and precious metals, and real estate—as well as to diversify within each investment category.

Looking ahead into 1988, we foresee lower interest rates, lower inflation, and as a result a tremendous bond rally. Smaller investors will be reluctant to re-enter the stock markets. They will also be looking at income-producing funds as alternative investments that will not have the volatility pressures of the market itself. As we see these interest rates falling, inflation staying low, and some tendency to increase taxes in 1988, we foresee that a new base will be built for financial instruments in this country.

If individuals invest prudently and look upon money management as a dynamic and long-term proposition; if they use the principles of the painless budget, and of dollar-cost averaging; and above all follow the fundamentals of asset allocation, they will not be as easily affected during a market tragedy. And, they will build the long-term wealth that all of us strive for and most assuredly deserve.

Judith Headington McGee

INTRODUCTION

J. K. Lasser's Personal Financial Planner 1988, the only self-assessment, financial planning, and investment book of its kind, will help you win the personal money management game in the 1990s. No other single volume gives you

- Up-to-date professional advice on how to establish and implement your own comprehensive financial plan
- A complete guide to 64 investment opportunities along with up-to-the-minute information on their prospects for 1988
- All the basics of money management and investment strategy—plus tips for making financial decisions the way the pros do
- Insights into your money-related needs, goals, values, and investing behavior—all factors that affect your ability to build and keep net worth
- Annual advice on allocating your resources in a way that fits your needs and priorities, and optimizes your portfolio's safety and return

In short, this book addresses the *heart* (Part I—how you feel about money and making money-related decisions), the *head* (Parts II and III—knowledge about financial planning and investments), and the *hands* (Part IV—how to implement your plan) of total financial planning.

If you are an experienced money manager, this book will help you accomplish your financial goals more quickly and cost effectively—saving thousands of dollars in unnecessary fees, disappointing investments, and inappropriate financial products. If you're only beginning to build your wealth, this book will give you the facts and confidence you need to build a sound defensive financial base for future offensive, wealth-creating investments. Although this book is no substitute for personalized legal and tax counseling, *J. K. Lasser's Personal Financial Planner 1988* will help you deal with all financial professionals—from planning advisors to product salespeople—more knowledgeably and effectively. And if you update your J. K. Lasser's money management library with each year's revised edition of the *Personal Financial Planner* you'll stay abreast of the new tax laws, changing financial regulations, winners and losers in the investment marketplace, and the overall economic environment for the coming year.

YOUR KEYS TO MORE EFFECTIVE MONEY MANAGEMENT

Throughout this book, you'll find the following symbols near critical parts of the text. They are your reminders to take certain actions, refer to other parts of the book, or seek advice from outside counselors in matters that are crucial to your financial health.

Throughout this book, you'll also encounter various lists of top-performing investments, as well as lists of special vehicles (such as exotic assets or mutual funds that invest for special objectives); charts showing the general characteristics of, and next year's prospects for, specific investment vehicles—your "almanac," in short, of current financial markets. Although we've endeavored to make these lists as complete and timely as possible, you should seek the advice of your own financial advisors before making any specific investment.

About the Authors

Judith Headington McGee, C.F.P., is founder and senior financial planner for Associated Investment Advisers, a firm that provides financial planning for clients in 11 western states from offices in Spokane and Seattle, Washington. She is past national president of the Institute of Certified Financial Planners Educational Foundation.

Don Adair is a freelance writer and marketing consultant to financial service firms.

Ronald L.Brock, J.D., a member of the Editorial Board of the *Real Estate Securities Journal,* the NASD, and the IAFP, teaches graduate courses in a variety of financial subjects at the University of California, Berkeley; and Golden Gate University in San Francisco.

Jerrold D. Dickson is the executive editor of Bailard, Biehl, & Kaiser's investment advisory letter, *You & Your Money,* and editor of *Futures Truth,* a monthly newsletter for futures traders.

Robert Irwin is the author of more than a dozen authoritative investment and real estate works.

Lasser's Personal Financial Keys

 This is the symbol for *investment strength*. It tells you how that particular investment vehicle adds growth (capital appreciation), current income, inflation protection, liquidity, or tax shelter benefits to your personal portfolio.

 This symbol represents *investment risk*—your warning that one or more characteristic weaknesses of that investment type may be at work in your portfolio. These risks include business failure, market (asset price) volatility, interest rate fluctuations, inflation losses, deflation losses, or loss of principal (or profits) due to asset illiquidity.

 When you see this symbol, you should seriously reflect on the human factors behind the financial decision in question. Although you'll find the symbol most often around discussions of risk, other emotional or lifestyle issues may be involved—so you'll want to review the factors discussed in Part I that apply to you.

 This symbol marks the asset allocation percentage limit appropriate to risk-sensitive or risk-averse investors.

 This symbol marks the asset allocation percentage limit appropriate to risk-tolerant investors.

 When time is of the essence, you'll see this symbol—your reminder that the timing of the action or decision in question is *critical*. Areas requiring quick reaction include market timing opportunities, special trading techniques, and calendar (tax-related or investment) deadlines.

These symbols remind you that the investment vehicle in question is extra sensitive to a market's *investment climate*—of significance to both "bullish" offensive- and "bearish" defensive-minded investors.

 This symbol appears wherever the investment vehicle has important *tax consequences*—for ordinary income or capital gains, or to flag useful tax-exempt or tax-deferred investments.

 This symbol is your reminder to *record this information* for future financial planning or tax-reporting purposes.

 This symbol appears whenever independent professional advice (CPA, attorney, tax preparer, or other) is critical to making an informed financial decision.

 This symbol tells you to take extra precautions (examine a deal more closely; do more homework about the market, the economy, or your own investment objectives; or read the fine print of the contract or prospectus) when you encounter the problem or opportunity described.

 This symbol marks every J. K. Lasser *money management tip*—hints for more efficient and effective portfolio management.

PART I

PERSONALITIES AND LIFESTYLES

Can you picture a world filled with money but no people? Of course not—people earn, save, invest, and spend money to satisfy human wants and needs. In Part I, you'll learn more about yourself as a breadwinner and investor, and see why people who ignore the human side of financial planning often finish second best.

1

CHAPTER 1

YOUR FINANCIAL ATTITUDES AND VALUES

A GLANCE AHEAD

In this chapter, you'll discover

- *Why people in the coming decades will be less economically secure than previous generations were*
- *How your attitudes about earning, saving, investing, and spending affect your wealth-building potential*
- *How financial planning is the only reliable way to increase your personal net worth—the money muscle you need to get the things you want*

THE ECONOMICS OF PERSONAL FINANCE

After a generation of spectacular growth, capped with the ominous stock market crash of "Black Monday," October 19, 1987, the U.S. economy is cooling off—entering a plateau of stablized growth between now and the end of the century. Two-income households are now the rule, not the exception; and homeownership, for those who failed to buy before the late 1970s, is a more distant dream than ever. Health care and college costs have outstripped inflation; and mergers, acquisitions, and foreign competition have made job security, like the traditional nuclear family, little more than a pleasant memory. It's an economy that will reward those people who understand their goals and build their assets accordingly, and will punish the ones who think that tomorrow—inevitably—will turn out like today.

Your task as breadwinner and investor in this environment is to develop an offensive plan that builds, and a defensive plan that protects, your personal *net worth*—the best measure of anyone's ability to live a secure and comfortable life. To begin that process, you must take a new look at an old problem most Americans wish would simply take care of itself: money—and what it *really* means to you.

Taking Your Money Personally

Money—or the lack of it—has always played a big role in the way we Americans define ourselves. We value educated, successful people, yet despite the increased demand, college costs have grown beyond the reach of all but the wealthiest (or brainiest) Americans. We value our leisure time and the nonmaterial side of life, yet we regularly subordinate our personal interests to the endless treadmill of "earn and spend"—seldom remembering to pay ourselves first (save and invest) from the product of our labor. The point is, money is the fuel for our society and our personal aspirations. It fires the engine of our economy, creating opportunities and wealth; greases the wheels of industry, creating jobs and life-enhancing products; and provides charities and our public sector agencies the wherewithal they need to serve us and protect us. Like it or not, money is the very "mother's milk" of a healthy and rewarding life.

Of course, what's true on a national scale is doubly true for individuals, couples, and families. We may earn and spend our money in a million different ways, but there are still only a few basic wants and needs.

Money as Power. Because of its ability to satisfy desires (achieve goals and mitigate or avoid calamities), a wealthy person has options that poor people lack—a fact that will come as a surprise to no one. But when that wealth is held by one person in a relationship (an employer versus an employee, one spouse versus another, a government official versus a needy citizen), that person can control the quality and direction of that relationship—at least to the extent that the other person feels dependent on the things that money can buy. From this perspective, money is more than a medium of exchange for goods and services—it is the vehicle of freedom itself.

Money as Magic. In a sophisticated, developed economy, money's ability to transform one thing into another seems to fulfill the alchemist's dream of turning base matter into gold. When you're wealthy enough, your ability to transform life's raw materials (time, talent, energy, and good health) into pleasure, prestige, and security is virtually unlimited.

Money as Emotion. When it comes to expressing your feelings, money can help even the most inarticulate voice sing out with affection. From purchasing a ready-made greeting card to bestowing yachts, diamonds, and vacations on a loved one, money has become, for some, the virtual language of love.

Money, Values, and Lifestyles

In his book *The Nine American Lifestyles,* SRI International researcher Arnold Mitchell describes how cultural values, beliefs, and personal drives combine with economic privilege or necessity to form a portrait of U.S. society. This typology, called "VALS" for the comprehensive "values and lifestyles" questionnaire used to gather Arnold's data, has rapidly become the basis for many marketing and financial decisions made throughout America. Here is a brief look at the nine VALS categories. Do you recognize yourself in one of them?

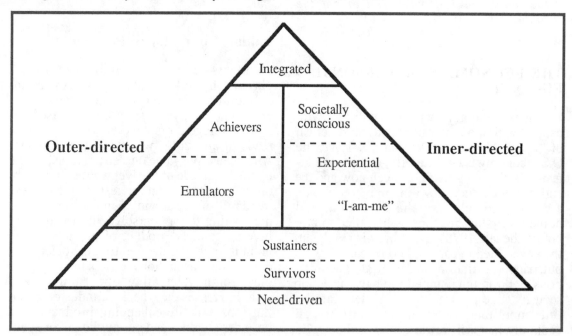

Figure 1-1 The VALS categories

The Need-driven Groups. Although they comprise a relatively small percentage of the total population (around 11%), the VALS *Survivors* and *Sustainers* receive a lot of press and reflect many people's worst fears about a depressed financial future. Survivors tend to be old (their median age is 65), female (women live longer than men), and desperately short of income—living from one paycheck (or relief check) to another. Although almost half of all Survivors own their homes, the houses are sometimes hovels and only a handful have assets in excess of $50,000—few of which contribute to their sorely needed income. Financial planning for Survivors tends to center around the concerns of the poor and elderly—meeting living expenses and those medical costs not covered by federal or private insurance.

Their younger, more numerous counterparts, the Sustainers, experience many similar problems, but, unlike Survivors, they have hopes of improving their condition. Because they seek to rise above their economic hardships (many are from disadvantaged minority groups), they view money as a tool for social mobility—sometimes getting in over their heads in debt when they try to move too fast. Although they, too, live paycheck to paycheck, their ability to earn and expand that income is significantly greater than the fatalistic Survivors. For these people, financial planning—learning to manage and build what few resources they have—can mean the difference between entry into the sunshine of the American middle class or another generation of poverty.

The Outer-directed Groups. Above this economic "underbelly" of U.S. society, the VALS typology splits into two segments: one inner-directed (concerned with personal and societal development) and the other outer-directed, comprised of those more concerned with material wealth and status.

At the base of the outer-directed segment, the *Belongers* resemble what most people might call the traditional blue-collar or "lower-middle" class. They prefer to live in small towns or rural areas in the company of like-minded citizens who reflect traditional, conservative values. Church or family ties provide their strongest sense of community, and as a rule they tend to like things pretty much the way they are—and "always have been." Financially, they are conservative spenders, avoiding consumer debt, and believe in building net worth throughout their lives—a whopping 82% own their own homes, with almost a third of those holding no mortgage! For Belongers, financial planning offers a way to keep what they have earned and preserve their treasured lifestyle for the generation that will follow.

Just above the Belongers on the VALS hierarchy are the youthful (median age under 30) *Emulators:* those who admire, pursue—but have not quite reached—life in the economic fast lane. Emulators tend to be hardworking and ambitious, prefer urban life, and fill the many clerical, service, and crafts jobs that lie just below the really remunerative professional positions to which they ultimately aspire—hence the name Emulator. Although their incomes are significantly higher than the need-driven types, they teeter on the edge of insolvency because of their drive to live—or at least appear to live—the good life. Financial planning for Emulators involves learning the basic disciplines of saving and investing—not just for security, but for the additional education, social mobility, and luxuries their values and lifestyle demand.

At the top of the outer-directed groups sit the objects of all this emulation, the VALS *Achievers*—the very model for the American dream. Achievers comprise the heart of the U.S. middle and upper-middle class: their median age lies well above aspiring Emulators and well below the less ambitious Survivor and Belonger groups. They tend to have solid marriages, children of all ages (including those in college), and just under a third of them boast at least some college themselves. They tend to be economically and politically conservative, distrust too much government or "social engineering," and are optimistic about the power of free enterprise to solve just about any kind of problem. Their average incomes are higher than any other group, and theyparticipate in the full range of financial and investment activities—including liberal use of debt to increase or sustain their chosen lifestyle. Of these, 87% own their own homes (including townhouses and condominiums)—the highest of any VALS group. About a third of all Achievers regard themselves as "financial experts"—a proportion, curiously enough, exceeded only by Sustainers, whose ideas about making and handling money undoubtedly reflect the lessons learned on meaner streets than Wall Street. Still, it's an example of how initial self-perceptions are not always best when it comes to the emotional subject of money. Financial planning for Achievers, consequently, is less an option than a necessity. Not only do they have more assets to employ and protect, but—by virtue of their investing and spending power—the rest of the economy depends heavily on their success as well.

The Inner-directed Groups. Parallel to the outer-directed Belongers, the first rung on the ladder of inner-directed lifestyles is the youngest of all (median age, 21 years), the *I-Am-Me* group; so-called because of its preoccupation with self-identity in a world that seems busy with other things. Although I-Am-Me's tend to hold lower-paying jobs, they view this situation as transitory, as if fate (if not their own effort) will eventually lift them to a higher quality of life—possibly because many grew up in the households of materially successful Belongers or Achievers. They tend to be socially aware, yet, because of their preoccupation with self, unengaged by social issues. They are spenders, rather than savers, and are ambivalent about financial security—probably because of their youth. Financial planning for people in this youngest, more intelligent, but somewhat alienated group means defining their career and life goals and moving forward in a way that will allow them to enjoy the fruits of their labor as they earn them—and discover who they are along the way.

Slightly older than the I-Am-Me's are the VALS *Experientials* with a median age of 27. These individuals are well-educated (38% are college graduates), politically liberal, and prefer to live in the West—mostly in small towns or suburbs. Although they are moderately concerned with money, their predominantly professional or other well-paying jobs allow them to focus on the less material aspects of life. As the name implies, Experientials are interested in experiencing first hand what life has to offer. They are more confident than the less mature I-Am-Me's, and tend to be active in social and political issues.

Financially, they respect the freedom money gives them and are pragmatic, if unstudied, money managers rather than big spenders or investors. For Experientials, financial planning means learning to make full use of a wider variety of financial markets—from individual stocks and bonds to mutual funds and real estate investments—as these are the appropriate vehicles for the financial independence their values and lifestyles demand.

Capping the inner-directed groups are the highly educated (58% are college graduate), liberal, and affluent VALS *Societally Conscious* group—the group with the highest number of intellectually oriented, professional, or technical occupations. Although they have benefitted greatly from the current socioeconomic "system," they tend to believe that our system needs repair and subscribe to views that most other groups would consider "progressive." Although their income and assets are often substantial, the Societally Conscious are not strongly motivated by material gain or the status normally given to wealth. For them, money is a tool for achieving personal and societal objectives. Consequently, their financial plans must reflect unusual flexibility—a balance between income and growth and the capability to shift assets quickly when a need or opportunity presents itself.

The Integrated (Combined Inner- and Outer-directed) Group. At the top of the VALS hierarchy stands the emotionally, intellectually, and financially mature *Integrated* group—a scant 2% of the U.S. population. This group has managed to combine and balance the outer-directed groups' striving for material success with the inner-directed groups' concern for social harmony and personal self-fulfillment. Obviously, such a rare and elusive group is difficult to pin down (even with the aid of the complex VALS questionnaire), and estimates about its composition, demographics, attitudes, and financial habits are still little more than conjecture. The VALS researchers, however, were able to make two startling conclusions about this most amazing and impressive group.

First, *Integrateds seem to be the ultimate destination of all VALS types.* As you may have noticed, the VALS typology formed not only a hierarchy (beginning with a bottom layer of disadvantaged, need-driven groups and ending with a group that has achieved concurrent material and psychological success), but it suggests paths of growth toward that destination. Thus, a Sustainer might pull him- or herself into the ranks of Emulators, accumulate enough wealth and success to become an Achiever, then seek to balance an overly material lifestyle with the inner-directed pursuits of the Experiential or Societally Conscious. When the pendulum has swung too far in the direction of self-actualization (suppose, for example, that the person begins to suffer financially from these expensive and less remunerative pursuits), a new respect for economic achievement will reassert itself—but in harmony with that person's new inner-directed insights. Thus the long-sought, if hazily defined, goal of becoming a truly integrated person will have been achieved.

Second, *a surprising number of both inner- and outer-directed people view themselves as already belonging to the Integrated group.* A curious result of ongoing VALS research is the number of people who, when queried during seminars, identify themselves with the Integrated group—even though they clearly belong to other VALS types. This convinced Arnold—as it convinces many others—that people *do* generally aspire to a balanced life: one that permits personal fulfillment and societal contribution within the framework of financial security and material comfort.

This very natural human desire to eventually "have it all"—to live a balanced, secure, productive, and rewarding life—is what successful financial planning, and this book, are all about.

Ways and Means of Attaining a Desired Lifestyle

At the beginning of 1987, *U.S. News & World Report* took a survey of the U.S. socioeconomic landscape and came up with this conclusion:

The U.S. is still the richest country in the world, with the resources to improve its competitive posture if it puts its mind to it. The American economy is about triple Ja-pan's and six times West Germany's. Over the past six years, the U.S. has produced 10 million new jobs while Western Europe has lost 1.4 million. Inflation has fallen to its lowest annual level in 25 years—a 1.1% rise in consumer prices last year [1986]. Interest rates and the dollar's value are down and may ease further, perhaps spurring economic growth. American productivity is improving faster, rising 4.4% in 1985. And quality is on the rebound in some industries.

Looking at even broader indicators of macroeconomic health, observers found that in the second quarter of 1987, even the U.S. trade deficit—a record for any nation in the history of the planet—began to look as if it might become manageable as a weakening dollar made U.S. goods more attractive on foreign markets. Even so vocal a critic of current U.S. trade policies as MIT economist Lester Thurow acknowledges that despite its awesome heft, the trade deficit is still a relatively small fraction of the total American gross national product (GNP)—the value of all the goods and services we produce in a single year. The effects of the October 19, 1987 stock market collapse, although dramatic, seem (at our date of publication, at least) to have left the larger economy unscathed.

What does this mean to the personal financial planner in the years ahead?

First, it means that while our personal financial health has always been tied to a robust national economy, that well-being is now equally dependent on financial, product, and service markets throughout the world. Need-driven, outer-directed, inner-directed, and well-Integrated breadwinners and investors must now think in terms of global markets, multiple-asset categories, and assets that assume both offensive and defensive postures in a personal portfolio, as well as the satisfaction of personal wants and needs.

Second, it means that most of the responsibility for this new and highly customized strategy lies with *you* —the breadwinner and investor—and no one else. You must sift through the veritable avalanche of financial product and service information and screen out the nuggets that apply to you: your needs, your plans, and your aspirations.

No government agency, no university professor, no broadcast financial guru, no storefront financial planner is going to do this for you. Only *you* can diagnose your own true wants and needs, money-related attitudes, earning capabilities, and investment resources. Only then will you be ready and able to devise and implement the wealth-building and wealth-protecting plan that's right for you.

FOUR STEPS TO MASTERING YOUR FINANCIAL FUTURE

This book is divided into four parts, each of which is crucial to designing and implementing a comprehensive and successful financial plan. Because your lifestyle, goals, and values will place you in a different position from other readers, you may use the book in the way that suits you best: as a textbook on both the fundamentals and advanced concepts of financial planning, or as a reference encyclopedia for "a la carte" investment decision making.

If you are a novice money manager, you may want to read the book straight through, skipping only those parts that deal with sophisticated investments, advanced trading techniques, or specialized products aimed at the needs of wealthier or more experienced investors. If you are a reader who already has substantial assets and experience in financial markets, you may read only those chapters that apply to the investment opportunities or asset allocation decisions you currently face.

In Part I: Personalities and Lifestyles

In Chapter 2, you'll learn the reasons why most successful people eventually turn to financial planning to take control of their lives and how those different situations lead to different needs, goals, and outcomes. You'll see how individual personalities affect one's ability to take, or avoid, the risks that are part of every financial decision and how certain investment vehicles fit some personalities better than others.

In Chapter 3, you'll see how spending needs and asset growth tend to follow predictable patterns over the course of a lifetime and how your personal financial plan can—and must—reflect reality at every stage of life. You'll discover that the wealth-building, wealth-protecting, and portfolio management tools that are right for you depend as much on your personality and goals as on the ups and downs of specific markets.

In Part II: Money Management and Investment Strategies

In Chapter 4, you'll explore every side of financial planning—from short-term cash management to long-range retirement and estate planning. You'll understand and compute your current net worth and find the strengths and weaknesses of your present financial position. Most important of all, you'll discover the secret of *multiple-asset allocation*—investing in a carefully chosen mix of financial markets that, by responding *independently* to world economic forces, help ensure the steady growth of your portfolio.

In Chapter 5, you'll master the interdependency of time and money: the mechanics of investing and the cyclical nature of financial markets. You'll learn how to plan investments in a way that makes time work for you and avoids the ravages of inflation—regardless of your earning capacity and desired lifestyle. You'll examine the differences between, and strengths and weaknesses of, debt and equity instruments; how to construct offensive and defensive segments of your personal portfolio; and how to find qualified and reliable advisors in the financial planning process.

In Chapters 6 and 7, you'll look further into the future to learn the do's and don'ts of retirement and estate planning—before your heirs and dependents are required to solve those problems for you.

In Chapter 8, you'll review the opportunities and pitfalls of the new era of "tax reduction and simplification" and see if you are really one of those who'll benefit from—or pay higher taxes because of—this often misunderstood legislation.

In Part III: Investment Guide to 68 Product Opportunities

Here's where you'll get to the very heart of your wealth-building plan: designing your multiple asset portfolio from an extensive menu of investment vehicles—analyzed and presented in a way that reflects a variety of goals and investing attitudes.

In Chapters 9 through 14, you'll explore the six basic asset categories: near-money instruments, such as money market funds and short-term certificates of deposit; domestic (U.S.) stocks; fixed-income investments, such as U.S. Treasury issues and corporate bonds; real estate (both individual and group investments); international securities that tap the breadth and depth of the new global economy; and commodities and precious metals. In addition, you'll learn which investments the experts pick as the best performers for growth, income, and safety in 1988 and how to establish the multiple-asset allocations that will build and protect your portfolio.

In Chapters 15 and 16, you'll learn about special (and often high-risk) investing techniques, such as stock market options and commodity futures, that can increase your overall gains through profits from short-term trading. You'll also discover those exotic, one-of-a-kind investments—such as motion picture limited partnerships and oil and gas investments—that can provide both tax and wealth-building benefits to the right kind of investors.

In Chapter 17, you'll see if the tried-and-true route to retirement security through purchased annuities is right for you; and which forms of insurance—from standard term and whole life to the newer universal policies—will protect your assets and your loved ones best.

In Part IV: Establishing and Executing a Financial Plan

In this last section, you'll learn the techniques and short-cuts of putting—and keeping—your financial house in order.

In Chapter 18, you'll learn to evaluate a prospectus (the legal description of a security) the way the pros do and find out that what isn't said is often as important as the information the investment company provides.

In Chapter 19, you'll eavesdrop on some of the nation's leading investment advisors as they debate the financial future: the likely movement of all key markets in the upcoming year. You'll learn where the "smart money" (institutional and the superrich investor) is going in 1988—and why—and use that knowledge to make your own asset allocations.

In Chapter 20, you'll find ways to get your own comprehensive financial plan under way: from locating specialist advisors to keeping appropriate records and coordinating the contributions of tax preparers, financial planners, family attorneys, and family members.

Finally, in Chapter 21, you will explore more fully the logic behind multiple-asset allocation as a wealth-building and wealth-protecting strategy. You'll learn where and when to use market timing and special investing techniques and when it's best to leave such methods to the experts.

CHAPTER 2

YOUR PERSONALITY AND FINANCIAL BEHAVIOR

A GLANCE AHEAD

People sometimes say one thing and do another—an expensive habit when the subject is money. In this chapter, you'll learn

- *How financial phobias and negative money feelings can undermine your wealth-building plan*
- *Why money-related homilies and folk wisdom—however beloved—make poor financial planning strategies*
- *About your own investing attitudes and behavior, and how to make those habits work for you*

Some people know how to get along with their money. They know how to get it and how to put it to work. They create financial strategies and stick with them. They know when to take financial risks and when to leave them alone. Their wealth just seems to grow, effortlessly. Just as importantly, they seem to know how and where to spend their money for maximum satisfaction. Others—the vast majority—only muddle through.

Why do some of us seem so comfortable with money while others are so clumsy? Obviously, it's not a question of intelligence—many very bright people are hopeless money managers. Background and upbringing can play a role, though not the only one. Aptitude and attitude are important too, although their influence, too, is limited.

The bare fact is that people do or don't do well with money for many complex reasons: emotions, attitudes, personality types, intellect—all can play a role.

Although there's no single way to turn poor money managers into good ones, there are many ways to make virtually any money manager better—to understand and modify the behavior that keeps him or her from achieving financial goals.

IN SEARCH OF THE RATIONAL INVESTOR

As long ago as the 1950s, economist Harry Markowitz established a theory for managing investment risk. Markowitz's landmark work came to be known as *modern portfolio theory,* and its underlying principles guide the multiple-asset allocation strategy that you'll use later in this book.

Using modern portfolio theory and multiple-asset allocation, investors can optimize risk and reward for long- and short-term paybacks. The concepts are time-tested, and everyone—big investors and small—can benefit from using them. Unfortunately, most investors don't.

The reason is quite simple: most people just aren't rational about money.

DISGUISING FINANCIAL PHOBIAS

Effective money management begins with intelligent household spending and progresses to offensive and defensive investment strategies, prudent tax, estate, retirement and insurance planning, and more. These elements join like links in a chain. If any one is too weak or underdeveloped, the entire system can fail—sometimes catastrophically. No wonder some people find the whole process simply too intimidating to contemplate.

Families that spend money capriciously never develop any real fiscal muscle. They get off on the wrong foot at once and never catch up with the crowd. Some people get further down the path toward security and wealth, but fall into well-worn planning potholes—inadequate insurance or incomplete wills. Others ignore the tax implications of their financial actions and literally give away much of their wealth. Some commit these fiscal sins out of an inability to face life's realities: the inevitability of death and taxes. Others become hypnotized by one or a few financial products or markets at the expense of all the others. Despite their sincere intentions, they never get ahead and can't understand why they don't.

Foremost among these all-too-human financial foibles is the investor who tries on a money management investment strategy that doesn't fit his or her investment and spending temperament.

BUILDING A MONEY MIND AND MONEY MUSCLES

Creating a more rational investment temperament is like building a stronger body: A portfolio needs room to grow, make mistakes, and develop its muscles. It requires care and feeding. It needs nurturing by someone who understands the ways of markets and its owner's point of view.

How Money Managers Go Wrong

Money managers go wrong when they use investing strategies with which they aren't completely comfortable. Sooner or later they begin tinkering—out of worry or impatience—and that's when a portfolio loses its ability to grow. Without realizing it, they trade away their assets until they end up with a few stocks or bonds that started out with lots of company, but end up as orphans: cashed in as soon as the first kid's college tuition comes due. What began as a grand scheme to build net worth becomes a discouraging exercise in complacency or anxiety.

Other underdeveloped investors become hyperinterested in their portfolio. They buy and sell on impulse—victims of hot tips or the movement of "the herd." They take bad advice and when it doesn't pay off, try to reposition themselves by selling losers and acquiring winners—buying high and selling low—the cardinal sin of all investing.

Invariably some irrational attitude or emotional foible interferes between themselves and profit, and their financial mind- and body-building program is undone.

How Money Managers Go Right

The key to successful money management is self-understanding. To be truly effective, your financial strategy must reflect who you really are, not who you would like to be and not who someone else thinks you should be. If your strategy doesn't fit your personality, you will unconsciously sabotage it. The irrational bad decisions of the many are what makes big profits for the few.

If this were a perfect world, we all would be free of emotional stumbling blocks. If it were simply a better world, we would recognize where we went wrong and smooth things out—we would all be perfect money managers.

But that isn't going to happen. And investors tend more to repeat than to learn from their mistakes; smart money managers avoid those mistakes to begin with. On the path toward this more rational, reality-based money management, everyone else gets stuck. When the barriers are shown in sharp relief, the financial path around them is much clearer and easier to take.

INDEX OF FINANCIAL COMFORT

Perhaps it is only fitting that George Washington's face should be forever associated with the image of money, for he was one of the wealthiest men in America. Historians have pointed out, however, that he had an obsession with wealth that made him exceedingly acquisitive, and he would insist upon the immediate payment of any money due him. At the same time Washington was a man of great integrity and had strong leadership abilities. When he voluntarily retired from office after his second term he furnished a worthy and time-honored example for later leaders of the nation.

We gave the Index of Financial Comfort to the subjects in the Success Group to discover just how comfortable or concerned successful individuals are with their financial situations. Are they worried that they'll never have enough to feel secure, or do they tend to feel comfortable and satisfied whatever their current positions? Of course, most score somewhere in between these extremes, but we did find a direct correlation between their attitudes on this test and their overall emotional well-being.

INSTRUCTIONS

In the Index of Financial Comfort, you will be presented with 20 statements about your feelings toward and experiences with money. Read each statement, and determine whether, for you, it is a true (T) or false (F) statement. Answer all the questions, and write your responses in the space provided. When you've finished, turn the page to find your score.

_____ 1. With each increase in my earnings, I still feel that I should be making even more.

_____ 2. No matter where my money is (vaults, investments, banks, at home) I worry about losing it.

_____ 3. I can't understand how people who make less money than I do can seem so satisfied.

_____ 4. Money is not worth getting upset about or arguing about.

_____ 5. When I finally receive money I've been looking forward to getting, it seems less valuable.

_____ 6. I get upset when I think of all the money I've wasted over the years.

_____ 7. I know I'd be happier if I had more money.

_____ 8. I often think about the things I would like but can't afford to buy.

_____ 9. I usually know to the dollar how much money I have in the bank.

_____ 10. Getting more money is one of my least important goals.

_____ 11. People who worry about money are incapable of enjoying life.

_____ 12. I become uncomfortable around people who have a lot more money than I do.

_____ 13. I often feel that others are trying to take advantage of me financially.

_____ 14. When I am out with people who make more money than I do, I think they should offer to pay.

From Rita Aero and Elliot Weiner, *The Money Test* (New York: Beachtree Books, 1985), pp. 120–123. Reprinted with permission.

_____ 15. The amount of money you make is not a good indication of how well you're doing in life.

_____ 16. I am not one to compromise my principles in order to increase my earnings.

_____ 17. To be truly content, I need to know that I'll be financially secure five and even ten years from now.

_____ 18. I've always managed to get everything I want without worrying about money.

_____ 19. When I don't have surplus money, I feel trapped.

_____ 20. It's taking me too long to get as rich as I want to be.

(Answers on next page)

SCORING

To find your score on the Index of Financial Comfort, compare your answers to those on the Scoring Key. Give yourself one point for each true or false answer that matches, and write the total number of matches in the box below. Now check the Norms Table to find the range in which you have scored.

SCORING KEY

1. F	6. F	11. T	16. T
2. F	7. F	12. F	17. F
3. F	8. F	13. F	18. T
4. T	9. F	14. F	19. F
5. F	10. T	15. T	20. F

TOTAL SCORE

INTERPRETATION

Contrary to popular opinion, people who are the most comfortable in their financial situations are not necessarily those with the highest incomes. Feelings of financial comfort and security come primarily from psychological factors—a sense of self-esteem, satisfaction with one's work, a network of supportive friends, and continuous personal growth. Psychologists believe, in fact, that it is an underlying emotional insecurity that creates financial dissatisfaction.

In the Success Group, individuals who indicate the highest levels of financial comfort have the strongest sense of control over their lives. They are not overly concerned with their business images and do not place great value on appearances. At the other end of the spectrum those who indicate the most dissatisfaction with their levels of success hold the view that their financial security depends a great deal on luck and other outside influences and not on who they are or what they do.

These people tend to be among the most serious-minded in the group, and they feel a great deal of anxiety about money. They are highly creative in their approach and are constantly inventing new schemes to enhance their positions.

Very low scorers feel a great deal of frustration and anxiety in their financial situations. This insecurity probably permeates everything they do. They have retreated into positions where the need for security as become an unattainable obsession. They believe that money equals financial comfort, and while it is certainly true that money makes life easier, the lack of money is not the problem here. This is one range where outside help—a psychologist or career counselor—can make a big difference in the quality of life and the chances for success.

Low scorers are in somewhat better shape than very low scorers—a little less anxiety, a bit more self-esteem—but they still have high levels of financial discomfort. Individuals who score in this range tend to place great emphasis on the appearance of success, so much so that it can unfavorably alter their values and judgment. If you score here, make sure that you understand the worth of all your assets, not just your bank account. While it is OK to want more money and security, it is not OK to feel helpless or not in control of your own well-being.

Medium scorers see their financial situation as a combination of positive and negative elements. Their negative feelings may stem from the fact that they are acutely aware that others have more than they do, or they may be concerned with financial security in an inappropriate and slightly desperate way. Although they are not contented, they do have enough personal power to bring about the necessary changes. If you score here, continue to develop your talents in order to increase your sense of worth and self-esteem. Security and satisfaction—and even money—will follow.

High scorers indicate that they are in control of their financial situations and have strong senses of control in other areas of their lives as well. This feeling of power brings with it a sense of self-esteem, which is important in achieving success. High scorers know the fallacy of trying to attain happiness through money. Benjamin Franklin expressed it best: "Money never made a man happy nor will it. There is nothing in its nature to produce happiness. The more a man has the more he wants. Instead of filling a vacuum, it makes one." This is the ideal range in which to score.

Very high scorers are completely contented with their financial situations, and they are almost totally free of anxiety and concern about their images and success. This range is so high however, that there may be a hint of complacency lurking. If you score here, you are clearly comfortable with your current positions. As long as you are not indifferent to success or completely lacking in ambition, this is a good range in which to score.

NORMS TABLE

Very Low	Low	Medium	High	Very High
0 to 6	7 to 9	10 to 13	14 to 16	17 and above

Overcoming Negative Money Emotions

Many people are simply too prejudiced against money to use it effectively. Negative attitudes based on traditional religious or cultural values ("Money is the root of all evil") stunt some people in their growth toward financial maturity; others grow up in families where attitudes of defeat and failure in business or as employees linger into adulthood. Psychologists tell us that schoolchildren who do poorly at math may grow up with an aversion to money. Sometimes, the simple fear of the unknown—the often arcane and threatening world of banks and brokers—can make otherwise competent people indecisive and ineffectual with their money. Here's an example with which you may identify.

Money and the Devil

As a child, Bill got contradictory messages about money. He was expected to go to college to escape the working-class background of his family. He was also taught *not* to trust people with money. "It is easier for a camel to pass through the eye of a needle than for a rich man to go to heaven," his mother told him. The idea stayed with him into manhood.

For many reasons, Bill's professional life was a series of false starts and financial stumbles. His jobs left him unsatisfied and immediate expenses seemed to absorb all his income. Despite his hard work and long hours, he could never put any money away. He was intelligent and skilled, but everything he did with money was a struggle. "I felt like I was always floundering in quicksand," he said later. "Just thinking about money wore me out."

Circumstances (a hard-won promotion and a desire to marry and start a family) eventually forced Bill to take good, hard look at himself. With the help of a knowledgeable financial advisor, he began to identify some of the issues that kept him fiscally trapped in the past. As he told the advisor about his goals for a home and family, he began to relive the negative money feelings of his childhood. In ways he couldn't understand, money always evoked feelings of inadequacy, disappoint-

ment, and failure. From parents who had sometimes displayed their own bitter feelings about the wealth of others, he learned that success somehow made people unworthy. Money was a kind of taint—to be disposed of as fast as you got it.

"One day," Bill said, "it occurred to me that the bad feelings I had as an adult were the same feelings I had as a little boy. Every time I started to get ahead, my mother's voice told me to toss it away. It's as if I had to wear my childhood clothes for the rest of my life! Those feelings just didn't fit anymore."

Bill's story is true—and it's typical of many stories heard every day by financial advisors. When people who fail with money want to know why, they invariably discover underlying emotional answers.

Money and Loneliness

Financial professionals see people all the time—usually women—who give their money away. Such "loans," as they call them, are to someone they care about—and for the best of reasons. These victims (you can't call them lenders) just can't say no, even when it's the right answer. The outcome is usually the same: if someone doesn't intervene, the victims run themselves bankrupt.

Often, divorced or widowed women use money as a surrogate husband. They keep it close to them for security, feeling compelled to hang onto anything that reminds them of better, stabler times. Although making wise money decisions always involves some risk, even the slightest risk upsets the fragile sense of security these victims work so hard to maintain. For them, money represents far more than the things that money can buy.

"I've lost so much already," said Rose, a tearful widow. "Between my loans to Teddy's (her son's) business and the cost of just getting through the month, I couldn't stand to lose anything more." Yet Rose loses money every day: her funds sit in a low-interest savings account, but her fear won't let Rose do anything else.

Money and Relationships

Some people squander money by using it as a vehicle for personal power. They buy friendships and allegiances, hoping to control the actions of others. This is usually the by-product of insecurity—a common syndrome in our society—and if this substitution of money for self-worth continues long enough, both elements lose their value.

Take the case of Carl, for instance: the hard-driving president of a newly established service firm in a large midwestern city. An enthusiastic but inexperienced entrepreneur, Carl tried to combine the kind of charismatic leadership style he admired in other chief executives with a liberal salary and benefits policy for his staff. For the first 18 months, Carl's ideas about money and management seem to pay off. The staff performed well and he got a real emotional charge from the inspirational "kickoff rallies" he held every Monday morning.

Unfortunately, Carl's company had been riding the crest of a soon-to-poop-out local business cycle. As orders dwindled, Carl found his staff less anxious to attend his morning sermons. They wanted more say about company operations. They complained privately about Carl's "rah-rah" management style, and he became the butt of office jokes. Naturally, Carl turned to the other half of his "winning" motivational plan to make up for what his personal charisma lacked. He gave big raises to loyal workers (meaning those who kept their mouths shut) and cut off the bonuses from those whom he felt were "backsliders" and "not on the company team." One by one, the more aggressive, independent-minded employees dusted off their résumés and found employment elsewhere.

Soon, Carl discontinued his Monday morning rallies altogether and depended almost exclusively on written memoranda and announcements of bonus and equity-sharing awards to get his message across. By the end of the company's third year in business, Carl found he had purchased the finest staff of overpaid "yes people" that money could buy—but he could count few true friends (and virtually no high producers) on the company's payroll. Business picked up as local economy improved, but Carl was so discouraged that he sold the company at a loss and accepted a salaried executive position with a larger competitor. It took several years for Carl to overcome his bad experience and again take an interest in rebuilding his personal wealth or risk his feelings on new, intense personal relationships. For Carl, money alone proved to be a poor way to influence the people on whom his self-esteem and success ultimately depended.

Of course, the issues of spending for pleasure versus security is as old as money itself. Even for a single individual, life can be a juggling act as he or she tries to balance the desires of today with the needs of tomorrow. And when two individuals join together in a common household, that juggling act can become a three-ring circus.

THE DOUBLE-EDGED SWORD OF MENTAL ACCOUNTING

Learning to discipline ourselves—as individuals and as couples—can require some mental gymnastics. Trying to protect yourself from the uncontrollable urge to buy a new car, for example, you might do the obvious—earmark some of your money for security purposes, such as retirement or a cash pool for layoffs or emergencies, and some for spending for capital investments (like cars) and everyday expenses. We create what researchers Hersh Shefrin and Meir Statman report is called "mental accounts." This phenomenon works as follows.

Arthur was wise and respectably rich: his net worth amounted to over $7.5 million, mostly made in the past three years. His wisdom lay in this: he put $1.5 million into U.S. Treasury bonds and gave them to his wife with the following admonition: "Barbara, these securities are now yours. They represent as much income as we will probably ever need for the rest of our lives. However, I will continue to speculate and try to make more money. But if, by any incredible chance, I should ever come to you and beg for these bonds again, under no circumstances should you give them to me. Instead, get your brother, the psychiatrist, on the phone, for you will know that I've gone crazy."

Arthur—like many other red-blooded emotional investors before him—broke his solemn, rational vow. His many speculations "went south" and he saw no option but to call on his wife for the million-and-a-half to protect the other $6 million. Fortunately, Barbara neither gave him the bonds nor called a psychiatrist. She simply complimented him for putting the money where he couldn't get to it in an emotional flurry. He was imposing discipline on himself, with her as a backup. His speculative bankroll took a beating, but their nest egg stayed intact.

That's exactly the same logic we use when we make automatic salary deductions to fund a pension plan or pay every month into a whole-life insurance policy to build cash value. Both are savings tools, and both depend first on discipline—and later, mechanical safeguards—to keep those savings in the nest. From this perspective, "mental accounting" is a wise and productive idea.

In the investment world, however, all dollars are used for building wealth. By their nature, speculative dollars are subject to more risk than other, "safer" money. The traditional prudent investor knows that if worst comes to worst, the safe account will still be there. This strategy—Arthur's strategy—protects people from squandering everything on impulse.

That sounds good from an emotional point of view, but it leads to a major investing paradox. The purpose of financial planning is to build net worth—your financial bottom line. To be truly effective in this effort, you must consider all assets and all liabilities as working together in one pot. Segregating them mentally into "safe" and "speculative" accounts only dilutes your wealth-building power. The laws of risking markets says eventually you'll lose, just as the law of safe investments says you'll make only pennies on every dollar.

Mental accounting, therefore, may protect important money from our worst impulses, but it inhibits financial growth.

For example, some people borrow from a bond at high interest to pay for a car, rather than "loot" a child's college education fund that pays 5% less than what they are paying for the loan. Their net worth, in the end, suffers from such false economy.

Of course there's only one reason for such a decision—the emotion-driven fear that they won't be disciplined enough to pay back the college fund. Overcoming such parent-child reasoning can be an expensive lesson: using the bank as a "parent" costs them 5% a year—an amount they could easily make up, even as undisciplined consumers. In personal finance, such rational and irrational thinking are all-too-common bedfellows.

MULTIPLE-ASSET INVESTING: SATISFYING EMOTIONAL AND FINANCIAL NEEDS

If mental accounting costs, rather than saves you money, how can human emotional foibles be made to serve your wealth-building plan? The best way to minimize risk—the technique used in modern portfolio theory and multiple-asset allocation strategies—is the diversification of investments. This is the opposite of the go-for-broke, all-the-eggs-in-one-basket" strategy used by many individual investors.

Because there's no "show-place-or-win" competition in the world of investing, investors can, and should, spread their money across a variety of asset categories—from money market investments, stocks and bonds, to real estate, foreign securities, commodities, and precious metals. The category mix should be adjusted periodically to respond to significant shifts in the market, but should not be tinkered with in an attempt to benefit from short-term fluctuations. Research shows that asset diversification results in better long-term gains than any other strategy.

The process of mental accounting, however, leads the investor to separate asset categories by risk in his or her head and apply different investment criteria for each account. The success or failure of each category is then judged entirely on its own standards as high- (or low-) risk/reward investment—not a part of an integrated, wealth-building multiple-asset portfolio. The portfolio is not perceived as a fluid, united whole (with the potential for and synergistic growth among the parts) but as a rigid, stratified structure with competing—not complementing parts. Such an investor might adopt a buy-and-hold strategy for mutual funds in his or her bond portfolio and trade in speculative stocks vigorously, reasoning that the two groups intrinsically satisfy different needs. Because different criteria are used to judge the success of each category, investors apply different strategies to each. The result is that the parts of the portfolio look as if they were controlled by entirely different investors. This is not the route to a high-performing (or even consistent) wealth-building portfolio.

To be sure, this "safe" versus "speculative" strategy does what it is supposed to do—accommodates our emotional need for certainty as well as gain, segregates money we can't afford to lose from money with which we are willing to gamble. Its downfall is that it prohibits complete diversification, because the boundaries between the accounts are emotional, not rational, and inhibit the growth a combination of markets can deliver.

A CATALOG OF EMOTIONAL ILLUSIONS

In their February, 1986 article "How Not to Make Money In the Stock Market" in *Psychology Today,* Shefrin and Statman report on a number of emotional barriers that appear like irrational camouflage to obscure our view of investment reality. When we are caught in the spell of such illusions, a wrong decision may seem unimpeachably right.

The "Hot Hands" Fallacy

An investor (or investment forecaster) who, like a successful racehorse handicapper, usually picks the winners, is said to have "hot hands"—a Midas touch with the market. The "hot hands" illusion is so compelling that even authoritative sources commonly use it to predict the future behavior of stocks and funds and even the performance of financial advisors.

The concept is predicated on the appealing notion that past—especially recent—performance predicts future results. Hot-handers regularly ask, "Which brokerage firm has the hottest five-year record? Which mutual fund has posted the best return to date? Which tip sheet has the highest percentage of winners?" The supposition is that those which have performed the best are good bets for the future.

Unfortunately, hot streaks, like points on a scoreboard, don't say anything about the next play—the secret to investing success. The performance of any investment or investor over a five- or six-year period (apart from cy-clical effects) says little about next year's return.

For example, in 1979 the Wall Street Fund had the hottest five-year record around. But in 1980 it began a slide that put it at the bottom of the mutual fund heap in the next four-year period.

Or take the case of Joe Granville. In the late 1970s and early 1980s, Granville's successful stock market predictions made him look like the Jeanne Dixon of the market. But when Granville advised investors to divest themselves of stocks on the eve of one of the greatest and longest-lasting stock market rallies in history, people stopped paying for his advice.

The Law of Small Numbers

We are conditioned to believe that when a coin is tossed ten times, it will land on "heads" 50% of the time and "tails" the other 50%—but that simply isn't true. The mathematical "law of large numbers on which this statistic is based depends on hundreds or thousands of tosses.In small samples, disproportionately large runs in either direction can occur.

In fact, the 50–50 logic applies only to the *very next toss* of the coin. Only in a very large sampling will the "law of large numbers" take over and the true probabilities begin to exert themselves.

Of course, skill, along with luck, is involved in picking the best funds—but many highly skilled men and women operate on Wall Street, all with access to the same information at the same time, and no single firm—or individual—has yet demonstrated a clear, systematic superiority in the ability to pick winners in the long run. In modern portfolio theory, the "random walk" of stock prices means that no one trader has a systematic advantage over another—no matter how good his or her track record.

Is Seeing Truly Believing?

Emotional illusions can be just like optical illusions: once your senses are fooled, close scrutiny only supports the idea that the thing is just what you think it is not. Three "errors of attribution" can lead us to see a predictable pattern in a set of random events, and it's important for money managers of all personality types to know exactly what they are.

The Illusion of First Impressions

When we form a first impression, explain psychologists Hillel Einhorn and Robin Hogarth, we have a natural tendency to look for, and find, evidence that supports our original conclusion. In this manner, first impressions become strong convictions. In the world of investing, a favorable emotional impression—from a parent's prejudice to an affinity for a company's logo, products, or industry—can keep an investor "sold" long after the accounting ink has turned red.

The Illusion of Control

The illusion of control leads you to believe that you have a greater effect on the outcome of an event than in fact you do. Witness (says psychologist Ellen Langer) the gambler's tradition of throwing the dice physically harder for high numbers and softer for lower scores. Many investors establish similar routines and rituals, which they hope will sway the odds in their favor. Rationally, of course, the actions of one investor have no influence on the larger economic world that governs the movement of prices. Only recently, with the advent of large institutional investors and computer-triggered trading, has it become possible for the actions of one block of shares to affect the value of the rest. Beyond that, the rituals and formulas of small investors still count even less than do a "magician's" smoke and mirrors.

The Hindsight Fallacy Illusion

After an event has taken place, says psychologist Baruch Fischoff, many investors mistakenly believe that it was not only predictable but also inevitable. In other words, the event becomes self-evident after its occurrence, and investors are quick to convince themselves they knew that it was certain. This 20/20 hindsight gives investors exaggerated confidence in their own ability to predict what's going to happen next—often with disastrous consequences..

Blinded by any or all of those illusions, investors easily convince themselves that a "sure thing" is out there for the taking. They abandon common sense, their own experience, and rational strategy to pursue riches with the same fervor as a gambler with a foolproof "system." The only proof of the fools, unfortunately, is in the way the system takes them for all they're worth.

THE EMOTIONAL BOTTOM LINE: RISK VERSUS REWARD

Some people jump out of airplanes; others climb cliffs, shoot river rapids, or drive race cars—all for the sake of a thrill.

And then there are those who like to take chances with money—financial thrill seekers—the ultimate in adventurous living. Intuition may tell you that these physical and financial thrill seekers should be the same people—but, interestingly enough, that's not the way it turns out. Financial advisors know that people who seek physical thrills tend to be no more carefree, or less carefree, with their money than anyone else is. Financial risk takers, it seems, get all the kicks they need taking chances with their assets. What's more, clear personality characteristics distinguish these fiscal daredevils, and you should learn to recognize one if you meet one—even in the mirror.

"The No. 1 goal in life of fiscal risk takers is to be successful," says Dr. Frank Farley, a University of Wisconsin psychologist who has done ground-breaking research into the thrill-seeking personality. "For the high financial risk takers, investments are a major focus in their lives, practically an obsession." Conversely, people who structure their lives to avoid financial risk tend to place a priority on happiness.

Said another way, taking financial risk seems to offer these investors the same stimulation and promise of big emotional rewards that physical risk taking does for others. Still, we should draw a distinction between what Farley calls "high financial risk takers" and more circumspect investors who are willing to assume some, if more reasonable amounts

For Love and Not Money: Some Investors Hold On to Stock for Its Emotional Value

YOUR MONEY MATTERS

By Francine Schwadel
Staff Reporter of THE WALL STREET JOURNAL

When American Telephone & Telegraph Co. offered holders of fewer than 100 of its shares an incentive to sell their stock recently, Elliot Groffman refused.

"It would be like selling a memory," says the 33-year-old New York lawyer, whose five shares were a bar mitzvah gift from his grandparents in 1966. He fondly recalls following his stock's performance with his grandfather, who died three years ago. "When I get statements from AT&T," Mr. Groffman says, "I think of him."

At a time when stock prices are driven largely by the cold calculations fo profit-hungry money managers, some people still base their investment decisions on emotions that have little to do with greed. Tax considerations certainly motivate many long-term holders of securities, but market specialists say others seem to be seeking psychic as well as financial reward.

A Test of Loyalty

A 1985 survey by the New York Stock Exchange indicates that almost half the 47 million Americans who own stock in publicly traded companies or mutual funds hold shares in only one issue or one mutual fund. And it's likely, says Richard Ross, executive director of the Center for the Study of Investor Behavior in Chicago, "that people own shares int hat company because they work for it, or used to work for it, or they inherited it or they have some other emotional attachment to it."

Sentimental stockholders like these "are saying,'I'm a loyal person,'"explains Maurice Elvekrog, a Birmingham, Mich.-based investment counselor who holds a doctorate in psychology.

And loyalty sometimes pays off. An investment adviser in the Detroit area tells of a woman whose father left her some stock in a small company in New York. Before he died in the 1920s, the man made his daughter promise always to invest her spare cash in the company's shares—a promise she kept for many years. The company turned out to be a predecessor of International Business Machines corp. And the woman, who died a few years ago, became very wealthy.

Similarly, Wayne Janus, a financial planner in Oakbrook Terrace, Ill., says one of his clients has seen the value of her stock in a Midwestern distributor of consumer products rise 62,000% to more than $9 million, not counting dividends, in the 20 years since her husband's death.

The husband, who had been chairman of the company, had told his wife never to sell, no matter what advice she received from her bankers, accountants or lawyers. "She felt he knew what he was talking about," Mr. Janus says. "There's probably no investment she could have made that would have done as well."

Of course, emotional investors can also get clobbered. William Thompson, a financial planner with the brokerage firm of Raymond James & Associates in Wilmington, Del., recalls a client a few years back who watched the value of his Sun Co. shares drop dramatically. (Sun shares have since bounced back; they recently rose above $70 a share, compared with a low of $26.75 in 1982.)

Oil stocks were taking a beating at the time, and Mr. Thompson tried to convince his client to diversify. But the second-generation Sun employee, who had retired, refused to sell any of his Sun shares, even though his yield was so low that he had to get a part-time job to supplement his pension income.

"It was emotion that stopped him from making a proper investment decision," says Mr. Thompson, who estimates that 80% of his clients have some sort of emotional attachment to their securities.

At Mr. Thompson's urging, another client, an AT&T retiree, agreed to sell about $25,000 of AT&T stock and buy tax-free bonds to boost his income, but a few days later, the client ordered Mr. Thompson to cancel the transaction.

"He said his wife was so upset that she had been vomiting in the sink for two days," Mr. Thompson recalls.

Charles Ricker, an investment adviser in Grosse Point, Mich., had more success with a client who had a big position in General Motors Corp. stock in 1980. At the time, the auto industry was on the skids, and General Motors had cut its dividend almost in half. Mr. Ricker says he didn't have much trouble persuading the client to sell some of his General Motors shares.

"Suddenly, he was faced with the reality of not having an income to match his life style," Mr. Ricker recalls.

Ties to Dad

Sentimental shareholders often have especially strong ties to stocks selected by their fathers. "They view (selling) as a repudiation of the father's judgment," says Mr. Elvekrog, the investment adviser and psychologist.

For James Feeney, a 48-year-old advertising executive in New York, selling the Bank of New York shares his father bought while working in the bank's trust department would be even worse than that. "It would be violating a tradition," he says.

Mr. Feeney, who expects to inherit some of the shares, already has promised his 77-year-old father that he will never sell. "It means a lot to him," says the younger Mr. Feeney. "That's the only place he ever worked."

The shares also mean a lot to the son, who now counts the bank among his clients. "It's a very special feeling," he says. "It gives me a nice link with the past."

Still, emotions work both ways, and sometimes they can trigger stock sales. Mr Feeney, for instance, says he sold some shares of MCI Communications corp. at a loss last year, after MCI fired his advertising agency. "I just wanted to get rid of it," he says. "I was teed off."

And Mr. Elvekrog recently liquidated the stock portfolio of a client in her 40s who had gotten a divorce. "She wanted to sell everything, " he says, "and start over."

Reprinted with permission, © 1987 Wall Street Journal

10 HIGHEST-RISK INVESTMENTS

1. Futures
2. Options—buying
3. Short selling
4. Collectibles
5. Diamonds
6. Leveraged contracts
7. Oil Drilling
8. Mutual funds—option buying
9. Options on futures
10. Strategic metals

10 LOWEST-RISK INVESTMENTS

1. Treasury obligations
2. Federally guaranteed money market funds
3. Passbook savings under $100,000
4. Certificates of deposit under $100,000
5. Zero-coupon bonds held to maturity
6. Corporate bonds rated AA or higher
7. NOW and super-NOW accounts under $100,000
8. Government agency notes held to maturity
9. T-bill money market funds (buy only T-bills)
10. Annuities issued by highly rated companies

of risk. The first type gets a charge out of going for greatness in one bold stroke. The second type knows that luck is an unavoidable element of every investment strategy and plans a balanced program of risk and rewards.

This ability to gauge your own tolerance for (and manage) risk is a key issue in developing a personal financial plan. You don't have to be a high roller to benefit from risk; in fact, the ability to assume *reasonable* risk is a sign of a healthy financial personality.

Profile of the Healthy Risk Taker

Experience shows that people who accept reasonable risk tend to be capable money managers. They are confident they can develop money-making ideas and can follow through on their investments. They spend an appropriate amount of time reading about money and investing, and have the personal leadership skills to commmunicate with and direct their financial partners and advisors.

Dr. Julian Rotter, a University of Connecticut psychologist, has uncovered an important clue to the ways people approach risk.

"If you think life is controlled by luck," says Dr. Rotter, "you'll either play your investments very safely or get enticed by a long shot, like the lottery. It's the people who think they have more control over destiny who will take risks when it seems the right thing to do."

This parallels the distinction that decision theorists make between risk and uncertainty. An "uncertain" decision is one in which the outcome cannot reasonably be estimated, like playing the Irish sweepstakes—the province of the lucky thrill seeker—or betting on an election. More rational players prefer "games" like the stock market, where risks can be reasonably assessed.

Like everything else in life, risk and uncertainty—luck and judgment—have their qualitative as well as quantitative components. Do you wake up in the morning feeling like things will go your way ? Are you confident of the job you're doing at work and feel secure as a result? Does it seem that when you put effort into a project, things usually turn out right?

Or do you have the sense that no matter what you do, nothing good will happen? Does it seem that getting and keeping a job has more to do with other peoples' actions than your own? Do you feel there really is hardly *anything* you can do about a situation to control its outcome?

Some people prefer to take a loss on a good risk than to be idle in perfect safety. Others hate loss so much that they will pass up a very good opportunity on the chance of a small loss.

Finding your own risk tolerance can mean the difference between successful, satisfying investing and a prolonged career of second-guessing your own decisions. Unfortunately, many people fail to perceive the true relationship between risk and reward—emotionally and financially—and build this failure into their financial plan from the start.

In Part III of this book, you'll find a key detailing the level of risk for each of the best investments for 1988; and in Part II, a discussion of risk in multiple-asset allocation. Chapter 3 describes the risk that is appropriate to investors in various stages of their lives and with differing long-term goals. Beyond these general guidelines, each investor must learn the level of risk with which he or she is comfortable. Too much risk leads to needless sleepless nights; too little leads to low returns and recriminations. Either result can undermine the emotional and financial satisfaction of even the most sanguine investor personality.

THE WINNING PERSONALITY

There are no quick paths through the emotional maze of effective money management. They are complex, subtle, and often change with each new situation.

If you've had trouble managing your money, or if you are unable to build a portfolio mix that intuitively feels right, you should look beyond the charts and numbers to the heart of your financial plan. Inside, you may find outdated money attitudes, irrational beliefs, and nonproductive behaviors that, with the help of a competent financial advisor, would break the bonds that hold you back.

PLANNING STRATEGY INVENTORY

Thomas Jefferson, the third president of the United States, was what we would today call a radical. He had the courage of his convictions, yet he preferred to work beneath the surface, using artful arguments and strategies to win adherents. Jefferson displayed what John Adams called "a happy talent for composition" and used this skill to draft the Declaration of Independence. Although he was curious about all facets of life, his fondness for structure and order is apparent in the meticulous records he kept on the plant life and weather conditions at his home in Virginia.

In order to measure some of these very subtle qualities, we developed the Planning Strategy Inventory. This test measures three aspects of the personality: the level of serious-mindedness, the level of need for stimulation, and the long- or short-term focus of plans. There are no right or wrong answers, yet the scores of the Success group demonstrate some very specific tendencies. Furthermore, we learned that men and women score differently, even when they are equally motivated and successful.

INSTRUCTIONS

In this Planning Strategy Inventory, you will be presented with 45 statements about personality and preferences. Read each statement and determine whether, for you, it is a true (T) or false (F) statement. Answer all the questions, and write your responses in the space provided. When you've finished, turn the page to find your score.

_____1. I read magazines as soon as they come in the mail rather than wait until later.

_____2. I dislike spur-of-the moment invitations.

_____3. I eat snacks whenever I'm hungry rather than wait for a set mealtime.

_____4. I keep a well-stocked kitchen instead of shopping each day for food.

_____5. I usually but tickets for sports, concerts, or the theater in advance rather than purchase them at the door.

_____6. I would rather have a less secure occupation that provided lots of time off than a work-intensive career with steady promotions.

_____7. I react at the time that someone wrongs me rather than wait for the appropriate moment.

_____8. I like to read about foreign countries that I visit before I arrive.

_____9. I am not the type who prefers a long courtship and engagement when I'm in love.

_____10. I would rather buy a new car on credit now than save up and buy it outright in the future.

From Rita Aero and Elliot Weiner, *The Money Test* (New York: Beachtree books, 1985), pp. 51-55. Reprinted with permission.

_____11. When I buy clothes, they reflect the very latest in fashion.

_____12. I take each moment as it comes rather than keep a detailed daily schedule.

_____13. I would choose a low-paying job with a secure future over a short-term but very high-paying one.

_____14. I would rather organize a party than go to one.

_____15. I spend more time thinking about where I'm going to be next year than I do focusing the details of my current work.

_____16. I would much prefer a home and family over a lifestyle with many lovers in different places.

_____17. I would rather spend three weeks in a Caribbean beach bungalow than spend the time touring all the islands.

_____18. I only "live it up" on special occasions and do not make a regular practice of it.

_____19. My friends all come from varied backgrounds, with dissimilar interests and careers.

_____20. I'd rather eat something I know I like than order an exotic dish I've never heard of.

_____21. I prefer rock and roll or jazz over "beautiful" or classical music.

_____22. I have just a very few close friends whom I speak with frequently.

_____23. I tend to read the same newspapers and magazines each month rather than switch around.

_____24. I would rather participate in a sporting event than watch one.

_____25. I like a career that provides a lot of contact with the public.

_____26. I think being an astronomer is just as stimulating as being an air controller.

_____27. I'd choose a fast red coupé over a distinguished gray sedan.

_____28. I prefer movies with true-to-life characters to those with outrageous ones.

_____29. I prefer to work under tight deadlines.

_____30. Most of my clothes are in very bright, warm, or interesting colors.

_____31. If I'm going to meet a business contact, I'd rather do it for information than for idle pleasure.

_____34. If I spend time watching television, chances are it's the news.

_____35. I often break up my workday with diversions like chatting with a friend on the telephone.

_____36. When I exercise, I think more about having fun and looking good than I do about a healthy body.

_____37. Even if my work isn't finished, I'm still able to relax and enjoy myself.

_____38. I find it difficult to delegate responsibility and prefer to attend to the details myself.

_____39. If one is going to travel in a foreign country, I think it is important to learn the language.

_____40. I rarely take my work home with me on the weekends.

_____41. Instead of taking my failures to heart, I'm able to shake them off.

_____42. I prefer films with light romantic themes to films with very serious social themes.

_____43. Even if everyone knows it's a safe investment, I still conduct my own investigation before risking my money.

_____44. When I have a fight with a loved one, I cannot let it go until it gets straightened out.

_____45. When I read the newspaper, I usually glance over the comics before I turn to the business news.

SCORING KEY

1. F_____	13. T_____	25. F_____	37. F_____
2. T_____	14. T_____	26. T_____	38. T_____
3. F_____	15. T_____	27. F_____	39. T_____
4. T_____	16. T_____	28. T_____	40. F_____
5. T_____	17. T_____	29. F_____	41. F_____
6. F_____	18. T_____	30. F_____	42. F_____
7. F_____	19. F_____	31. T_____	43. T_____
8. T_____	20. T_____	32. T_____	44. T_____
9. F_____	21. F_____	33. T_____	45. F_____
10. F_____	22. T_____	34. T_____	
11. F_____	23. T_____	35. F_____	
12. F_____	24. F_____	36. F_____	

SCORING

To find your score on the Planning Strategy Inventory, compare your answers to those on the Scoring Key. Give yourself 1 point for each true or false answer than matches.

This test is acutally divided into three subsets, so to compute your final scores, total the number of matches for questions 1 through 15 and write it in the appropriate box below. Repeat this process for questions 16 through 30 and 31 through 45.

Total 1–15

Planning Orientation

Total 16–30

Arousal Avoidance

Total 31–45

Serious-Mindedness

Norms Table
Planning Orientation, Arousal Avoidance, Serious-Mindedness
(Note: All three tests have the same norms.)

Very Low	Low	Medium	High	Very High
0 to 4	5 and 6	7 and 9	10 and 11	12 and above

INTERPRETATION

The Planning Strategy Inventory is really three tests in one, and each section evaluates a separate but related personality characteristic. These three subtests measure a short- versus a long-term focus on goals, a need for stimulation, and a tendency toward serious-mindedness. Each section has its own Norms Table and interpretation.

Planning Orientation—The questions in this section of the test measure a tendency to plan ahead and organize long-range goals as opposed to an inclination to become involved with short-term tasks and achievements.

Very low and *low scorers* want to see results immediately instead of waiting for events to be resolved sometime in the future. Some individuals may be so attached to immediate gratification that they find long-term career or business planning frustrating. Thus they expend most of their time and energy dealing with smaller, immediate goals, which may or may not lead them to major success.

High and *very high scorers,* on the other hand, orient themselves toward the future and gain satisfaction from long-term planning and anticipated achievements. Although they are highly motivated, very high scorers have lower income levels than their medium-range colleagues. They may run the risk of being so future-oriented that they lack the necessary spontaneity to take advantage of today's opportunities.

Statistical data from the Success Group indicate that *medium scorers* focus on a combination of long- and short-term plans. From this focus comes the ability and willingness to take advantage of immediate opportunities, while an overall strategy is held in mind. Scorers in this range are the most likely to realize the successful outcome of their goals.

Arousal Avoidance—The questions in this section measure an individual's tendency to avoid stimulating situations as opposed to having a desire for excitement.

Very low and *low scorers* are drawn to new and stimulating situations. In business these individuals enjoy excitement and change, and they often prefer careers that require travel and flexible schedules. Arousal-seeking individuals are exposed to a great deal of stress, and they must have adequate stress-coping skills. Individuals who are highly visible, outgoing, and successfull in business tend to score in this range.

High and *very high scorers* find satisfaction in fixed schedules and stable careers. They like to predict their daily routines and may react negatively to surprises. Individuals who score here tend to believe that situations sometimes control them, and therefore they like to keep the lid on outside influences. Very high scorers also prefer long-term planning that provides them with security. It does not, however, allow them the flexibility they need to uncover new opportunities.

Medium scorers straddle both extremes, but in this section of the test the middle is not the ideal position for success. The most successful individuals are those with the lowest levels or arousal avoidance. They are eager to deal with stimulating situations and have an internally directed sense of control over their lives. The men in the Success Group tend to avoid arousal more than do the women; perhaps men are more susceptible to the stresses that come with their careers.

Serious-Mindedness—This scale measures the individual's preference for activites that are lighthearted and sometimes frivolous as opposed to those that are focused and task-oriented.

Very low and *low scorers* might be described by their colleagues (if they can be found at work) as fun-loving and pleasure-seeking . They are drawn to excitement, and they view stimulating situations as important experience. Extremely low scorers can find it difficult to commit to long-term projects and may be excluded from business opportunities because they do not appear dedicated.

High and *very high scorers,* on the other hand, might be accused of taking life too seriously and being less that fun to be around. Men in the Success Group tend to score in this range more often than do successful women. Very high scorers are a motivated and ambitious group of individuals, but they may be harboring the fear that their world will come crashing down if they relax and enjoy life too much. Individuals in this range are very knowledgeable in business, and they tend to have workaholic personalities. They produce great successes—but at high personal cost

Medium *scorers,* therefore, are in the range that leads to success. High serious-mindedness is associated with a low level of financial comfort, so much that the individual is driven toward success without a feeling of control. Individuals who score low, on the other hand, find it difficult to apply themselves to the disciplined structure necessary for the fulfillment of their goals.

CHAPTER 3

LIFESTYLES AND FINANCIAL LIFE CYCLES

A GLANCE AHEAD:

In this chapter, you'll take the first steps toward financial independence. You will learn

- *About the stages of your financial life: accumulation, preservation, and distribution*
- *How your current stage affects your money management strategies*
- *How goal-setting provides a practical strategy for changing money behavior.*
- *How to set long- and short-term financial goals*

THE STAGES OF LIFE

Our lives tend to pass through a few distinct and fairly well-defined phases, and each brings with it unique opportunities and responsibilities. Effective money managers know that age and outlook play a big role in the way their financial plans are structured.

- Doug and Cynthia are just getting started. They've decided to postpone having children, but they are starting a fund for a planned-for child's education. If they choose to stay on career tracks that make having children too burdensome, they'll use the education fund for retirement. They are trying to decide whether to buy a home or rent and want to know what type of investment profile best suits their needs.
- Jim and Jean are in their early 40s and have a household income of around $80,000. In two years, their oldest daughter, Sara, will leave for college; her two brothers and a sister have decided go to college too. The Smiths put some money away for education, but not enough. Now they have 24 months to prepare for the shock of college tuition and Sara's living expenses.
- Bill hopes to retire from his job as plant foreman in 10 years. He and his wife Rose own a piece of river property, on which they haven't built yet. Their children are grown and Bill and Rose are in good health, but aside from the land and the family home, they don't have many assets. They don't want to lose what they have, but they feel they need to implement a fairly aggressive financial strategy in order to be ready for retirement.

Their values and lifestyles are all from mainstream America, yet they have unique goals, values, and financial needs. Just as your view of the land around you shifts when you walk to a different spot, your perception of finance changes with your age and your circumstances.

Most people progress through distinct financial stages: the *education* years, the *accumulation* years, the *preservation* years, and the *distribution* years. On paper, as in real life, these are not segregated by clear boundaries; rather, they overlap as we gradually grow from one phase into the next.

The Education and Accumulation Years

In all societies, youth is the time for learning. By the time young people in our culture have reached their mid-20s, they are expected to have learned the skills they need to support themselves. They are no longer financially dependent on their parents; they have made their first self-supporting steps into the world.

Life's next decade should be devoted to establishing a career and laying the groundwork for future financial security. Needless to say, the education process continues—in the laboratory of life if not in the classroom. During these years, young people should learn the basics of household financial management and begin taking the first steps toward defining their financial strategies. One great joy of this stage of life is that money put aside now has time to build to far greater value than like amounts invested later: the 25-year-old who begins investing $2,000 a year in an IRA at 10% annual interest will see that sum grow to $973,703 at age 65; postponing the IRA by ten years reduces earnings to $361,887.

The years between 25 and 35 are pivotal to future success. During them, you should build a sound financial base; except for the fortunate few who came into the world well positioned, it's not generally a good time for speculation. Your efforts should be focused on building a good savings program, acquiring a home, preparing for the education of children, establishing a long-range financial plan.

This also is the time when some people begin to develop entrepeneurial skills; if you want to start your own business, do it now. Don't wait until until you are too entrenched in someone else's enterprise to seek your own financial fortune.

Establish credit and protect it during these formative years; use leverage prudently to develop net worth. Don't be afraid of debt— leverage will get you into your first home or get your business on its feet—but don't abuse consumer debt. Remember: use debt

for assets that appreciate (grow in value over time), not for those that depreciate, or become less valuable. Learn to save for a new refrigerator instead of opening a revolving charge account.

While this is a time for caution, don't let fear paralyze you; there is still time to rebound from mistakes.

The Accumulation and Preservation Years

As you move into your 40s and 50s, you should be in a position to capitalize on the base you carefully built in the preceding decade. By now, most people are ready to seriously prepare for the retirement years by putting a full-scale multiple-asset investment program into place.

These years can be a mixed bag. The earning power we have generated may be offset by the expense of helping children get educated and established. Some people who have accumulated net worth may use it as a cushion while they prepare themselves for a career change, or they may invest it in a new business venture.

Most people, though, should use these years to prepare for a comfortable retirement. During the early years of this phase, people tend to be fairly aggressive with a portion of their assets so that the accumulation process is accelerated. They can take advantage of good credit to move quickly when an outstanding business or investment opportunity presents itself.

Later, as they approach the age of retirement, most people grow more conservative and reduce financial risk and debt. They get their house in order for the golden years by gathering and consolidating their assets. Those who plan to work right through the retirement years may stay aggressive, but most people are beginning to look for stability.

The Preservation and Distribution Years

The goal of the accumulation years was to stimulate the growth of your assets so they pay off in regular income at retirement. With retirement comes a continued shift to the preservation mode. People tend to reduce the number of investments they hold; they look for less complicated and more liquid investments. Good money managers aim to preserve what they have by reducing risk and debt, and they begin to prepare their affairs for the time when they will no longer be able to care for themselves.

They also look ahead to the responsible distribution of their assets. Most people like to leave something for their families and many leave assets to their church or a favorite charity; there's a good feeling when you can leave something behind as a way of making the world a better or more comfortable place. The successful completion of each phase results from good planning, self-discipline, and the mastery of appropriate skills. Part II describes specific tools and strategies to accomplish the goals of each of your life's financial stages.

MAKING IT WORK

All people have visions of how they would like their life to be; for most people, comfort and financial security are a big part of the picture. Need is one of life's least pleasant realities, and we are reluctant to imagine ourselves burdened by poverty—especially in old age. We know we don't need millions, but we want to know our everyday dreams of comfort and peace of mind can come true.

Learning how to transfer that vision to reality can be tricky. In fact, it's almost like magic, since it means making something intangible (an idea) into something concrete (reality). A very lucky few will resolve the dilemma by inheriting money, winning the lottery, or cashing in on a long-shot investment, but for most of us the payoff comes only after we've learned some skills and invested some time and money. Even those lucky "big winners" will have to learn successful money management if they are to enjoy their good fortune.

The Habit of Winning

Any athlete will tell you that the toughest team to beat is the one that prepares—and plays—to win. Those teams have learned how to win; they have established winning as a habit.

Financial success works the same way. People who succeed learn the methodology of success. Success becomes a habit, and those who have the habit wear success comfortably. Yet people who have failed in the past often continue to fail—which explains our fascination with people who beat the odds by coming back from defeat: it just doesn't happen that often!

Success is not a mystery. It's a way of life built with skills and behaviors that can be learned and practiced. Like any practical knowledge, it's best learned from the bottom up. The biggest hurdle faced by most of us is believing that it can be done.

Planning for Success

Successful companies use a planning process that forces them to look to the future and to periodically review their progress. They start by looking at where they are; then they define where they want to be. To get from here to there, they create a strategy that consists of goals and objectives. This is called a *strategic plan*. It works because it takes a large, intangible vision and breaks it down into manageable objectives that can be accomplished with relative ease. Most importantly, since a dream doesn't become a goal until it has a deadline, a timetable is applied to the process.

Successful families and individuals follow the same process. They decide where they want to be, and create a strategic plan to get themselves there.

Successful plans are built on goals that have three essential qualities: (1) they are well-defined and understood by everyone who will be affected by them; (2) they are specific and measurable, not vague and open-ended, and (3) they are time-dated. One final criterion: goals should be written down.

Three common myths keep people from creating successful plans:

1. Most people think plans are rigid and monolithic. They are afraid a plan will lock them into a direction with which they may become uncomfortable. To keep their options open, they don't plan.

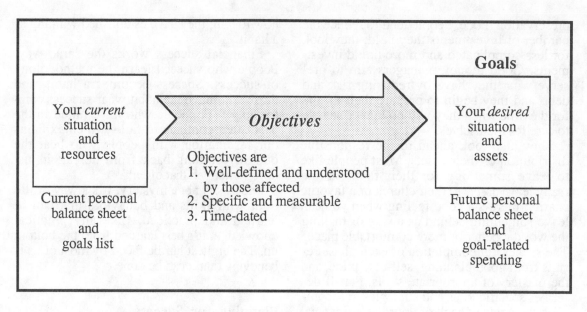

Figure 3-1 The Strategic Financial Planning Process

2. Other people see a plan as a mountain of goals that demand total mastery. In this view, anything short of mastery is failure. Because they are afraid to fail, they don't plan.
3. Finally, it's easy to make the mistake of believing that plans are concerned only with far-distant events. People think that a plan will force them into a grim present of never-ending sacrifices on only the distant promise of a future security.

These are the excuses for *not* planning. Plans, in reality, are not *things*, they are *tools*, road maps—as it were, to the future you desire. An effective plan changes to accommodate the planner's changing goals and circumstances; what you want at age 25 is often entirely different from what you want at age 40.

A good plan operates in three time dimensions: near term, mid term and long term. We all want some short-term perks—after all, the future is an uncertainty and the present is all we have. An effective plan will improve your chances of having what you desire in the near term, even as it creates the groundwork for a prosperous future. Fear of present sacrifice is

no reason to postpone the implementation of a plan.

Effective money managers know that plans have two main purposes. A plan gives shape and focus to your dreams—that's the obvious reason for planning. What can be even more important, though less understood, is that a plan is the most effective way to learn the habits of success.

Occasional failure is inevitable—no one ever accomplishes everything they hope to—but people who expect to win pick themselves up after a failure, dust themselves off, and move on to the next success. They know that big successes are built on a foundation of small ones.

Hope and fear are twins: no one moves ahead in life without some fear about the journey. But those who let fear stop them never move on at all.

Setting Goals

Goal setting starts with your vision of how your life should be. Define it however you choose: it will be different for everyone. Perhaps you want to retire to a mountain cabin, or at the oceanside. Maybe your vision calls for a lifetime or travel, or education, or service to your community. Whatever your vision is, write it down.

Now, give your vision a time frame. Don't be afraid. Step right up and say, "I would like to be retired and living in my dream home on an 18-hole golf course by the year 2017, when I will be 60 years old." Write it down.

Next, give your vision a specific, measurable value. If it's a financial goal, give it a price tag.

Now you have a well-defined long-range goal that is time-dated and has a measurable value—and you have written it down. You have come a long way toward transferring your vision from the intangible realms to the real world.

Everyone has more than one goal. Some goals will be near term—a new car next year, remodeling the kitchen. Some will be mid term—a college education for the kids, a trip to Europe. Other goals will be long term—your retirement home, enough income at retirement to live comfortably. Each goal should be well defined and understood by everyone who will be affected, have a measurable value, and have a deadline.

Creating Objectives

To activate your goals, you must identify a set of actions, or objectives. As each is accomplished, you will have moved another step closer to your goal. These bite-size objectives make your big goals attainable. That's their beauty and their purpose: by its nature, a goal is distant and may feel unattainable; an objective operates in the present.

Perhaps college education for your children is a mid-range goal. Quantify your goal by determining an estimated cost. Then determine how much money must be set aside each month to accumulate that amount in the appropriate time frame. That is your objective; be sure to phrase it in action terms— "We will save $125 each month toward an education fund."

Remember that success begets success; one of the most important reasons to set objectives is to establish a habit of success, so don't make objectives you won't reach. People who have failed learn to succeed by setting small objectives and reaching them— they change their behavior.

You may have to make very small objectives in the beginning: "I will put aside $1 each day;" "I will read one article each week on effective money management;" "I will avoid impulse buying by making a list each time I go shopping for groceries." As you gain the momentum that comes with continued small successes, you can move on to larger objectives.

Objectives must have the same qualities as goals: they must be specific and understood, they must be measurable, and they must be time-dated. Objectives are milestones on the highway to your goals; they give you something immediate to shoot for and they tell you how you're doing.

Reviewing the Plan

Some people mistakenly believe that plans are chiseled in stone. In fact, plans must adapt to all kinds of changes, or they have no value.

Not once in the history of the world have economic conditions stood still: economic forces roll along in gigantic cycles that absorb all manner of disruptions, including war, famine, and political upheaval. In everyday terms, interest rates and inflation are two of the factors most likely to affect an individual plan, Although there are ways to plan for shifts in either condition, good money managers know they must be prepared to revise their strategies when conditions change.

An occcasional review will help you keep your plan in line with your changing priorities, and a review may show that (1) you need to make a renewed effort or (2), you're doing better than you thought. A review is a rejuvenating experience, that can stimulate your thinking and help you develop even more effective strategies for arriving at your long-term goals.

A Goal Accomplished

If a plan is a road map, goals are destinations, and objectives are signposts, what happens when you arrive?

10 Steps to Setting Financial Goals

A goal is nothing more than some desired future state. A *financial* goal is simply the expression of that goal in monetary terms: What will it cost to attain that goal? Because of this close connection among dollars, satisfaction, and security, setting financial goals is the first—and most important—task in financial planning.

Complete each of the following items, writing your answers on a separate sheet of paper. Take as much time as you need to thoroughly consider each question. Be sure to consult others who may be involved in each goal's achievement, such as a spouse, life partner, children, parents, or other dependents.

1. How long will it be before you retire?
2. How much income will you need each year to support the retirement lifestyle you envision?
3. What average rate of return do you consider "too risky" for your overall investment portfolio? What is the lowest rate of return you would accept on a long-term investment?
4. How much annual income do you need right now to maintain your desired lifestyle?
5. How much of your current income (in dollars or as a percentage of total income) is committed to outside expenses unrelated to your cost of living? (Examples are: legal judgments, continuous medical expenses, and support of relatives not residing in your household.)
6. Do you have now, or expect to have in the future, income, or a lump-sum cash distribution from a trust or inheritance?
7. If the primary breadwinner in your household could no longer work, what could the remaining spouse or life partner earn annually?
8. List each household member who will depend on you for advanced (college or career) education. Estimate the annual cost of that education, including living expenses, and multiply that cost by the number of years that person will be attending school. Write this amount beside the person's name and note the number of years remaining before the first installment is due.
9. List any short- to moderate-term (one to five years) goals you have in mind beyond your current living expenses. Typical goals include the purchase of a new car, recreational vehicle, vacation house, and home remodeling or expansion plans. *Do not* include money earmarked for specific wealth-building or income-producing investments, such as a rental property or the startup cost of a small business. Beside each item, list the item's estimated cost and how much time remains before you will have to pay for it. What percentage of your current discretionary income would you be willing to set aside right now to obtain each item on your list?
10. On a scale of 1 to 10 (10 being high) write down how strongly you feel about preserving your wealth and guaranteeing a continued income for your dependents in the event of your death. What percentage of your current income would you be willing to set aside right now to ensure that outcome?

To analyze your financial goals, compare the amounts of money you will need at specific times in the future to the amount of money you are prepared to set aside right now for their attainment. When you consider (1) how important a goal really is to you, (2) the rate of return you expect (or will accept) from your investments, and (3) the amount of time available to achieve the desired goal, you will have a much better idea about the feasibility and priorities of your financial objectives.

Remember, too, that time can work both for and against you. Although a long-term investment has more time to accumulate a desired amount (especially when annual returns are compounded), inflation can erode the purchasing power of those future dollars.

Part II of this book will show you how to turn your financial goals into specific elements of a comprehensive financial plan.

Effective planners know that goals give life purpose and direction, so they never stop planning—no matter how many important goals they've accomplished. Goals flow into one another; as one is reached, another presents itself. Accomplishing one goal is merely the trigger for setting another.

Some people believe that reaching a major goal entitles them to enter a state of grace where they will never again be touched by struggle or difficulty. But reaching a goal is like climbing a mountain peak: you can appreciate the view of the height you've achieved, but the next peak—the one that looked unattainable from the ground—now beckons.

Your new goal has presented itself and the skills you've learned will take you onward and upward to new heights.

Building a plan that accommodates several important goals in many intermediate time frames can seem overwhelming when you're standing at sea level looking up at mountain peaks, but you'll build the skills you need in the process of making the climb. In succeeding chapters, you will learn the principles and techniques that can put all those needs and desires into one neat package, and provide the fiscal muscle you need to accomplish them.

PART II

MONEY MANAGEMENT AND INVESTMENT STRATEGIES

Even the finest automobile is useless without roads, fuel, and a competent driver. Similarly, wealth means little if you don't know how to acquire it, protect it, and use it as a vehicle for a more secure and rewarding life. In Part II,

you'll discover the underlying principles of effective financial planning, learn how to make time and the new tax laws work for you, and how to preserve more of your assets for your retirement and your heirs.

CHAPTER 4

WHAT IS FINANCIAL PLANNING?

A GLANCE AHEAD

In this chapter, you'll survey the general principles behind effective personal financial planning:

- *Facts and myths about money management*
- *How to measure your net worth and track it from year to year*
- *How to build discretionary income for investing and for enjoying the finer things in life*

FINANCIAL PLANNING: FACTS AND FICTIONS

People often equate income with wealth: the more someone makes, the wealthier he or she appears to be.

In truth, income has less impact on financial net worth than most people think. It's one of many economic fallacies promoted by a society that is more concerned with increased consumer spending than building wealthy citizens. Your job as an effective financial planner is to overcome a lifetime of such prejudices and to learn the skills and habits of a successful money manager.

The Main Goal of Financial Planning

How many times have you said, or heard someone say, "No matter how much I make, I always seem to spend it all"?

The great tragedy in our society is that many of us will reach our senior years unnecessarily impoverished. Literally millions of dollars will have passed through our hands in a lifetime, yet we will have failed to put any of it aside. We may survive, but existence on Social Security and Medicare is no picnic. To make matters worse, few of us will have pensions sufficient to fill the gap.

The bad news is, in order to enjoy a secure and rewarding financial future, you've got to prepare today. The good news is you can begin with far less than you think—provided you start right now. If you want to take an early retirement; enjoy first-quality medical care, travel, and leisure; send your children to good schools; have a home on the beach; and live the other, innumerable benefits of a quality life, you need to make a plan.

A financial plan is a map of the road to success. It tells you how to get from where you are now in terms of assets and potential, to where you want to be—next year, 5 years, or 20 years in the future. Financial planning is a process that reflects who you are, where you want to go, and how you want to get there. In short, it encompasses all the economic factors that affect your progress through the many stages of life.

Financial planning helps you manage your income so that you will accumulate the money you need to invest. It encourages (indeed, requires) practical goal setting and realistic risk assessment and management. It gives you a framework for investment strategies and the resources and capabilities you need to profit from the changing economy.

If your ultimate goal is a healthy financial maturity, the best way to achieve it is through a healthy—and muscular—financial plan.

How Financial Planning Works

Financial planning attacks the barriers to your future well-being simultaneously. First, it gives you a clear snapshot of where you are. This includes guidelines for a budget that will help you find the money you need to begin investing.

When you have mastered your current financial circumstances, planning then helps you establish strategies to achieve your goals.

Figure 4-1 illustrates the various components of a personal financial plan and how they interact at any given time.

Cash in. This component consists of your paycheck, your income from rents, child support, gifts, inheritances, and interest and dividends you receive from investing. It's all the cash you receive within a given period of time.

Inexperienced money managers often make the mistake of thinking that there are different "cash ins" for each purpose. For example, they believe that dividends go only toward stock investments or rents go only toward new housing or other real estate investments. In a sound financial plan, however, all income is considered "cash in" and, consequently is fair game for the best mix of investments.

Cash out. This component is your expenditure of income. The two biggest categories are usually living expenses and liabilities such as taxes and mortgage payments. What's left over is discretionary income, and building this resource is an important objective of any financial plan.

Discretionary income. This component is the money left after paying living expenses and liabilities. You can spend it on entertainment, travel, give it away, or invest it for the future—anything your heart desires. If you invest it, however, it builds your asset base, which in turn can build more discretionary income and—ultimately—net worth.

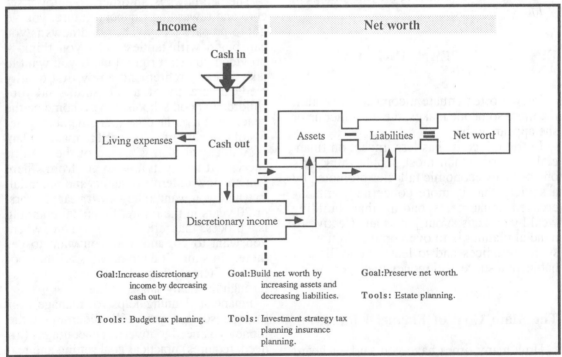

Figure 4-1 How Financial Planning Works (Understanding Net Worth)

Liabilities. Your liabilities include taxes and debt, such as mortgages and all the interest on all loans.

Assets. Your assets are what you own, even if someone else (such as a bank) has a claim against them. Assets may be productive or nonproductive. Productive assets generate income in the form of dividends, interest, rent, or other cash payments that flow back as "cash in." Nonproductive assets are those that, while possibly appreciating in value (such as your house), do not contribute to "cash in" until they are sold.

Net Worth. Your net worth reflects the assets you own "free and clear"—your wealth at any given moment. Building and preserving net worth is the ultimate objective of all financial planning. To calculate your net worth, subtract all your liabilities from all your assets. We'll show you how to do this shortly.

STRATEGIES FOR INCREASING NET WORTH

The basic goals of a financial plan are to

1. Increase discretionary income by increasing cash in and, where possible, decreasing cash out, consistent with a desired lifestyle
2. Build net worth by developing effective tax and investing strategies
3. Preserve existing net worth with effective tax, estate-planning, and insurance strategies

Measuring Where You Stand Today

A map of a strange city is useless unless you first know where you are. Similarly, your financial plan cannot proceed without a realistic understanding of your net worth—your balance of assets and liabilities—as they exist today. In financial planning, this "road map is called the *personal balance sheet*, and it reveals important facts about your current fiscal status.

Your Personal Balance Sheet. Your balance sheet is very much like stopped action on a videotape. If you hit the "pause" or the "freeze frame" button on a VCR, the picture suddenly halts so that you can examine one frame at a time. A personal balance sheet is one "frame" of your financial life.

Of course, this single picture changes as often as your finance situation changes. By following its progress from one period of time to another, you can see if your net worth is growing or declining.

It doesn't take much time or work to create a personal balance sheet—and the reward is vastly greater than the effort. Simply create two columns, side by side, on a blank sheet of paper. In the left-hand column list all your assets, starting with your most liquid assets, such as cash, and move downward through long-term assets—those that would take a lot of time and trouble to sell off, such as your house or a business. In the right-hand column, list all your liabilities, progressing again from current (outstanding bills) to long-term debt, such a home mortgage. Figure 4-2 gives you an example of a typical personal balance sheet.

Personal assets. Here are the elements of the asset side of the balance sheet, beginning with current (liquid) assets.

Cash. This element includes not only cash but items that can be quickly turned into cash, such as savings and money market accounts, certificates of deposits (CDs), contracts or notes receivable, and the cash value (if any) of your life insurance policies.

Marketable securities. Your marketable securities are stocks, bonds, mutual funds, and other investments that can be sold quickly. (Restricted stock is an example of a nonmarketable security, since it can't be sold until a specified time. Include that kind of investment under long-term assets.)

Personal property. Your personal property includes cars, furniture, clothing, and other nonproductive personal property. They could be sold for cash if necessary, otherwise, they don't produce income.

PERSONAL BALANCE SHEET

For_____(name)

Date_____

ASSETS:
    Cash on hand_____
    Checking accounts_____
    Savings accounts_____
    Money market funds_____
    Life insurance cash values_____
    Notes/accounts receivables_____
        TOTAL:_____

MARKETABLE SECURITIES:
    Stocks_____
    Bonds_____
    Government securities_____
    Mutual funds_____
        TOTAL:_____

TOTAL CURRENT (LIQUID) ASSETS:

PERSONAL PROPERTY:
    Automobiles_____
    Household furnishings_____
    Art/antiques/collectibles_____
    Clothing, furs_____
    Jewelry_____
    Other possessions_____
        TOTAL:_____

REAL ESTATE:
    Residences_____
    Other properties_____
        TOTAL:_____

PENSIONS:
    Vested pension benefits_____
    IRA/Keogh_____
    Tax-sheltered annuity_____
        TOTAL:_____

LONG-TERM ASSETS:
    Equity in business_____
    Pending inheritance_____
    Limited partnerships_____
        TOTAL:_____

TOTAL ASSETS

Note: Assets shown at fair market value.

LIABILITIES (current balance and interest rate):
    Mortgage (residence)_____
    Mortgage (other)_____
    Car(s)_____
    Charge accounts_____
    Education loans_____
        TOTAL:_____

TAXES: Due within 12 months
    Federal taxes_____
    Property taxes_____
    Social Security_____
        TOTAL:_____

      TOTAL LIABILITIES_____
      TOTAL NET WORTH_____

      TOTAL LIABILITIES AND NET WORTH_____

      CURRENT RATIO_____
      NET WORKING CAPITAL_____
      DEBT-TO-EQUITY RATIO_____

CASH FLOW

MORTGAGES (monthly payments):
    Residences_____
    Other properties_____
        TOTAL:_____

OTHER LOANS (monthly payments):
    Car(s)_____
    Charge accounts_____
    Other_____
        TOTAL:_____

Figure 4-2 Personal Balance Sheet

Personal Balance Sheet (continued)

Disability Income Insurance

Insured	Policy Number	Plan	Company	Issue Date	Monthly Income Benefit	Elim. Period	Benefit Period	Annual Premium

Life Insurance

Insured	Policy Number	Ownership	Beneficiary	Cash Value	Face Amount	Cost per $1,000	Annual Premium

Financial Resources
Cash Reserves (passbook, certificates of deposit, etc.)

Bank	Branch	Amount	Interest Rate	Term	DateDue

Real Estate (residence, second home, industrial, commercial, land)

Type	Original Cost	Current Value	Date Acquired	Mortgage	Mortgage Rate	Principal and Interest Payments	Property Tax	Equity

Stocks (common, preferred, options, mutual funds)

Shares	Name of company	Date Acquired	Cost	Current Price per Share	Current Value	Dividend	Yield

Bonds (government, municipal, coporate)

Number of Bonds	Name of Company	Coupon	Date Acquired	Maturity Date	Cost	Current Price	Current Value	Current Income

Keogh, IRA (circle one)

Grantor	Trustee	Trustee Address	Account Number	Value of Account	Investment Vehicle	Rate of Return

Real estate. Use current market values and include your home as well as any rental properties.

Pension. Include IRA/Keoghs as well as annuities.

Personal Liabilities. Here are the elements of the liability side of the ledger—claims against your personal assets.

Current debts. Your current debts are debts such as payments on your mortgage, on credit cards, education loans *that are due within the next 12 months.* List the interest rate you are paying on each to determine which area of debt is most heavily burdened with interest payments.

Taxes. Include all taxes due in the next 12 months. List city and state taxes as well as federal and Social Security taxes.

Long-term liabilities. Includes the balances of all loans, including balloon payments. List any other long-term commitments.

Long-term assets. Include anything that can't be converted into cash within the next 12 months or that does not have a ready market value. Include limited partnerships.

Total assets. Your total assets are the sum of both short- and long-term assets.

Analyzing Your Balance Sheet. You now have a snapshot of your current financial position. If you're already familiar with the balance sheet, you can quickly tell what your net worth is, if your financial position is healthy or ailing, and how much cash or cash equivalents you have to meet emergencies or capitalize on new opportunities.

If you are new to balance sheets, here's how to analyze yours.

Net Worth. Your net worth is the difference between total assets and total liabilities—and it *is* possible to get a negative number if you owe more than you own. Subtract your total liabilities from your total assets to compute this value.

People often are surprised when they see their actual net worth in black and white. Some people have tended to underestimate how well they've done while others are reminded of how far they have yet to go.

Knowing your net worth gives you a reference point for future decisions—a foundation for subsequent financial planning. If you update the numbers every six months and recalculate your net worth, you can tell whether you are winning, losing, or tied in the game of wealth. Comparing balance sheets over a longer period of time can tell you if you are obtaining your financial goals.

Measuring Your Financial Health

 Health is something we usually associate with our physical bodies, but it also is relevant to finance. Having a healthy balance sheet generally means that your current assets exceed your current liabilities—that there is enough money coming in to meet your short-term debts. An unhealthy situation exists when current liabilities exceed current assets because an interruption of that income stream could result in insolvency and possibly even bankruptcy itself.

To determine your fiscal health, you need to compute two simple ratios—your "current ratio" and your "debt-to-equity ratio."

Current Ratio. The current ratio is the relationship of your current assets to current liabilities. To obtain it, simply divide the sum of your current assets by the sum of your current liabilities. For example, let's take the balance sheet of Robert, owner of a successful restaurant.

Total current assets = $250,789
Total current liabilities = $78,426
$250,789 ÷ $78,426 = 3.19%

This calculation yields a current ratio of 3.19%, which means that Robert has more than three times the assets needed to meet his current liabilities—a very healthy financial situation. A ratio of 1:1 or better is satisfactory, but if the ratio is less than 1:1 it means your liabilities are outrunning your assets.

Debt-to-Equity Ratio. Your debt-to-equity ratio influences your ability to acquire new financing. Banks use this ratio to calculate the assets you could use to cover losses in the event of a personal financial setback. The lower the debt ratio, the better bankers like it. However, too low a debt ratio may mean that you have too much nonproductive cash. Too few investments mean that your money isn't working hard enough for you.

Determine your debt-to-equity ratio by dividing your total liabilities by your total assets.

Robert's total liabilities are $422,567, and his total assets are $1,465,000.

$$\$422,567 \div \$1,456,000 = 0.2884$$

Robert's balance sheet shows 3.46 times as many assets as needed to meet liability commitments—a robust financial condition.

Net Working Capital. Net working capital is the money you have available for new investments or other spending. It is a short-term measurement of your financial strength—your "muscle" to get the things you want. Because some of it may be in the form of life insurance cash value or stocks you don't want to sell, the entire amount may not be fully available to you now. However, net working capital represents potential spending or investing resources you could obtain by converting everything to cash and paying off your current liabilities.

To find your net working capital, subtract your total current liabilities from your total current assets. For example, Robert's total current assets are $250,789 and his total current liabilities are $78,426. Subtracting the second amount from the first gives Robert a net working capital of $172,363— certainly enough to accommodate a wide range of unforeseen problems or opportunities.

 Using the Financial Ratios. These formulas are not complex, and they can be easily computed each time you update your personal balance sheet. If you have a computer with spreadsheet capability (such as Lotus 1-2-3 or Excel), you can quickly configure the sheet so that each time you enter new figures, the computer automatically recalculates your ratios.

Checking the ratios, as well as your net worth, will give you an immediate fix on your financial position. You can then compare your ratios every six months to see how you are progressing toward your financial goals.

PREPARING A FINANCIAL PLAN

Once your balance sheet is complete, you can move forward to develop a comprehensive financial plan. Remember, a financial plan is like a living organism. It may possess fixed goals such as long-term growth, but it may also require changing strategies to achieve them. The purpose of any financial plan is to increase and preserve net worth, which, as you have seen, is the best true measure of your financial health.

Net worth is built by (1) increasing the amount of resources you have available for investment, and (2) properly allocating those resources into asset categories and investment vehicles that fit your investing personality, lifestyle, stage of life, and personal goals. You'll begin by increasing the resources available for asset building.

Building Discretionary Income

Discretionary income is the key to increased investing power. Unless you win a lottery or inherit a fortune, you can and must find practical, day-to-day ways to make money available for building your asset base.

Of the several options available, all revolve around increasing your flow of cash. Cash flow, of course, can be positive or negative. Positive cash flow—a continuous, incoming stream of dollars—contributes to discretionary income. Negative cash flow diminishes it.

One way to build discretionary income is to earn more money and for people with high income potential, building one's value as a breadwinner is an important component of a healthy financial plan. For nonearned income, you can increase the contribution made by your productive assets—those that generate interest or dividend income. You can control your expenses, by reducing the drain on current income, this control automatically puts more dollars in the investment kitty.

As you learned at the beginning of this chapter, your income does nothing to contribute to net worth unless you keep enough of it to build your assets. Since most of us have a tendency to spend as much as we earn, good financial planning often begins with good budgeting.

Budgeting for Fun and Profit

If you wait to plan or invest until you've finally saved some money, you've missed the entire point: *Financial planning not only uses your money effectively, it helps you get that money in the first place.* The money you need to start an investment strategy almost always can be found among existing assets and income. Budgeting is the process that helps to uncover it.

Every fit and healthy person knows that a sound diet and exercise program perpetuates itself because you feel better every day—you are tangibly rewarded as you go along. A good budget produces tangible, immediate results too, and that's encouraging. Bad budgets produce more pain than reward, which is why so many of them are so quickly abandoned by so many people.

A basic "low-pain" budget is built on a time-tested formula we call the 10/20/70 plan. It is amazingly simple, yet more effective than budgets that are much more complicated. It works by helping you put your money into three separate "accounts." Here's the first element, or account, of the 10/20/70 budget. (See Figure 4-3.)

The Put-and-Keep Account

Each month, write your first check to yourself, for 10% (or more) of your after-tax earned income. It must be the first commitment you make after the charitable or religious contributions to which you have committed yourself.

This 10% goes into an account to which you will continually add for investment funding. Consequently, you never spend it—at least until you clear down the investment vehicles it obtains. It's called your "put-and-keep" account because once you put it there, you will never touch it. It is used to build,

and to keep building, your asset base.

There's nothing new about paying yourself first. In the past, people called their put and keep accounts their "savings" and kept them in passbook accounts, which earned very little interest. Whenever they needed something expensive, they would use this money. After a while, they rightly got the feeling that they were never getting ahead.

Your "put-and-keep" account isn't the savings account of yesteryear. It's money that you accumulated to invest for long-term security and future income needs when your earning power will be reduced. It's even possible to defer taxes on this money through real return annuities and single-premium life insurance contracts—vehicles you'll learn about later in this book. If necessary, impose some discipline on yourself by setting up an automatic payroll deduction or automatic bank draft to make sure that 10% of your total income is invested in your "put-and-keep" account. Once the habit is established, it can help make you wealthy faster than you think.

How Your "Keep" Account Will Be Structured. The cash flow you tap to build net worth will be earmarked for eventual short- or long-term spending (such as retirement) or for the logical and orderly transfer of your estate to your heirs. How you structure the assets that achieve these goals is greatly influenced by your tolerance for risk and by the other components of the offensive and defensive segments of your portfolio.

Just what is a portfolio and how does it relate to your financial plan? A portfolio is nothing more than a collection of investments, although some financial planners break the collection down into portfolios of similar or complementary investments. Your portfolio will always require attention, even if you are the most passive investor. To start, you have to allocate funds to several basic asset categories, choosing appropriate investment vehicles (and specific securities) in each. You then have to rebalance that portfolio periodically (usually once a year) by transferring profits from the asset categories that did well to those whose time has yet to come. If you are an active portfolio manager, you will be trading individual securities within each asset category in hopes of adding marginal profit to the general profits delivered by market growth—but handsome long-term profits don't depend—and should never depend—on "market timing" or other short-term trades.

 Eventually, you will invest a portion of your put-and-keep funds into each of the six basic asset categories identified in Part III: (1) near-money and money market investments; (2) U.S. equities, or individual stocks or stock market mutual funds; (3) U.S. fixed-income or interest-bearing debt investments, such as Treasury bonds, Treasury notes, and municipal or corporate bonds; (4) real estate investments, either in individual properties or group investments, such as limited partnerships or real estate investment trusts (REITs); (5) international securities, such as international mutual funds; and (6) commodities and precious metals—stock in mining companies, metal bullion, or coins.

If you wish to manage your put-and-keep account actively, you will eventually use the special trading techniques that try to profit from short-term fluctuations in the market prices of these basic assets, typically using options and futures. If your financial plan involves unusual tax or personal situations, you may even be a candidate for some of the so-called exotic investments, such as precious gems, strategic metals, collectibles (like art), or a whole range of special-venture limited partnerships.

Put-and-Take Account

When your investment account is taken care of, you will place the next 20% of your after-tax earned income into your "put-and-take" account. This account stores the kind of money you need for emergencies or big-ticket expenditures such as vacations, new car down payments, and home improvements. The money placed here is meant to be saved until it's needed. If you use it for dinners in nice restaurants, you won't have it for the things you really want.

The "put-and-take" account can also save marriages. Many couples have different ideas about how money should be spent— most all marital disagreements begin over money-related issues. A lot of this friction can be eliminated by dividing some of your "put-and-take" money into separate "his" and "hers" *subaccounts*. Each spouse then spends his or her money independently, without argument or justification.

One husband called his put-and-take kitty his "toy" account. His wife placed approximately 5% of their budget in this subaccount—enough that by the end of the year her husband had not only bought all the "toys" he had in mind, but had enough money left over to buy his wife and children special gifts. Not only did this family reduce their level of tension about money, but the amount they *did* spend had never before achieved so much happiness and satisfaction for them.

Another couple targeted a trip to Japan as a three-year goal. They named their put-and-take account "Japan" and even began a contest over who could contribute the most after their basic 10 and 20% deductions had been made.

To keep them productive, you can invest your "put-and-take" dollars in short-term money market accounts or money market checking accounts for reasonable returns without diminishing liquidity. Chapter 9 presents some other vehicles for liquid, short-term investments.

Living Expenses

You should earmark 70% of your monthly income for living expenses. This percentage includes money for the mortgage payment, taxes, and daily living expenses—plus a fudge factor for unforeseen but non-emergency expenses. Any funds not spent in these categories will be channeled into your put-and-keep or put-and-take accounts at the end of the month, the year, or on a quarterly basis.

With this low-pain 10/20/70-plan budget, you control your money instead of it controlling you. Your budget helps you redirect the money that flows into your household every month and apply it to the things that will support your desired lifestyle, and also build discretionary income. It provides a framework not only for managing your income—wages, salaries and commissions—but also for man-

The 10/20/70 Budget

10% (or More)	20%	70%
Put-and-Keep	*Put and Take*	*Living Expenses*

10% (or More)

Put-and-Keep

This is your wealth accumulation account.

Use for long-term needs. *(Never use for consumer spending.)*

Retirement capital

Tax planning dollars

When invested, these are your wealth–building accounts:

    Mutual funds
    Stocks
    Bonds
    Limited partnerships
    Pension funds
    IRA
    Land
    Real estate
    Oil/gas
      etc.

20%

Put and Take

This is your spending account.

Use a bank account or credit union close to you so that it can be used for withdrawals easily.

Preplanned consumer spending

    Education
    Furniture
    Travel and fun!

    New car

    Dreams . . .

Debt reduction if off budget (list)

_____
_____
_____
_____
_____
_____
_____

70%

Living Expenses

This account reflects your absolute needs.

Use your personal checking account.

Fixed Expenses

    House payment
    Medical and dental
    Food
    Utilities
    Car expenses
    Property taxes
    Home maintenance

    Insurance
      Home
      Auto
      Life
      Medical
        etc.

    Career improvement
    Day care expenses

    Children's allowances
    Wife's allowance
    Husband's allowance

    Clothing
    Charity/contributions

    Miscellaneous debt

Figure 4-3 The 10/20/70 Account

GOOD WAYS TO RAISE MONEY
FOR A FIRST PORTFOLIO

1. Begin a "10/20/70" put-and-keep account.
2. Start using employer's automatic paycheck transfers.
3. Convert income-producing assets to growth assets.
4. Sell nonproductive asset (such as little-used automobile, RV, boat, etc.) for cash.
5. Earmark next income tax refund for "investments only."
6. Borrow the money if spread between interest paid and investment rate of return is favorable.
7. Borrow against the cash value of a whole-life policy.

aging the capital that is generated by your assets.

Asset Management

You have two kinds of assets—productive (adds money to your income stream) and nonproductive. By increasing your productive assets, you can generate income that contributes to the cash flow that actively builds net worth.

Nonproductive assets are those intended for personal enjoyment. They may include jewelry, personal property, furniture (including antiques), cars not used in business, clothing, and even your home—if you do not intend to sell it to obtain retirement funds.

Productive assets are those that pay interest, dividend, rents, or royalties. One of the advantages of 10/20/70-plan budget is that you may find it reduces your need to generate income through investments. If you can afford to reinvest your interest and dividend payments, your net worth will grow faster. Of course, your "put-and-keep" account does not depend on these asset management decisions. It will keep on chugging along, adding a solid 10% of your income each month to your net worth-building muscle.

Controlling Cash Flow

Your 10/20/70 budget can also help in yet another important way: to analyze and gain greater control over the two important elements of cash flow.

You already know that cash flow is nothing more that the difference between money income and outflow. The higher the income-to-outflow ratio, the better your potential financial health—although *what* you do with that surplus is often as important as the surplus itself.

Just looking at the total cash flow, for example, is not particularly helpful, from a planning point of view. To gain control over it, you need to know its components and assigning a weight to each, starting with the income side.

Linda, an attorney and solid VALS Achiever (see Chapter 1), had a total income of $70,000. Of that total, $50,000 came from her law firm salary and the remainder from dividends, interest payments, rents, and other investments. To determine what percentage of her total income is generated by professional earnings, she divided the total cash in ($70,000) into her salary ($50,000). This year, her wages represented 71% of her cash flow income.

This calculation gave her a handle on how well her investments are doing—what contribution they were making to her total wealth-building potential. This became particularly important as Linda contemplated her future and began to see the need—and advantages—of income produced from nonwork sources.

Still, your budget—or anyone's budget—won't be workable if you can't get a handle on the 70% that goes to monthly expenses. To determine how expenses influence cash flow, and how well yours conform to the norm for your lifestyle, you can apply some simple tests. The best example is your mortgage: is it proportional to the rest of your income/expense posture?

Case Study 1: The Reasonable Mortgage Payment. Linda's annual expenses happened to be $56,000, and her mortgage payments were $18,000 annually. By dividing her expenses ($56,000) into her mortgage payments ($18,000), she learned that her mortgage represented 32% of her total expenses. Most lenders consider this amount reasonable, although criteria for "reasonableness" can differ greatly from lender to lender, region to region, and the method by which a person's primary income is earned—including the other ratio tests for financial health.

Case Study 2: The Unreasonable Mortgage Payment. Now suppose Linda's adjustable-rate mortgage increased her payments to $29,000 annually. Her mortgage now represents 52% of her total expenses. Such a percentage is of far more concern to her lenders because it may indicate she is overleveraged—owes too much money in comparison to the income she has available to service her debt.

The Bottom Line: A Liveable Mortgage Payment. When mortgage payments are as high as the one in Linda's second case, the money to pay them may have to come from her discretionary income. In fact, imbalance in any debt component can set up negative cash flow—more cash going out than coming in—and deplete discretionary income. In such circumstances it's virtually impossible for Linda or anyone in her situation to put aside anything for the future

 You should apply this same analysis to all debt components on the liability side of your balance sheet, including insurance, car expenses, and your food budget. When you subject your monthly expenses to this kind of scrutiny, you will probably find "financial fat" that can be trimmed without too much pain—or risk to your wealth-building discretionary income.

THE SATISFACTIONS OF FINANCIAL PLANNING

The first comment most financial planners hear from new clients is that for the first time, the clients finally know they have control over their money. They are no longer subject to the unexpected and uncontrollable twists of everyday life and are putting money into the bank, rather than taking it out.

No matter how insignificant the amount may seem, every dollar you put into your "put-and-keep" account contributes to your financial wealth. All you need to keep even a modest sum growing is that greatest of all allies to any investment—time.

TOP LOW-RISK CAPITAL GROWTH
INVESTMENTS FOR 1988

1. Blue-chip common stocks
2. Convertible bonds
3. International stocks
4. Growth stock mutual funds
5. International mutual funds
6. Single-family home (real estate)
7. Rental property (limited partnerships)
8. Balanced mutual funds
9. Index mutual funds
10. Closed-end funds

TOP INFLATION HEDGES

1. Gold and silver bullion
2. Gold and silver coins
3. Gold stocks
4. Futures—precious metals and oil
5. Mutual funds—gold and silver
6. Single-family home (real estate)
7. Rental properties
8. Common stocks
9. Foreign currencies
10. International stocks

TOP DEFLATION HEDGES

1. Treasury obligations
2. U.S. savings bonds
3. General-obligation municipal bonds
4. Money market funds
5. Certificates of deposit (under $100,000)
6. Short-selling stocks
7. Credit union savings accounts (under $100,000)
8. Passbook savings accounts (under $100,000)
9. Corporate bonds (AAA-rated)
10. Annuities (AA-rated companies)

MOST LIQUID INVESTMENTS

1. Treasury obligations
2. Listed common stocks
3. OTC common stocks
4. Mutual funds
5. Checking accounts
6. Money market funds
7. Wheat, corn, and soybeans futures
8. Financial futures

CHAPTER 5

TIME AND YOUR MONEY

A GLANCE AHEAD

Time heals all wounds, as the saying goes, even an anemic pocketbook—and that's the miracle of effective money management. The inner workings of time and money can turn a handful of dollars into true wealth. All it takes is commitment, patience, and knowledge of a few financial basics.

In this chapter, you'll discover

- *The power of compounding to double, triple—even quadruple—any investment*
- *Why inflation is the number one enemy of future spending power and how your real (after-inflation) returns can be increased*
- *How the time-tested technique of dollar-cost averaging can build your "put-and-keep" account*

HOW COMPOUNDING REALLY WORKS

The amount of "put-and-keep" dollars you set aside each month may seem too small to do much good, but that's because you see your investment "frozen" at the moment of its birth—like the snapshot of a baby that has a lot of growing to do. When you learn to visualize those dollars compounded over many years, you will see them as an ocean, not a few meager drops in the bucket.

Time is the powerhouse that turns dollars into fortunes. At the root of its power is the concept of compound interest, a powerful financial tool available to everyone. Interest makes money grow, and compound interest makes it grow fastest of all. Here's how.

Simple Versus Compound Interest

"Simple" interest is the basic interest charged on any amount of money loaned. If you loan $10,000 at 10% simple interest per year, each year you will receive $1,000 back on your money. At the end of five years, you will still have your original $10,000 plus five yearly interest installments of $1,000 each, for a grand total of $15,000.

"Compound" interest pays interest-on-the-interest as well as on the principal. Interest accrues periodically—it may accrue daily, weekly, monthly or quarterly—and as it accrues, it is added to the principal and future interested is computed on this total. Thus you end up receiving interest not only on your principal, but on previous interest as well. $10,000 loaned out at 10% compounded annual interest yields $16,105 after five years, a bonus of $1,105 over simple interest.

Of course, if you were to set aside $1,000 each year and add it to your $10,000 principal, the rate of growth would be even faster.

Figure 5-1 shows how compounding works when $1,000 is invested annually at different interest rates over a number of years. A mere $1,000 invested annually at 10% compounded interest over 30 years yields an impressive $180,942!

Years	5	10	15	20	25	30
7%	6,153	14,783	26,888	43,865	67,676	101,072
8%	6,335	15,645	29,324	49,422	78,954	122,345
9%	6,523	16,560	32,003	55,764	92,324	148,574
10%	6,715	17,531	34,949	63,002	108,181	180,942
11%	6,912	18,561	38,189	71,265	126,998	220,912
12%	7,115	19,654	41,753	80,698	149,333	270,292
13%	7,322	20,814	45,671	91,469	175,850	331,314
14%	7,535	22,044	49,980	103,768	207,332	406,736
15%	7,753	23,349	54,717	117,810	244,712	499,956
16%	7,976	24,732	59,924	133,840	289,087	605,161
17%	8,206	26,199	65,648	152,138	341,761	757,503
18%	8,441	27,755	71,938	173,021	404,272	933,317
19%	8,682	29,403	78,849	196,845	478,430	1,150,386
20%	8,929	31,149	86,441	219,859	566,374	1,418,256
21%	9,182	33,001	94,780	255,017	670,632	1,748,630
22%	9,441	34,961	103,934	290,346	794,164	2,155,837
23%	9.707	39,237	113,982	330,640	940,464	2,657,402
24%	9.979	41,565	125,010	376,464	1,113,628	3,274,734
25%	10.258	37,038	137,108	428,680	1,318,487	4,033,865

Figure 5-1 The effects of compound interest.

The "miracle of compounding" can be seen even more clearly in Andrew Tobias's book, *Money Angles*. Tobias notes that Benjamin Franklin's will, leaving 1,000 pounds sterling each to the cities of Boston and Philadelphia, with instructions that the cities lend it at interest to worthy apprentices, exceeded $3 million 192 years later.

That's the power of compound interest!

The Rule of 72

Unfortunately, one of the problems with compounding is figuring out just how fast your money is growing. You can look it up in tables or compute it with algebra yourself, but mathematical shorthand provides a quicker answer. It's called the rule of 72.

To determine how long any amount of money invested at compound interest basis will take to double, simply divide the interest rate into 72. If you're receiving 10% interest, for example, your money will double in 7.2 years:

$$72 \div 10 = 7.2$$

Here are some common interest rate calculations using the rule of 72:

Formula:	Rule	÷	%	=	Years
	72	÷	20	=	3.6
	72	÷	15	=	4.8
	72	÷	12	=	6
	72	÷	10	=	7.2
	72	÷	7	=	10.3
	72	÷	5	=	14.4
	72	÷	3	=	24

Lending money at compound interest is one way to make time the ally of your wealth-building plan. But time can be the enemy of your investment too, particularly if the rise in general price levels around the country are going up faster than your investment pays you back. This enemy is called *inflation*.

INFLATION—THE ENEMY OF WEALTH

Just as compounding builds wealth, inflation tears it down. Compounding interest gives you more dollars, but inflation makes them worth less when you receive them. Inflation can rob you of everything you hope to gain through the use of compounding, and every investor should know how to hedge against it.

Before 1970, few people in this country worried much about inflation. Of course, stories had been told of great inflationary periods, like post–World War I Germany, when 500,000 German marks bought one loaf of bread, or the hyperinflation that racked many Central and South American countries in the 1960s and 1970s. But those were distant experiences until, in the late 1970s, inflation took this country by storm. Soaring well into double digits, the menace of inflation finally got our attention

Although rebuffed by the monetary recession of the early 1980s, inflation is always a threat. Unless you hedge against it in your investments, you run the risk of earning high interest rates—but at very low *real* (after-inflation) rates of return.

The Real Rate of Return

When calculating your return on an investment, be sure to consider the real rate of return—the true measure of your investment's future purchasing power.

To find the real rate of return you must know two things: (1) the nominal rate of return (the interest paid) and, (2) the annual rate of inflation. The nominal interest rate is easy to find, it's the interest you are getting from the borrower.

 The rate of inflation is measured by the CPI (Consumer Price Index) published by the federal government, although more sophisticated investors tend to follow the WPI (Wholesale Price Index). To find the approximate real rate of return, simply subtract the annual CPI or WPI from the interest rate you are receiving. The results might surprise you.

Suppose, for example, you have $10,000 to lend. You get 10% compound interest and think you are doing well. But real rate of return is only relative. If inflation is 9%, your

real rate of return is just 1% (10 – 9 = 1). Not such a great investment!

Are Inflation Worries Realistic?

If you are like a great many people, you may feel that worrying about inflation is a waste of time. They feel that inflation is waning, that the double-digit inflation of the late 1970s was an anomaly. It won't return, and there's really no reason to worry about inflation for another 40 years. Such thinking will probably get you in trouble.

The truth is that inflation has specific economic causes, and those causes often recur. Inflation *will* return again. The question is only when. Here are two economic theories that may convince you.

Money Supply Theory. In the 1500s, when Europe was getting huge shipments of gold from South America, a finance minister warned the Spanish queen that the arrival of new gold would cause a terrible inflation. Everything would become more expensive, and nobody would be better off. The queen laughed. How could more gold be bad? Gold was money. It was struck into coinage as soon as it arrived. More money meant more wealth. Who would be hurt by that?

Very soon afterward, however, the minister's warning proved true. Spain experienced a terrible inflation. The more money Spaniards made—the more things seemed to cost. The queen summoned the minister—but now she was speaking as a student of economics, not a monarch. "Why did this happen?" she asked.

"It is simple," the minister explained. "When gold coins were scarce, everyone hoarded them. They were precious. Hence, they bought many goods and services. But when gold from South America resulted in tens of thousands of new gold coins, each became less precious. People thought less of them and asked for many when before only a few were needed."

The queen realized she too was as guilty of this "inflationary psychology" as anyone else. "Easy" money—the expansion fo the money supply—did not produce more goods and services; it simply increased the medium used for exchange. With the same number of

Spaniards and products available, the only thing that could increase was prices.

In this country, something similar happens. When the federal government creates more money (through an expansion of credit, bank deposits, or printing paper money), the value of that money as a commodity decreases just as the increase in gold in early Spain devalued gold coins. Too many dollars mean less buying power for each of them—and that is the definition of inflation.

It's the job of the Federal Reserve to control the money supply so that enough enters the economy to spur growth, but not so much as to cause inflation. That, at least, is the plan—but plans don't always work out.

During 1986 and 1987, the money supply rose at such alarming rates that many people began to predict a return of inflation. Will it? To make an intelligent guess, you'll need to understand, like the Spanish queen, the psychology that tends to drive people's expectations about prices.

"Price Shock" Deflation. In addition to money supply inflation, economists today recognize inflation caused by commodity shortages. When there was a worldwide shortage of oil in the 1970s, the Organization of Petroleum Exporting Countries (OPEC) cartel used it as an excuse to multiply oil prices by a factor of 8 (from $5 a barrel to $40). By prolonging that shortage through intentionally low production, OPEC kept oil prices high long after any physical shortage had disappeared.

Since oil is used both as a product and as a fuel to power vehicles that move products, the price of virtually every commodity in the country shot up. The inflation of the late 1970s and early 1980s was caused, in part, by the shock of that oil price increase.

PUTTING TIME ON YOUR SIDE

If we accept the fact that inflation is likely to be an on-again, off-again phenomenon, we must have some strategy that allows us to invest and gain reasonable *real* returns.

Unfortunately, virtually all financial markets respond to inflation. The stock market generally falls in value when inflation threatens, although most companies eventually find ways to fortify the prices of the stocks. The commodity market, conversely, rises at once.

TWO KINDS OF INFLATION

The inflation of the late 1970s provides an excellent example of two kinds of price instability—money supply and price shock inflation. The huge overnight increase in the cost of oil is a textbook example of price shock inflation; but the worst inflation in recent U.S. history had a strong money supply component too. Because the Vietnam War drained resources away from President Johnson's Great Society programs, the government tried to pay for both without raising taxes. The only way to do that was to create new money, and the resulting surge in the money supply spurred not only increased borrowing and consumption, but the *expectation* that such a condition would go on indefinitely. Consequently, people demanded more and more money from products and wages even though both productivity and output increased at a much slower rate. When the OPEC price shock occurred in the 1970s, the United States was vulnerable to this inflationary "double whammy."

Similar occurrences can happen with any commodity when cartels or other forces, such as trade quotas, act to control the free market. Commodity prices have been dropping steadily, or increasing at a very slow rate, since 1980. However, early in 1987 they once again began rising at a rate faster than the rise in GNP. This was taken as a sign, by many prominent economists, that inflation was on the way back.

The bond market falls as interest rates rise (in response to inflation) because the value of older bonds (issued at lower rates) diminishes.

Of course, inflation isn't the only factor affecting these markets. The health of the economy (growth of GNP), the size of the national debt, the foreign trade imbalance (export of U.S. jobs and dollars), and other items also are involved. However, over the long term, inflation tends to affect most investments most adversely.

How does one "put-and-keep" money safely in an economy that, over the years, will see prices shoot up and down? How do you build wealth steadily when there are periods during which inflation will rob you of your money's buying power?

The answer is to let time work *with,* and not against you. If you assume that over the long haul, even with the ups and downs of inflation, overall market trends will be up—as historically they have been—you can put time and the overall power of the economy on your side. As markets move up and down in response to inflation and other factors, inexperienced investors typically move their money impulsively. When a market is high, such investors imagine that everyone is making money, and they jump in and "buy high." When a market is low, they think that everyone is going broke, and they bail out, selling when asset prices are low. As a result, these impulse investors have the worst of both worlds: they buy low and sell high—the cardinal sin of all investing.

 It's usually impossible to say when high prices are "too high" and when low prices are "too low." It is very easy to say how the market did yesterday or what the rate of inflation was last month. But how do we know what either will be tomorrow? Trying to anticipate trends and move investments around accordingly can end up being the most expensive lesson you've ever learned in the futility of amateur financial fortunetelling. Market timing can ultimately wear down the most determined investor, finally sending him or her to the sidelines with a near-empty "put-and-keep" account suitable only for savings accounts, savings bonds, or one last night on the town.

Winning Through Dollar-Cost Averaging

Fortunately, there is a solution that puts time back in your corner. It works in virtually any market, and while its results on any given day may not be spectacular, over the long run it almost always turns up a winner. It's called *dollar-cost averaging* and it's been called the greatest investing tip of the century.

Dollar-cost averaging began in the 1920s as a way to keep up with the then skyrocketing price of stocks. Although it's tempting to say that averaging ignores market cycles, it's more accurate to say that averaging plays right through them.

Figure 5-2 shows what dollar-cost averaging does. It flattens out the day-to-day and month-to-month see-saw of market prices so you can take advantage of a long-term upward trend.

How Dollar-Cost Averaging Works. The principle is simple: each month (or every six months or at whatever period is comfortable for you), invest a constant amount of money—come rain or shine, even if the market is in the doldrums. Suppose you have $300 a month of your "put-and-keep" money to invest in stocks. You decide to put the money into XYZ Mutual Fund—a growth fund. Initially the shares sell for $10 apiece. You buy into the fund, getting 30 shares the first month. The next month you buy another $300 worth, although the actual number of shares you buy will depend on the current price per share. Six months later you discover that the fund has soared. The market has turned up and the fund took advantage of it. Now the shares are selling for $20 apiece. If you buy $300 worth again, you will only be able to get 15 shares. You are now faced with a decision—and a temptation. Because the market is up and the fund has done so well, your natural impulse is to put more money in—to raid your other investments and spend $600, for example, this month. but because you are working on a dollar-cost plan, you resist the impulse and buy only the same $300 worth of the fund. You buy more shares of a winner, but fewer than before because the price is high.

Now suppose that nine months after you bought into the fund, things have taken a turn

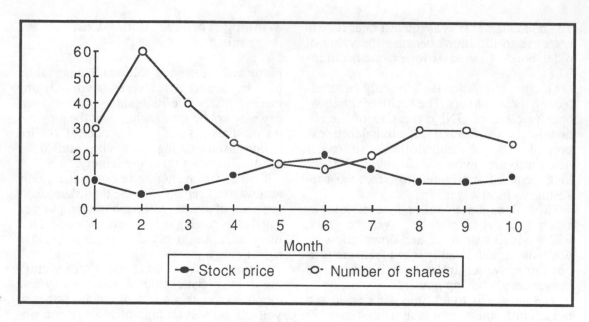

Figure 5-2 Dollar-cost averaging

for the worse. The fund is now back to $10 per share. Your urge is to bail out—to sell before the stock drops lower. However, you resist the impulse again buy your standard $300 worth of the stock. This time you end up with 30 shares. You bought into a "loser" when the price was low and consequently bought more shares than before.

After a year you take a look at your investment. How have you done? The following chart describes your stock purchases.

Five-Year Chart of Investments with Dollar-Cost Averaging

Month	Amount Invested	Stock Price	Shares
1	$300	$10	30
2	300	5	60
3	300	7.50	40
4	300	12	25
5	300	17.50	17
6	300	20	15
7	300	15	20
8	300	10	30
9	300	10	30
10	300	12	25
Totals:	$3,000	$13 (last price)	292

Have you lost money over the year or made it? After all, the stock went as high as $20 and as low as $5. Your natural impulse would have been to buy at $20 and sell at $5. But, instead of buying high and selling low, you steadily bought $300 worth of stock per month regardless of the price. How well did this strategy serve you?

At the end of the year, you have 292 shares. At $13 per share, that means that you have $3,796, or a profit of $796. That's a little over 25% on your original investment—not too shabby—and considerably better than you would have done following your "normal" investor instincts.

Some people, of course, point out that you could have made much more by selling when the stock was at its high of $20. Yes, you could have. But remember too, the whole point of dollar-cost averaging is to come up with a plan that allows you to win *regardless* of market cycles. You might have sold when the mutual fund stock was at $20 and made a killing. But you might just as easily have sold when it dropped down to $5 and lost a lot. The point is, you can't really tell which time is the right time to buy or sell. Who knows when high is "high enough" and when low is "too low"? Thus, by buying steadily and using time as your ally, you break through the crests and troughs and end up with a very healthy profit.

The Logic Behind the Numbers. The reason it all works is mathematical. With a dollar-cost averaged investment of $300 per month, you bought more shares of XYZ Mutual Fund when the price was low and fewer shares when the price was high. Thus you were buying more at the low end and less at the high end. It's easy to see why you came out on top: You bought low and although you did not "sell high," at least you did not spend more money "high" than you should have. Another way to gauge the value of dollar-cost averaging is by looking at the average cost per share of the fund. The average price per share during the year was roughly $12. But your average cost per share was only a little over $10. Again, a recipe for winning in any market.

Of course, there is one more factor to consider. Earlier, you learned that dollar-cost averaging allows you to break through the ups and downs of the market to take advantage of its generally upward trend. The fact that your cost per share is lower than the average price per share means you are in a good position to make a profit. When you want to sell, the price of the stock at that time must be higher than your average cost. In the preceding example, you invested $3,000 to acquire 292 shares. To make a profit, you would have to receive a price per share of more than $10.27—but this probably won't be difficult.

Here's where that historical upward trend in the market pays off. since prices tend to rise (if for no other reason than inflation), there is a good chance that when you want to sell, the price of the stock that month will exceed your average cost. If it does not, you may be experiencing another short-term price fluctuation, which you will have to wait out. Given the forces of time and statistics, however, the wait should not be too long.

Time Diversification Theory and Dollar-Cost Averaging

 "Time diversification" is one of the newest ideas in modern portfolio theory—it embraces the twin concepts of dollar-cost averaging and multiple-asset allocation. Time diversification theory holds that to reduce risk and maximize total return, investments should be held through a complete market cycle, which usually lasts at least four to six years. Recent academic evidence suggests that when it comes to reducing total risk, time diversification is more important than the traditional diversification of buying many different securities. Thus, it gives you further guidelines for deciding how long is "long enough" to hold your investment.

SELECTING YOUR BASIC INVESTMENT STRATEGY

Once you have made your commitment to invest a consistent amount of money each month in your "put-and-keep" account, you must decide where it should be invested. Should it be in stock, bond, commodities, or something else?

You need a basic strategy that unites the time factors of investing to investments you'll choose. The first task is to match your portfolio to the time available and your financial goals. Are you in the stage of life where you want to build wealth, or do you need to preserve it and invest for current income? One calls for an offensive investing strategy; the other implies a defensive strategy. Neither, however, negates the value of multiple-asset investing or dollar-cost averaging. Most investors should build elements of both tactics into their portfolio strategies.

Defensive Players

Defensive players use their money to protect existing assets. They are most concerned about not losing what they already have. They do not want to risk giving up their hard-won principal.

Unfortunately, too many people think they must be defensive players. They remember the hard work it took to acquire their "put-and-keep" money. At parties, they tend to repeat stories about this person or that who lost his or her shirt in the market, or who got wiped out by a chancy investment. Defensive players basically distrust all investments and consequently distrust their own ability to succeed in investing. "Never mind shooting for big profits—just take the money and run!" seems to be their motto.

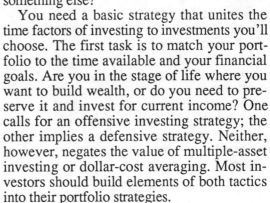

Many kinds of investments are suitable to defensive players and the defensive segment of any portfolio. Generally speaking, debt-based assets provide the benefits of safety and income. Many debt-based investments are "stable" (they offer no growth), but they are dedicated to preserving principal. Debt assets include T-bills, CDs (certificates of deposit), money market accounts, and insurance plans. More aggressive debt assets include trust deeds and notes, direct loans, and commercial paper. Having large cash reserves is also a defensive play because it keeps you out of other markets, and hence keeps you immune to all risks but inflation.

The big advantage of debt-based assets is that the principal is always protected, sometimes by government insurance or other guarantees.

The big drawback to debt is that should inflation rise while you are locked into a fixed-income asset, it can undercut the buying power of both the dollars you are earning and those you are protecting. The cruel part of debt assets is that during periods of intense inflation, the defensive players who can afford it least—the elderly and those on fixed incomes can end up with dollars that are worth only half as much as when they began.

Offensive Players

Offensive players don't worry too much about keeping what they have! Their goal is to get more. They think of their current money as a tool to build a bigger asset base. Offensive players are always "in the market" and keeping their eye on the bouncing ball— market prices and new opportunities.

Equity-based assets are usually the best play here. They offer growth—the rapid increase of principal—that is generally unrelated to interest (unless that interest rate gets too high). Equity-based assets can make money quickly, but they can lose money just as fast. Even with mutual funds and dollar-cost averaging, if you buy into a fund that eventually bottoms out at a price far lower than your average cost, you will end up losing money.

Typical equity investments include publicly traded stocks, stock options, real estate, equity-based mutual funds, and certain tax shelters left over after the 1986 Tax Reform Act, including domestic oil and gas. They also include commodities, bullion, and rare coins.

When you buy an equity investment, your main objective is to make money—to experience capital gain. You are on the offensive. You are specifically looking for growth. The typical questions you will ask yourself are

- *"How good is the market for this type of investment?"* Not all equity issues are easily traded.
- *"Is there liquidity? Can I get out after I make my profit?"* Stocks, for example, are highly liquid. Stock options, however, tend to be slightly less liquid. Bullion is extremely liquid. Rare coins are more limited in liquidity. And real estate should always be considered a long-term investment.
- *"Are my assumptions about growth realistic?"* You don't expect stocks in general to soar during a recession, you'll have to look for peculiar stocks or wait until the business cycle picks up. And you won't see commodities doing well during *dis*inflation. Existing bonds are going to do well when interest rates are falling and do poorly when rates are rising. You have to realize that, over time, the general road "up" is not without its potholes.
- *"Can I trade, or may I buy and hold the investment?"* Is it something that takes constant attention, such as investing in commodities, or can you sit back and check in every six months or so?

Figure 5-3 shows the two different approaches, offensive and defensive, and the equity and debt investments they represent.

Toward a Combined Investment Strategy

Most of us are neither defensive or offensive players exclusively. How we "play the markets" tends to be determined by our positions in life, goals, and other elements of investor personalities, as discussed in Part I. The traditional view of the investment life cycle is that at the beginning we *accumulate,* in the middle we *protect,* and at the end we seek to *dispose* in an orderly and efficient manner. Younger people are typically attuned to spending and to accumulating wealth. They have little, are more likely to take risks, and are often hungry to get more. They have time to recover from the mistakes, so they tend to be offensive equity players.

As people get older, they tend to become more conservative. Those who have accumulated some wealth are anxious to protect it. They tend to shift their strategy to the defensive, and debt assets play a larger role in their portfolios.

Of course, not all assets acquired during the accumulation stage are or should be offensive. It is important to build a solid financial base on which a more aggressive investment strategy can be pursued. Such a pyramid starts with the construction of a sound, conservative, defensive foundation; moves to the middle of the structure containing assets of different traits; and, finally, peaks at the apex of aggressive, growth in-

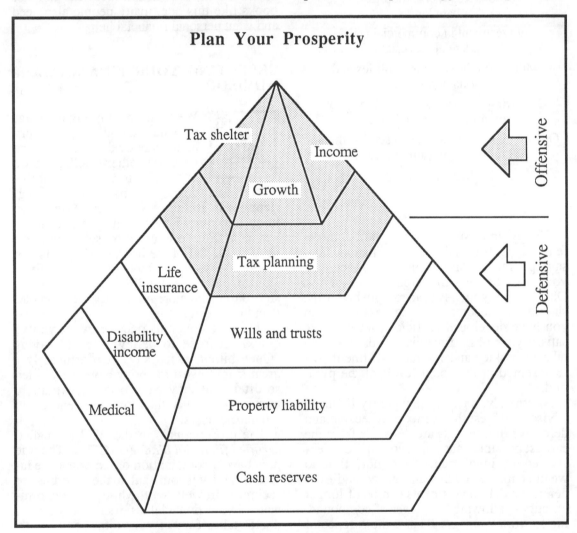

Figure 5-3 Offensive and defensive investing approaches

vestments. A typical financial pyramid might look something like this:

LIFETIME FINANCIAL PYRAMID
Greater Risk

Rare coins

Art and stamps

Bullion and jewels

Speculative options
(uncovered)

Stock, R&D, commodities,
bare land

Investment in commercial and
residential real estate

Mutual funds, stocks in utilities and
solid companies

Investing in bonds and annuities and
owning your own home

Opening a savings account, establishing an
IRA and buying life insurance

Lesser Risk

The pyramid suggests that you begin defensively by first building a base that includes savings, retirement account, insurance, and your own home—all defensive strategies. Only when you have accomplished this, should you become more aggressive. when you have developed sufficient net worth to satisfy your basic financial needs, you can take on riskier and riskier investments, as represented in the upper levels of the pyramid.

Alternately, many contemporary financial advisors suggest that a mix of offensive and defensive investments are desirable from the earliest possible date. Thus your more offensive equity investments have more time to weather market cycles and grow, and even defensive debt investments can be of longer duration—allowing the power of compounding to work its magic. This is the essence of the multiple-asset allocation philosophy you'll encounter throughout this book, and understanding its offensive, defensive, and time-related components is important to your financial success.

Ultimately, the strategy—or mix of strategies—you choose to follow should depend to a great degree on your level of comfort with risk. As we have seen, some people are comfortable only when they have all their bases covered; others are always out there scrambling for more even after they have acquired considerable wealth.

Your goal should not be to artificially select a model and then force yourself to fit it. Rather, it should be to find a model that best suits your own investing personality, lifestyle, values, and goals. Although you can do so on your own and with the help of books like this one, many people also need and want personal financial help.

SELECTING YOUR FINANCIAL ADVISOR

 We seem to be living in an age of financial advisors. Every hour on television or radio one guru or another is telling us we can make fortunes in gold or diamond or penny stocks or agriculture in Brazil or something else. If we jump into one of these trendy or exotic investments very often find ourselves out on a limb, at the tail of the herd, or simply losing money. Most investments pitched on television or otherwise loudly promoted are designed to make more money for the promoter than the investor.

If you've done this once or twice, you've quickly learned to believe the old saying "Once bitten, twice shy." Unfortunately a great many investors today have been bitten so often that they have become extremely mistrustful of even the most experienced and reliable advisors.

The professionals in the field are called *certified financial planners* (CFPs). The true pros have a combination of experience, education, and wisdom that makes the cost of seeing them well worthwhile. They coordinate all your financial affairs the way a good doctor takes care of your total body health. They handle not only investments but also insurance, estate planning and retirement planning. By coordinating these elements, they can achieve benefits (including product discounts, economies of scale, and better-tailored product choices) that wouldn't be available if each were handled separately. Best of all, they can create a realistic financial plan suited specifically to your needs. And they are investments that allow you to maximize the advantages of time in your "put-and-keep" account.

To begin your search for an advisor, it's important to know with whom you're dealing. Almost anyone can call him- or herself a financial planner, but only those who belong to the International Board of Standards and Practices for Certified Financial Planners, Inc. (IBSPCFP) may use the CFP, certified financial planner, designation. The organization has stiff educational requirements for obtaining the CFP designation and enforces a strict code of ethical high standards. Although competent advisors may be found without the CFP designation, an advisor who has this credential is usually your best bet.

Interviewing Your Financial Planner

Once you've narrowed the field of candidates, you should interview your financial planner in depth. Of course, really top-flight financial planners are very, very busy and you may not be able to gain access to them unless you already have a substantial net worth. However, many capable CFPs are just starting out and may be willing to take on less established clients—and some of these will eventually become the superstars of tomorrow!

When meeting with a financial advisor, here are some areas to inquire about.

Background. How long have the planners been in business? What special educational preparation do they have? To what professional organizations do they belong, what licenses and certifications do they hold? (Remember that planners with professional licenses to maintain may hold to a higher standard of performance.) What did they do before becoming financial planners?

Client Interest and Specialization. To earn the CFP designation, planners must have a broad-based financial knowledge, although many planners specialize. Some financial planners focus on pension and estate planning, others specialize in corporate planning, tax work, or particular investments.

To a large extent, a planner's specialty reflects the kind of clientele with which he or she is most comfortable. Some planners work primarily with people just getting started; others prefer to work with established investors or those on the threshold of retirement. Others work mainly with certain professionals, such as doctors, lawyers, or senior executives. Select an advisor who recognizes and appreciates your own special needs and whose clientele reflects your profile. Be sure your advisor's view is broad enough to oversee all your needs.

References. Don't be shy about asking for professional references. They may be testimonial letters of praise from former or current clients, or sample financial plans set up for other clients, with a track record of results. By asking for references, you may get some idea of the clientele with whom the planner works and a sense of how he or she works. If you want verbal assurance, ask for several clients to contact. Don't be satisfied with the first or only name you're given.

Professional Help. Most financial advisors work at the hub of a wheel, the spokes of which include bankers, attorneys, accountants, and specialists in different kinds of investments. The true value of your financial planner may depend on the quality of the other professionals he or she can bring to service your account.

Costs. Good financial advice is not free. The financial planner is a business person who works to make a profit. However, if the advisor makes money for you, then you won't resent paying the bill. The real question therefore, is how much value can and should the advisor add?

Financial planners generally charge in three different ways:

1. *Fee only.* Some financial planners work for a set fee. Such a planner may create a financial plan, suggest investments, create an estate plan or do whatever else you may need. A planner need not be licensed, but in that case he or she would not be able to implement the portions of the plan that re-

quire the services of a licensed professional, such as stock brokers or insurance dealers.

The fee is usually based on time spent and the complexity of the work. It can be a flat amount, an hourly amount, or a percentage of your net worth or income. Fees may range anywhere from a few hundred dollars to several thousand dollars, depending on the assignment.

2. *Commission only*. Since many people balk at paying fees, many planners charge on a commission-only basis. Commission-only financial planners are licensed to sell specific investment products that may include securities, insurance, or even real estate. They collect commissions on the individual transactions that take place in implementing and administering your plan.

Some investors believe there is a built-in conflict of interest when financial planners collect a commission on the investments they suggest. As a result, a third type of financial planner receives both a fee and a commission.

3. *Fee and commission combination*. Many planners set a fee for the services they pro-vide, then receive commissions on products they sell to you. This arrangement tends to protect the client from the possibility that a planner will favor one product over another, since his or her income is not wholly dependent on commissions. Because some of the financial planner's income is coming from commissions, however, the planner is able to charge a much lower fee than a financial planner who operates simply on a fee basis. Many people prefer this arrangement, and it has become the most common form of compensation in the business.

Whatever arrangement you select, make certain the financial planner fully discloses all sources of compensation. Full disclosure is one of the tenets of trust on which financial planners—and any reliable profession—must operate.

The financial planner may be one of the most important people you can meet in your lifetime. He or she may become a counselor, researcher, educator, and family friend. Your financial planner can put you on the road to financial wealth and protect you from life-wrenching, costly mistakes.

CHAPTER 6

RETIREMENT PLANNING

A GLANCE AHEAD

This chapter takes a long look into the future. In it, you'll discover

- *Why the Social Security system may let you down when you need it most*
- *Why IRAs continue to be a good bet for retirement planning*
- *How to make Keogh and corporate retirement plans work harder for you*
- *The role of insurance in retirement planning*
- *How to make the most of your retirement fund*

SOCIAL SECURITY: WHO'S SECURE AND WHO'S NOT?

Jonathan arose from bed one bright, sunny morning and his head hurt just a little. The night before had been his 30-year retirement party at work. He had received a gold watch, champagne, and an abundance of best wishes from his lifelong friends.

Later in the morning, Jonathan received and opened his mail. First he was surprised to see that a credit card he recently applied for had been declined. How could that be? Jonathan's first reaction was surprise, followed closely by strong irritation and resentment. After all, Jonathan had always paid his bills promptly. On the rare occasions when he had used credit cards, the issuers periodically offered to raise his credit limit, although he had always declined such offers.

This rejection of a routine credit card request was difficult to understand. Jonathan called the issuer to inquire. The reason? Jonathan was no longer employed and could not therefore continue to show a dependable source of repayment from current and future income. What? When the credit card company checked for verification of employment, it was informed that Jonathan's income was ending as of his retirement date. Since no other source of income was shown on Jonathan's application, the application was summarily rejected.

A second piece of mail drew Jonathan's attention. This envelope was from his group insurance carrier. Jonathan's health, dental, and life insurance policies, previously covered under a company-sponsored group insurance plan, had all lapsed as of the date of Jonathan's retirement. Jonathan would have to apply afresh, with a new medical examination, new application forms, and new related requirements. Also, 100% of the new premiums (much higher than when the company plan was in effect) would have to come out of Jonathan's postretirement pocket.

Is Jonathan's story an isolated hard-luck incident? Not at all! Most Americans currently express serious concern over lack of retirement planning. Most people in our country lack the resources to pay for their individual idea of "comfortable" retirement. Social Security is never enough. That should come as no surprise: it was never intended to substitute for private retirement plans and personal savings.

It's no secret that Social Security may not provide much comfort for your retirement. For people who have prepared for retirement, Social Security payments will provide a supplementary income at best; those who are forced to rely on Social Security will wish they had planned for other resources.

In 1935, Congress established Social Security as a form of supplementary income for retirees. Today, the program, which is funded by taxes, covers 90% of the population. Money paid into the system by workers and their employers is not invested; it's dispersed directly to recipients. This system has two obvious flaws: (1) as life expectancy figures continue to rise, increasing numbers of retirees will be supported by a proportionately smaller work force; and (2) the younger siblings of the post-World War II baby boom generation are going to be hard pressed to keep up with the demands of the system when their older brothers and sisters begin to retire in the second decade of the next century.

"Ten years ago, for example, four workers supported one retiree," write C. Colburn Hardy and Howard J. Weiner in their book *Personal Pension Plan Strategies for Physicians:* "Today, the ratio is three to one, and . . . it will soon be two to one."

Even if Social Security payments held still, the system would be a fiscal disaster. Unfortunately, they don't. Payments are indexed to inflation, and most of those who have retired to date have earned back everything they contributed within the first five years. "The payback time is lengthening," write Hardy and Weiner, "but by every standard, Social Security is a terrific deal. Even new retirees will receive, during their first year away from work, about $2 for every $1 paid in the year before."

Accordingly, the tax levied against workers to support Social Security has leapfrogged from 1% of the first $3,000 of salary of wages in 1935, to 7.51% of a base of $45,000 in 1988, a total of $3,379.50 for anyone with an income of at least $45,000. Employees and their employers both pay the 7.51% tax. Self-employed persons pay at a 13.02% rate in 1988.

WHAT YOU CAN DO

Individuals who are employed by companies with good retirement programs have a head start on the Social Security dilemma: with good tax and investment planning, they have a very good chance of enjoying a prosperous retirement. Workers who don't have a retirement program can prepare by funding an individual retirement account (IRA); and the self-employed can invest their dollars either in an IRA or a Keogh (Keoghs were established in 1962 to give self-employed people many of the benefits of a corporate retirement program), or both.

Whatever form it takes, a pension plan is the "must-do" item in any good financial plan because it provides tax benefits that aren't available through other investment tools. Think of a pension plan as a tax-deferred savings account: you can deduct the contributions when you make them, which may lower your tax bracket, and tax payments on the assets that build internally are deferred until you begin to withdraw funds at retirement, when you will probably be in a lower bracket.

A pension plan allows you to cut your tax bill, enjoy the benefits of compounded interest, and shelter your assets until you need them. This could become incredibly important to you if Congress chooses to limit future Social Security benefits in order to preserve the system.

Potholes in the Road to Retirement

Assume, as you begin your retirement-planning process, that the following statements will apply to you if you do little or nothing to ensure that your retirement goals are met:

1. I will not have enough money.
2. My lifestyle will go steeply down hill as I grow older.
3. Credit will be routinely denied me.
4. My family will suffer economically and emotionally.

5. When my health deteriorates, my assets will be liquidated and lost.
6. Social Security, Medicare, and similar programs will be cut back.
7. Inflation will soar.
8. My private pension, if any, will fail to pay off as previously expected.
9. Taxes will increase much faster than I have anticipated.
10. New income opportunities for me will no longer exist.

If this list does not inspire you to do something, better check your pulse. The later stages of life can and should be as vital as the early ones. Sometimes, some of us need to be scared into doing what we know needs to be done. If this works for you, put the scariest scenarios you can think of down on paper and force yourself to read them out loud once a month until you do something about them. Do what works for you!

After you find yourself sufficiently motivated to act, develop your own personalized list of goals that you really *want* and perceive you *need* to achieve.

Goals That Matter to You

 When you set goals for retirement, don't simply parrot a book filled with actuarial tables, pension fund statistics, and similar "dry" data. Use goals that are relevant to *your* daily habits, to *your* family, and to *your* future hopes and dreams.

For example, if you enjoy traveling to resort destinations and staying in first-class hotels, your retirement travel budget will need to be much larger than if you are happiest camping close to home in public parks.

Regardless of your personal situation, always aim high. Costs are very likely to exceed your estimates—perhaps not every item, but the ones you especially want 10 or 20 years from now, when they have become rare and expensive.

Goal-setting Checklist. Use the following list to guide your goal setting:

1. *Write down your goals*. Print clearly for review.
2. *Review your goals*. Are they comprehensive? If not, add more to your list!
3. *Discuss your goals with your family*. Your spouse *and* your children are old enough to understand that they should be involved as completely as possible in the planning process.
4. *Date your list of goals*. Time passes more rapidly than any of us care to admit. If a year has passed, it is time to update your goals.
5. *Evaluate your performance*. Lists are useful tools. However, if you fail to *act* from year to year, you have merely engaged in an academic exercise of no value to you or your loved ones.
6. *The indispensable goal: increasing your net worth*. Every financial move you make should, in retirement planning, be geared toward increasing your financial net worth. Most people focus only on *income*. However, it is the accumulation of assets that increases income over time. Therefore, include *growth* in your goals each and every year.

Twenty Questions Toward a More Secure Retirement

We hope you are reading this book long *before* your intended retirement date if this passage is relevant to you. Anticipate your retirement needs according to the following precepts, and remember to be overly pessimistic.

The 20 questions posed here are meant to trigger your own thinking about your personal situation. Each person's retirement goals and plans must be individualized. You are unique. Your needs may be similar to others, but they are never identical. Design a plan that fits *you*.

 1. When should I begin retirement planning? The answer to this first question is always *now!* It is never too early. It is also never too late. Regardless of your age, condition, or resources, it can help to stop and take a fresh look at your situation. Compare notes with your friends. What can you learn from both their mistakes and their successes?

The conventional wisdom is that retirement planning occurs sometime between ages 40 and 65. Such a narrow viewpoint fails to serve the needs of the majority. Retirement planning is an integral part of the financial planning process, and should be approached as a lifelong habit. Try your best to resist setting limits on planning. Rethink your lifetime financial plan as often as possible.

Change is constant. Retirement in the twentieth century is very difficult for many people. However, retirement in the twenty-first century will present challenges we have not even dreamed of yet. Read as much as possible. Talk to as many of your friends as possible. Never limit the input you have access to. For example, a neighbor may have found out a great deal about health insurance. A co-worker may have successfully insulated his or her home with state-of-the-art technology to save future energy costs. Such information all adds up to improving your future standard of living.

The answer to the question "When will I retire?" is probably "Later than I would like" if you would like to retire from your current job early, or "Earlier than I would like" if you would like to keep working and there is a mandatory retirement provision where you are employed. In other words, assume that you will *not* retire when you want to retire.

2. What is my projected net worth now? It is part of the necessary self-discipline of the planning process to periodically and regularly evaluate where you stand. One of the most important measurements you must make is a calculation of your net worth. Figure it out at least annually (preferably semiannually). Net worth comparisons over time help you track what is working and what is not working in your financial strategy.

3. What will my net worth be at retirement? Figuring out your net worth at retirement is the toughest part because you cannot perfectly predict the future. However, you should take a good guess. Here's a hint—do not use compound interest growth (as discussed elsewhere within this book) in

order to calculate net worth at time of retirement. Instead, use simple interest because if you are later fortunate enough to experience compound growth of your money, this will be a bonus and you won't be disappointed by overestimating.

4. What is my income now? Be conservative in estimating current take-home income. Be certain to deduct all potential taxes. Review your withholding assumptions to be comfortable with the logic behind them. If your accountant advises you to withhold more or less, change accordingly. If you are uncertain about your present tax position, check with a qualified accountant (preferably a certified public accountant, or CPA). Gross income is an important benchmark of how well you are doing but net take-home pay is the real income test and it should always be "after tax." Measuring after-tax income means you compute how much you owe in taxes, deduct that sum from gross income, and determine your own "bottom line" from your paycheck. If you stop at what the pay stub says, you may forget other tax dollars that need to be paid before you have arrived at a true net take-home pay figure.

5. What will be my income at retirement? No one knows what Social Security benefits will be 20 or 30 years from now. We also lack any dependable knowledge about future inflation trends. Since everyone's crystal ball is at least a bit cloudy, it is helpful to assume no increase in current Social Security benefits for your own retirement planning. If most of your relatives are receiving approximately $500 per month in current Social Security benefits, plug that number into your own projections. What interest from savings, what income-producing investments do you have? What private retirement plan(s) apply? When you total it all up, you have a conservative projection of your income at retirement. If you're like most people, you won't be comfortable with the idea of living on that amount for the rest of your postretirement life.

6. Can I live comfortably on that income? Assume the answer is no. It may seem enough today, but you should assume that inflation will be higher, your needs will increase, and anything that can go wrong will go wrong at the worst possible time (Murphy's law). Think about a business in which you can participate as an owner. This may be a family business with someone you know and trust, or a sole proprietorship you start on your own, part time. Businesses provide a means of tax savings in the early years and, if successful, a means of supplementing retirement income in later years.

7. If not, what are my alternatives?

- Plan now and review your retirement plan annually.
- Check your insurance policies and inquire into annuities.
- Review the investment opportunities in Part III of this book that seem right for you.
- Review Social Security benefits likely to flow to you.
- Review all your retirement assets, and project likely income streams.
- Determine family resources, including extended family assets and liabilities that are relevant to your situation.
- Review all your retirement data with spouse and/or financial advisors.
- Determine relevance of business opportunities and act on them.

8. What are my financial resources now?
It can be tough to face the facts when the facts are relatively negative. For example, if you are an upper-middle income household, yet have little or no savings and few retirement assets, it is time to wake up and do something about it! At the very least, you must start to save a significant percentage of your income immediately and keep on doing it! Do the following:

- List all cash assets, including checking and savings accounts in banks, savings and loan associations, credit unions, and similar institutions. List account numbers, and verify current balances and interest rates.
- List all other investment assets, including stocks, bonds, mutual funds, real estate, and all other appropriate items. Verify balances and interest rates, when applicable.

- Determine present and future projected income (cash flow projections).
- Compare the bottom line with your projected expenses for retirement. If you are dissatisfied, start saving more and put it into the safest investments you can find within your predetermined investment strategy.

9. What should I be doing to prepare now?
You should be acting in your own best interest for your financial future. That means maximize savings and asset growth while minimizing taxes and the spending of after tax dollars on potentially deductible items (especially important when a business owner is determining strategy). Review and revise as frequently as necessary and no less often than once each year.

10. What will I do for retirement health care?
If you have no health insurance, buy some. Shop for it—then buy it. If you accumulate assets and have no health insurance other than Medicare or the state equivalent, you are inviting the vultures to your sick bed. Government health entitlement programs, such as Medicare, are also best considered in the "never enough" category for planning purposes. Assume it won't be sufficient, and take care of it yourself.

11. What will I do for retirement credit?
Establish more than you think you want or need *in advance of retirement*. Remember our story at the beginning of this chapter. When you need credit is the only time you probably won't be able to get it. Therefore, establish all you want and then some *prior* to your retirement date. Then you know it will probably be there when you want it.

12. How can I improve my retirement tax planning?
Review your tax status with your accountant. Be certain that you have a comprehensive checklist of itemized deductions available to you if you are paying significant sums of tax each year. Do your tax planning early and often during the year. When you think you have your situation well in hand, ask for a second opinion. Look at tax-deferred exchanges if you are considering the sale of real estate assets. Compare lump-

sum distributions with forward-averaging alternatives if you have retirement plan proceeds to deal with. Read a great deal on the subject and educate yourself as fully as possible.

13. Do I have family who can and will help when needed? Our American work ethic presumes a fierce sense of personal independence in every aspect of life. It is therefore difficult for many people to appreciate the increasing likelihood that as we age we may one day need to depend on our families, at least physically, even if we are fortunate enough to avoid financial dependency late in life.

14. Will I be asked to help other family members? The reverse should also be anticipated and planned for. Are you in a position to help others? Who is most likely to ask for such assistance? Make a list and discuss it with your spouse or other closest relative, such as a grown child who may inherit such an emotional and/or familial obligation. How will you manage? Determine your own financial and emotional limits—then make those limits clear to the family members involved. Never *assume* major commitments for someone else without expressly asking the other person. Provide for such contingencies with wills, trusts, and similar planning vehicles.

15. Have I prepared a budget with increases each year for cost of living, inflation, and unexpected financial demands on net worth? If you have not yet projected your own cost of living for future years, please do it now! It's never too early to plan for the future. By assuming conservative increases in your own cost of living, inflationary assumptions, and contingencies, you prepare yourself psychologically as well as financially for the rough times that we do not anticipate.

16. Who are my advisors, and are they adequate? This issue is difficult. We all tend to deal with friends or referrals from someone whose advice we respect, and sometimes such friends or referrals are limited in their relevant expertise. It is therefore important that you write down on a sheet of paper a list of those people you rely on for the following:

- Financial planning
- Legal advice
- Insurance
- Pension administration
- Other relevant or specialized advisors

Then evaluate each advisor on your list for accountability, availability, relevance to this time in your life, expertise (perceived level of competence), reputation, and cost. If you feel you are under- or overrepresented, then modify your team of advisors. Remember, no one else but *you* is responsible for your own financial planning and financial future.

17. Have I asked for all the information I need? One of the biggest problems facing our adult U.S. population is that we were not taught much, if anything, about financial responsibility in our earlier years. Even public broadcasting rarely airs prime-time specials on "How to Balance Your Checkbook" or "Paying Yourself First." Financial planning precepts are not yet in the forefront of our national consciousness.

On an individual level, remember that no advisor can be a perfect mind reader. If you don't ask, you probably won't be told the information you need to know. Therefore, go into meetings with advisors (or telephone calls) with prepared lists of questions, checklists, or agendas. Keep a file on the information you need to make intelligent decisions about your own financial future.

18. Have I established sufficient credit to access my assets when, as, and if needed after my retirement? Remember our story at the beginning of this chapter? When you need credit, you will generally find it more difficult and more expensive, if not downright unavailable. The time to establish sufficient credit is while you do *not* have any immediate need for it. Think of the responsible use of available credit as another means of ensuring liquidity in the event of unforeseen misfortune. Do it now—not later.

What type of credit should you establish? The most important type of credit to obtain while working is "unsecured," which means that no assets are specifically tied to the obligation. Such credit becomes a general obligation when used. This formula includes common bank-type credit cards, prestige-oriented credit cards with no preset spending limits, and "signature" lines of credit from banks or credit unions, wherein your signature is all that is needed to use the credit line that has been established in advance of its use. Shop rates and terms. Interest rates can double between competing banks. While pending legislation may change the industry practice, banks and other card issuers can currently charge upward of 20% to the customer for funds that cost the institution less than 6%. The least expensive issuer found in the United States was recently charging approximately 10% as a means of attracting new business. The point is that shopping is important. Also, annual fees are attached to many cards and/or credit lines. Be certain you know *all* the costs associated with your credit before you accept it. It is axiomatic that one should always select a creditor as carefully as one selects a debtor.

19. Am I adequately insured both as an individual and as a family? For health? For life? For other insurance needs? Relying on insurance for your "safety net" in the event of death, disability, and for many other negative possibilities requires serious and conservative planning. Deal only with insurance companies who have the highest available ratings in the industry. Read your policies carefully. If you are insuring for a specific result, *write* to the company and your agent and *specify* the purpose of your purchase. If the policy is issued but you have trouble collecting for the intended purpose, you will then at least have a "letter to the judge" showing the parties knew your intent and accepted your premium dollars with such full knowledge.

20. Have I reviewed this checklist within the past year? Everything changes. The best habit you can establish for your own financial health and well-being is to review this checklist consistently. Perform a review no less frequently than once each calendar year. Pick a date. Mark your calendar.

Involve your family as appropriate. Being informed is critical to becoming prepared.

INDIVIDUAL RETIREMENT ACCOUNTS (IRAs)

IRAs were a big loser with the 1986 Tax Reform Act (TRA), but for many people they continue to be a solid retirement investment tool. Prior to TRA, anyone could enjoy the tax benefits of an IRA, even if they were already participating in a tax-sheltered pension plan. But TRA changed the rules. Almost anyone who wants still can make IRA contributions, but not everyone can take those contributions as deductions (see Figure 6-1).

Individuals with adjusted gross incomes of less than $25,000 and couples who file jointly with less than $40,000 income still may claim their contributions—up to $2,000 for an individual and $2,250 for a spousal IRA. Partial deductions are allowed on incomes falling between $25,000 and $35,000 for single people, and $40,000 and $50,000 for couples filing jointly.

Almost anyone may make an IRA contribution of up to $2,000, regardless of income and the earnings may be deferred until retirement. However, the contributions are not deductible if income requirements are not met. Still, since the new tax law has eliminated most other forms of tax shelter, an IRA can still have value as a long-term savings vehicle that offers tax-deferred growth.

The rules for IRA withdrawal were unchanged by TRA: they are permissible at age 59 1/2 and mandatory at age 70 1/2. If you chose to withdraw money from an IRA before age 59 1/2, you will pay a penalty that equals 10% of the amount of the IRA, plus taxes. As distasteful as that may seem, you might pay less for early withdrawal than if you were to borrow a like amount from a bank.

Some people underestimate the value of an IRA because of the relatively low contribution ceilings and so-so interest rates, but don't forget what compounding does over time for even small amounts of money. Besides, those IRA contributions that can be deducted can help lower your total tax bill.

The phaseout of the IRA deduction applies to taxpayers covered by an employer pension plan.

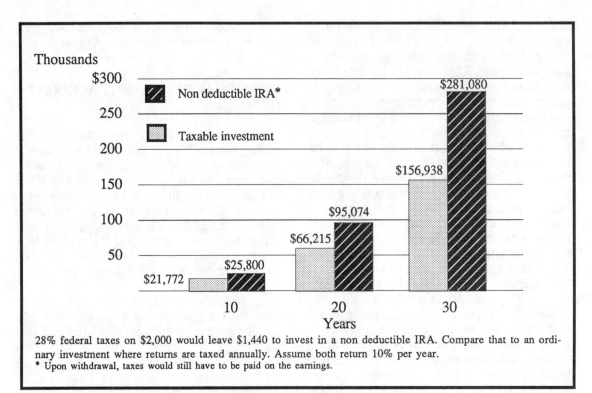

Thousands

28% federal taxes on $2,000 would leave $1,440 to invest in a non deductible IRA. Compare that to an ordinary investment where returns are taxed annually. Assume both return 10% per year.
* Upon withdrawal, taxes would still have to be paid on the earnings.

Figure 6-1 IRAs can *Still* Make Sense

Rollover IRAs allow the transfer of a part or all of the proceeds of a corporate pension plan or a Keogh so that they can be held, tax free, until age 70 1/2, when you must begin making withdrawals. Some limitations exist: if you choose to withdraw all the assets from your pension plan, you must do so within 12 months, and you must fund the rollover IRA within 60 days of the last distribution. If you take a partial distribution, you must roll over at least 50% of the fund's total assets.

You may take advantage of a rollover IRA in two situations: (1) when you leave one company and are waiting to qualify under the pension plan of another, and (2) when you take early retirement and receive a lump-sum payment from your pension plan.

KEOGHS AND CORPORATE PENSION PLANS

Keogh plans and corporate retirement plans offer many similar benefits. This wasn't always the case: corporate plans once offered many advantages not available to self-employed individuals and the owners of small, unincorporated business. Corporate plans may only be used by corporations; Keoghs are available to sole proprietors and partners, but may not be used by an incorporated business.

The costs of setting up a corporate program are higher than those of a Keogh, but they are offset by three advantages: (1) lower taxes, (2) the capacity to shelter larger amounts of income, and (3) greater flexibility in the way the corporation makes contributions on behalf of employees. And you can borrow against a corporate plan, an option that's not available with a Keogh.

The 1986 Tax Reform Act changed the rules on borrowing from a pension plan. You may borrow up to $50,000 or half of your vested assets up to $50,000, whichever is less. That amount is amortized over 5 years, with interest and principal included, and the interest is not deductible. If you are an employee, and not a stockholder of a company in which you have a retirement plan, you may borrow for a second home loan with a 15-

year payback. A Keogh account offers none of these options.

Keogh plans are generally regarded valuable for sole proprietors, very small companies wishing not to incorporate and start up businesses wishing not to incur unnecessary expense. Of course, the relative advantages and disadvantage of incorporation must also be considered by the as-yet-unincorporated business.

Whichever type is chosen, significant tax benefits result.

The Tax Benefits of Keogh and Corporate Retirement Plans

The first benefit you'll enjoy when you set up a Keogh or a corporate pension plan is an immediate reduction in your tax bill. Both plans qualify for tax-deferral considerations—hence the terminology *qualified retirement plan* (QRP). QRPs offer dollar-for-dollar deductibility, and their earnings are not taxed until they are withdrawn. This simple example shows how it works. Assume a two-income household making $100,000 annually with their own business in 1988.

1. *Without a QRP:*

$100,000	income
10,000	in itemized deductions
7,800	in exemptions (4)
$82,200	taxable income at 33% marginal tax bracket, yields a $19,664 tax liability

2. *With a QRP:*

$100,000	income
13,044	in Keogh contributions
10,000	in itemized deductions
7,800	in exemptions (4)
$69,156	taxable income at 28% marginal tax bracket, yields a $15,496 tax liability—taxes saved: $4,168.

Pension plans funds for future wealth: $22,000.

The twin benefits of QRP planning are obvious: it creates a tax-favored pool of retirement funds and frees up significant amounts of capital for investing. And, since the earnings are compounded, a modest annual contribution can blossom into a sizable retirement fund if given enough time.

Using Life Insurance in a Retirement Plan

A debate is going on regarding the value of including a death benefit insurance plan in a retirement plan. By including an insurance policy within a retirement plan you are, in effect, buying insurance with pretax dollars. You may also adopt a waiver of premium that guarantees that your policy will continue to be paid if you are disabled. However, you will pay taxes on the term portion of your universal or whole-life policy, and if you choose not to liquidate your policy at retirement but to roll it out to yourself instead, you will pay taxes on that amount. A policy within a retirement plan has built annuitizing (payback) rates for a lifetime income. If you wish to annuitize your plan at retirement, you will enjoy the annuity rates that were in effect at the time the policy was written. Your whole-life policy will guarantee you a cash value for investment purposes and, since you have been paying taxes on the term portion of your policy, the death benefit will pass through tax free to your heirs.

The amount of your retirement plan that can be spent on insurance is limited: up to 40% of a profit-sharing or 401(k) plan (see following discussion), or 50% of a so-called money-purchase-defined contribution plan.

OTHER RETIREMENT PLAN OPTIONS

Despite the wide use of Keogh, company, and insurance-based pension plans, other means for a secure retirement are available.

SEP-IRAs

A self-employed individual or the owner of a small business who doesn't want the cost or administrative burden of a qualified retirement plan may chose to establish a Simplified

Employee Pension Plan (SEP-IRA). Under a SEP plan, employees establish their own IRAs, to which the company may make contributions. The company eliminates the headaches of managing a more complicated plan, and retains the ability to make tax-sheltered contributions to its employees' retirement plans. SEP contributions are limited to 15% of compensation or $30,000, whichever is less. However, the 1986 Tax Reform Act added one more advantage to SEP-IRAs, called the SAR-SEP.

SAR-SEPs

The SAR-SEP provision allows the employee to elect to make a separate, nondeductible contribution to his or her SEP-IRA, subject to the 15%/$30,000 limit. This separate contribution may not exceed $7,000 (indexed to inflation) and is funded via a payroll deduction. The contribution is not counted as taxable income to the employee.

401(k) Plans

401(k) plans are a type of qualified profit-sharing plans. Employees can reduce their income by having their employer invest part of their gross salary into the plan. Employee contributions are usually matched in part by the corporation. The maximum possible contribution is $7,000. The contribution is actually made by and credited to the employer, who gets the deduction, but the contribution is not counted as income to the employee. The employee may select from a number of methods of making the contribution, but all have the effect of sheltering the contribution from taxes—which means that actual take-home pay is not as significantly affected as if the same amount were set aside in a savings account or bank certificate of deposit.

HOW TO TAKE YOUR PENSION PLAN PROCEEDS

The contributions you make over the years to your pension plan—whether it's an IRA (except for the new nondeductible contributions), a Keogh, or a corporate plan—are tax deductible, so you will be taxed on your withdrawals. But as long as your money stays in the pension plan, it continues to grow, tax deferred. If you have other assets, you should use them before you begin to dip into your pension. Once you begin the distribution of your pension funds, however, IRS rules force you to continue to take them according to a fixed schedule. You may take them faster than you had planned, but if you take them more slowly the government may sock you for a 50% tax on the difference between the required sum and the amount you actually took. You may not begin taking funds from any qualified retirement plan, including IRAs, before age 59 1/2 without being assessed a penalty of 10% on the amount withdrawn. Exceptions may be made in the event of disability, termination of employment, or death. (See Figure 6-2).

 You may take your pension funds in three ways: in a lump sum, a fixed sum from an annuity, or a variable sum over a predetermined number of years based on life expectancy. You must consider a number of factors before you commit to one method or another: How big is your pension fund? What kind of lifestyle do you want to support? How much total taxable income do you have, including income from Social Security, from a spouse who may continue to work, from other investments you have made over the years? You may find that the most difficult aspect of setting up a realistic distribution program is overcoming your fear of using the assets that you have been working so hard to build and preserve over the years. Suffice it to say that you no doubt will have worked hard for that money and the time to enjoy it is at retirement—that's the whole point.

IRA Withdrawals

You may begin to withdraw funds from your IRA when you are age 59 1/2. Once you begin to make withdrawals, you are not allowed to make further contributions, although if you continue to have earned income you may contribute to your younger spouse's IRA. You may take your IRA distributions in a lump sum, through an annuity, or by payments whose terms and timing are governed by IRS regulations.

Keogh and Corporate Plan Withdrawals

If your retirement plan is written to allow it, you may continue to make contributions to your Keogh or corporate plan after you have begun to take withdrawals. With certain exceptions, you must begin taking withdrawals at age 70 1/2.

Note: It may be wise to initiate withdrawals before age 70 1/2 for more flexibility and control over the withdrawal period and amounts. Consult your financial advisor to discuss your options. Many prefer not to be forced into annuitizing their assets into a fixed return. They may prefer to ad-

Current Age	Life Expectancy in Years		Current Age	Life Expectancy in Years		Current Age	Life Expectancy in Years		Current Age	Life Expectancy in Years	
	Men	Women		Men	Women		Men	Women		Men	Women
30	42.8	47.4	46	28.7	33.0	61	17.5	21.0	76	9.1	11.6
31	41.9	46.5	47	27.9	32.1	62	16.9	20.3	77	8.7	11.0
32	41.0	45.6	48	27.1	31.2	63	16.2	19.6	78	8.3	10.5
33	40.0	44.6	49	26.3	30.4	64	15.6	18.9	79	7.8	10.1
34	39.1	43.7	50	25.5	29.6	65	15.0	18.2	80	7.5	9.6
35	38.2	42.8									
			51	24.7	28.7	66	14.4	17.5	81	7.1	9.1
36	37.3	41.9	52	24.0	27.9	67	13.8	16.9	82	6.7	8.7
37	36.5	41.0	53	23.2	27.1	68	13.2	16.2	83	6.3	8.3
38	35.6	40.0	54	22.4	26.3	69	12.6	15.6	84	6.0	7.8
39	34.7	39.1	55	21.7	25.5	70	12.1	15.0	85	5.7	7.5
40	33.8	38.2									
			56	21.0	24.7	71	11.6	14.4			
41	33.0	37.3	57	20.3	24.0	72	11.0	13.8			
42	32.1	36.5	58	19.6	23.2	73	10.5	13.2			
43	31.2	35.6	59	18.9	22.4	74	10.1	12.6			
44	30.4	34.7	60	18.2	21.7	75	9.6	12.1			
45	29.6	33.8									

Figure 6-2 Life Expectancy

just on the life expectancy tables over a longer period of time—any time after age 59 1/2 and before age 70 1/2.

Methods of Distribution

Rollover IRA. As discussed earlier, you may roll over all or a part of the proceeds of your corporate pension plan or Keogh into a rollover IRA where they may remain, tax sheltered, until you are 70 1/2. Rollover IRAs are useful if you don't need the money right away and if you are under 65.

Annuity. If you want a regular income from the proceeds of your pension plan and you want them where they're very safe, you might consider an annuity. When you purchase an annuity, the IRS judges that purchase to be "qualified," which means you don't pay taxes on the money you used to make the purchase. You will be taxed on subsequent withdrawals at the full rate, however. Annuities are an insurance product, so pricing and terms are dependent on insurance company costs, the interest rate you earn at purchase, and your life expectancy. Annuities come with some big drawbacks: (1) you pay the full tax rate on withdrawals; (2) in the event that both spouses die, there may well be nothing left over for the heirs; and (3) since they provide fixed payments only, the value of an annuity may be eroded by inflation. However, if you are nervous about a more aggressive approach, if you want a guaranteed income and if you plan to live until a ripe old age, an annuity may be best for you.

IRS Actuarial Tables. This last option allows you to withdraw a portion of your pension assets and leave the balance in the pension fund to continue to grow. It offers you the greatest potential for continued growth of your assets at retirement, but isn't helpful if you have an annuity and may actually be disadvantageous if you or your spouse outlive by many years your actuarial expectations.

The IRS publishes an actuarial document called the Income Tax Unisex Annuity Tables, on which it bases the amount and timing of withdrawals. Withdrawals are scheduled to be based on an increasingly higher percentage of the remaining assets with an anticipated termination 3 1/2 months before the end of the last year of the schedule, which is based on your life expectancy. This plan has the advantage of continuing to reward you if the investments within your pension portfolio continue to perform well. You may actually earn surplus payments, which can be reinvested.

CONCLUSION

In the last analysis, *you* are the sole person responsible for your own financial future. Do not rely on the government, your parents, your rich uncle, your employer, or anyone else to ensure that your goals are met. You must take personal responsibility for *all* your financial matters. Plan now, review your plan regularly, and enjoy the active, comfortable, and secure retirement you've earned.

CHAPTER 7

ESTATE PLANNING

A GLANCE AHEAD

Estate transfer should be the defensive cornerstone of your financial plan—not a sudden source of anxiety for your heirs. In this chapter, you'll discover:

- *How important estate planning is, and its relevance to your wealth-building and wealth-preserving plans*
- *What tools are available for the orderly transfer of wealth*
- *What the tax consequences are of the estate planning tools you choose*

ESTATE PLANNING SHOWS YOU CARE

The primary purpose of estate planning is to pass your wealth on to your heirs—without excessive tax penalties and in a way that minimizes their natural emotional pain and their need to make hard economic decisions when they may not be capable of addressing them.

People who die or become permanently disabled without having planned the transfer of their estate often—and unnecessarily—doom people whom they care about to costly, chaotic, and emotionally draining legal battles. By failing to look ahead to the first of life's great certainties, death, they leave their wealth vulnerable to the second, taxes, in the form of federal death tax and, often, to state inheritance tax. To make matters worse, an unplanned estate is usually illiquid and must be converted to cash by auction, often at a fraction of its value. In addition to costing money, transferring an unplanned estate costs time through years of probate and expensive attorney's fees. Here's an all-too-typical example of just such a needlessly compounded life tragedy.

Jane was 40 years old, married, with two children. Her father had passed away eight years ago and her mother, Ellen, had lived comfortably in their wholly owned family home until Ellen's death last week. After the funeral and the departure of friends and relatives, Jane began to look into her mother's legal and financial affairs.

After consulting her family attorney, Jane learned that the home was not mentioned in Ellen's will. In fact, Jane's mother had neither reviewed nor revised her will since Jane's father had passed away. The home, purchased in a desirable neighborhood for $20,000 in the late 1940s, was now worth over $500,000. In addition, because they had always filed their own tax returns, neither Jane nor Ellen had ever had professional tax-planning advice.

Until now, Jane had never thought about returning to live in her parents' home. Because the larger, more valuable, and well-located house had no mortgage, it seemed logical to sell her own, modest house and move into the house in which she had grown up. She was shocked and dismayed, then, when the attorney informed her of the horrendous tax bill that now loomed between her and this happy prospect. She was amazed and hurt that her parents had not formally bequeathed the family home to their daughter—even though they had stated often that it was clearly their intent to do so. The title to the home had never been changed. They apparently thought such details would happen "automatically." The same state that had collected their taxes and their Social Security all their lives surely wouldn't neglect them now—or would it?

In short, Jane would be forced either to sell the home to raise cash for taxes or begin a long and complex legal battle that would have been nearly as expensive. For Jane, the lost opportunities for estate planning with her parents became a nightmare problem in the "here and now."

TEACHING YOUR MATURING CHILD TO PLAN AN ESTATE

It is a great idea to start your adult children in acquiring the "habit" of financial and estate planning by helping each child at the age of majority (18, in most states) to do the following:

1. Help your near-adult child create a valid will. This will may be holographic (completely handwritten and hand dated), or a witnessed will (with valid forms that may vary with your state of residence). Consult with a practicing probate attorney to be certain the will is valid in your jurisdiction.
2. Help your near-adult child create a financial plan. It doesn't have to be complicated. Just include a savings goal, educational planning, and perhaps goals related to travel or buying a new car. Discuss basic investments that are available without a large amount of initial capital, such as mutual funds It's never too early to educate yourself or your children in the basics of financial planning.
3. Relate your child's interests to the planning process. For example, if your child is interested in architecture, discuss real estate and planning for the purchase of a house or condominium. Encourage your child to read more about the subject. If your child is a computer buff, check out a few high-technology stocks or stock mutual funds. Purchase a few shares of stock or mutual fund *with* your child.
4. Trust your own child! Ask your child to hold something of value in trust for you. Offer to enlist your child as a trustee on your behalf. This can provide an excellent exercise in trust formation and administration. The subject of the trust does not matter. It can be a favorite ring, pocket watch, VCR, or television set. You can draft the trust agreement together. Keep it simple: "I (*insert name*), trustor, as owner of the property(*identify the property*) that is the subject of this trust, hereby appoint (*insert child's name*), as trustee, for the benefit of (*insert your name again*) as beneficiary. The terms of the trust are as follows: (*list how the item is to be cared for*). Include date and place of signing. You might even have both your signatures notarized. Be certain to identify the subject matter of the trust precisely in the trust terms. This entire trust can be a single page. This exercise can help demystify the whole process of estate planning. It can be simple and yet memorable for the whole family. Most importantly, it can be formative and educational in raising "planning-smart" adults.

ESTATE PLANNING IS A "HERE AND NOW" PROPOSITION

Fortunately, the tools for effective estate planning are simple and easy to use. There's no excuse for denying yourself or your heirs the peace of mind that comes from knowing that every reasonable contingency has been anticipated.

Traditional western culture has always mandated each generation to leave the next a little better off. With the advent of progressive income taxes, governmental policies aimed at redistributing wealth, and an increasingly consumption-oriented (savings-averse) society, Americans tend to postpone thinking about passing on accumulated wealth to their heirs. When they do think about the later stages of life, they often approach retirement planning from the idea of gradually "zeroing out" (using up) their assets. But, this kind of long-range planning is amazingly *short*-sighted.

First, the possibility—however remote—of untimely death, disabling accident, and disease is always possible in life's equation. Like it or not, no one is guaranteed the full span of years that retirement planning is based on.

Second, we cannot count on others to do things for us the way we would do them ourselves—including (and especially) the government. In many ways, a fundamental tension exists between (1) individuals who seek to acquire, enjoy, and transmit wealth to loved ones and (2) the state, which is mandated to intervene, collect, and redistribute that wealth in pursuit of social goals, as evidenced by our progressive income tax and estate tax systems. Life, liberty, and the pursuit of happiness includes the ability to earn and keep assets over time. Unless *you* provide for the orderly transfer of asset ownership to your heirs, you may limit their ability to "pursue happiness" in the way you—and they—have in mind.

THE TOOLS FOR PLANNING YOUR ESTATE

If secure, comfortable, and unencumbered heirs are the ultimate destination of your life's economic journey, then your estate transfer plan is the "road map" for getting there. Furthermore, it is a map that must be reviewed and updated throughout your life because both the means (resources) and ends (specific heirs) may change, as well as the legal and economic environment on which your plan is based. To help you on this journey, a number of estate-planning, transfer, and wealth preservation tools are available. These include wills, trusts, durable power of attorney, various forms of life insurance, a variety of family business organizations, and options for using the marital deduction to reduce your taxable estate.

Wills and Will Substitutes

All of us know about wills and, once we begin to accumulate a little wealth or have children, most of us write a will. A will is simply a legal statement describing how you want your assets distributed at your death. In it, you name your beneficiaries (those who receive your assets) and an executor—a person who has agreed to act on the behalf of your estate. A "holographic" will is written entirely in your own handwriting, dated, and signed by you—but is not witnessed. Holographic wills are better than nothing, but a properly drawn and witnessed will is your best bet for ensuring that your final wishes are respected.

A will's executor is more than a ceremonial office holder, so the person you choose should have good judgment and some experience with life's financial affairs. An executor's duties are many and varied, and run from such simple tasks as taking inventory of your safe deposit box and obtaining your income tax and canceled check records for the last three years, to making some very substantial decisions about the valuation and tax elections of your estate.

Dying without a will ("intestate") leaves you unable to implement many estate-planning tools and creates enormous problems for your heirs. For example, should you and your spouse die intestate before your children are 18 years old, the probate court-appointed guardian and attorney must manage your assets—and collect their fees—from wealth you had intended for your children. When your children reach 18, they will be entitled to the balance of your estate. A sizeable estate thus runs the risk of being wasted in youthful, undisciplined spending or in poor investments. Obviously, drawing a will and hiding it where no one will find it is the same as dying intestate, so make sure your spouse, family attorney, or other trusted individual will know where to find it.

If you are married and have a will, however, you will probably leave your assets outright to your spouse, with your children identified as contingent beneficiaries—the main contingency being your spouse's simultaneous demise. Some wills allow the beneficiary, usually a spouse, to "disclaim" all or part of the inheritance, putting the disclaimed amount into a trust (for which the spouse would then act as trustee) that provides income for life or a specified amount of time. The trust can also provide benefits to your children, or pass to them after the demise of the surviving spouse. With this device, you can specify the age at which your child will receive all or part of an inheritance, and taxes on your estate would be eliminated.

 Although books are available for do-it-yourself wills (which are certainly better than nothing), a will of any complexity should be drafted by an attorney with advice from a competent financial planner or tax counselor.

Certain legal arrangements—particularly property titles— have the effect of becoming "will substitutes." For instance, holding property as "joint tenancy with right of survivorship" means that, should either joint tenant die, the property will pass directly to the other without probate or any specifications to that effect in the deceased person's will. When the joint tenant is a spouse and the property is a house or other real estate, complications involving a will (or no will) are avoided.

Various other options exist, of course, for titling property—and each has an effect on estate transfer.

Tenancy in Common. The arrangement called "tenancy in common" can be a husband and wife or any number of people. Each co-owner has individual title to his or her undivided interest, an equal right of possession, and may convey the interest separately. Should the co-owner die, his or her interest must pass by will to the heirs—there is no right of survivorship.

Community Property. Community property is used as the method of title in most community property states, while "tenancy by entirety" is used in most "severalty" states. The ownership applies only to married people, and although interests are equal, management responsibility usually rests with the husband, which means the wife's rights are subject to the husband's managerial pre-

---

TEN KEYS TO ANTICIPATING AND PREVENTING ASSET LOSS AT DEATH

1. Identify *all* your assets annually with realistic market values.
2. Review the ownership status of all your assets.
3. Ask yourself and your advisors, "Must ownership change at my death?"
4. If ownership must change at your death, then change ownership *now*!
5. Provide for legal entities needed to maintain assets beyond your death.
6. Ensure an adequate cash estate by buying insurance policies.
7. Supplement insurance with pensions, retained corporate earnings, and so on.
8. Clearly identify management succession within each entity.
9. Regularly review your actions with knowledgeable advisors.
10. Check your will and other documents for *clarity*, *legal validity*, and *consistency*. Be certain that your documents do not give rise to obvious conflicts of interpretation. If your wishes are clear, it will be easier to achieve the results you desire.

rogatives. Property held this way must be conveyed jointly. Should one spouse die, half the property belongs to the survivor "in severalty" and the other half goes by will to the decedent's "devisee" (the beneficiary of real property) or, by succession, to the surviving spouse.

Tenancy by Entirety. Again, the form of ownership known as *tenancy by entirety* applies only to married people. Title to the entire property rests with both spouses who enjoy equal rights of possession. Neither spouse can convey the property (that is, end his or her tenancy) without the other spouse's consent, so any purchaser of the property must buy it in its entirety. On one spouse's death, consequently, the survivor receives the whole title.

Joint Tenancy. Although this form is often used by a husband and wife, any number of people can be joint tenants. Although all joint tenants have equal ownership interest and rights of possession, there is only one title to the property. When one co-owner conveys his or her interest, the joint tenancy is broken (except when the property is community property and the joint tenancy is used as a legal convenience) and is replaced by a tenancy in common with the new purchaser. Should a joint tenant die, the co-owner's interest dies too, and cannot be bequeathed in a will. Instead, the surviving spouse (or other joint tenants) gains the property by right of survivorship.

Because joint tenancy is widely used between spouses holding property, some additional discussion of its pros and cons in estate planning is necessary.

 On the positive side, joint tenancy is straightforward and easy to use when the estate is small. There is no delay in transferring title, and some administrative costs and state inheritance taxes can be avoided. This simplicity has great emotional attraction to many married couples because the survivor has immediate and complete control of the asset—often the family home. If the property was not used to secure the deceased spouse's debts, it may not be seized by creditors.

On the negative side, if the joint tenant is not a spouse, a gift tax may be levied on the transfer. Also, if the decedent wishes to dispose of the property by some other way, the automatic right of survivorship gives the property to the other joint tenant, regardless of the will's provisions. In some instances, estate executors have faced cash shortages because much of the property was tied up in joint tenancy arrangements, and not subject to immediate sale. Finally, if the estate is planned to avoid double taxation (once at the first spouse's death and again at the death of the second spouse), joint tenancy will thwart this goal. Because the surviving spouse gains title to the property, and not a trust, the property will be taxed again as part of his or her estate.

Family Trusts

A trust is a legal entity that involves three "parties"— although they do not have to be three separate people. A trustor (also called the *grantor)* gives the property to the trustee, who watches the property on behalf of the beneficiary according to the terms of the trust agreement. A trust may be thought of as a "depository" in which assets are placed to accomplish a specific goal, such as sheltering wealth from estate or inheritance taxes. As a trustor, your primary duty (in addition to furnishing the assets) is to specify what you want the trust to accomplish and ensure that it is established in conformity with current laws—including the 1986 Tax Reform Act, which reduced some of the benefits of certain kinds of trusts.

Trusts may be created in two ways. An *inter vivos,* or living, trust is established while the trustor is still alive. It may run for a specified amount of time or may continue after your death. If the trust is revocable, you may cancel it, alter its terms, or regain control of the assets assigned to the trust. Unless you make this distinction, the trust will be irrevocable and you will lose these potentially important rights.

Testamentary trusts, in contrast, are created by your will and come into being on your death. The assigned assets, therefore, must flow through your will, through probate, and then into the testamentary trust—

sometimes a lengthy process during which the value of those assets might be diminished.

Revocable living trusts are useful when the trustor wants or needs a capable, discreet third party to manage his or her assets—even after the trustor's death or disability. Also, assets in trust at the time of death escape certain estate administration costs. Irrevocable living trusts can help the grantor save on federal income and estate taxes.

Both types of living trusts also have certain drawbacks. Revocable trusts cost money—at least to the extent that the trustee requires compensation for asset management duties—and assets in revocable trusts are taxed as part of the trustor's estate. Irrevocable trusts incur trustee's fees, must file income tax returns each year, and, of course, are not subject to alteration once they are made.

Here's an example of a living trust in action.

Jeff was a successful executive whose will left his estate outright to his wife, Heather. When their son was born, however, Jeff became concerned that the child might not be competent to handle his inheritance should his mother die before his father. Jeff's strategy was to continue to designate Heather as the beneficiary of his life insurance policy and other assets should he die first. However, if Heather predeceased him, the assets she would have received at Jeff's death would be assigned to a living, revocable trust. This arrangement allowed Jeff to reclaim the assets should his situation change.

As time went by and Jeff's wealth and income became significant, he began to be concerned about estate taxes as well as management and preservation of the assets. For selected assets, he transferred ownership to an irrevocable trust with his wife and children named as beneficiaries. A portion of the income from these trusts was used to help pay for his children's education and his wife's charitable activities. When Jeff finally passed away (before his wife), the trust paid its full income to Heather and, when she died, passed the assets in their entirety on to their now grown-up children.

Chapter 8 of this book gives you additional information about the tax consequences of trusts and custodial accounts under the 1986 Tax Reform Act.

Durable Power of Attorney

An "attorney" is someone legally entitled to conduct business on your behalf. If the power of attorney is limited, the person can conduct only that business specified in your agreement. If the power of attorney is general, the person's authority is much broader but still assumes you are competent to review and approve the person's decisions. If you become incapacitated, the "attorney-in-fact" can no longer handle your affairs. If the agreement contains what is known as "durable" language (made possible by passage of certain recent state laws), it allows the attorney-in-fact to make decisions regardless of your competence. As you can see, this "dura-

ble" feature has enormous implications in estate planning because it can prevent an unwanted court-appointed guardianship in case you are incapacitated or disabled.

In essence, the durable provision assumes you should be able to specify in advance the person you want to make critical decisions regarding your medical care, well-being, and wealth should you ever become incapable of making those decisions for yourself. Especially helped by this option are elderly people who fear senility in the closing stages of life, people with debilitating or degenerative diseases, people in dangerous occupations where sudden incapacity through accidents is a real possibility, or people facing major medical treatment the outcome of which might render them temporarily or permanently incapacitated.

For example, Helen, age 62, is scheduled to undergo exploratory surgery next month. She has been advised of the risks of the operation and the slight chance of her mental incapacitation as a result of the procedure. She consults her family attorney and is advised that her state has passed a law authorizing the addition of "durable" language to a general power-of-attorney document. She asks her adult daughter to act as attorney-in-fact, in an agreement that includes the words "this power of attorney shall become effective in the event of the disability or incapacity of the principal." Helen's operation goes well, and her recuperation is much quicker owing to the fact that she had no worries about how her affairs would have been handled had she survived the surgery with diminished mental capacity.

Because a will only becomes operative at your death, it is not the appropriate vehicle for granting a durable power of attorney. Consult your family attorney for the language necessary to create this important part of your estate preservation plan.

Insurance: The Direct Way to a Cash Estate

Although many people joke about persistent insurance salespeople, few financial service professionals have done more to get people to think—and do—something about the far end of life's cycle. These same people, while procrastinating in their own estate-planning efforts, are usually the first to make the most often overheard statement at funerals: "For the family's sake, I sure hope he (or she) had some insurance!"

Estate planning normally includes a life insurance component to ensure that enough liquid assets are available to at least cover debt and death expenses without burdening your heirs. Although insurance products are discussed in detail in Chapter 17, you should also know how certain insurance options can affect your estate transfer plans.

Life Insurance as an Estate Benefit. The primary purpose of any type of life insurance (whole, term, universal, and any of the new variable forms) is to replace your income when you are gone. If you have adequate sources of income for your dependents beyond your breadwinning capacity, life insurance is not a particularly valuable product. Indeed, "self-insurance"— investing money now to obtain a specific amount of cash in the future—is one way to replace or supplement an insurance policy and avoid recurring premiums. Unfortunately, it requires principal to invest (a larger amount for a larger payback), so conventional insurance is the means most people choose to provide both liquidity to their estate and an alternative source of income for their dependents.

 A quick way to gauge the contribution of a life insurance policy to your estate is to compare its value to the return of a similar investment. For example, let's say your annual income is $40,000 and your spouse makes $30,000 per year. Together, your combined $70,000 yields a comfortable lifestyle with enough left over to fund retirement and your childrens' college-related investments. How much life insurance should you buy to ensure that your family's quality of life will not suffer if you are gone?

After a few rough trial-and-error calculations, you will eventually determine that a policy that pays $500,000 on your death, invested for an 8% per year return, will replace your $40,000 per year income exactly. Your next task would be to shop for a policy whose premiums for that amount will not significantly reduce the lifestyle you are trying to protect.

Irrevocable Insurance Trusts. One way to combine the benefits of both trusts and insurance is by creating "funded" or "unfunded" insurance trusts—a trust that owns an insurance policy on your life. A funded trust is established when you irrevocably transfer the life insurance policy plus enough money (or assets capable of producing enough money) to pay the policy's premiums. An unfunded trust holds the policy only; you or your beneficiary must pay the premiums to keep the policy current. The purpose of the trust is to remove your life insurance benefit from your estate, minimizing your federal tax exposure.

Although the transfer of both the policy and the payment of its premiums constitute a gift and are subject to gift tax, the costs are usually less than the $10,000 annual gift tax exclusion, and no tax consequence results. Your tax advisor can tell you about other tests your irrevocable life insurance trust must meet, and whether funded or unfunded trusts will work best for you.

Life Insurance Assignment. Federal death tax laws consider the proceeds from a life insurance policy to be part of your estate if you possess what they term "incidents of ownership" in the policy, or if the policy benefits the executor or others in your estate. The only way to avoid this classification is to eliminate those "incidents of ownership" by assigning the policy to someone else. One way to do so is to assign the policy to an irrevocable insurance trust, as described earlier, but this is not the only avenue open. A policy may be assigned to your children, but—because "incidents of ownership" include the right to designate a beneficiary, receive cash values, borrow against cash values, and other owner's privileges—you should be sure your spouse would not depend on the proceeds for income subsequent to your death.

 Time is also a factor in insurance policy assignment. To escape death taxes, the assignment must have been completed at least three years prior to your death. Again, your tax advisor should guide you as to the precise terms of the assignment, including the best method for making premium payments.

Family Business Organizations

Lawyers, physicians, dentists, and entrepreneurs have long seen the wisdom of structuring the ownership of certain assets through a family or professional business. The key idea, as it is with a trust, is to separate, for purposes of tax reduction or managerial control, income- or wealth-producing assets from the single individual who would otherwise face a higher than necessary income or estate tax liability. Although no single form of ownership is perfect for all assets, individuals, and situations, those available are quite flexible and may serve your estate-planning needs admirably.

General Partnership. In this form of business, all general partners exercise managerial control over the asset and share total liability for the business's operation. The terms of the general partnership agreement govern the actual workings of the partnership and, for estate-planning purposes, should state explicitly the succession of the

managing partner's duties if the principal partner dies or becomes disabled. Although the partnership must file a tax return, the individual partners are each responsible for paying their own taxes and there is no inherent double taxation, as with a corporation (to be discussed shortly).

The drawback to a general partnership as an asset-holding vehicle, of course, is that all partners have legal managerial control and unlimited liability. This agreement may not be suitable for family businesses involving children or an inexperienced spouse or other nominal general partners.

Limited Partnership. A limited partnership consists of at least one general partner (who assumes managerial control and liability for the business) and a specified number of limited partners, whose liability is limited to the value of their share of the assets and who take no active part in running the business. In a family business, the general partner is usually the principal breadwinner and the limited partners are dependents (spouse and children) or other relatives. For estate-planning purposes, the partnership agreement should spell out the procedure for the orderly succession of a new general partner should the current general partner die or become disabled. As with the general partnership, there is no inherent double taxation.

Corporation. A corporation is a legal entity that operates in perpetuity; that is, it does not depend on *specific* people for its organization, as with general and limited partnerships. It issues stock, which is the form and evidence of ownership. In "closely held" family corporations, family members (and perhaps one or two others, such as a family friend, attorney, or accountant) usually hold all the stock. Most family corporations are organized according to Subchapter S of the Internal Revenue code, which applies to small businesses—"small" with regard to the number of shareholders, not necessarily the value of its assets, which can be quite large. Shareholders' liability is limited to the value of the stock they own.

 One big disadvantage to the family corporation, beside the cost of organization, is the double taxation of the income its shareholders receive. Because it is a separate legal entity, a corporation pays taxes on its income before it can distribute those earnings to its stockholders, who are taxed again when they declare that income on their personal returns.

Other forms of business are available, such as joint ventures, but those just described are most widely used. Although your attorney and tax advisor should guide your decisions about the feasibility and desirability of assigning assets to a family business, the following general steps are recommended for everyone.

1. *Identify all assets that may be accounted for in a family estate plan.* Only then will you know which might be reasonably assigned to a family business.

2. *Obtain current fair market value of your assets, paying for independent appraisals when necessary.* It is important to establish asset value when ownership of a personal asset is transferred to the family business.

3. *When assets and their value have been identified, consider the tax consequences of doing nothing.* Avoid the false economy of continuing with the formation and maintenance of a family business just because you have made a tentative decision to do so. If you are not helped economically by the decision, it's foolish to pursue it.

4. *Compare the costs and benefits of alternate forms of ownership.* If a family business still seems like a reasonable asset-holding arrangement, explore the costs and benefits (*pro forma* analysis) of several alternative approaches. Don't form a Subchapter S corporation, for example, simply because it worked for a friend or relative in a similar situation. Different organizational, tax reporting, and clerical costs are associated with each form of business.

 5. *Be certain each family member involved is aware of what you're doing.* All relatives involved in a family business should understand their roles, obligations, liabilities, and the tax consequences of participation—especially if they file their own returns. In some cases, minor children may need to have their interest held by a custodian. Consult your legal and tax advisors about the requirements of the form of business you select.

THE JOYS—AND REWARDS—OF PLANNED GIVING

Sharing your success with others—loved ones, favorite charities, or educational institutions—can be an important part of a full and rewarding life. Giving money or assets away spontaneously, however, may be costlier than you think. Because tax consequences and asset preservation are constant factors in financial planning, economic gifts—like the investments that made them possible—deserve forethought and attention to relevant details if you want your gift to have its full and desired effect.

Writing a check on your liquid assets is not the only way to help the people or organizations you have in mind, and the vehicle you select can have important consequences on both the magnitude of the gift and your own ability to continue giving.

Giving Through Your Will

The easiest way to transfer a lot of money or a sizable asset to a desired beneficiary without unduly perturbing your current finances is to simply mention the beneficiary in your will. Gifts bequeathed this way can be cash, a fraction of your estate, specific securities, or a trust, to name only a few. Charitable donations made this way are a tax deduction from your estate.

Using Life Insurance Benefits

You may name a person, people, or a organization to receive the proceeds of your life insurance policy. If you name the charity as both beneficiary and owner of the policy, you can deduct the premiums from your current taxes.

Income-producing Gifts

Like the revocable living trusts discussed earlier, you may also establish trusts and funds that pay the earnings of your income-producing assets to a charity. For example, a charitable remainder trust pays income from designated assets to the charitable organization until the benefactor dies, then donates the assets themselves (the "remainder") to the charity. The gift tax is deferred because the asset is not transferred to the beneficiary until after your demise, and you receive immediate income tax deductions for the income donations your asset makes. Your tax advisor can suggest other forms of income-producing gifts, such as charitable annuities, charitable lead trusts, or pooled income funds, that might be right for you.

Life Estate

If you want to donate title to property now, but need to retain the use of the property itself, you might consider a life estate. Under this plan, you can deed a property, such as a house, apartment building, or farm, to a charitable organization and return the use of it yourself for your lifetime or the lifetime of your surviving spouse. This yields immediate tax savings for you and reduces your ultimate estate tax liability.

Giving Personal Property

Personal as well as real property may also be suitable for planned giving. Instead of selling an unused automobile, recreational vehicle, boat, antiques, books, jewelry—even livestock, such as saddle horses or breeding animals—you might consider giving them to charity and deduct their value from your current taxes. Valuation of such donations, however, can be a tricky business, and you should use the beneficiary's valuation for tax purposes whenever it is available.

Giving Securities

One of the worst ways to give money derived from appreciated stocks, bonds, and other investments is to sell the security, pay taxes on your gain, then donate the remainder. It is far wiser to donate the securities directly to the charity and take your deduction for the fair market value of the gift. This approach gives you a substantial tax break and makes more money available to the beneficiary. If the security has lost money during the holding period, sell it for the tax-deductible capital loss and donate the receipts to the charity, deducting the contribution from your current taxes.

The Marital Deduction

A married person may greatly reduce or eliminate estate tax by using the marital deduction. Property passing to a spouse is generally free from estate or gift tax because of an unlimited marital deduction. For maximum tax saving, you may want to reduce your taxable estate to the exemption floor with marital deduction property. The unified tax credit ($192,800 for decedents dying in 1987 and later years for taxable estates in excess of $600,000) will then eliminate tax on that amount at the time of your death. By leaving your spouse less than the maximum deductible amount, you may also reduce the tax at the time of his or her death as well.

To qualify for the marital deduction, the property must generally be given to the spouse outright or by equivalent legal arrangements. Life insurance proceeds may qualify as marital deduction property if your spouse is named as unconditional beneficiary of the proceeds with unrestricted control over any unpaid proceeds. If your spouse is not given this control or general power of appointment, then proceeds remaining on your spouse's death must be payable to this or her estate. Otherwise, the insurance proceeds will not qualify for the marital deduction.

A variant of the marital deduction is called the A-B trust, wherein the estate, after your death, is divided into two parts: the "A" part for the surviving spouse, and the "B" part, or nonmarital trust, for your children. The A trust includes the survivor's share of your community property and any other property you may wish to transfer to that trust, hence qualifying it for the marital deduction. (There may be some tax on the A trust amount if it exceeds the unified tax credit.) The B trust would then contain, within the limits of the unified tax credit, funds to educate your children or provide emergency funds for the maintenance, medical care, and support of your surviving spouse. On the death of that surviving spouse, the remainder of the B trust would then be distributed to your children (in any manner you may designate) without further taxation.

A FINAL WORD ON YOUR FINAL ARRANGEMENTS

An orderly, efficient transfer of your wealth to your heirs is the ultimate act of love. Because the economy, tax laws, your resources, and the needs and capabilities (as well as the number) of your heirs will change over time, estate planning is not so much an event as an ongoing—indeed, a lifelong—process. Keep the people you love apprised of your activity and the location of important documents. Use the members of your financial planning team—your CFP, tax preparer, family attorney, and others—to make sure the efforts of a lifetime are not wasted when the people you love need them most.

The checklist at the end of this chapter may be helpful in beginning this process.

ESTATE-PLANNING CHECKLIST

Documents and Information to Be Furnished to Your Advisor

Estate planning for _____ (name)

Item

Check column
where item is
to be furnished

Part I Family facts
1. Birthdates of children: _____ _____
2. _____ _____
3. _____ _____

Part II Inventory of assets and liabilities
1. Copies of deeds relating to home and real estate _____ _____
2. Verification of ownership of stocks and bonds _____ _____
3. Verification of ownership of bank accounts _____ _____
4. _____ _____
5. _____ _____

Part III Income
1. Copies of personal income tax returns _____ _____
2. Copies of trusts _____ _____
3. _____ _____
4. _____ _____

Part IV Gifts
1. Copies of agreements _____ _____
2. _____ _____
3. _____ _____
4. _____ _____

Part V Business interests
1. Copies of agreements _____ _____
2. _____ _____
3. _____ _____
4. _____ _____

Part VI Your life insurance
1. Copies of all policies _____ _____
2. _____ _____
3. _____ _____

Part VI Your life insurance
1. Copies of all policies _____ _____
2. _____ _____
3. _____ _____

Other information or documents to be furnished
1. _____ _____
2. _____ _____

CHAPTER 8

TAX PLANNING WITH THE NEW TAX LAWS

A GLANCE AHEAD

Your tax return is a historical document; it reflects only what you did (or failed to do) to reduce your taxes in the preceding year. Consequently, tax savings begin on or before January 1 of the tax year—not 16 months later, when you prepare your return on April 15 of the following year when your tax is due. In this chapter, you'll learn

- *How the 1986 Tax Reform Act has affected financial planning for everyone*
- *How homeowners can keep interest deductions that others have lost*
- *How the disappearance of long-term capital gain advantages affects investment strategies*
- *New sources for tax-deferred and tax-exempt income*

TAX PLANNING AFTER TAX REFORM

Yes, there are tax savings in the post-TRA (1986 Tax Reform Act) environment. But you have to know where—and how—to find them. In a nutshell,

1. *TRA swept away tax shelter plans that offered up-front deductions for writeoffs from salary, interest, and dividend income.* The passive activity rule is designed to discourage you from investing in tax shelters whose deductions can be used to offset other income. Such "paper" or tax losses now apply only to other passive income, such as rents. The new rule is, if you don't actively participate in the business, your income (both positive and negative) from the investment is passive.

2. *Long-term capital gains are no longer favorably taxed.* In the post-TRA world, capital gains are now subject to ordinary income rates. Investors should no longer concern themselves with strategies for long-term capital gain. Current income—including dividends that can be reinvested profitably and taxed at the new lower rates—is the order of the day.

3. *Shifting income to children may not provide substantial tax savings.* Starting with 1987 returns, investment income of children under age 14 in excess of $1,000 is taxed at the parent's top marginal rate; although with the reduction of tax rates, the discrepancy between high and low rates has narrowed. The new law also prevents you from shifting income to beneficiaries of 10-year Clifford and "spousal remainder" trusts—both previously popular ways to split income with family members in lower tax brackets.

4. *Equipment investments no longer earns tax credits.* The TRA disallows investment credit and has severely cut back depreciation deductions for automobiles. It has

also taken away accelerated deductions for real estate and has reduced deductions for many leasehold improvements.

5. *Consumer credit is more costly.* Only certain types of interest payments remain fully deductible. Deductions for consumer interest payments, in fact, have been cut back substantially and will be eliminated in 1990.

Nevertheless, the post-TRA environment still offers tax savings opportunities for homeowners, investors, corporate executives, families, and senior citizens—if you start planning for them now.

TAX SAVINGS FOR HOMEOWNERS

Homeowners have always had substantial tax benefits, and after TRA most of these advantages continue. For example, the tax deferment benefits of personal residence sales and the $125,000 exclusion for homeowners age 55 or over still apply. Interest paid on home mortgages is also fully deductible, provided certain rules are followed. However, taxable sales of personal residences will be subject to higher taxes because of the repeal of the capital gains deduction. Even so, your home may be a source of additional deductions—and of cash for investing or other uses.

Tax Savings Through Home Equity Loan Deductions

Qualifying residential mortgage interest on up to two residences is exempt from the phase-out limitations for personal interest. The tax rules for deducting qualifying residential mortgage interest distinguish among mortgages made before, on or after August 16, 1986.

Interest on Mortgage Debt Incurred Before August 17, 1986. If debt secured by your principal residence or a second residence was incurred on or before August 16, 1986, the interest is fully deductible. It does not matter how you used the loan proceeds. Such pre-August 17, 1986, loans are not subject to the following limitations applied to

mortgage debts incurred after August 16, 1986. However, if you increase the debt that was secured as of August 16, 1986, such as by taking a line of credit or refinancing the mortgage, the increased debt may be subject to the new tax limits for debts incurred after August 16, 1986. When this book went to press, Congress was considering a bill allowing a full interest deduction for a refinanced mortgage originally incurred on or before August 16, 1986, provided the new mortgage does not exceed the outstanding principal debt immediately before the refinancing.

Interest on Mortgage Debt Incurred After August 16, 1986. Whether interest is deductible on a new mortgage or refinancing after August 16, 1986, depends on

1. The cost basis of the residence, including improvement costs
2. Existing mortgage debt, if any
3. In some cases, how you use the loan proceeds

If debt secured by the residence does not exceed cost basis plus improvements, the interest is deductible even if you use the loan proceeds to pay personal consumer debts. If you want to borrow above cost basis plus improvements (but not over fair market value fo the house), the interest is deductible if you use the loan proceeds to pay medical and educational expenses. If you use the proceeds for other purposes, the interest on the excess debt (debt above cost plus improvements) is treated as personal interest and is subject to the phase-out limitation.

For example, suppose the cost basis of your principal residence is $100,000. Fair market value is $125,000. Your residence is subject to a purchase money mortgage of $60,000. You may refinance up to $100,000 (including the original $60,000 plus an additional $40,000). The interest paid on the new mortgage is deductible regardless of the type of personal needs to which you apply the loan.

Now suppose you refinance for $110,000. To deduct interest on the $10,000 of the debt above $100,000 cost, you must show that the $10,000 proceeds are used to pay medical or educational expenses, or make improvements to the home. If the $10,000 proceeds were used for other purposes, interest on that $10,000 debt would be treated as personal intest and thus subject to the phase-out limitations.

The Two-residence Limit. The rules for deducting residential mortgage interest apply to loans secured by your principal residence and one other residence. A principal residence may be a condominium or cooperative unit, a houseboat, or house trailer. If you own more than two houses, you decide which residence shall be considered your second residence. Interest on debt secured by the designated second residence is deductible under these rules. Interest on any other home will be subject to the limits for personal interest. A residence that is rented out for any part of the year may be designated as a second residence only if it is used for personal non-rental purposes for the greater of 14 days or 10% of the rental days. By making the designation, you ensure that interest is fully deductible as residential interest. If you do not make the designation, part of the interest allocated to your personal use is deductible only as personal interest subject to the phase-out percentages, and interest allocated to the rental activity is treated as passive activity interest subject to limitations.

A married couple filing jointly may designate as a second residence a home owned or used by either spouse.

If a married couple files separately, each spouse may generally deduct interest on debt secured by one residence. However, both spouses may agree in writing to allow one of them to deduct the interest on a principal residence, plus a designated second residence.

Cooperatives. In the case of housing cooperative, debt secured by stock as a tenant-stockholder is treated as secured by a residence.

Post-TRA Tax Consequences of Selling Your Home

Because wealth building for most people involves buying or repurchasing (trading up) a home, we won't go into detail here about strategies for liquidating a personal residence. You'll find complete guidance for minimizing tax exposure from such transactions in *J. K. Lasser's Your Income Tax 1988.*

Most people may avoid or defer tax on all or part of a profit from the sale of a home depending on the owner's age:

1. *Age 55 or over.* If you are age 55 or over, you may elect to avoid tax on gain of up to $125,000. To claim this exclusion, you must (1) elect to avoid tax, (2) be age 55 or older before the date of sale, and (3) have owned and occupied the house as your principal residence for at least three of the five years preceding the day of sale.

2. *Under 55, or 55 or over but do not want to avoid the tax.* You may defer tax by (1) buying or building another residence for use as your principal residence, (2) buying or building within two years of the sale of your old house, buy or build at a cost at least equal to the amount you received from the sale of the old house, or (4) by making an even exchange (or pay additional cash) for a new principal residence.

If you sell your house at a loss, you may not deduct the loss. However, you may claim a loss (1) if you convert the house from personal use to some profit-making purpose before the sale, (2) if you sell a house acquired by gift or inheritance that you did not personally use but rather offered for rental or sale shortly after acquisition, or (3) if you sell stock in your cooperative apartment in which there were nonstockholder tenants when you acquired your stock.

You must report details of a 1987 sale on Form 2119, which you attach to your Form 1040. On Form 2119, you compute gain on the basis of a new residence and may make the election to exclude gain. If you do not qualify for tax deferral or exclusion, enter taxable gain from Form 2119 on Schedule D.

The IRS may tax you on the unreported gain from the sale of your residence during a three-year period that starts when you notify the IRS (1) of the cost of your new residence, or (2) of your intention not to buy one, or (3) of your failure to acquire a new residence before the required time limit. If you don't notify the IRS, you may be assessed the tax on unreported taxable gain at any time.

If you will receive some or all of the sales proceeds after the year of sale and you do not qualify for deferral or elect the exclusion, you must report your gain on the installment basis, unless you elect to report the entire gain in the year of sale. Sales of residential property on the installment basis are not subject to restrictive rules applied to sales of rental property of more than $150,000.

TAX SAVINGS FOR INVESTORS

With the repeal of the capital gain deduction, the substantial tax benefits of realizing long-term capital gain are no longer available. Long-term capital gains are now subject to ordinary income tax rates. In 1987, however, a 28% tax ceiling is placed on the tax on long-term capital gains. In 1988, the distinction between short- and long-term capital gain remains effective, although the scheduled ordinary tax rates for 1988 apply equally to both types of gains. Although capital gains in 1988 are fully subject to ordinary income tax rates without the application of the 28% alternative tax, the $3,000 limitation on deducting capital losses from other types of income remains as a substantial limitation on capital losses. If you have substantial capital losses limited by the $3,000 rule, it will remain advisable to realize income from capital asset transactions.

As long-term capital gains, interest, and dividends become taxable at the same tax rate, your investment strategies should change. In holding securities, you will generally not pay as much attention to holding periods as with pre-TRA investments. Your test for judging the investment return will be the same for gains, interest, and dividend income, which is the net after-tax return over a given period. If the projected after-tax return on a stock held for investment will give only 5% over a two-year period, for example, an investment that will return net interest after tax of 7% during the same period should be the preferred investment, all other things being equal.

Investing in Mutual Funds

Many people buy a ready-made tax liability simply by investing in a mutual fund that has already realized significant capital gains during the year. With a mutual fund, your investment is taxed on the basis of the current value of its portfolio. At the end of the year, the gains realized by the fund before your investment are distributed to you as a capital gain distribution. You then have to pay tax on the return of your own money—not a wise move in any financial planner's book! However, an experienced fund advisor can tell you when to make your investment. Or you can postpone investing until the stock goes "ex-dividend," whereby the buyer of the shares does not receive the current dividend but wait until the *next* dividend is declared by the fund's managers. By that time, your buying price will be based on an asset value that is reduced by capital gain distribution.

Averaging Cost for Sale of Mutual Fund Shares. A U.S. Treasury regulation sets rules for averaging the cost of purchases made at different times if only part of your holdings are sold. The election applies to open-end mutual fund shares held by an agent—usually a bank—in an account kept for the periodic acquisition or redemption of shares in the fund. Averaging avoids the difficult task of identifying the exact shares being sold where shares were bought at different times and prices. There are two averaging methods: single and double category.

Under the single-category method, all shares in an account are totaled. The basis of each share is the total basis of all shares in the account at the time of a sale or transfer, divided by the number of shares in the account. For purposes of determining the holding period, the shares sold or transferred are considered to be those shares acquired first.

Under the double-category method, at the time of each sale you divide all shares in an account into two classes: shares held long-term and shares held short-term. Shares are deemed to be transferred from each class without regard to stock certificates. You may tell the agent from which class you are selling. If you do not so specify, the long-term shares are deemed to have been sold first. If the number of shares sold exceeds the number in the long-term class, the excess shares are charged to the short-term class.

IRS Publication Number 564 provides details of these methods.

 You make the election to average on your tax return for the first taxable year to which you want the election to apply. Note on your return which method you have chosen. Keep records to support the average basis used on your return. The election applies to all shares of the particular mutual fund in which the election is initially made.

You may not average shares of a mutual fund acquired by gift if the adjusted basis of such shares in the hands of the donor was greater than their fair market value at the time of the gift.

Reducing the Tax on Dividend Income

Because TRA encourages investors to look for current income instead of shelters, new ways to minimize taxes on that income have also surfaced.

- **Sell Stock on Which a Dividend Has Been Declared But Not Yet Paid.** During the period a dividend is declared but not paid, the price of the stock includes the value of the dividend. If you plan to sell stock in this position and figure that the tax on the dividend reflected in the selling price will be less than the tax on the dividend received, transact the sale before the stock goes ex-dividend.

- **Invest in Companies That Pay Tax-free Dividends.** Some companies pay tax-free dividends. A list of companies that do may be provided by your broker. When you receive a tax-free dividend, you do not report the dividend as income as long as the dividend does not exceed your stock basis. A tax-free dividend reduces the tax cost of your stock; dividends in excess of basis produce capital gain.

- **Invest in Companies that Pay Stock Dividends.** A stock dividend is generally taxable income.

TRA and Real Estate Tax Planning

The new tax law has caused radical restructuring for many commercial real estate investments, as follows:

- *Passive activity income or loss.* By law, income and losses of rental operations are treated as passive activity income and loss. This definition has its advantages and disadvantages. The disadvantage is that losses are not deductible from salary, interest, and dividend income. The advantage is that rental income may be offset by other passive activity losses.
- *Installment sales.* Sales of dealer property and sales of rental property of over $150,000 are subject to restrictions. If you find you are subject to these rules, it may not be advisable to transact an installment sale. You may have to report income in a year when you do not have cash from the buyer to pay the tax on the income. Consult your tax advisor if you are contemplating such a transaction.
- *Dealer or investor status.* Your status as a dealer or investor will affect how you deduct interest and whether you can use the installment sales method on sales of property.
- *Leasehold improvements.* Leasehold improvements made by you as a lessee must be depreciated although the lease term may be shorter than the depreciation period.
- *Tax credits.* Benefits from tax credits are available for rehabilitation and low-income housing.

The ideal real estate investment should provide a current income return and an appreciation in the value of the original investment. As an additional incentive, a real estate investment may in the early years of the investment provide income subject to little or no tax. That may happen when depreciation and other expense deductions reduce taxable income without reducing the amount of cash available for distribution. This tax savings is temporary and is limited by the terms and the amount of the mortgage debt on the property. Mortgage amortization payments reduce the amount of cash available to investors without an offsetting tax deduction. Thus, the amount of tax-free return depends on the extent to which depreciation deductions exceed the amortization payments.

To provide a higher return of tax-free income, at least during the early years of its operations, a venture must obtain a constant payment of mortgage that provides for the payment of fixed annual amounts that are allocated to continually decreasing amounts of interest and increasing amounts of amortization payments—the buildup of owners' equity through mortgage reduction. Consequently, in the early years a tax-free return of income is high while the amortization payments are low. But as the amortization payments increase, nontaxable income decreases. When this tax-free return has been substantially reduced, a partnership must refinance the mortgage to reduce the amortization payments and once again increase the tax-free return.

For example, let us say, a limited real estate partnership of 100 investors owns a building that returns an annual income of $100,000 after operating expenses are deducted, but before a depreciation deduction of $80,000. Thus, taxable income is $20,000 ($100,000 minus $80,000). Assuming that there is no mortgage on the building, the whole $100,000 is available for distribution. (Since the depreciation requires no cash outlay, it does not reduce the cash available for distribution.) Each investor receives $1,000. Taxable income being $20,000, only 20% ($20,000 ÷ $100,000) of the distribution is taxable. Thus each investor reports as income only $200 of the $1,000 distribution; $800 is tax free.

Now, suppose the building is mortgaged and an annual amortization payment of $40,000 is being made. Consequently, only $60,000 is available for distribution, of which $20,000 is taxable. Each investor receives $600, of which 1/3 ($20,000 ÷ $60,000) or $200 is taxed, and $400 is tax free. In other words, the $60,000 distribution is tax free to the extent that the depreciation deduction of $80,000 exceeds the amortization of $40,000—namely, $40,000. If the amortization payment was increased to $50,000, only $30,000 of the distribution would be tax free ($80,000 minus $50,000).

The tax-free return is based on the assumption that the building does not actually depreciate at a rate as fast as the tax depreciation rate. If the building is depreciating physically at a faster rate, the so-called tax-free return on investment does not exist. Distributions to investors (over and above current income return) that are labeled "tax-free distributions" are in fact a return of the investor's own capital.

The preceding advantages are available for investments made by you individually or in partnership with other associates. They are also available to investors in limited partnerships. However, before investing in a limited partnership, consider these disadvantages of this form of business:

1. Investors in limited partnerships are by law generally treated as receiving passive activity income or loss. Furthermore, as a limited partner, you may not take advantage of the $25,000 rental loss allowance, as you are not considered an "active participant." In view of the passive activity rules, if you and others join together to buy rental property, you should not organize as a limited partnership if any losses are anticipated. Limited partnerships are advisable only if income is expected or where two or more investment activities will produce income and loss, which will offset each other.

2. Although limited partnerships are organized to prevent double taxation, which occurs in doing business as a corporation, there is a danger that the partnership may be taxed as a corporation if its operations resemble those of a corporation.

3. Partnership operations do not provide for the diversification of investments or for the free transfer of individual interests. Investors may find it difficult to sell their interests because of transferability restrictions and a lack of an open market for the sale of their interests. This liquidity problem may be overcome by buying interests sold through public exchanges. Interests in master limited partnerships (MLPs) are offered on the public exchanges. The organization of MLPs has been sparked by the passive activity loss restrictions. MLPs are designed to provide passive income to investors who have passive activity losses that will offset the income. However, MLPs are controversial: the U.S.

Treasury has urged Congress to pass legislation that would tax MLPs as corporations.

Investing in REITs. The tax treatment of real estate investment trusts (REITs) resembles that of open-end mutual funds. Distributions are taxed to the investors in the trust as ordinary income, but no dividend exclusion is allowed on such distributions. Distributed long-term calital gains are reported by the investors as long-term gains. If the trust operates at a loss, the loss may not be passed on to the investors.

A REIT may not necessarily invest in equities. It may operate for interest return by providing loans to other real estate investors. Before investing, check the scope of the REIT's operations and current market conditions and projections.

Investing in REMICs. The TRA encourages the creation of real estate mortgage investment conduits (REMICs). A REMIC is formed to hold a fixed pool of mortgages. Investors are treated as holding a regular or residual interest. A corporation, partnership, or trust that meets statutory tests is allowed to be treated as a REMIC. In addition, a segregated pool of assets may also qualify as a REMIC as if it were an entity meeting the requirements.

A REMIC is not a taxable entity for federal income tax purposes. The income from the REMIC generally is reported by holders of regular and residual interests. However, a REMIC may be subject to tax on prohibited transactions and may be required to withhold on amounts paid to foreign holders of regular or residual interests.

The pass-through status of the REMIC applies regardless of whether the REMIC was formed as a corporation, partnership, or trust. For example, where a REMIC is organized as a partnership, the partnership provisions do not apply to any transactions involving the REMIC or any of the holders of regular or residual interest. At the time this book went to press, the Treasury had not released regulations governing REMICs, so it is important to look for new developments in this area. Income from a REMIC is reported on Schedule E.

Exchanging Real Estate Without Tax. You may trade real estate for investment for other investment real estate and incur no tax until the time you sell the exchanged property at a price exceeding the tax basis of the property. A tax-free exchange may also defer a potential tax due on gain from depreciation recapture and might be considered where the depreciable basis of a building has been substantially written off. Here the building may be exchanged for other property that will give off larger tax deductions.

The postponement of tax is equivalent to receiving an interest-free government loan in the amount you would have owed in taxes had you sold the property. With no part of your capital depleted by tax, you can reinvest the full value of your old property.

Although a tax-free exchange has this major tax attraction, there are limitations on its use. The primary problem is bringing together suitable exchange properties and investors interested in trading. This difficulty may sometimes be overcome by brokers specializing in real estate exchanges. Another serious limitation attaches to exchanges dealing with depreciable property: It is posed by the tax rule that requires you to carry over the basis of the old property to the new property. A tax-free exchange may be advantageous in the case of land, which is not depreciable. It may be exchanged for a depreciable rental building. The exchange is tax free, and depreciation may be claimed on the building. A tax-free exchange is not desirable if the transaction will result in a loss, because you may not deduct a loss in a tax-free exchange. To ensure the loss deduction, first sell the property, then buy new property with the proceeds.

Timing Your Real Property Sales. Generally, a taxable transaction occurs in the year in which title or possession to property passes. By controlling the year in which title and possession passes, you may select the year in which to report profit or loss. For example, suppose you intend to sell property this year, but you estimate that reporting the sale next year will incur less taxes. You can postpone the transfer of title and possession to next year. Alternatively, you can transact an installment sale, giving title and possession this year but delaying the receipt of all or most of the sale proceeds until next year.

TAX SAVINGS AT WORK

The 1986 TRA left intact the basic tax-saving features of employee pay plans but reduced the scale and extent of the tax savings in the following ways:

1. The new tax law reduces the amount of salary income that you may defer in 401(k) plans and imposes stricter nondiscrimination rules.
2. It restricts averaging opportunities. Special averaging for lump-sum distributions is unavailable to people under the age of 59 1/2 who were not age 50 as of January 1, 1986.
3. It imposes penalties on withdrawals from retirement plans before age 59 1/2 unless because of death or disability, or unless other approved exceptions apply.
4. Eliminates long-term capital gain benefits and so reduces the tax-saving potential of incentive stock options.
5. It imposes 15% penalty on excess retirement distribution.

Despite these developments, pay plans provide one of the few opportunities for deferring or sheltering income.

Pension and Profit-sharing Plans

A company-qualified pension or profit-sharing plan offers these benefits:

1. You do not realize current income on your employer's contributions to the plan on your behalf.
2. Funds contributed by both you and your employer compound tax free within the plan.
3. If you receive a lump sum, tax on employer contributions may be reduced by a special averaging rule.
4. If you receive a lump-sum distribution in company securities, unrealized appreciation on those securities is not taxed until you finally sell the stock.

When you are allowed to choose the type of payout from a qualified plan, make sure that you compare (1) the tax on receiving a lump-sum distribution with (2) the projected tax cost of deferring payments over a period of years or (3) of rolling over the distribution to an IRA account.

Cash or Deferred Pay Arrangements: 401(k) Plans

If your company has a profit-sharing or stock bonus plan, it has the opportunity of giving you additional tax-sheltered pay. The tax law allows the company to add a cash or deferred pay plan, called a 401(k) plan, which can operate in one of two ways:

1. Your employer contributes an amount for your benefit to a trust account. You are not taxed on your employer's contribution. Although there is no income tax, the contribution is subject to Social Security tax.
2. You agree to take a salary reduction or to forgo a salary increase. The reduction is placed in a trust account for your benefit. The reduction is treated as your employer's contribution. In addition, your company may match part of your contribution. The new law limits total salary reduction deferrals to $7,000, although this limit may be increased starting in 1988 by an inflation factor. Taking a pay reduction may be an ideal way to defer income and benefit from a tax-free buildup of income.

Income earned on the trust account accumulates tax free until it is withdrawn. By law, you may not withdraw funds attributable to elective salary reduction contributions until you reach age 59 1/2, are separated from service, become disabled, or show financial hardship. Withdrawals are also allowed if the plan terminates or if the corporation sells its assets or its interest in a subsidiary and you continue to work for the buyer or the subsidiary. However, the hardship provision and age 59 1/2 allowance do not apply to certain "pre-ERISA" money purchase pension plans (in existence June 27, 1974). Furthermore, after 1988, hardship withdrawals may include only an employee's elective deferrals; the hardship withdrawal may not include employer contributions or income earned on the employee's elective deferrals.

If withdrawals are allowed before age 591/2, such as for hardship, you are subject to the 10% penalty for premature withdrawals unless you meet one of the exceptions allowed.

A lump-sum distribution may be eligible for special averaging under IRS rules. Lump-sum distributions exceeding $750,000 may be subject to the excess distribution penalty.

If you are allowed to borrow from the plan, certain loan restrictions apply.

 Finally, you should know that the law imposes strict contribution percentage tests to prevent discrimination in favor of highly compensated employees. If these tests are violated, the employer is subject to penalties and the plan could be disqualified unless the excess contributions (plus allocable income) are distributed back to the highly compensated employees within a specified time.

Saving Taxes on Insurance Plans

Company-financed insurance for employees is a common way to give additional benefits at low or no tax cost. For example, group insurance plans may furnish not only life insurance protection, but also accident and health benefits. Premium costs are low and tax deductible to the company while tax free to you unless you have nonforfeitable rights to permanent life insurance or, in the case of group term life insurance, your coverage exceeds $50,000. Even where your coverage exceeds $50,000, the tax incurred on your employer's premium payment is generally less than what you would pay privately for similar insurance.

Where you want more insurance than provided by the group plan, your company may be able to help you get additional protection through a split-dollar insurance plan. Under this type of plan, your employer purchases permanent life insurance for you. The company pays the annual premium to the extent of the yearly increases in the cash surrender value of the policy, and you pay only the balance of the premium. At your death, your employer is entitled to part of the proceeds equal to the cash surrender value of any lesser amount equaling the total premiums he paid. You have the right to name a beneficiary to receive the remaining proceeds, which under most policies are substantial compared with the employer's share.

You annually report as taxable income an amount equal to the one-year term cost of the declining life insurance protection to which you are entitled, less any portion of the premium provided by you.

Despite the tax cost, you may find the arrangement an inexpensive way to obtain additional insurance coverage with your employer's help. Split-dollar insurance policies entered into before November 14, 1964, are not subject to this tax on the employer's payment of premiums.

Educational Benefits for Employees' Children

The IRS has published guidelines under which a private foundation established by an employer may make tax-free grants to children of employees. If the guidelines are satisfied, employees are not taxable on the benefits provided for their children. Advance approval of the grant program must be obtained from the IRS, and the grant must also meet a percentage test regarding the number of grants awarded versus the number of eligible children.

SAVING TAXES THROUGH FAMILY INCOME PLANNING

TRA discourages income splitting among family members by

1. Reducing the difference between the lowest and highest brackets. When the range between tax brackets was 11 to 50% (and

sometimes as high as 70%), there was an obvious incentive for diverting income from high breadwinner brackets to the lower brackets of dependents. If the projected two-rate structure is adhered to by Congress, the 13% spread between the 15 and 28% tax brackets may not offer the same motivation for such transfers.

2. Taxing investment income exceeding $1,000 of minor children under the age 14 at the top bracket of parents.
3. Repealing the income-shifting feature of short-term (10-year, or Clifford) trusts.

Although the tax-saving advantages of family income splitting have been tarnished by these developments, certain tax savings are available.

Escaping Gift Tax Liability

Because family income planning generally requires the transfer of property, you must consider possible gift tax liability. The gift tax rates and credit are the same as those of the estate tax. However, gift tax liability may be avoided by making gifts within the annual exclusion of $10,000 (or $20,000 for joint gifts). Gifts over this exclusion may also avoid tax after applying the unified gift and estate tax credit described at the end of this chapter.

If you make interest-free or low-interest loans to a family member, you may be subject to income tax as well as a gift tax.

Unfortunately, to realize the full potential of income splitting, you must do more than make gifts of income: you must actually transfer property from which the income is produced. For example, you do not avoid tax on interest by instructing your savings bank to credit interest to your children's account. Unless you actually transfer the complete ownership of the account to your children, the interest income is earned on money owned by you and must be reported by you. The same holds true with dividends, rents, and other forms of income. Unless you transfer the property providing the income, the income will be taxed to you.

You may not split earned income; income resulting from your services is taxed to you.

You may not avoid this result by setting up trusts to receive your earned income.

Custodian Accounts for Children

Custodian accounts set up in a bank, mutual fund, or brokerage firm can achieve income splitting, although certain tax consequences apply to each type of account. Trust accounts are considered revocable under state law and are ineffective in splitting interest income. Also, limitations are placed on the custodian. He or she may not take proceeds from the sale of an investment or income from an investment to buy additional securities on margin. Although the custodian should prudently seek reasonable income and capital preservation, he or she generally is not liable for losses unless they result from bad faith, intentional wrongdoing, or gross negligence.

When the minor reaches majority (depending on state law), property in the custodian account is turned over to the child. No formal accounting is required, although a separate bank account should be opened in which proceeds from sales of investments and investment income are deposited pending reinvestment. Such an account will furnish a convenient record of sales proceeds, investment income, and reinvestment of same.

Income from a custodian account is taxable to the child as long as it is not used by the parent who set up the account to pay for the child's support. Tax-exempt income from a custodian account is not taxable to the parent even when used for child support. Income from a custodian account in excess of $1,000 is taxed at the parent's tax rate if the child is under 14.

When setting up a custodian account, you may have to pay a gift tax because transfer of cash or securities (above the $10,000 single, or $20,000 joint, annual exclusion) is a gift. If you die while acting as custodian of an account before your child reaches majority, the value of the custodian account will be taxed with your estate. This problem may be avoided if you appoint someone other than yourself as custodian.

Other Types of Investments for Minors

Because a minor generally lacks the ability to manage property, you may wish to control the property you give—although such active management may disallow the gift for income shifting purposes. You could appoint a fiduciary for the child, but this will only add to the investment's cost. Alternatively, you might choose a property that does not require investor participation and that can be transferred by a minor, such as

1. Bonds, which may be purchased and registered in a minor's name. Coupons or the proceeds on sale or maturity of bonds may be cashed or deposited in a minor's name.
2. Insurance policies written on the lives of minors. These policies recognize the minor's ownership of the policy and may cover the lives of others. Depending on the age of the minor, state law, and company practice, it may be necessary to appoint a guardian for the purpose of cashing in or borrowing on insurance policies given to a minor. A gift of a life insurance policy or annuity will usually qualify as a gift of a present interest in property for the annual gift tax exclusion.
3. Mutual fund shares that may be purchased and registered in the name of a minor. The problem of management is minimized by the investment company's supervision of the fund. Most funds also provide automatic reinvestment of dividends in additional shares.

Other Income-splitting Possibilities

Making a gift of appreciated property that will eventually be sold may reduce income tax. To shift the profit and the tax, the gift must be completed before the sale or before the donor has made a binding commitment to sell. By making a gift of interests in the property to several family members, it is possible to spread the tax among a number of taxpayers in the lowest tax bracket. Of course, the IRS may claim that the gift was never completed if, after sale, the donor controls the sales proceeds or has use of them. You

should also remember that appreciation on property passed by inheritance will escape income tax: the heir takes a basis equal to estate tax value, usually fair market value at the date of death. Furthermore, appreciated property encumbered by mortgage may result in income tax to the donor when a gift of the property is made.

If you own a business, tax on your business income may be reduced if you can shift it to members of your family. You may also avoid estate tax on the value of capital interests transferred to children. If you keep within the annual gift tax exclusion for each donee, there will be no tax consequence.

Business income may be shifted by forming a family partnership or by making your family stockholders in a corporation. Generally speaking, a Subchapter S corporation in which stockholders elect to report income may be used more freely than a partnership to split income. A minor child will not be recognized as a partner unless he or she is competent to manage his own property, or unless control of the property is exercised by another person as a fiduciary for his or her sole benefit.

Life Insurance Tax Advantages

Insurance may provide tax-free accumulation of cash. During the time you pay premiums, the value of your contract increases at compound interest rates. The increase is not subject to income tax. In addition, when your policy is paid at death, the proceeds are not subject to income tax.

To shelter life insurance proceeds from estate tax, you must not have ownership rights. If you have an existing policy, you must assign your ownership rights, such as the right to change beneficiaries, the right to surrender or cancel the policy, the right to assign it, and the right to borrow against it. An assignment must occur more than three years before death to exclude the proceeds from your estate.

If you create a trust to carry a policy on your life by transferring income-producing property the income of which is used to pay the premiums, you are taxable on the trust income. Similarly, if your spouse creates the trust to carry the policy on your life, he or she is taxable on the trusts income. This tax rule does not apply to the trust funding of life insurance covering the life of a third party other than your spouse. For example, a grandparent transfers income-producing property to a trust to pay the premiums on a life insurance policy for a son. The grandchildren are named as beneficiaries. The grandparent is not taxed on the income earned by the trust on the transferred property because the trust purchased insurance on the son's life, not on the grandparent's.

The trust may receive insurance proceeds where there is a concern that the beneficiary may be unable to manage a large insurance settlement. Insurance proceeds are not subject 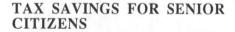 to income tax whether paid directly to named beneficiaries or to a trust.

More information on types of insurance policies available, their investment value, and their tax consequences, may be found in Chapter 17.

TAX SAVINGS FOR SENIOR CITIZENS

When you reach age 65, you receive an increased standard deduction allowance, provided you do not itemize deductions. If your or your spouse's sixty-fifth birthday is on January 1, 1988, you claim the extra standard deduction amounts on your 1987 tax return. For tax purposes, you are considered to be 65 on December 31, 1987. You may also be entitled to a tax credit; and if you are age 55 or over and sold your principal residence at a gain, you may elect to avoid tax on up to $125,000 of profit, provided you meet certain tests and file an election, as discussed earlier in this chapter.

Tax Credits for the Elderly and Disabled

In 1987, the credit for the elderly is available mainly to people 65 or over who do not receive Social Security or Railroad Retirement benefits or people under 65 who are permanently and totally disabled and receive disability income. The credit for elderly and disabled is combined with the credits for dependent care and mortgage credit certificates. The total credits may not exceed regular tax liability without the Alternative Minimum Tax and self-employment tax and penalty taxes for premature retirement distributions.

Taxes and Social Security

Social Security benefits are not paid automatically. You must register at the local Social Security office three months before your sixty-fifth birthday to allow time for your application to be processed and to locate all necessary information. Even if you do not plan to retire at age 65, you must register to ensure your Medicare coverage. For each year you delay retiring past 65, your potential Social Security benefits increase.

If you are under 70, Social Security benefits are reduced by earned income (wages and self-employment income). If you were 65 or older but under 70 in 1987, you could earn $8,160 without losing benefits. If you were under 65 for the whole year, you could earn $6,000 without losing benefits. These ceilings are subject to inflation adjustments. Once you earn more than these ceilings, benefits are reduced. For each $2 you earn, you lose $1 in benefits. A special monthly rule applies in the year you reach retirement age. After 1989, you will lose $1 in benefits for each $3 you earn above the earnings ceiling.

For those age 70 or over, benefits are not reduced by earnings. You can work, earn any amount, and receive full Social Security benefits.

As long as you continue to work, regardless of your age, you will pay Social Security taxes on your earnings. You may also receive any amount of income from other sources than work (private pensions or investments, for example) without affecting the amount of Social Security benefits. However, benefits may be taxable if your income exceeds a base amount. The maximum taxable amount is 50% of benefits.

There are two steps in figuring taxation of Social Security benefits: (1) deciding whether your income exceeds the base amount for your filing status, and (2) calculating the amount of benefits subject to tax. Your tax advisor or *J. K. Lasser's Your Income Tax 1988* will show you how to make these computations.

 The Social Security Administration has been criticized for not keeping up with workers' earning records. Don't risk a problem by ignoring your own record. Once every three years you should mail Form SSA-7004, Request for Statement of Earnings, to the Social Security Administration, Wilkes-Barre Data Operations Center, P.O. Box 20, Wilkes Barre, PA 18703. (This form is available at your local Social Security office and the headquarters in Baltimore.) You will receive a response in about 6 weeks. Social Security forms state that if you wait more than 3 years, 3 months, and 15 days after an error is discovered to request a correction, a change may not be possible. The agency waived the deadline in 1981 since it had fallen behind in its record-keeping, but you should still try to correct any errors immediately.

If you are age 55 or older, your local Social Security office can give you an estimate of your retirement benefits.

SAVING TAXES IN OTHER SITUATIONS

Members of the armed forces stationed outside the United States and those returning from foreign duty, veterans of the Vietnam conflict, members of the reserves, and anyone receiving income from foreign sources all face special tax situations under TRA. Resident and nonresident aliens also face tax consequences for money earned in the United States. If you fall into one or more of these categories, you should consult your tax advisor or *J. K. Lasser's Your Income Tax 1988* before filing your return to ensure you have taken advantage of every possible deduction, credit, and benefit—and met every obligation—specified by the 1986 TRA.

WHAT HAPPENS AFTER YOU FILE YOUR RETURN?

Although the time to minimize your taxes is *before* you prepare your return, your opportunities for savings (and potential for new liabilities) continue while the IRS examines your return.

First the IRS checks your return for arithmetic accuracy. If a mistake is found, you receive either a refund or a bill for additional tax. Naturally, the IRS looks first for errors that most typically result in a higher tax, such as reported medical expenses without the adjusted gross income limitation, or use of auto mileage rate for business travel that exceeds the allowable IRS rate. The IRS also screens returns that claim refunds from tax shelters. If your return is selected for more thorough review, you will be notified by letter—although this may not happen for a year or two after you file. Your chances of being audited are greatest in the following circumstances:

- If you claim tax shelter losses
- If you report complex investment or business transactions without clearly explaining them
- If you receive cash payments in your work that the IRS thinks are easy to conceal, such as cash fees received by physicians or tips received by cab drivers and waiters
- If your business expenses are large in comparison to income
- If your cash contributions to charity are large in relation to income
- If you are a shareholder of a closely held corporation whose return has been examined
- If a prior audit has resulted in a tax deficiency
- If an informer gives the IRS grounds to believe you are omitting income from your return

An examination may take place at a local IRS office or at your place of business or home if your return is complex and involves many outside records. If the questions can be cleared up by correspondence, you may not have to appear at all. If your return is complex, if a large potential tax liability is involved, or if you are unfamiliar with how the return was prepared, it's advisable to have an experienced tax practitioner represent you during the examination. If you disagree with the examiner's findings, many appeal steps are possible, from an immediate interview with the examiner's supervisor (if the audit was conducted in an IRS office) to eventual litigation in Tax Court, federal district court, or U.S. Claims Court.

A FEW WORDS ABOUT INCOME TAX RETURN PREPARERS

An old joke goes, "anyone with a business card who is more than 50 miles from home is a 'business consultant.'" The same is true for tax return preparers—although they can be as close as the nearest corner and often carry no business cards at all.

In short, anyone who prepares someone else's tax return or refund claim for a fee is a tax return preparer. Although tax preparers, like financial planners, can have extensive qualifications (such as CPAs or attorneys), many do not. Enrolled Agents (EAs) are preparers who have established a working relationship with the IRS, but their experience is often limited to general return requirements. Some employees of local tax preparation services are neither accountants nor EAs, but simply people who moonlight as seasonal tax preparers. As with most financial products and services, the rule is "Buyer beware."

The IRS requires any tax preparer to provide certain minimum services and levies penalties if those services are not performed:

1. If preparers understate the tax on a client's return, they can be fined $100 if the act was negligent; $500 if it was willful. For example, the IRS has applied the $100 negligence penalty to a preparer's failure to list interest shown on a taxpayer's 1099s that resulted in a substantial underpayment of tax. A mathematical error made in totaling interest payments was not penalized, but a penalty was applied to a preparer who incorrectly totaled the amount of itemized deductions and used the wrong tax table. Although the total understatement of tax was not substantial, the errors, taken as a whole, were considered negligent. Failure to ask a taxpayer whether he or she had records to support a claimed entertainment expense was penalized, but not where the preparer asked for records that the taxpayer lied about having. A preparer is not subject to penalties for failure to report additions to tax for an underpayment of estimated tax.

2. Preparers are subject to a $500 penalty if they endorse or negotiate a refund check issued to a taxpayer whose return they have prepared. To avoid the penalty, a business manager for celebrities or a professional who handles personal funds must act only as an agent in depositing the client's refund check.

3. Preparers must furnish a completed copy of the return or refund claim to the taxpayer when (or before) it is presented for the taxpayer's signature. A $25 penalty is imposed for each failure.

4. Preparers must keep for three years, and have available for IRS inspection, a completed copy of each return or claim prepared, or a list of the names and identification numbers of taxpayers for whom returns or claims were prepared. A $50 penalty is imposed for each failure.

5. Preparers must sign the return and include their identifying number or the identifying number of their employer. A $25 penalty is imposed for each failure.

In addition to the penalties imposed, the IRS may also seek to enjoin fraudulent or deceptive practice or to enjoin a person from acting as an income tax return preparer. The IRS publishes a list of enjoined preparers in its weekly *Internal Review Bulletin.*

For additional information about income tax return preparers, see the Professional Edition of *J. K. Lasser's Your Income Tax.*

PART III

INVESTMENT GUIDE TO PRODUCT OPPORTUNITIES

In the deregulated and reregulated financial markets of the late 1980s, investment products change almost daily. In Chapters 9 through 14, you'll learn which products comprise the six basic asset categories over which you'll spread your wealth-building portfolio. In Chapters 15, 16, and 17, you'll discover the advanced trading techniques and special investments that are tailored to unique portfolio needs.

CHAPTER 9

CASH AND MONEY MARKET INSTRUMENTS

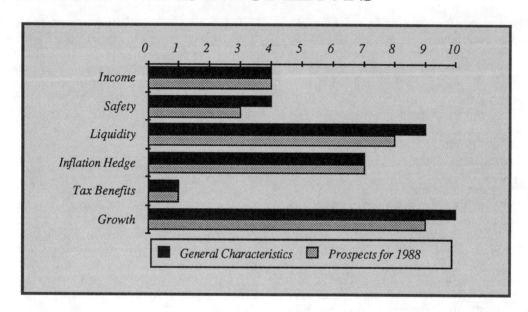

Income / Safety / Liquidity / Inflation Hedge / Tax Benefits / Growth

■ General Characteristics   ▨ Prospects for 1988

PERSONAL
FINANCIAL
KEYS FOR CASH
AND MONEY
MARKET
INSTRUMENTS

Liquidity

Inflation

Ordinary income

OUTLOOK FOR
1988

High Volatility

Record deficits

Erratic Fed
Policy

Potential
inflation

Need Liquidity

A GLANCE AHEAD

The collapse in oil prices in 1985 and 1986 left many wealthy Americans in the peculiar position of being "asset rich" and "cash poor." In the headlong rush to accumulate wealth, they failed to understand the importance of liquidity. All investments are ultimately valued in the terms of the cash they will fetch.

Cash provides the grease that enables the wheels of our increasingly complex economy to roll. The high inflation and interest rates of the late 1970s led to deregulation of the financial markets. A variety of new money market instruments developed to meet the demands of savvy investors who want and need to have their money working at all times—earning interest—while remaining liquid enough to take advantage of new market opportunities..

In this chapter you'll discover the most important of these new products as well as updates on the more familiar savings alternatives. You'll learn

- How money market instruments provide portfolio liquidity so you'll be prepared for
    Emergencies requiring immediate cash
    New opportunities
    Quick asset allocation adjustments
- How money market instruments can be used to earn more income on even your personal bill-paying accounts.

OUTLOOK FOR THE 1988 MONEY MARKETS

Volatile economic cross currents, including the stock market collapse of "Black Monday," October 19, 1987, mandate holding a substantial cash reserve for 1988. After years of slow growth, low inflation and declining interest rates, 1987 witnessed a return of higher rates in both. Long-term economic problems, such as the trade and federal deficit, remain unresolved, and higher financial reserves are best in such situations.

The consensus economic forecast for 1988 calls for continued slow growth and moderately rising inflation and interest rates. However, several key factors could change this outcome. By mid-1987 the status of the dollar became the most important factor in the health of the investment markets. As 1987 drew to a close, uncertainty surrounded the fate of the dollar. After two years of sharp weakness, the dollar declined by over 60% relative to the yen, bringing only marginal improvement in the trade deficit.

Many analysts also continue to warn about the size of the federal budget deficit. The economic recovery and expansion that began in 1982 has already become the longest peacetime expansion in history. Despite this favorable environment, the budget deficit is huge. If the economy slows and the federal revenues fall off, the Treasury will be forced to borrow even greater sums in the credit market. This will have the effect of "crowding out" less creditworthy borrowers from the private sector. Rising rates could choke off the recovery.

Federal Reserve monetary policy slowed dramatically in 1987. The growth rates for both major monetary aggregates, M2 and M3, slowed below the bottom end of the Federal Reserve's target range. M2 is carefully watched by most analysts. M2 and M3 are expanded monetary aggregates from the classic M1, which historically has been the primary aggregate for defining "money." M1 is currency in circulation, commercial bank demand deposits, NOW accounts, credit union share draft accounts, mutual savings bank demand deposits, and nonbank travelers checks. The Federal Reserve indicated in 1987 that it was no longer monitoring M1 for policy purposes.

M2 is the total of M1 plus savings accounts, time deposits under $100,000, money market funds, overnight repos issued by commercial banks, and overnight Eurodollars. M3 is M2 plus time deposits over $100,000 and term repurchase agreements.

The technical definition of each aggregate is not really important for most people. What is important is the trend of growth for each. Money supply provides the liquidity for the economy. Slow money expansion inhibits the economy's growth. Slow expansion limits inflationary pressures, though.

On the other hand, politicians prefer to have robust growth. High rates of money supply expansion foster ever greater economic growth—up to a point. That point is when inflationary fears outrun production. If production does not keep up with money supply growth, you have the classic inflation scenario: too much money chasing too few goods.

The Federal Reserve attempts to steer a course between the extremes of too slow money expansion and recession and too fast money expansion and inflation. Through July 1987 there was no net growth in monetary reserves. A continuation of this trend will stifle the economy. If money supply is too restrictive in a growing economy, interest rates will turn higher as producers fight to obtain capital to keep up with customer demand.

This is the core of the classic business cycle. As interest rates turn higher, marginal producers are forced out of the market. Eventually, the economy slides into a recession as business slows. It is vital to monitor Federal Reserve policy. President Reagan appointed Alan Greenspan as Federal Reserve chairman in 1987 to replace Paul Volcker, who had been chairman for seven years.

It is expected that Greenspan will follow a slightly more expansionary policy than his predecessor. However, he is an unknown quantity at this time. Given the importance of Fed policy for the economy and interest rates, any changes from past trends will be important signals for the investment markets.

The *Wall Street Journal,* and most major city dailies, report on the Federal Reserve's weekly money supply figures, which are released each Thursday. Watch to see if M2 and M3 growth stays within the Fed's target ranges. A sustained rise above the target ranges has inflationary implications. A drop below the target ranges would signal recessionary potential for a recession.

Cash in the form of short-term money market instruments provides an important hedge against rising inflation and interest rates. While bonds, real estate , and even stocks can be hurt by these rising rates, your fully invested money-market reserve should preserve its value. These accounts also provide you with the liquidity to take advantage of emerging trends in other asset categories.

Keep a minimum of 30% of your total near-money reserves in short-term U.S. Treasury bills (or in money market funds that invest only in Treasury bills). Remember, the main purpose of your cash reserves is insurance against uncertainty, and in uncertain times that insurance is doubly important.

INVESTING IN CASH AND MONEY MARKET INSTRUMENTS

Cash is legal tender for all transactions. Money market instruments are short-term investment vehicles that provide income to the owner of the cash in exchange for "loaning" the cash to another party for a short time. Money market instruments are frequently referred to as "cash equivalents" or "near money investments." They have very short-term maturities, never more than six months, and typically are very liquid—very easily reconverted back to cash.

 Cash itself earns no income. It has to be loaned at interest or invested in an appreciative security to grow. Cash is the last word in liquidity. In order to entice investors into making their cash less liquid—even in highly liquid economy market accounts—an institution must pay a reasonable penalty in interest. The less liquid the account becomes, the more interest they must pay. While the interest paid on cash and short-term debt varies widely, the value of cash itself varies only with the rate of inflation. When interest rates rise, environments, the yields paid on cash and money market instruments will also rise. Unlike long-term fixed-income instruments (see Chapter 11), there is no risk to principal from outside forces such as rising rates that tend to devalue bonds. The only penalty you pay is higher interest you don't receive.

There are two types of near-money or cash equivalents: deposit accounts (such as passbook savings) and short-term debt called "paper" (such as commercial paper). Deposit accounts in federally chartered institutions are insured to $100,000. Short-term debt paper is typically not insured and pays higher interest.

Risks

 Although greenbacks can be lost or stolen, cash (demand deposit account) is very safe—although there are some risks. The principal risk is that of the bank's failure as a business. If your bank or money market fund fails due to malfeasance or simply poor business judgment, you may lose some or all of your uninsured principal. The short-term nature of money market instruments protect them from the heavy loss of purchasing power due to inflation, but interest rates typically grow more slowly than inflation, so stocks or real estate are better inflation hedges.

All investments are subject in part to political risk. The falling dollar of 1986 and 1987 diminished the purchasing power of the dollar relative to other countries' currencies. A change in tax laws or the regulatory environment may adversely affect the profitability of cash in your portfolio. The adverse affects of foreseeable political events are less onerous for cash and money market vehicles than other assets simply because they are so liquid.

There are ways to ensure even greater protection by investing in only those instruments that are evaluated and rated by independent credit services such as Standard & Poor's or Moody's. The federal government provides depositors' insurance for federally chartered savings and loans institutions as well as for banks.

Near-money in Relation to Other Assets

Cash is unique because all other asset categories are valued in terms of the cash they can generate. In a diversified portfolio, cash provides a hedge against inflation because the rates on money market instruments will rise as inflation increases. Don't confuse this rise with profiting from inflation, though. It is more a preservation of capital than profiteering from other people's spending habits!

In the initial phases of an inflationary spiral, the interest rates on short-term instruments tend to lag behind the rate of inflation. Once inflation becomes well established, short-term rates tend to rise quickly to reflect the current rise in prices. As we've seen by the disinflationary experience of the 1980s, short-term interest rates will fall much slower than the inflation. Over a full inflation-deflation cycle, then, the purchasing power of your cash (plus interest earned, of course) should remain fairly constant.

 Although cash is generally considered to be a stable, non-speculative preserve, the financial markets have developed products that enable you to speculate on short-term rates. The futures market offers the chance to buy certificates of deposit, commercial paper, three-month Treasury bills (T-bills) and other short-term instruments in a highly leveraged form (see Chapter 15).

The major components of the broad category known as cash and money market instruments includes passbook savings accounts, credit union share deposit accounts, NOW and super-NOW accounts, certificates of deposit, commercial paper, banker's acceptances, repurchase agreements, and money market funds.

**Lasser's Recommended Allocation Range for 1988
Cash and Money Market Instruments:**

 Allocate as little as 15%.

 Allocate as much as 30%.

Passbook Savings Accounts

Passbook savings accounts are short-term interest-bearing deposits with banks or thrift institutions. They were the staple of the savings industry until the 1970s. Banks and savings and loans institutions would acquire most of their funds for loans from low-yielding passbook savings accounts. They'd pay 5.25% for the deposits and then loan money out at a higher rates. Their profit came from the difference.

PASSBOOK
SAVINGS
ACCOUNTS

Moderate income

Very safe

Very liquid

Poor for
inflation

No tax benefits

No capital
growth

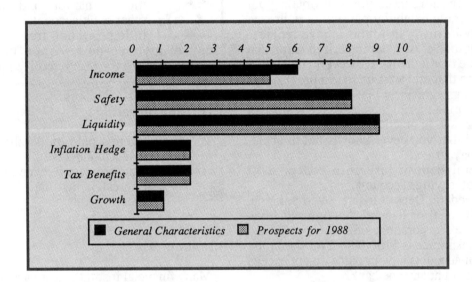

The passbook savings account has understandably withered in importance for many consumers. However, the deregulation of the financial industry has also presented many Americans with such a confusing array of alternatives that the old passbook simplicity and convenience is attracting new customers. To this day, billions of dollars are safely ensconced in passbook savings accounts.

The inflationary experience of the 1970s created a whole new savings and banking environment. Money market mutual funds began offering substantially higher yields than passbook accounts in a form that was accessible to most consumers. When inflation was raging at 10%–15%, a passbook account paying 5.25% became a losing proposition, even with the higher minimum balances required by money market accounts.

Most savings institutions still offer passbook accounts. The ceiling on passbook interest was eliminated in 1986. However, most savings institutions have already created numerous products to compete with the money market funds. (See NOW and super-NOW accounts, and certificates of deposit, later in this chapter.) As a result most passbook accounts still only pay about 5.25%.

You should investigate all the different types of savings accounts your bank offers. Other products may pay higher interest with no more fees than a passbook account and a reasonable amount of liquidity.

Usually no fees are assessed on a passbook account unless the activity is considered abusive. Banks will advise you not to consider a passbook account a substitute for a checking account. Frequent withdrawals within a month (usually more than three) will trigger a fee. Accounts with *no* activity (especially deposits) may be closed by the bank unilaterally after a certain amount of time, usually six months.

Passbook savings accounts are covered by federal depositors insurance at federally chartered institutions.

Investment Potential

The days of the passbook savings account as your largest cash holding are long past. Its chief value now is for short-term savings while you are deciding on where to place your funds. Such an account pays current income with no potential for capital gains.

A passbook savings account is the classic secure, nonvolatile, liquid investment. Under normal circumstances you can obtain your money immediately by presenting your savings book (many institutions have replaced the "passbook" with computerized cards that resemble credit cards). However, you should be aware that all banks include a provision in the savings agreement that allows them to require as much as 30 days advance notice for withdrawals. In practice, this provision is not invoked, but you never know what financial crisis may strike.

Federal deposit insurance covers most passbook savings accounts.

The Federal Deposit Insurance corporation, FDIC (banks) or Federal Savings and Loan Insurance Corporation, FSLIC (savings and loans) insurance is $100,000. You should be sure that accounts in your name do not exceed that amount at any one bank.

Passbook savings accounts offer no protection of your guaranteed return from inflation.

They are not designed to offer variable interest rates that could offset higher inflation.

Strengths

 Passbook savings accounts are very liquid. They are insured by an agency of the federal government up to $100,000. They are convenient for short-term savings. You are not required to lock up your money for any fixed period. The concept is simple and widely understood in an increasingly complex financial world.

Weaknesses

 Passbook savings accounts typically pay much lower rates than money market funds or even other bank accounts. They offer little protection from inflation. Many institutions now require minimum monthly balances for you to receive interest.

Tax Considerations

 Interest paid on passbook savings accounts is fully taxable at your ordinary income rates. The interest is also taxed by most states.

Summing Up

Many financial institutions are actually discouraging passbook savings accounts by assessing fees for small amounts. Formerly the backbone of the savings industry, passbook savings are fading as realistic alternatives in a more sophisticated financial world.

Passbook savings offer a simple, safe, short-term "parking place" for your funds when they are between more profitable destinations. However, the emphasis is on *short-term*. There are equally safe alternatives that pay better yields.

Credit Unions

Credit unions are a nonprofit cooperative savings organization. This means that the members own the institution and have some common bond. Typically they are started by a company's employees, a church, a community, or even civic or fraternal organizations.

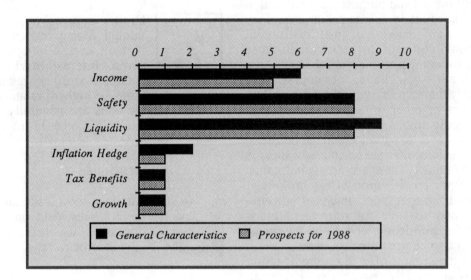

General Characteristics ■   Prospects for 1988 ▒

Credit unions offer services similar to other savings institutions, such as savings and checking accounts, time deposits such as certificates of deposit, and in recent years even credit cards, mortgage loans, and discount brokerage services. Generally smaller organizations, they offer more personal and informal contact and transactions.

Many credit unions are offered as fringe benefits for employees of a company. Often the employer provides free office space and other amenities. In addition, many credit unions use volunteer workers to accomplish some of their required tasks.

 Many people find the informal, close-knit credit union environment more amenable for obtaining credit than large banking establishments. Loans are usually offered at lower rates than profit-oriented enterprises because their costs are lower (credit union profits are not usually subject to federal taxes).

There is usually no cost to join other than meeting the "common bond" requirement. Credit unions have become so widespread that most people qualify for at least one. Information on credit unions around the country is available from the Credit Union National Association, P.O. Box 431, Madison, Wisconsin 53701.

Federally chartered credit unions are covered by insurance issued by the National Credit Union Administration. Depositors (not accounts) are insured up to $100,000. Most state-chartered credit unions are also required to have equivalent insurance. However, not all are. You can write NCUA at 1776 G Street, NW, Washington, DC 20456 for details on those credit unions that are federally insured.

A credit union works much like any other savings institution, although the terminology is different. Your deposits are called *shares*. The interest earned on a credit union account is called *dividends,* though it is treated as interest for tax purposes. Checking accounts are called *share draft accounts*.

Investment Potential

For all intents and purposes, a credit union savings account is the same as a savings account at any banking or thrift institution. You should compare the returns with those offered by competitive organizations. As a part owner, you have, of course, the intangible benefit of working with fellow employees or other organization members. Many credit unions offer their members a very real chance to participate in the business.

Credit unions offer the potential for income on your savings. There are no capital gains (unless your credit union offers brokerage services). Employer credit unions offer a convenient way to save for retirement plans through payroll deductions. Loan payments can often also be structured this way.

The interest rates offered on credit union accounts are usually competitive. However, keep in mind that savings accounts are not good protection from inflation.

Minimum accounts are small, and no (or very nominal) fees are charged. If your account is less than $100,000, you should have no problem with liquidity.

Strengths

 Credit unions offer personalized attention no matter how small your account is. Accounts in federally chartered credit unions are insured to $100,000. Your

money is liquid. Credit is readily available with minimal hassle. You can become personally involved. As a member of a cooperative, you may be entitled to receive an annual payout from the credit union if it meets certain performance criteria.

Weaknesses

 Higher returns are available through money market vehicles. Not all credit unions are insured. Interest (dividends) is taxable as ordinary income. After tax returns may be higher in municipal securities. Credit lines are generally smaller than may be available at other institutions.

Tax Considerations

 Although most credit unions call their money paid on deposits *dividends,* it is taxable at ordinary income rates.

Summing Up

Credit unions offer a safe, liquid (if unexciting) haven for savings. The small, informal structure of most offer a chance for increased personal involvement. Deregulation of the savings industry has enabled many credit unions to expand their range of services.

They will never offer the highest return available but convenience may outweigh other considerations.

NOW and Super-NOW Accounts

The first effort to provide interest on checking accounts was the NOW account. NOW stands for negotiable order of withdrawal. *Basically it is the same as a checking account, but renamed to enhance its product value in the marketplace.*

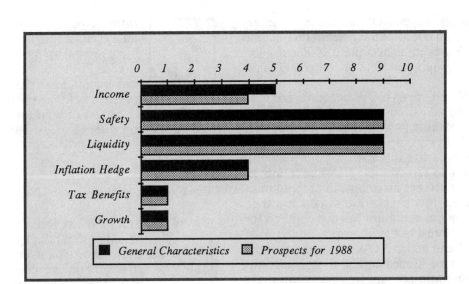

Many consumers don't realize or remember that interest-paying checking accounts haven't been around for very long. In the 1970s the money market funds launched by the mutual fund industry threatened to "put a stake in the heart" of the banking industry. Banks and savings and loans institutions were limited to paying 5.25% interest on normal passbook savings accounts and nothing on checking accounts. Thus, the NOW account was born as a defensive measure.

The money market funds became instantly popular, and a huge amount of cash moved from savings institutions into the hands of the mutual fund industry. To combat this, the savings industry united to promote legislation freeing them from interest rate ceilings.

In the 1970s, NOW accounts were limited to paying only 5.25%. With the advent of bank-sponsored money market deposit accounts that paid a fluctuating market interest rate, the super-NOW account was created. A super-NOW account is not bound by the 5.25% limitation imposed on NOW accounts. Initially super-NOW accounts could pay mar-

ket rates only on those accounts with a minimum balance of $2,500. This minimum was phased out until it was eliminated altogether on January 1, 1986. However, banks have continued to impose additional fees and restrictions on super-NOW accounts.

In fact, most banks no longer advertise or talk much about NOW accounts. Common sense has prevailed, and most banks merely term the accounts "interest-paying checking accounts." The fees vary widely. It would be wise to comparison-shop before plunking down your money. Most super-NOW accounts still require a minimum balance, or additional fees are assessed.

NOW and super-NOW accounts are available only from banks and thrift (savings and loan) institutions, which will be glad to explain their programs to you. As mentioned earlier, fees can vary widely. You should speak to several banks to find a program that most closely fits your financial needs. For example, some fees go up if you write more checks. Others allow you a set number of checks each month without triggering those extra charges. You may be surprised to find that some banks charge very high fees for certain very basic accounts. The bottom line is "Shop around!"

Investment Potential

NOW and super-NOW accounts pay interest. They do not offer the potential for capital gains. However, an account can obtain good returns through the effect of compound interest.

NOW and super-NOW accounts are very stable and they offer no leverage. There is no market volatility to worry about. Your principal is always secure, and the only thing that fluctuates is the interest on your account. Most people regard their NOW accounts as long-term savings programs. In order to minimize fees, few checks are drawn and then only when the minimum balance required for the best interest rate is observed.

NOW and super-NOW accounts are very liquid. As mentioned earlier, most banks impose minimum account limitations on these accounts. If your balance falls below the minimums, you're assessed additional fees.

NOW and super-NOW accounts are covered by federal insurance up to $100,000. Since they pay a flexible interest rate, NOW and super-NOW accounts provide some measure of protection from inflation. The lack of growth potential limits the potential for outperforming the inflation rate.

Strengths

Now and super-NOWs are very safe. They are insured for $100,000 by an agency of the federal government. Make sure your savings institution is fed-

erally chartered. They are very liquid accounts. The variable interest rates afford some inflation protection. They pay safe and secure current income.

Weaknesses

Interest paid is typically less than comparable uninsured vehicles such as money market funds. Fees are complex and can amount to a substantial portion of earnings. They offer no growth potential. There are no tax advan-tages. Taxes must be paid on interest as earned. There is no deferral.

Tax Considerations

The 1986 Tax Reform Act eliminated preferential treatment for any interest paid on bank accounts. You are taxed at ordinary income levels for any interest earned on Now and super-NOW accounts.

Summing Up

NOW and super-Now accounts are standard services offered by banks and savings institutions. You can generally obtain higher rates with lower fees through money market funds. However, money market funds are not insured by an agency of the federal government.

NOW and super-NOW accounts usually are not limited to writing checks over $100 like most money market funds. If a secure, convenient, flexible checking account is what you need, check these out.

U.S. Savings Bonds

U.S. savings bonds are debt instruments backed by the full faith and credit of the U.S. government. In order to receive the highest allowable rate, you must hold the bond for a minimum of five years. The initial rate is 5.5% in the first year. It rises gradually after that until you've held it five years, when you're eligible to receive the maximum rate.

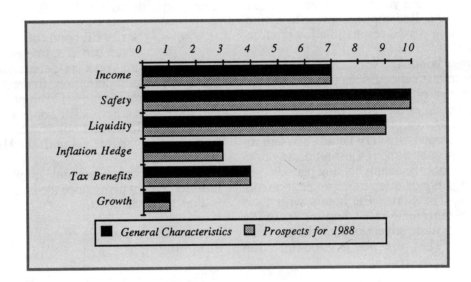

For many years during and after World Wars I and II, U.S. savings bonds were a part of almost everyone's savings. Before the inflationary experience of the 1970s, U.S. savings bonds offered competitive yield when the convenience of buying in small amounts, the absolute safety of principal and interest, and the long-term tax deferral features are considered.

However, the classic Series E savings bond, with its fixed low-interest rate, became a victim of the deregulation of the financial markets. When U.S. savers were able to obtain money market interest rates rather than being locked into the low fixed rates paid by bank savings accounts and Series E savings bonds, they moved quickly and decisively. The market for savings bonds dried up.

Congress recognized the problem and in 1982 authorized the new Series EE bonds. EE bonds pay a floating interest rate, which is 85% of the average rate paid by five-year U.S. Treasury bonds. The interest is paid on

redemption, not as current income. There is a fixed minimum rate after the bonds have been held for five years of 6% (prior to 1986, the minimum rate was 7.5%).

In addition to the Series EE Bonds, there are HH bonds, which pay current interest of 7.5%. HH bonds cannot be purchased for cash. You can acquire them only by exchanging your EE or E bonds. The idea is that EE bonds serve as a tax deferral device to enable you to accumulate a nest egg, which can be converted to HH bonds when you need to start receiving current income.

Information on savings bonds is available from any bank or savings and loan. You can buy savings bonds with no sales charge from these same institutions or from the Federal Reserve Bank. Series EE Bonds are available in ten denominations ranging from $50 to $10,000 face value. They are sold on a discount basis. You pay 50% of the face value ($50 for a $100 bond). The bond value increases with time as interest accrues. Their stated maturity is 10 years, though historically the government has permitted virtually unlimited extensions beyond that.

Investment Potential

U.S. savings bonds earn interest income. There is no capital growth potential. They are long-term investments. Bonds must be held a minimum of five years to receive the maximum payout. Redemptions prior to a five-year holding period results in a lower effective yield.

Savings bonds are very safe, secure, non-volatile investments. Prices do not fluctuate with interest rates—though the interest paid on the bonds does. Your principal is thus very secure.

Savings bonds are very liquid. You can redeem them at any savings institution any time after an initial six-month holding period.

Savings bonds offer little protection from inflation. The Series EE bonds with their floating interest rate feature provide moderately more protection than the previous Series E. They are not a good inflation hedge.

Strengths

Principal and interest is guaranteed by the full faith and credit (including taxing power) of the U.S. government. They are very liquid. Series EE bonds interest accumulates on a tax-deferred basis. They offer great flexibility in denominations. There are no sales charges. Many companies offer payroll deduction plans for accumulating savings bonds.

Weaknesses

There is no capital growth potential. Interest paid is low relative to competitive products. Minimum holding period is five years to receive the maximum rate.

Tax Considerations

Series EE bonds offer a number of tax benefits. Interest accumulates on a tax-deferred basis until redemption. Interest paid on redemption is exempt from state and local taxes. Series EE bonds can be exchanged for Series HH bonds without incurring taxes on the interest until the HH bonds are redeemed.

Series EE bonds are not appropriate for most retirement plans since the interest earned is already tax deferred.

Summing Up

The changes made in 1982 have substantially enhanced the investment attractiveness of savings bonds. However, the maximum interest rate paid is still only 85% of government-guaranteed five-year U.S. Treasury bonds.

The advantages of small minimum investments, high safety, good liquidity, and tax deferral of interest earnings make savings bonds a viable alternative for a portion of your long-term savings. Investors who have the time to devote to alternative investments can achieve higher yields, though.

Certificates of Deposit

A certificate of deposit is a loan from an investor to a bank or thrift institution for specified time at a set interest rate. Certificates of deposit (commonly called CDs) are perhaps the most widely used money market instrument for individual investors.

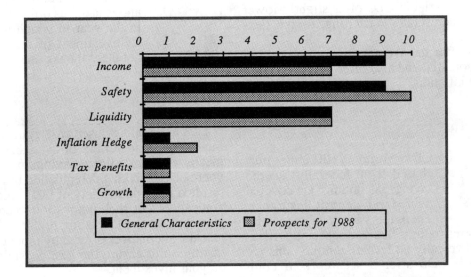

CDs are bank deposits and are covered by federal insurance up to $100,000 per account. "Jumbo" CDs are a minimum of $100,000 and therefore may subject the purchaser to some risk not covered by federal insurance.

Banking deregulation has resulted in a wide variety of options for CD investors. Interest rates vary with the length of the CD. Longer maturities and larger CDs generally pay higher rates. It is possible to find just about any combination to meet investors' needs. "Designer" CDs are offered by many savings institutions. These offer investors the opportunity to invest whatever sum they want in the form of a CD. For example, if investors have an odd sum, they can obtain a CD specifically built around their requirements.

The most common CDs include 31- and 91-day maturities in which the yield is tied to the 13-week Treasury Bill rate. Six-month and 30-month CDs generally pay higher rates, usually through some formula tied to Treasury bills.

As in any interest-bearing investments, there are a number of ways to calculate inter-est. For example, the interest may be figured as simple interest or may be compounded. It is important to ascertain exactly how the interest is calculated to ensure accurate comparison with competitive products. The time period used in compounding may change the effective annual interest rate received. A 7% CD rate compounded daily will yield a 7.25% annual rate compared to only 7% if compounded annually.

While the most common method for investing in CDs is direct purchase from a savings institution, brokerage firms pool CDs from disparate institutions around the country. They then offer investors the opportunity to invest in the pools. However, these pools generally invest in jumbo CDs, which are not wholly covered by federal insurance.

Investment Potential

You invest in CDs for income. Jumbo CDs and CD pools offer institutional investors some chance for capital gains that result from interest rate fluctuations, but individual investors normally do not participate in this sophisticated, high-level process.

CDs range from as little as 7 days to as much as seven years. Most CDs offer fixed interest rates for the specified maturities. In recent years, yet another option has been offered: variable interest rates based on a preset formula. Variable CDs offer slightly lower current interest rates in exchange for this flexibility.

CDs offer the average investor no capital gains potential and also offer little protection against inflation.

Strengths

 CDs under $100,000, purchased from federally insured savings institutions, are covered by federal deposit insurance. The wide variety of maturities and interest rates offers you substantial flexibility. Typically no fees or commissions are assessed. CDs offer a secure fixed compounding of income over the selected maturity. CDs do not require large investments. They are available for sums as little as $100.

Weaknesses

 Liquidity is limited for most CDs. Early withdrawal typically entails substantial penalties. Banks usually have the option of denying early withdrawal.

Long-term CDs at a fixed rate may suffer purchasing power loss in an inflationary environment.

Tax Considerations

 All earned income is interest and is taxed as ordinary income in the year in which it is paid. Reinvestment of interest does not defer the tax due.

Summing Up

CDs are a widely used cash equivalent vehicle. The wide variety of available options means you can tailor a savings plan to suit your needs. Banking deregulation has already resulted in a wide variety of CD vehicles and you can expect such innovation to continue (see next section). It is important to investigate the alternatives offered by more than one institution to ensure the best possible return on your investment.

Speculative Certificates of Deposit

The basic CD is simply a loan from the investor to a savings institution for a specified maturity at a set interest rate. While that is still the dominant form of CD, innovations are rampant. A speculative CD offers variable returns based on a preset formula. The depositor trades a secure return for the potential of higher returns if certain conditions are met.

SPECULATIVE
CERTIFICATES
OF DEPOSIT

Moderate income

Moderate safety

Moderate
liquidity

Good on
inflation

No tax benefits

Some growth
potential

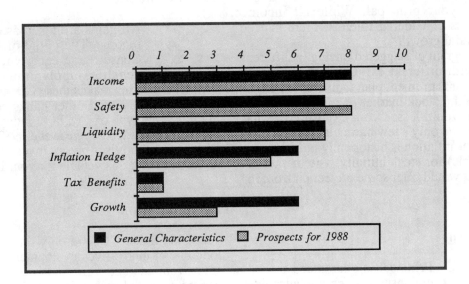

A widely used variant on that theme is the adjustable-rate CD. Rather than offering a fixed interest rate, an adjustable CD's interest rate is tied to the rate or performance of another investment vehicle, usually a 91- or 180-day Treasury bill.

In early 1987 Chase Manhattan Bank was the first to offer a CD tied to the performance of the stock market. The most common complaint about CDs is the lack of growth. This is most evident in a low-interest-rate environment. The attraction of 20% annual growth, such as the stock market has experienced since 1982, makes marketing low-interest-rate CDs more difficult. Chase Manhattan Bank responded with its "market index" CD. Other banks are already gearing up to match this innovation soon.

A market index CD is a hybrid between the safety of a CD and the potential for greater returns if the stock market appreciates. In exchange for a lower initial interest rate on the CD, the investor buys the chance to earn a higher return by tying it to the Standard & Poor 500 stock market index.

Chase initially offered two choices for the CD purchaser: a 4% minimum annual interest rate or a zero-minimum return. At maturity the investor receives the higher of the two possible outcomes: the minimum guaranteed rate or a percentage of the rise in the S&P 500. The amount of stock market participation depends on which option is taken and the maturity of the CD.

For example, if the 4% guarantee is selected, the investor's potential higher return alternative would be 25% of any rise in the

S&P for a 3-month deposit or 40% for a 12-month deposit. If the zero guarantee is selected, the S&P participation ranges from 40 to 75%.

Investment Potential

A market index CD at this time is a short-term investment. This puts a premium on market timing since the longest maturity is only one year. It gives you the opportunity to participate in stock market growth without risking your principal. While all income earned is considered interest, there can be substantial growth.

A program of staggered buying in different CDs with different expiration dates would give your retirement plan a diversified exposure to the stock market over time. This approach would lessen your exposure to what happens on only a few particular dates.

Slight inflation is historically bullish (very favorable) for stock initially. The market index CD would offer some protection from inflation.

Strengths

 Principal is guaranteed by federal insurance for amounts under $100,000. The market index CD gives you diversified exposure to stocks. You're betting on the market as a whole, not just one or a few stocks. Great flexibility is offered. You can choose the level of risk for your return that is most suitable to your situation. Minimum investment is only $1,000.

Weaknesses

 There are substantial penalties for early withdrawal. Liquidity is limited as there is no secondary market. The initial offering by Chase Manhattan Bank was ineligible for IRAs. The one-year maximum means that market timing, never an exact science, is crucial.

Tax Considerations

 All gains are taxed as ordinary income. The initial offering by Chase made early withdrawal penalties apply immediately. This makes these CDs ineligible for IRAs. Chase, and other banks considering this same type of CD, have indicated that this will be changed by year end 1987. Check with your tax advisor *before* investing if you are considering this vehicle for your IRA.

Summing Up

Market index CDs are only the latest in a long line of innovative developments in CDs. Improvements and variations on the theme can be expected as long as the deregulation environment exists. It is vital to carefully investigate the wide variety of products being offered to ensure that you obtain the best return for your situation. The market index CD is an important step in the development of risk-averse investment products.

Commercial Paper

Commercial paper is a money market instrument issued by corporations, financial companies, or state/local governments to cover short-term cash needs. Investors loan money to the issuing entity for a specified time period at a set interest rate. Normally the paper is issued on a discount basis. This means that the buyer pays less than the face amount and on maturity receives the full face amount. The difference is the interest earned.

COMMERCIAL PAPER

Good income

Fair safety

Fair liquidity

Fair on inflation

No tax benefits

No capital growth

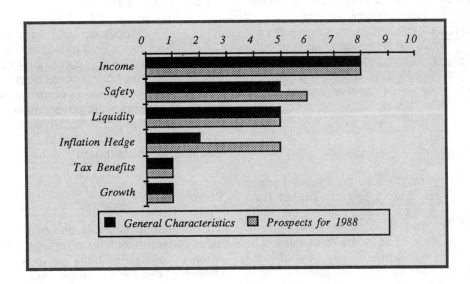

Commercial paper is available with a wide variety of maturities ranging from a few days to 9 months. It is usually backed by a bank line of credit, but it is not secured by the assets of the issuer.

 Although commercial paper is not required to be registered with the SEC, regulations do require that it be sold only to "sophisticated investors." A sophisticated investor is one who is experienced. High income (over $100,000 per year) or substantial net worth (over $500,00 exclusive of home) are sufficient proof of "sophistication" for the SEC. Because of this requirement, you will not find commercial paper offered through advertisements in your local paper.

It can be purchased direct from the issuer or through banks or brokerage firms. Purchasing direct saves commissions and fees.

Minimum denomination is usually $100,000, though some issuers do sell amounts as low as $25,000.

Independent credit-rating services such as Standard & Poor's or Moody's rate some commercial paper. There is no federal insurance.

Institutions issue commercial paper to borrow money at rates below what they could get from banks. It competes in the money market with Treasury bills, certificates of deposit, and banker's acceptances. Money market funds are heavy buyers of commercial paper. They offer substantial benefits to nonprofessional investors. These benefits include convenience, diversification, and liquidity.

Since there is no established secondary market for commercial paper, selling the paper before maturity presents a significant liquidity problem for individual investors. The issuer may take back the paper but you should expect to pay a fee for that service.

There have been few defaults historically, but it bears repeating that commercial paper is not secured by the issuer's assets. Therefore, *buyer beware*.

Investment Potential

Commercial paper is a short-term debt instrument. Individual investors have little chance of obtaining capital gains by selling the paper before maturity. Gains made on maturity are considered interest income.

Short-term interest rates are subject to wide volatility. While the short-term nature of commercial paper is some protection from the ravages of inflation, a nine-month commitment may lock your funds up at a time of rising rates.

Strengths

 The yield on commercial paper is usually slightly higher than that of Treasury bills and certificates of deposit. Defaults are rare. The short-term nature of commercial paper limits the risk to your principal. If you have the time and expertise, you can earn the higher returns that commercial paper offers without having to give up the fees that money market funds assess for buying it.

Weaknesses

 Liquidity is limited for individual investors. Initial investment amounts are substantial, usually $100,000, though denominations as low as $25,000 are available in limited numbers. There is no insurance for commercial paper. Therefore diversification is even more important than with CDs. The money market is both volatile and complicated. It takes much time to understand all the maturity options available. With no federal insurance and no asset backing the paper, it carries higher risk than Treasury bills or CDs.

Tax Considerations

 Money earned from commercial paper held to maturity is deemed interest income. It is taxable at ordinary income rates. The lone exception is commercial paper issued by local or state governments. Interest earned on this paper is usually free from federal taxes (check with your tax advisor to be sure in each situation).

Summing Up

Commercial paper is one of a number of money market vehicles offering good returns when compared to bank savings accounts. However, there is a definite tradeoff with the higher risk inherent in commercial paper. Unless they have the time to monitor and understand the money markets, most investors are well served to pay the management fees of money market funds.

Banker's Acceptances

Banker's acceptances are a type of letter of credit, developed to aid international trade. They facilitate imports and exports by providing a third-party guarantee of payment. For example, a manufacturer in a foreign country wants to sell a product in the United States. The company makes arrangements with a U.S. importer on price and shipping. Given the distances and problems of multiple jurisdictions involved, the exporter wants to get paid at once. The importer is faced with the same considerations and wants to ensure that he or she receives the product and can distribute them to outlets.

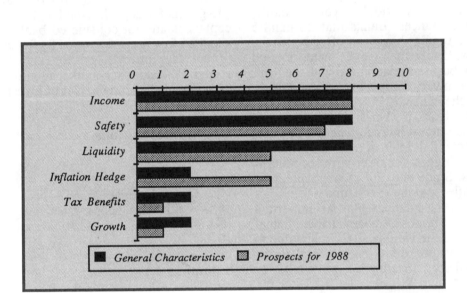

The financial portion of the transaction is handled through banker's acceptances. A bank accepts a record of the financial particulars for a fee. The bank either holds the note (the banker's acceptance) to maturity or sells it to an outside investor. The exporter receives its funds from either the bank, if it holds the paper, or from the investor who buys the acceptance. On maturity (usually 30 to 180 days), the importer pays the bank, which directs the funds to the investor.

Obviously neither a bank nor an investor will invest without earning fees for their participation. When the note is originally accepted, it is discounted from face value. This means that the exporter receives less than the face value of the note. The purchaser of the acceptance pays less than face value of the note. The difference between the discounted value paid and the face value on maturity is the interest earned on the transaction. Treasury bills are sold in the same discount manner. Interest earned is the difference between the discounted purchase price and the face value at maturity.

Banker's acceptances are one of a number of money market instruments that have attracted more individual investor interest over the past few years. Deregulation of the financial markets has resulted in wider availability of many sophisticated money market vehicles for individual investors. Banker's acceptances have historically been of interest primarily to institutional and professional investors. Many individual investors now include banker's acceptances in their short-term money market portfolios.

Investment Potential

Banker's acceptances are short-term, high-yielding, money market instruments although there is no central market auction. To buy a banker's acceptance, you need to approach individual banks and ask if they handle acceptances and whether they sell them to individual investors. You will also need to learn what denominations are available and what interest they pay.

Fees may vary widely. Not all banks handle acceptances. Banks that do handle them on a regular basis can offer better fee structures. Unlike many investments, a good long-term business relationship with the bank should mean very competitive fees and ready access to the market.

Returns from banker's acceptances are considered interest income. There is no capital gain potential. Interest rates are generally among the highest for short-term secured instruments. Since they are of short maturity, there is little exposure to inflation risk.

Banker's acceptances play an important role in the portfolios of money market mutual funds. While the yield is slightly less due to management fees, these funds offer daily liquidity and diversification.

Strengths

 Banker's acceptances are generally high yield compared to competitive money market instruments: T-bills and CDs. Banker's acceptances are secured by both the bank and the importer(s). In addition, the short maturities makes for a relatively safe investment.

Weaknesses

 Banker's acceptances offer limited liquidity for individual investors. Institutional investors have access to secondary market, but individual investors generally are limited to selling back to the issuing bank for an additional fee. Banker's acceptances are not considered bank deposits and therefore are not covered by federal insurance. Nonuniform nature and lack of accessible secondary market require greater educational effort on the part of investors.

Tax Considerations

 Income earned is taxed at ordinary income rates.

Summing Up

Banker's acceptances will fluctuate with short-term interest rates. They provide an avenue for further diversification of a sophisticated investor's cash portfolio.

Repurchase Agreements

A repurchase agreement (popularly called a repo*) is an agreement between two parties (usually large institutions) in which one party that needs short-term cash sells a portfolio of securities to another party for a short time period ranging from three days to as much as 3 months. The receiving party agrees to pay a set amount for the securities contingent on the selling party agreeing to buy them back* at a higher price *within the specified time period.*

REPURCHASE
AGREEMENTS

Good income

High safety

Good liquidity

Fair on
inflation

No tax benefits

No capital
growth

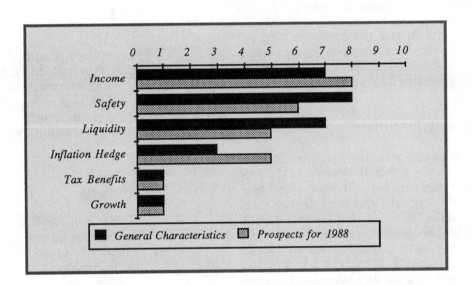

Until recent years repurchase agreements have been solely in the domain of very large institutions and of little interest to the average investor. The deregulation of financial markets has resulted in more interest in repurchase agreements (repos) by more and more investors.

Almost daily, the financial press reports on the latest transactions under taken by the Federal Reserve to add or delete monetary reserves. The level of monetary reserves determines the relative liquidity of the economy. A major tool employed by the Fed in "fine tuning" the national money supply is the use of repos.

Of more direct interest to many investors is the use of repos by most money market funds. Even funds that advertise that they invest solely in government securities for reasons of safety often employ repos backed by government securities rather than direct investment in the securities.

In other words, the securities that are sold are like collateral for a short-term loan to the selling party. Why would anyone want to do that? Often an institution's portfolio will contain securities that it wants to hold long term rather than actualize a taxable gain. By selling the securities as a repo, it can obtain cash without having to actualize a gain or loss immediately.

Even though the seller agrees to buy back the securities at a higher price, the buying party's profit on the transaction is considered interest, not capital gains.

Repos are debt instruments. Numerous problems, involving just exactly who is the owner of the securities that back a repo have resulted from the failure of a few government securities dealers. Even now it is unclear exactly who owns the securities used to secure repos. This is one reason that professional management in a diversified portfolio such as that offered by money market funds is the most logical way for most people to invest in repos.

 When researching money market funds, it is important to clarify the extent to which repos play a part in their portfolios. As already mentioned, some funds that actively trade in repos advertise that they invest solely in government securities. If safety is your primary concern and you are willing to give up some yield, consider sticking with those funds that only invest directly in government securities. All money market fund managers are compensated by a management fee deducted from the income generated by the funds assets.

Investment Potential

Repos pay high current income. There is no capital gains potential. Because of the way they are structured, the difference in the price paid by the original buyer (the one who loans money to the seller) and the higher buyback price does not constitute capital gains.

The very short maturities of repos limits their price volatility. There is an active market for repos of all maturities among large financial institutions. The complexity and very high cash requirements make repos impractical for most individual investors.

Even though repos often are backed by government securities, they should not be confused with the safety associated with Treasury obligations. In a case resulting from the failure of a one bank that had sold repos backed by government securities, it was held that the securities backing a repo actually belonged to the bank that initiated the repo transaction. In other words, the holders of the repos were left holding the bag, not the securities! But every case is different, as repos are structured in a variety of ways.

Repos of any sort are not backed by government depositor's insurance. The greatest risk to repo traders is the stability of the firms with which they do business. There is no independent rating of repos.

Strengths

 Repos pay high relative income. Very short maturities limit capital risk. Repos are very liquid among large institutions.

Weaknesses

 Complexity and high sums required to trade repos makes investment impractical for most individual investors. Uncertain legal status makes risk evaluation difficult. There is no capital gains potential.

Tax Considerations

 Gains from repo transactions are considered interest income. They are taxed at ordinary income levels.

Summing Up

The popularity of money market funds makes the indirect investment in repos by individuals a near certainty. Deregulation of the financial markets limits the appeal of retail repo agreements since they are not covered by depositor's insurance.

If maximum safety is your chief priority, you should buy only in money market funds that invest directly in Treasury securities. However, professionally managed diversified funds are able to pay slightly higher yields if they invest in repos. The risk is only moderately greater than direct investment in Treasury securities.

Taxable Money Market Funds

A money market fund gathers together a group of investors who pool their funds to invest in short-term money market vehicles. The fund managers buy large lots of various money market instruments such as jumbo CDs (certificates of deposit), banker's acceptances, commercial paper, or Treasury bills. Each investor buys a proportionate share of the fund.

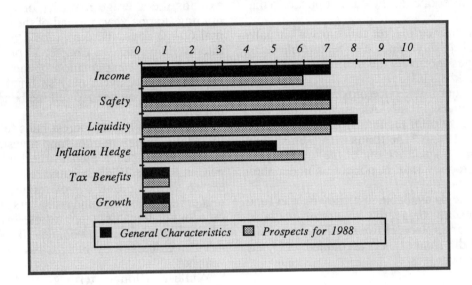

The advent of money market funds is a classic "chicken or egg" question. Did the rise of money market funds lead to deregulation of the financial markets, or did deregulation lead to the sharply increased interest in money market funds?

Either way, money market funds are here to stay as an important part of the financial markets. When inflation ran to double-digit levels in the early 1970s, bank savings accounts were paying 5 or 5.25%. So investors were actually losing purchasing power.

Large investors always had the option of investing directly in money market instruments such as commercial paper, Treasury bills, or banker's acceptances. The high minimum investments (often $25,000 or more) and extensive study needed to safely purchase the highest-yielding instruments prevented many investors from taking advantage of the higher yields.

Creative financial entrepreneurs recognized the need and demand for a way for average investors to participate in these markets. They developed the open-end money market fund.

Typically, each fund share is $1. So a $1,000 investment buys 1,000 shares. Interest is usually paid in whole and partial shares on either a monthly or quarterly basis. Since the interest is normally reinvested rather than withdrawn each time, your money appreciated on a compound basis. That is, you earn interest on previously earned interest in your account.

While minimum investments vary, most funds accept as little as $500 initially and as little as $100 for subsequent investments.

You are buying short-term debt instruments. The shorter the term, the lower the risk if interest rates rise. For example, if the average maturity in your money market fund is 12 months (and no money market fund should ever have an average maturity any longer), a rise in interest rates will cause a loss in principal because a full 12 months elapses before all the instruments in the fund would mature.

On the other hand, if your fund's average maturity was 90 days, a rise in short-term interest rates would be more quickly reflected in a higher average yield since the fund could roll its investments over to higher-yielding instruments sooner as the current portfolio matures.

Most money market funds offer virtually instant liquidity. Many also feature checking privileges (normally the minimum amount of the check is $100).

All major full-service brokerage firms offer money market funds. All major mutual fund groups also offer the funds. They are sold on a no-load basis. The funds earn their money by taking a small fee out of the interest paid by the money market portfolios under their management.

The yields available to money market fund investors are competitive with those available in the marketplace. However, there is usually a slight difference that is accounted for by the management fees.

Investment Potential

Money market funds pay current income. There is no capital gains potential. Money market funds by definition are short-term investments. This doesn't mean they can't be held for the long term, but rather that the average maturity in their portfolios is short. They are an attractive alternative to savings institutions' savings accounts.

Money market funds are very liquid. You can get your money out in 24 hours. The only potential exception would be in cases of poor or dishonest management of the fund. For example, if your money market fund manager extends the average maturity of the fund's holdings to one year, instead of the more normal 60–90 days, there may be a problem if interest rates rise. See Chapter 11 on fixed income for a full explanation of the potential loss that bond buyers may suffer if interest rates rise and you need to sell the bond before it matures.

In the early 1980s interest rates fell steadily. Many money market fund investors who had become accustomed to the high yields paid in the late 1970s became restless. In order to stem the outflow of money seeking higher returns, some fund managers started to buy longer-term debt securities. Instead of buying just short-term vehicles like 3- or 6-month vehicles, they bought two- or three-year notes.

While this longer term gives the fund a higher yield, it also has greater risk. If interest rates went up, the notes would drop in value, diminishing the true asset value of the fund. If fund redemptions became heavy, the fund could theoretically be unable to pay each shareholder promptly.

---

10 TOP PERFORMING U.S. GOVERNMENT MONEY MARKET FUNDS

1. Capital Preservation Fund
2. Carnegie Government Securities Money Markets
3. Dreyfus Money Market Instruments/Government Securities
4. Kemper Government Money Market Fund
5. Massachusetts Cash Management—Government
6. Merrill Lynch Government Fund
7. UST Master Funds—Government Money
8. Vanguard Money Market Reserves—federal
9. UMB Money Market—federal
10. Kidder Peabody Government Money Fund

We say "theoretically" because to date there has been no instance of a money market fund being unable to meet all redemption requests. However, this is a potential problem and you should be careful that your fund does not engage in such practices. One way to protect yourself would be to purchase funds that are restricted by their charters to buying securities with maturities of six months or less. Another alternative would be to carefully monitor the average maturity of your money market funds holdings. This information is available directly from the fund, and many newsletters such as the Donoghue *Moneyletter,* carry the information routinely.

Money market funds, like money market instruments themselves, have a wide range of risk. The safest funds are those which invest solely in 90-day Treasury bills. Since maturities are short and the investment is in direct obligations of the U.S. government, there is little chance of default. The only risk would be as a result of fraud.

Higher yields and hence more risk are available from funds that invest in short-term corporate securities such as commercial paper. The guarantee of payment is dependent on the financial stability of the company issuing the paper.

The length of maturity is another risk factor. The shorter the average maturity, all other things being equal, the safer the investment.

Money market funds, especially those with the shortest average maturities, provide some protection from inflation. Inflation will cause interest rates to move higher. Money market yields will move higher with interest rates.

The funds actually offer greater safety than direct investment in the money market instruments since you are buying a diversified portfolio. If a single issuer runs into financial difficulty, a well-managed fund with only a small percentage of assets in one company's paper will be only slightly affected.

The major risks in money market funds are the risk of failure on the part of an issuer of a money market vehicle or the risk of incompetent management. All funds must provide prospective investors with a detailed prospectus detailing what the fund invests in, the prior track record, and information on the funds management.

All money market funds must be registered with the SEC. They must comply with stringent financial requirements.

Strengths

 Money market funds are very liquid. Yields fluctuate with interest rates and provide a measure of protection from inflation. The wide range of funds offers you great flexibility in choosing the fund that most closely fits investment needs and risk tolerance. Fees are minor. Yields are typically higher than those of bank passbook savings accounts. Substantial diversification minimizes risk. Investment minimums are small for most funds. Funds are closely regulated by the SEC. Most funds offer checking privileges.

Weaknesses

 There is no government insurance. Poorly managed funds may yield substantially less than the average money market instrument.

Tax Considerations

 Interest earned on money market funds is taxable at ordinary income rates. Interest earned on funds that invest solely in U.S. Treasuries is exempt from state and local taxes.

Summing Up

Money market funds are here to stay. In only a few short years they have become an established part of the financial world. For most investors, money market funds offer an attractive alternative to the yields paid by passbook savings accounts.

The great variety of funds ensures that investors large and small can tailor their savings to closely fit their own objectives and risk tolerance.

In times of rising interest rates, money will flow into those funds with the shortest average maturities invested in the safest vehicles. In times of declining rates, money will flow to those funds with longer average maturities.

Tax-Free Money Market Funds

Tax-free money market funds are no-load mutual funds that invest only in short-term municipal debt issues. You buy into the funds at $1 per share. Interest is paid in whole and fractional dollar shares on a monthly basis. Reinvestment of interest results in compounded earnings. Most funds compound interest daily and pay monthly. The interest payments are referred to as dividends *because of the mutual fund structure.*

TAX-FREE
MONEY
MARKET FUNDS

Good net income

Fair safety

Fair liquidity

Fair on
inflation

Excellent tax
benefits

No capital
growth

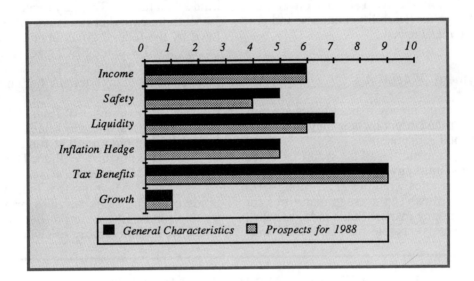

One of the negative effects of inflation is "tax bracket creep." Many Americans were bumped into higher tax brackets without a concomitant increase in their standard of living. Consumers who never before thought they were candidates for tax-exempt bonds and money market instruments realized that on an "after-tax" basis the yields on short-term money market funds meant more take-home pay.

Tax-exempt money market funds invest in short-term municipal debt instruments. Normally the average maturity of tax-exempt funds is longer than the average for taxable funds. This is because there is only a small supply of legitimate tax-exempt money market paper. The funds generally fill out their portfolios with previously issued bonds that mature in the near future.

Residents of many states are able to buy "double-tax-free" money market funds. These funds invest solely in debt securities issued by the state and local governments within the state. Income from municipals bonds is exempt from federal taxation. Income paid by municipal debt securities issued by the state in which you are a resident is also exempt from taxation.

Another way to avoid state income taxes on your money market funds is to buy funds that invest only in U.S. Treasury debt securities. Interest paid on federal government debt instruments is exempt from state and local taxes. Interest paid on state and local debt securities is exempt from taxation at the federal level.

The 1986 Tax Reform Act changed many features of the law for investors. General-obligation municipal bonds are the only source of tax-free income to escape changes. Congress did limit the quantity of "private activity" bonds that may be issued by state and local governments. There also were changes in exactly how these latter debt securities are to be taxed. For example, the type of municipal bond you buy could affect your Alternative Minimum Tax Calculations.

Tax-free money market funds are sold by major brokerage houses and most large mutual fund groups. There is no commission charged when buying a tax-exempt money market fund. Fund managers take a small percentage of the income paid by the securities in the portfolio they are managing for their fees. You receive a slightly lower yield in exchange for flexibility, liquidity, and professional management.

Investment Potential

Tax-exempt money market funds are purchased for the current income they pay. There is no capital gain potential.

The short maturities of the securities in the portfolios limits any risk to principal that rising interest rates would cause for long-term bond portfolios. The average maturities for tax-free money market funds is higher than for the average taxable fund because fewer

"money market-type" debt securities are offered by state and local governments.

If you are a resident of a large state, you can avoid state taxation as well as federal taxation by buying funds that invest solely in the debt securities of the state and political subdivisions of your state.

Risk is moderately higher than that for taxable funds because of the longer maturities. The market for municipal securities is less liquid than that for Treasury securities.

All money market funds are closely regulated by the federal government. They must be registered with the SEC, meet stringent financial requirements, and provide a detailed prospectus to all investors in the fund.

 A number of financial newsletters rate the relative safety of money market funds. The best known is William Donoghue's *Moneyletter*.

Most tax-free money market funds offer the same services provided by taxable funds. Checking privileges, 24-hour liquidity, and the ability to switch among a

---

10 TOP TAXABLE MONEY MARKET FUNDS

1. Vanguard Money Market Reserves
2. Cash Management Trust of America
3. Kemper Money Market Fund
4. Paine Webber Cash Fund
5. Scudder Cash Investment Trust
6. Transamerica Cash Reserve
7. UMB Money Market—Prime
8. Dreyfus Liquid Assets
9. Fidelity Daily Income Trust
10. Liquid Capital Income Trust

10 TOP TAX-EXEMPT MONEY MARKET FUNDS

1. Vanguard Muni Bond—Money Market
2. Fidelity Tax-exempt Money Market
3. Kidder Peabody Tax-exempt Money market
4. Dreyfus Tax-exempt Money Market
5. T-Rowe Price Tax-exempt Money Fund
6. Scudder Tax-free Money Fund
7. Standby Tax-exempt Reserve Fund
8. Tax-free Money Market
9. UMB Tax-free Money Market
10. USAA Tax-exempt Fund—Money Market

---

family of funds by telephone are typical services.

Tax-free money market funds are an attractive alternative to passbook savings accounts. Minimum investments are normally small. One major difference is the lack of federal insurance protection for the funds. Municipal securities are rated by major services like Standard & Poor's or Moody's. They are less secure than Treasury obligations.

The short maturities limit market risk. Incompetent management can affect returns. The funds offer some measure of protection against inflation. Their yields will increase as interest rates are pushed higher. The diversified portfolios limit the effects of interest rate volatility.

Strengths

Tax-free funds are very liquid. Most offer checking account privileges. Professional management provides diversified portfolios that minimize the potential problems of default by a single issuer. Short-term maturities minimize market risk. Rolling over (reinvesting) constantly maturing securities enables money funds to continually offer competitive yields. Interest income earned from funds that invest solely in municipal debt securities is exempt from federal taxes.

Weaknesses

There is no government insurance for investor funds. Yields will lag behind sharp interest rates rises. Poor management

may result in lower returns. There is no capital gains potential.

Tax Considerations

Interest paid on municipal debt securities issued before August 7, 1986, is exempt from federal taxes. Certain limitations apply to "private activity" bonds issued after than date. Carefully read the prospectus and consult with your tax advisor prior to selecting a tax-free money market fund.

Summing Up

The 1986 Tax Reform Act lowered the value of tax-free income by lowering the tax rates. In other words, you don't save as much as you used to! However, municipal securities are about the only safe investment for obtaining a tax-exempt cash flow. With more investors being pushed into the higher tax bracket as incomes increase, tax-free money market funds will attract even more interest.

CHAPTER 10

DOMESTIC EQUITIES

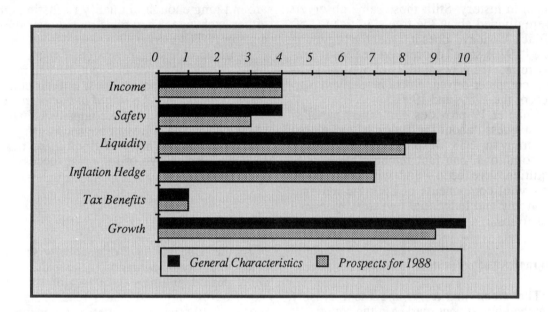

Growth

Volatility

Ordinary
Income, capital
gain

OUTLOOK
FOR 1988

High volitility

Probable uptrend

Higher risk

Will rise if:

Slow GNP
growth

Low inflation

Low interest
rates

Danger signs:

DJIA below
1500

Rising rates

Rising
inflation

Weak dollar

A Glance Ahead

In this chapter, you'll discover the wide variety of U.S. equity (domestic stock) investments that are offered to the public. You'll learn

- *The role of stocks in the U.S. economy.*
- *How stock ownership differs from bond ownership*
- *What an initial public offering (IPO) is*
- *The vital role stocks play in any diversified portfolio*
- *How listed and over-the-counter (OTC) stocks differ*

- *How the mutual fund industry has expanded its public offerings to suit the needs of most investors*

In January 1982, the United States was mired in a deep recession. Real interest rates (adjusted for inflation) were near an all-time high, the U.S. dollar was sliding ever lower, and U.S. prestige internationally was waning. As summer approached, the stock market's slide seemed irreversible. The June 14, 1982, issue of *Business Week* headlined its investment section "Running Scared from Stocks."

141

Few analysts recognized that the pervasive pessimism was setting the groundwork for one of the greatest bull markets in history. That summer the stock market as measured by the Dow Jones Industrial Average (DJIA) started from below 800. By August 1987 the DJIA had run to over 2,700!

On October 16, however, the market made its largest single-day drop to that date, losing 108 points. Observers thought the overvalued market had finally made its long-awaited "technical" correction. They were wrong. The following Monday, October 19, the DJIA fell 508 points for the largest single day crash in history. Still, those same observers were divided about the true significance of "Black Monday:" does it signal the beginning of a "1920s-style" depression or does it simply reflect the new volatility of our interlocking, computer-driven, global investment markets of the 1980s and 1990s?

Chapter 19 provides our expert panel's "best guess" about the future of the global economy in 1988. Despite a host of conflicting opinions, one fact remains clear: U.S. equities have been—and will continue to be—vital components of both the national economy and individual investors' personal portfolios.

DOMESTIC STOCK

The stock market is the most closely watched investment market in the country. It plays an important role in all sectors of the economy. Companies that need to raise money to start, expand, or diversify their business sell partial ownership in their corporation to interested buyers. The buyers in turn receive "shares" representing an equity interest in the corporation.

If the business is profitable, the shareholders expect to receive their fair share of the earnings. This share can take the form of dividends or appreciation of the price of the stock itself.

Stock market price cycles are closely related to underlying economic cycles. Perhaps the most widely watched cycle is the four-year presidential cycle. The stock market tends to move higher in the two years prior to a presidential election. In the years following the election, the market tends to be weaker.

There are two primary types of stock: common and preferred. Common stock is the purest form of part ownership in the company. Preferred stock holders trade some of the potential for future growth for the greater guarantee of steady dividend payments.

Stocks come in many forms. The stock of most well-known large companies are traded on the major stock exchanges: the New York Stock Exchange (for more established, seasoned issues) and the American Stock Exchange. But many companies have not been around long enough to qualify for listing on either exchange. They trade on the over-the-counter (OTC) market.

In times of rising prices (bull markets), many corporations see an opportunity to raise capital by selling part interest in their company to the public. An *initial public offering* (IPO) is the first sale of a company's shares to the public. Many investors watch this market closely in the hope of finding the next IBM or Xerox—two of the most successful IPOs in history.

Risks

As the "crash of '87" dramatically shows price volatility—fluctuation in value during a short period of time—is a fact of life for stocks. New untested issues tend to be far more volatile than older mature companies, although that is not always the case. When even seasoned companies become involved in takeovers or unanticipated events (such as Union Carbide in the Bhopal disaster, or Johns-Manville in the asbestos scare), the price of their shares also swings widely.

An individual stock issue has many potential risks. The health of the company's business will affect the share price. For example, with the advent of the automobile, the carriage-making and buggy whip business began a long decline. When transistors were in-vented, vacuum tube manufacterers were in trouble. New technology has always been the investor's biggest friend—and often a potential enemy—depending on which shares are owned.

Perhaps the most important factor in the price of an individual issue, though, is the state of the stock market as a whole. Even during the Great Depression certain companies managed to show steadily increasing earnings. Earnings and other economic "vital signs" were good for many companies who were hurt in the crash of '87. However, few stock issues were able to buck the falling trend of the market as a whole. It is vital to know the market's trend when selecting individual stocks.

Historically, stocks are considered good inflation hedges. However, the late-1970s experience with high inflation demonstrated the limits to this assumption. When inflation hit double-digit rates, it so distorted business pricing that the stock market actually fell sharply.

Rising interest rates generally tend to hurt stock prices eventually. Initially, rising rates are often a sign of increased economic activity, which is beneficial to stocks. As economic activity increases, company earnings turn higher. Eventually higher interest rates become competitive with the return on many stocks, drawing money away from the market. And, as credit becomes tighter, marginal companies lose their access to the credit markets. As they cut back employment or fail, their suppliers also become financially troubled. The whole process can snowball into a recession—the downward side of the business cycle.

A key advantage of most stock ownership is liquidity. For the most part, listed stocks are very liquid. Most OTC issues also have liquid markets, though it pays to find out *how* liquid before investing in an OTC issue. A liquid market merely means there is a ready supply of buyers and sellers for each issue. More obscure, untried companies naturally have fewer buyers and therefore have lower liquidity.

All investments are subject to some degree of political risk. Wars, embargos, tax policies, and many other political events can and do affect the markets and even individual issues. It is important to guard against the adverse affects of unanticipated political developments by diversifying over several stocks. As those investors who were overconcentrated in stocks on "Black Monday" will at-test, you should also diversify over several asset categories for maximum protection.

Ratings, Insurance, and Government Regulation

Stocks offered to the general public must be registered with the SEC (Securities and Exchange Commission). Registration consists of disclosure of pertinent facts regarding the business. The offering prospectus for the stock issue contains these details. Most companies ($1 million or more in gross assets) are required to file annual financial reports (Form 10-K) with the SEC. This report details total sales, revenue, and pretax operating income. It also includes a breakdown of sales for various products for the past five years.

The SEC does not pass judgment on the stability or worthiness of corporations that register their stock. However, various private companies examine public records and rate a companies financial condition. The largest rating companies are Standard & Poor's, and Moody's Investor Services.

The Securities Investor Protection Corporation (SIPC) insures customer accounts of member firms in much the same manner as the FSLIC for thrift institutions or the FDIC for banks. All brokers and dealers registered with the SEC must join the SIPC. The SIPC guarantees securities and cash in customer accounts to $500,000, with a limit of $100,000 on the cash portion. Unfortunately, this only protects investors from fraud or brokerage business failure—not from losses they experience in the market.

Stocks Compared to Other Assets

In the initial stages of inflation, stocks provide a good counterbalance to bonds. For example, in April 1987 as inflation picked up, the bond market began a long, hard slide. The Consumer Price Index, the Producer Price Index, and the prices of gold and of oil had all jumped higher in the first few months of the year. While bonds were falling, the stock market climbed sharply higher.

In balanced portfolios, the gains of the latter helped offset the losses of the former.

As inflation grows however, stocks begin to get hurt, especially when compared to tangible commodities such as gold. In the late 1970s, the stock market's real rate of return failed to make any upward progress. At this stage of the economic cycle, stocks ran contracyclically to gold. That is, gold appreciated as inflation increased.

The stock market can be an important leading indicator of the economy. In fact, stock prices are one of the 11 components of the U.S. Commerce Department's Index of Leading Indicators. This means that stock prices will generally begin to rise before other areas of the economy show signs of improvement. An example of this was the strong stock market move that began in the recession summer of 1982, when most analysts still viewed the economy's prospects as bleak.

The market will also tend to turn lower well before the rest of the economy although this is not a completely reliable indicator. The average lead time of the Index of Leading Indicators is 10 months of downturn before the onset of a recession so there is plenty of time for other factors to intervene.

The popularity of stock trading has resulted in an abundance of investment vehicles. (Later chapters give details on trading the stock market and even individual stocks on the options and futures markets.)

The major avenues for U.S. domestic stocks investing include individual, listed, IPO, and OTC issues, as well as a variety of mutual funds—investment companies that buy and trade these securities for their subscribers. In addition, we have described different types of mutual funds that invest in stocks in some manner.

Lasser's Recommended 1988 Stock Market Allocation:

 Allocate as little as 20%.

 Allocate as much as 40%.

Listed Common Stock

Common stock represents shares of ownership in a public corporation. Common stock holders usually have the right to vote on the company's board of directors and other important corporate decisions. Stock owners receive dividends as declared by the board of directors. Listed stock is stock traded on the New York Stock Exchange and the American Stock Exchange.

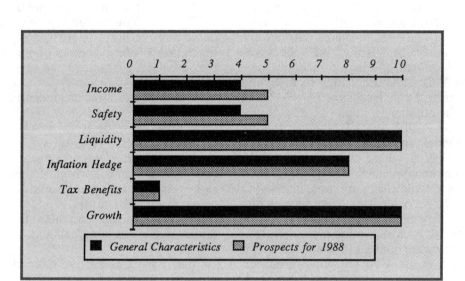

Common stocks receive more attention than any other investment class in the country. Even local newspapers, radio, and television all carry regular reports on the latest fortunes of the stock market because the market so often reflects the current and future state of the economy.

When corporations are formed, those people who invest either money or time receive proportionate ownership shares in the enterprise. These shares are stock in the company. In "closely held corporations," the outstanding stock is owned by only a few people, often family members or long-time business associates. These shares do not have an active market and are not easily bought or sold. Many companies, however, decide to broaden ownership in their companies. The chief reason is usually to raise additional capital to pay for business expansion. To do so, they sell shares of stock to the public. This action is called "going public." These shares represent ownership interest in the company.

As a part owner of the company, the stock owner shares in the wealth of the company in two ways. First, he or she may receive dividends if the board of directors elects to pay them. Profits generated by the business tend to influence the price of its shares. If a company's earnings increase after you buy its stock, those shares of stock will be worth more to another investor, increasing the price you can ask for your shares. And finally, a common stock holder is entitled to his or her proportionate share of the company's assets in case of liquidation, after the company's bond and preferred stock holders are paid.

The value of a share of common stock is based on a wide variety of considerations. Primarily, you invest in a company based on your perception of its prospects for future earnings and dividend growth. A company with a growing profitable business will naturally be more valuable as the earnings accrue. This increased wealth may be reflected either in further expansion as a result of reinvestment of the earnings, or in increased dividends paid to shareholders.

No matter how well the company's business is doing, if the economic environment is depressed the price of your stock may actually go down even with record earnings. Other factors that may affect a stock's price include interest rates, inflation, general investor psychology, and investment fads (the company may not be an "in" industry group).

Once a company has established an earnings record, a sufficiently diverse shareholder base, and enough shares outstanding, it may qualify for "listing" on a stock exchange. As noted, the major exchanges are the New York Stock Exchange (NYSE) and the American Stock Exchange (ASE). There are also a number of regional exchanges, such as the Pacific Stock Exchange. Listing requirements are most stringent for the NYSE. This is where older, more established, mature companies are found. Companies in mature industries are more inclined to pay out a larger percentage of earnings in dividends. They generally represent the cream of U.S. industry. Most major corporations whose names are household words like IBM, Kodak, Xerox, and General Motors are listed on the NYSE.

The American Stock Exchange also has requirements for companies to be listed. Since they are less stringent than the NYSE, companies listed on the ASE tend to be newer, more aggressive, more speculative ventures. Since earnings are reinvested to stimulate further rapid growth, dividends are low or nonexistent.

Investment Potential

Stocks are an excellent source of long-term total returns. The existence of well-established stock exchanges facilitates liquidity. Independent objective price information is readily available through newspapers, radio, and even television. Statistical information and professional investment advice are easily accessible. Publicly owned companies are required by law to thoroughly describe the financial details of their business in the annual 10-K reports that are filed with the SEC. Most companies also send shareholders an annual report detailing the most important elements of these 10-K reports. Computer databases such as those offered by Dow Jones or Media General make accessible literally thousands of pages of financial information to anybody with a computer and the funds to pay for computer time.

 While the main attraction of stocks is the capital gains potential, many stocks offer competitive income through dividends. You should remember that dividends, unlike bond interest, are paid at the discretion of the directors of a company—they are not a guaranteed part of your ownership benefits.

A major attraction of stocks is the great variety of investment objectives that can be met through judicious stock selection. Growth stocks—those which are in developing and growing industries and that reinvest the major portion of their earnings rather than paying dividends—offer the chance for substantial long-term gains. Short-term traders can also find volatile stocks to suit their temperament.

 Conservative risk-averse investors can select "blue-chip" issues from the New York Stock Exchange with relative long-term safety. Blue chips are companies with long, proven earnings records, stable management, and nonvolatile stock prices, companies that are leaders in the business world.

A number of listed stocks meet other objectives, such as the need for current income with the potential for capital appreciation. For example, utility stocks offer high yields.

As noted earlier, a number of independent companies rate stocks for their financial stability. These include Standard & Poor's, Moody's, and Value Line. In addition, a wide range of stock advisory newsletters provide specific trading advice.

Strengths

 Listed stocks are very liquid. The wide variety of listed stocks offers alternatives to meet most investment objectives. Stocks offer substantial growth potential. A vast amount of information on listed stocks is accessible. A wide variety of brokerage services and fee structures is available to choose from. Stocks are not a zero-sum game. In a rising market, everyone can profit. One investor's profit is not another's loss. A number of professional management services are available for investors who do not have the time to devote to stock investing.

Weaknesses

Price fluctuations (volatility) affect all stocks regardless of the soundness of the issuing company or the stability of the current market. Special circumstances such as suspension of trading in a stock may limit liquidity. The general economy affects stock prices. Unforeseen political developments may negatively affect certain stocks. Dividend income is not as secure as bond interest, because directors may elect to cut or suspend payments. Adverse market trends may exist for years.

Tax Considerations

The 1986 Tax Reform Act eliminated preferential long-term capital gains treatment effective in 1988. In 1987 long-term capital gains are subject to a maximum 28% tax rate. Capital gains and dividends are taxed as ordinary income.

Interest on margin loans secured by stocks is tax deductible up to the amount of investment income earned. Losses from stock trading can be carried forward. It is important to consult your tax advisor for specifics that may concern you.

Summing Up

Listed stocks are the favored long-term investment for pension funds. The S&P 500 index is the most widely used criterion against which money managers measure their relative performance.

Listed stocks represent the best of U.S. industry. Both the New York Stock Exchange and the American Stock Exchange set minimum requirements for companies to list their stocks. These requirements consist of minimum length of time in business, size of financial assets, and spread of shareholders over the country.

U.S. domestic equities remain the single most widely used investment for most Americans. The wide variety of companies offers investors the opportunity to select issues that fit their particular investment needs. Some investors will choose the less volatile stock of more mature companies that pay a steady dividend. Others, looking for a large, quick profit, concentrate their portfolios on young, untested issues that generally pay little or no dividends but that offer the potential of rapid share appreciation. These companies reinvest their earnings in the company in an attempt to maximize growth.

The mutual fund industry has been a major beneficiary of this latest and longest-running stock market boom. Mutual funds have become so specialized that it is possible for investors to tailor their own portfolios with a variety of mutual funds that specialize in certain market sectors. For example, certain funds invest only in gold shares and bullion, some silver funds invest solely in silver shares and bullion, and a variety of stock sectors such as high technology, basic industry, capital goods, utilities, retail stores, energy, natural resources and more. Of course, the older distinctions between mutual fund objectives—growth (even aggressive growth) versus income—still apply.

Over-the-Counter (OTC) Common Stock

OTC STOCKS

Poor income

Low safety

Moderate liquidity

Fair inflation hedge

No tax benefits

Good growth

Over-the-counter stocks are securities that are not traded on a major stock exchange. Trade is conducted through a complex telephone and computer network that brings together a wide variety of dealers throughout the country. Dealers choose to "make a market" in a particular stock by offering constant bids (to buy) and ask (to sell) prices for issues their clients have chosen to trade.

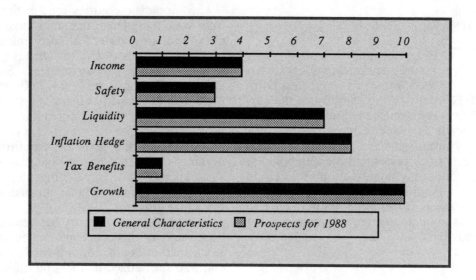

As we remarked earlier, every investor dreams of finding a fledging IBM or an infant Xerox in which a modest investment will yield huge profit. The nation's stock exchanges, however, are not the best place to find such start-up companies: stocks listed on the exchange must meet certain requirements—minimum lenth of time in business, an established record of earnings, so many shares outstanding, and a diversity of shareholders. Instead, the over-the-counter (OTC) market offers companies in their formative years, companies that do not qualify for listing on the exchanges, the chance to raise capital from the public. And it is to the OTC market that investors turn to trade in brand new, fast-growing companies.

When shareholders buy stock in a company, they look to profit from appreciation in the value of the stock as well as from dividends paid out of business profits. Most newer companies in dynamic industries, however, strive to maximize growth by plowing earnings back into the company rather than pay dividends to shareholders. Investors in growth stocks, therefore, need the organized and liquid marketplace that the OTC market provides to accurately assess and capitalize on opportunities to make profits through stock trading.

Over the last 20 years, the OTC market has significantly upgraded its efficiency and responsiveness to investor needs. Governed by the National Association of Securities Dealers (NASD), the OTC market offers a competitive and liquid investment opportunity.

Historically, price information on OTC issues was spotty. Accurate timely price quotes are now obtainable through the NASD's Automated Quotation (NASDAQ) system. Member dealers are tied into the computerized NASDAQ system. The dealers offer to buy and sell selected stocks on a regular basis. Their bids and offers are carried on the

NASDAQ system. This display of information gives investors a reliable picture of the market for various issues. An OTC stock can have as few as one or many dealers who make markets in the issue.

This "market maker" system differs from that for listed stocks, where exchange member "specialists" have a monopoly for making a market matching buyers and sellers in assigned stocks. Although much debate rages over which system is more fair for investors, the very existence of readily accessible quotes greatly facilitates trading. NASDAQ prices are updated continually throughout the day on a ticker much like that used by stock exchanges.

Stocks must meet certain minimum requirements to qualify for inclusion on the NASDAQ system. Very small or highly speculative, risky issues that NASD trades for less than $1 per share are called "penny stocks." Even though no NASDAQ system exists to bring continuously available quotes to the public, market makers have a highly organized and sophisticated network through which they can buy or sell these issues.

Investment Potential

Liquidity varies widely for OTC issues. Some stocks are heavily traded with many market makers and a substantial number of institutional investors. Other issues may only have one or two market makers and a limited following among investment analysts. Less liquid markets are called "thinly traded." It may be difficult to buy or sell large blocks of these issues in a short time period.

Generally speaking, the OTC market is the home of less seasoned more speculative, and more volatile stocks. The primary attraction of this market is the potential for substantial capital gains, although it is accompanied by higher risk. Since most OTC issues have shorter track records, it is more difficult to determine a stock's trading "character," such as its price volatility or sensitivity to economic news.

Some of the companies traded in the OTC market may very well turn out to be tomorrow's IBM and Xerox corporations. But in a universe of over 50,000 stocks, picking the right one is a challenging task.

OTC stocks are mostly growth oriented and therefore pay little or no income. Some exceptions exist, such as insurance companies or regional banks that still trade over the counter. As a general rule, though, investors seeking current income are better served elsewhere.

Historically, the price of growth stocks benefit during the early stages of inflation. Specific industry groups such as gold or silver mining stocks are direct beneficiaries of inflation and provide an excellent hedge against inflation.

Strengths

 In the right economic environment, new, small, growth-oriented companies offer good capital gains potential. Many OTC stocks are very liquid. Investors can readily find out the number of shares outstanding and the number of market makers for these issues—two important clues to liquidity. Performance for NASDAQ system stocks is easily tracked. Substantial financial and investment information is available for actively traded OTC issues. Competing market makers ensure fair pricing.

Weaknesses

 Volatility is a fact of life for OTC issues. Generally they have fewer institutional investors and are subject to sharp, unexpected price moves. Small, untested companies are vulnerable to competitive moves made by larger, better-capitalized competitors. Bankruptcies are more common in developing companies. OTC stocks are vulnerable to adverse economic events as well as adverse developments in their own industries. Transaction costs are harder to find out, since many OTC issues are bought and sold with dealer markups rather than clearly disclosed commissions. Developing companies are more vulnerable to investment fads that come and go. Low or no dividends means there is no protection on a downward trend.

Tax Considerations

The 1986 Tax Reform Act eliminates preferential capital gains treatment in 1988. The maximum long-term capital gains tax rate in 1987 is 28%. Dividends are taxable at ordinary income rates. Beginning in 1988, capital gains are also taxed as ordinary income.

Interest from margin loans secured by OTC stocks is tax deductible up to the amount of investment income earned. Losses from stock trading can be carried forward with certain limits, so you should consult your tax advisor for details about your own situation.

Summing Up

The OTC market offers investors the chance to buy shares new developing companies. Although some well-established corporations trade on the OTC market (note especially regional banks, for example), this market is typcially the domain of the "up and coming" issues.

Traders of OTC issues need to know a number of things that do not affect listed stocks. For example, the liquidity of an OTC issue cannot be taken for granted. It is important to know how many "market makers" there are for each issue. The more market makers, the more liquid the stock.

Prices are less accessible for many OTC issues than for listed stocks. Stocks traded on the NASDAQ system are more widely quoted. The NASDAQ index is a widely followed measure of the performance of these issues. This index complements the Dow Jones Industrial Average, which measures the performance of 30 of the leading well-established corporations on the New York Stock Exchange.

Initial Public Offerings (IPOs) of Common Stock

Initial public offerings (IPOs) are the first public issue of company's stock. When a company decides to go public, it contracts with an investment banker to underwrite its offering. Together, they decide such questions as the number of shares and price of each share for the offering. For example, XYZ Corporation may decide to try to raise $100 million through a public offering of 10 million shares at $10 per share.

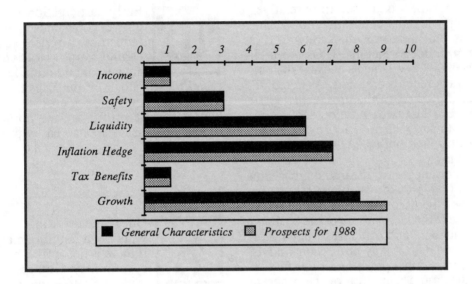

During bull markets (that is, rising markets) demand for "hot new issues" outstrips supply as investors rush to buy the latest offerings of highly touted stocks in the hope of quick and large profits. It is not unusual to see "hot issues" rise as much 25 to 50% within hours after their initial release to the public. The most important factor in this phenomenon is investor psychology rather than the actual financial and investment prospects of individual issues.

The underwriter puts together a "syndicate" made up of brokerage firms to distribute the offering to the public. An initial prospectus (called a "red herring") details the financial status of the company and its prospects and risks and is filed with the SEC. Once approved by the SEC, this prospectus is printed and made available to potential investors so they can evaluate the facts about the company and decide whether they want to invest.

The demand for IPOs varies directly with market conditions. In rising markets, investor euphoria results in overwhelming demand for issues underwritten by established quality firms. In fact, demand is often so great that only very good, sizable customers for participating brokerages can get stock before it trades in the secondary (previously purchased stock) market. In flat or falling markets, however, this condition reverses and some IPOs become difficult to sell regardless of the actual future prospects of the company.

IPOs are offered without a broker's commission to the public. The broker is paid by the issuer to market the new issue. Soon after release of the offering, the new issue begins trading in the secondary market. Usually this market is the OTC market, since most IPOs are relatively new enterprises that do not meet the criteria for exchange listing. Exceptions arise when a long established privately held company decides to go public, such as Ford

Motor company's first public offering in the 1950s.

The underwriting syndicate works to maintain a minimum offering price. Typically this effort ends about four weeks after the offering and market forces take over. This price "floor" provides some downside protection for initial investors.

Investment Potential

Since most new issues are from relatively new companies, the chief attraction is their prospects for future growth. Rarely do IPOs offer any dividend income. IPOs are high-risk speculative investments because their operating track records are short. As noted, the "red herring" draft of the prospectus details the financial status of the company, gives facts about management such as experience in the industry, and outlines business risks for the company.

An important part of the initial prospectus is a detailed breakdown of just how the money will be used. There are three major uses of the capital: expansion of the business, paying founders and officers, or paying off accumulated debt. Many professional advisors recommend that you avoid IPOs that intend to use more than 25% of the proceeds for things other than investment in the business itself. However, in euphoric markets this restriction is routinely ignored by investors who want to "get in on the ground floor." (It would be more accurate to say that the public is getting in on the mezzanine or second floor, since the company's founders own the "ground floor"—and the potentially most valuable stock!)

Good-quality, well-managed companies in growth industries offer good long-term capital gains potential. However, because of the euphoria that often surrounds these offerings in a bull market, it is not unusual to see large short-term gains. These "hot" issues are in short supply and are usually only obtainable by long-time proven clients of syndicate members.

Less fortunate investors who want to buy the stock must acquire it in the secondary market, where the stock often trades at a substantial premium to the offering price. The unrealistic euphoria surrounding these offer-ing is demonstrated by the fact that over 60% of all IPOs trade below the initial offering price within one year of issue. Nevertheless, the dream of large, quick profits motivates investors to buy on offering day.

These high-risk speculations do offer some inflation protection. Growth stocks normally keep ahead of moderate inflation.

Strengths

 Early participation in dynamic growth companies in expanding industries can yield substantial capital gains. Hot-issue IPOs are very liquid initially. The demand for the stock far outstrips the supply. There are no commission costs for purchase. Quick, sizable profits are the norm in bull markets for issues sponsored by proven underwriters.

Weaknesses

 Once underwriting support is withdrawn liquidity may dry up if there is not sufficient investor community interest. It is impossible to know in advance which issues will draw substantial investor trade after the offering period. Lack of dividend income provides no downside protection in adverse markets. A short management track record, financial stability, and earnings increase IPO price volatility. The large fees paid to underwriters means that initial investors are paying a hidden premium for the company. For most individual investors, hot issues are virtually impossible to purchase at the initial offering price.

Tax Considerations

 IPOs are subject to the same taxes as any common stock. The 1986 Tax Reform Act eliminated preferential long-term capital gains treatment in 1988. For 1987, long-term capital gains are subject to a maximum tax rate of 28%. Capital gains thereafter and dividends (if any) are taxed as ordinary income.

 Interest on margin loans secured by stocks (most IPOs do not qualify for margin) is tax deductible. Losses from stock trading can be carried forward, within limits. Consult your tax advisor for specifics for your situation.

Because of the high-risk speculative nature of IPOs, they are not appropriate for retirement plans governed by ERISA.

Summing Up

IPOs are a highly speculative type of stock. During bull markets (such as the one since 1982), IPOs become the "hottest game in town." Many IPOs come to market and shoot up the price within minutes of the time actual trading begins. This quick and volatile activity attracts many investors willing to take substantial risks for quick profits.

 Statistics point out the dangers of IPO investing. Most IPOs trade below their offering price sometime within the first 12 months of issue. Since many IPOs trade significantly above their offering price within hours of release, only savvy, well-heeled, and well-informed investors should pursue this avenue regularly.

Preferred Stock

PREFERRED STOCK

Good income

Fair safety

Fair liquidity

Poor inflation hedge

Corporate tax benefits

Moderate growth

Preferred stock is a hybrid investment combining features of corporate bonds and stock. Preferred stock is primarily of interest to institutional investors such as pension funds and insurance companies because 80% of the dividends paid is tax exempt for them. Unfortunately, that exemption does not exist for individuals.

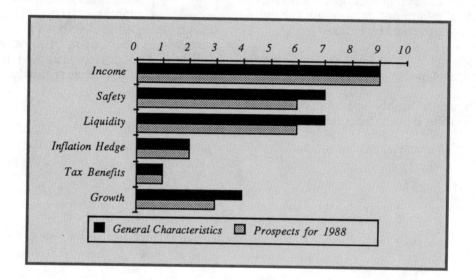

Despite its unique characteristics, preferred stock is an equity investment—not a debt investment, as are bonds. However, because the dividend is typically a set percentage of par value, preferred stock trades in a way that is similar to corporate bonds. When interest rates rise, preferred stock prices fall. Preferreds appreciate when interest rates decline.

Although it is an equity investment, preferred stock does not normally carry voting rights. The chief attraction for individual investors is the slightly higher yield that some preferreds offer. This is because the dividend paid to preferred holders is not a legal obligation, as is the interest on a corporate bond. Rather, preferred dividends are paid at the discretion of the corporation. If the company's earnings fall, it can elect not to pay dividends in a given payment cycle.

However, when dividends are declared, preferred holders must be paid before dividends are paid to common stock holders.

Most preferred stock dividends are cumulative, which means that if dividends are not authorized in a given year they accrue until such time as the company is able to pay them again. A cumulative preferred shareholder would receive all arrears before any dividends are paid to common stock owners.

Preferred stock is purchased through full-service brokerage firms. Since there is little short-term trading in preferreds, and there are many types of preferred stocks, including cumulative, preference, participating, or floating rate, discount brokerage houses catering to individuals are not normally well equipped to deal with them. A commission is charged for both the sale and purchase of preferred stock.

The prices of preferred stocks are quoted daily in the *Wall Street Journal* and in larger dailies. There is generally less volume in preferred issues, because they are primarily purchased by corporations that hold them for the tax-exempt income.

Investment Potential

Although preferreds are technically an equity investment, their primary attraction is the current income they pay, which makes them competitive alternatives to bonds. Their dividends take precedence over dividends for common stock. In the case of liquidation, preferred stockholders have priority over common stock holders. On earnings and assets, bond holders take precedence over both preferred and common. When interest rates decline, capital gains also are possible. Preferreds are normally long-term investments. Thin markets limit the appeal of short-term trading.

Although primarily designed for institutional investors, preferreds can offer slightly higher yields for individual investors. Because they are considered "less safe" than bonds due to their lower-priority claim on a company's earnings and assets, their yield sometimes is higher than bonds. Large, full-service brokerage firms have preferred specialists who ferret out these undervalued situations for their clients.

Preferreds are generally less volatile than common stock. However, with interest rates becoming increasingly erratic, preferreds are prone to wider swings. Many preferreds are very thinly traded. This limits their liquidity.

Preferreds are rated by number of independent services such as Standard & Poor's, Moody's Investor Services, and Value Line Investment Survey.

Strengths

Preferred stocks normally yield higher dividends than do common stock. They have priority claim over common stock on a company's earnings and assets. Dividends paid on preferred stock are 80% tax free to corporations. Preferreds appreciate when interest rates fall.

Weaknesses

Preferred stockholders usually have no voting rights. Preferred dividends are paid at the discre-tion of the company's board of directors. They are not legal debt obligations. Preferred stocks offer no protection against inflation. Preferreds are subject to the market risk arising from interest rates changes. Preferred stocks also carry business risk. If the financial condition of the underlying company deteriorates and its rating is lowered, the preferred stock will decline in price even if interest rates do not move. Preferred stock usually does not appreciate with improving company prospects, as does common stock. The low volume and activity in many preferreds limits their liquidity.

Tax Considerations

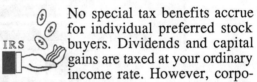

No special tax benefits accrue for individual preferred stock buyers. Dividends and capital gains are taxed at your ordinary income rate. However, corporate buyers have substantial tax benefits: 80% of all dividends paid is exempt from federal taxes.

Summing Up

Preferred stocks escaped major damage from the draconian tax law changes of 1986. Their dividends are still 80% tax free to corporations, though that is down from 85%.

Preferred stocks have enjoyed a bull market since 1982, with the decline in interest rates. In the first six months of 1987, the sharp upsurge in rates drove preferred prices down.

The primary beneficiaries of preferred stock are institutional investors. Individual investors can find comparable after-tax yields and greater liquidity in corporate or municipal bonds.

Growth Mutual Funds

A mutual fund is a pool of individual investors' contributions that is professionally managed that may invest in a variety of securities. Different funds are designed to meet different investor objectives. A growth fund invests in stocks of companies that are expected to appreciate due to increased earnings. Mutual funds have enjoyed a surge in popularity with the strong stock market since 1982. Record amounts of money have been invested in stock funds by investors seeking to participate in the market growth.

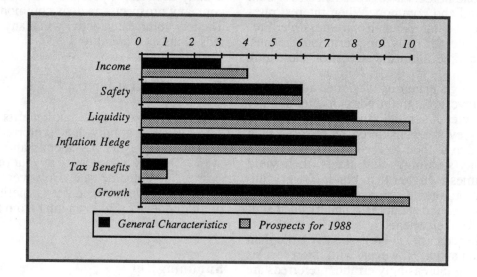

There are even many different types of growth funds. For example, aggressive growth funds invest in small, developing companies with short track records. These stocks are often traded on the over-the-counter market (OTC). Other growth funds specialize in locating undervalued stocks of companies listed on the major exchanges.

 You can find a fund that most closely matches your investment objectives and risk tolerance. Funds that specialize in newer small companies will be higher-risk investments than funds that concentrate on established firms.

Mutual funds can be purchased through brokerage firms. In fact, the major full-service brokerage firms usually have in-house funds managed by employees of the firms. Funds purchased through brokerage firms are called "load" funds. The load is the commis-sion paid to the salesperson for handling the transaction. Loads run from as low as 2% to as high as 10%.

No-load funds are usually purchased direct from the investment company that manages the fund itself. A no-load fund does not assess a sales charge. Your full investment is invested in stocks.

There is little difference in performance between the two types. Some investors feel more comfortable with investments that their brokers follow. Others are content to manage their investments without the "hand holding" that a full-service broker can provide.

Mutual fund prices are widely available. The *Wall Street Journal* regularly publishes fund prices. Most financial magazines, such as *Business Week*, *Money*, and *Changing Times*, devote substantial space to mutual fund coverage.

The boom in mutual fund investing has spawned an active newsletter advisory industry. Many newsletters are devoted to providing trading advice for mutual fund investors.

Investment Potential

The main objective of growth-oriented mutual funds is capital gains. Although some growth companies may pay income, it is usually negligible.

When you buy a mutual fund, you are buying a proportionate share of the net asset value of the holdings of the fund. The net asset value (NAV) is computed by subtracting the fund's liabilities from the value of the cash and securities it holds. If the stocks in the fund's portfolios appreciate, you make money as the net asset value goes up.

Mutual funds are very liquid. Federal law requires a fund to pay you for withdrawals within seven days of your sell order. Some funds offer ancillary services such as periodic payouts.

The volatility of a growth fund is directly related to the volatility of its stock portfolio. Because funds are invested in a diversified portfolio, their volatility is less than that for individual issues.

 All mutual funds are registered with the SEC. They must meet stringent financial and disclosure requirements. Prior to investing, a fund must provide you with a prospectus that gives a detailed report on the fund's investment approach, objectives, and track record. The fund is required to keep you apprised of developments on a regular basis.

The safety of your investment is a function of the type of stocks in which the growth fund invests. A growth fund that concentrates on "blue-chip" stocks is safer than one that seeks to uncover small, untested companies.

Growth funds are subject to market risk. If the price of the stocks invested in fall, so will the value of the fund.

Also, a business risk attaches to all funds. If the fund's management proves inept at selecting stocks, your investment may suffer even if the stock market is moving higher.

Growth funds provide some protection from inflation. Stocks have historically been good inflation hedges in times of moderate inflation.

Strengths

 Growth funds offer the potential for substantial capital gains. They enable small investors to achieve the safety of diversification. No-load funds assess no commission charges. An investor in individual issues cannot enjoy that luxury. Well-managed growth funds have enabled investors to achieve above-average gains over the long term. Growth funds offer very high liquidity. The variety of growth funds offers investors great flexibility in matching their investing objectives and risk tolerance.

Weaknesses

 Management fees may offset much of the gain in the funds portfolio. You are dependent on the ability of the fund manager to select good stocks. A poor manager may significantly underperform the market averages. The commissions paid for load funds come off the top. If you invest $1,000 in a growth fund with an 8% sales charge, your actual investment in the stock of the fund will only be $920. Growth funds do not invest in companies that pay high dividends. High dividend yields afford some protection against falling prices.

Tax Considerations

 The 1986 Tax Reform Act eliminated the preferential tax treatment for capital gains. Capital losses can be used to offset capital gains, and these losses can be carried forward.

Summing Up

Growth mutual funds represent the backbone of the mutual fund industry. Growth funds are designed to provide above-average growth over the long term. Unfortunately not many funds have actually outperformed the S&P (gained better returns than the index) for a 10-year stretch.

 There are many sources of information on mutual fund performance. Before investing in a fund, it is prudent to research the fund's performance. Almost all mutual fund prospectuses contain the so-called mountain chart that shows in graphic form how much richer you'd be if you had invested 10 years ago. When you see such charts, remember that compounding interest in a savings account can be made to look like a similar "mountain" of growth—so study the other aspects of potential performance as well.

Long-term investors should evaluate a fund's performance over a complete market cycle. Buying a fund that has done well in the past few years may show its performance only in a bullish market. Many aggressive funds shine during bull markets but then lose so badly when the market turns downward that their overall performance is mediocre.

Consistent performance over a 10-year span is far more important than occasional years of outstanding returns.

Income Mutual Funds

Equity income funds are mutual funds that invest in stocks that pay competitive dividends. The primary objective of these funds is current income. However, the fund managers are happy to take capital gains if the opportunity presents itself. Many stock groups pay good current income in the form of dividends and still have the promise of capital appreciation.

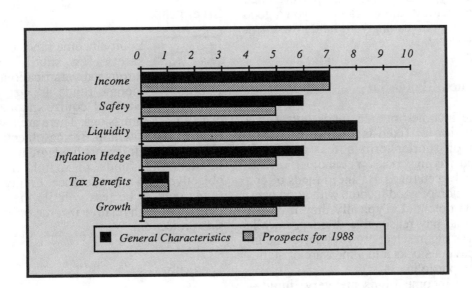

■ General Characteristics   ▨ Prospects for 1988

A number of mutual funds are designed to ferret out high-dividend-paying stocks. Just as with growth stocks, a wide variety of equity income funds offer programs to meet differing investment objectives and risk tolerances.

For example, investors who are primarily interested in income and only secondarily concerned with the growth will select funds that concentrate on certain types of stocks such as utilities or preferred stock. On the other hand, investors who are willing to forgo the highest possible dividends in favor of income plus a greater growth potential will focus on funds that buy shares in established companies in mature industries. These stocks generally pay good dividends—though less than those paid by utilities. However, a strong economic climate will benefit these companies more, and hence there is a greater growth potential.

Mutual funds offering good income are generally less volatile than pure growth funds. If you decide to invest in this type of fund, you'll be trading off greater growth potential for more predictable current income.

 Equity income mutual funds are available both as load funds (sold through brokers), and no-load funds, sold directly by the fund itself. A no-load fund usually buys and sells through the mail, Although many funds offer telephone switch (interfund transfer) and selling privileges.

Load funds typically charge sales commissions of 2 to 8%, charged as soon as you invest. As noted for growth funds, a $1,000 investment in an 8% load fund would leave $920 invested in the fund after this commission had been taken.

No-load funds charge no commission. They have no salespeople to pay and attract customers through the mail and through advertising.

Both types of funds assess management fees, which vary widely. They can amount to as little as 0.25% to as much as 2% of the funds assets on an annual basis. You should carefully check a fund's fee structure before investing.

The leading financial periodicals, such as *Business Week*, *Money*, *Changing Times*, and *Barron's*, frequently feature articles on different types of funds. The performance rankings in these articles can give you a good starting point in making your fund investment decisions.

Investment Potential

Some income-oriented funds invest in a combination of fixed-income instruments (bonds or shorter-term notes) and high-dividend-paying stocks. Yet another alternative is balanced funds. Balanced funds offer a combination of good income with good capital gains potential. Typically they invest in stocks that pay reasonable dividends while also investing in select growth issues. The income-paying stocks add a measure of stability to the portfolio.

Equity income funds are very liquid— many shares can be sold with just a phone call. Federal law requires that payments be made within seven days of your sell order.

The diversification of a typical equity income fund provides a measure of safety. Problems with a single issue should not have a major effect on the portfolio's performance. The government does not insure mutual funds.

Income funds are best suited to long-term investments. Generally investors are seeking a reliable income for the future. They are appropriate vehicles for retirement plans.

Equity income funds are subject to market risk. Even though the dividend income provides some protection on the down side of a market trend, a falling stock market will be reflected in income fund share prices. And there is an added risk of poor management. Wrong stock selection or trading decisions by the funds investment advisor can adversely affect the performance of the fund.

Income funds do not provide good protection from inflation. Dividend growth rarely is sufficient to offset even moderate inflation. Rising interest rates may hurt equity income funds more than growth funds initially. This is because some income-oriented stocks, such as utilities, tend to trade like bonds, moving inversely to interest rates.

Strengths

Equity income funds offer good safety for small investors through diversification. Equity income funds are very liquid. No-load equity income funds charge no commissions. There are a wide variety of funds with differing objectives and philosophies. Investors have great flexibility in selecting funds to match their own objectives and risk tolerance. Equity income funds tend to be less volatile than growth funds. The high relative income offers downside protection.

Weaknesses

Equity income funds offer less capital gains potential. Poor investment decisions by the funds investment advisor will adversely affect the value of your fund. Some funds' high fees affect investors' return. Rising interest rates often hurt equity income funds more directly than they hurt growth funds. Equity income funds do not provide protection from inflation.

Tax Considerations

The 1986 Tax Reform Act eliminated the dividend exclusion. Income and capital gains are taxed at ordinary income rates. Capital losses can be used to offset other capital gains. Excess losses can be carried forward.

Summing Up

 Equity income funds are ideal alternatives for conservative investors willing to forgo maximum capital growth for greater stability and more current income. The low interest rates, low inflation, and moderate economic growth of the past five years has aided equity income funds growth.

 As always, it is important to monitor the Federal Reserve's money supply policy. Rising interest rates will hurt income funds directly.

Sector Mutual Funds

Sector funds are mutual funds that are restricted to investing in a particular industry sector. Until recent years, this specialization was usually restricted to a few sectors such as utilities, gold, or high technology. Now, however, there are many offerings, including the sectors of energy, natural resources, biotechnology, real estate, brokerage, property and casualty insurers, regional banks, health, chemicals, telecommunications, software, computers, electronics, leisure, paper and forest, capital goods, transportation, automotive, restaurant, and many more!

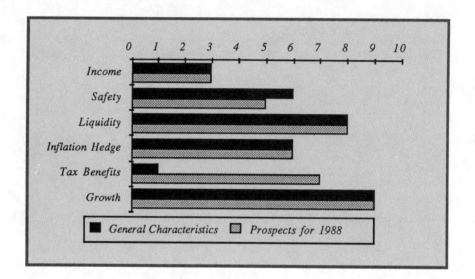

The cover story of the May 1987 issue of *Changing Times* was entitled "The Hottest Idea in Mutual Funds: Sector Funds." Sector funds are a method for getting "selective diversification." The funds concentrate on a clearly specified industry but buy a diversified portfolio of stocks within that industry. Some analysts believe that by switching your portfolio among a number of industry groups as the economic cycle unfolds, you can significantly outperform the averages. The idea is that certain industry groups perform better at different times in an economic cycle.

Sector funds, like most mutual funds, are available in two forms. Load funds assess a sales charge, no-load funds do not. The net asset value of each mutual fund is calculated at the close of every business day. When you buy a load fund, a sales charge of 2 to 8% is tacked on to the net asset value. A no-load fund sells at the net asset value. Load funds are purchased through brokers who provide ongoing service. No-load funds are purchased directly through the mail.

Sector fund prices are carried daily in the *Wall Street Journal*. Major financial magazines devote substantial space to mutual funds. *Forbes* features a detailed rundown on fund performance every August. *Money*, *Business Week*, and *Changing Times* also feature performance rankings.

Investment Potential

Sector funds are generally considered most appropriate as short-term investments. That is part of their attraction. Most sector funds are part of a "family" of funds managed by same sponsor that offers the right to switch among the different funds by telephone. Even some load funds allow you to switch for no or nominal fees after an initial investment in one of their funds. It is a losing proposition to trade load funds without this proviso on a short-term basis. You need to hold a load fund for five to seven years before it would make sense to trade it unless you can switch without paying the full load charge again.

Sector funds offer the greatest flexibility of all mutual funds because there are so many alternative ways to structure your portfolio. Some investors build a diversified portfolio filled with nothing but sector funds. Others switch among sectors depending on their advisors' timing advice.

Sector funds, like all mutual funds, are very liquid. Because they have relatively short track records, it is difficult to judge the ability of their managers. Some sectors, like high technology or biotechnology, tend to be very volatile. The mutual funds specializing in those sectors are more volatile and hence more risky.

Sector funds generally provide capital gains, although there are exceptions. Utility funds pay high current income. Most sector funds, though, are growth oriented and pay little income. Sector funds are appropriate for actively managed retirement plans, especially in the early years.

Strengths

Sector funds offer great flexibility to design a diversified portfolio that fits your objectives and risk tolerance. Astute selection of sector funds can yield returns far above the average market return. Sector funds offer excellent liquidity. Properly chosen sector funds offer outstanding protection from inflation. No-load switch funds offer a low cost method of short-term trading.

Weaknesses

Sector funds place a premium on good timing. If your investment is in the wrong sector at the wrong time, it can significantly underperform the market. Sector funds depend heavily on good research for their performance. The fees charged for some sector funds may offset portfolio gains. Most sector funds pay little or no income. Track records for most sector funds are too short to see how they've performed throughout an entire bull/bear market cycle.

Tax Considerations

No special tax advantages apply to sector funds, Although the dividends of some utilities are not taxable. Your fund will apprise you of such dividends but they will not be substantial. All capital gains and dividend income are taxed as ordinary income.

Summing Up

Sector funds are here to stay. They have drawn an increasing share of investor funds over the past five years. Every month more funds are announced specializing in heretofore unexploited areas. Active investors willing to devote substantial time to industry analysis will benefit greatly from the use of sector funds.

Investors who have expertise in a particular industry will also find these funds of value. If you cannot, or are not willing to spend some time researching the matter, a diversified growth fund would be more appropriate for you.

Index Mutual Funds

Poor income

Fair safety

Good liquidity

Good inflation
hedge

No tax benefits

Excellent
growth

Index funds are mutual funds that are designed to emulate the performance of one of the major stock indexes such as the Standard & Poor's 500 or the Dow Jones Industrial Average.

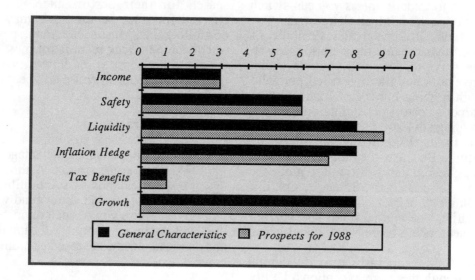

Index funds developed as a result of the inablility of most investment managers to beat the market averages consistently.

Prices for index funds are carried daily in the *Wall Street Journal*. Other financial periodicals such as *Money, Business Week*, and *Forbes* regularly devote space to these funds. An active and diverse newsletter advisory field, specifically devoted to advising investors about mutual funds, has bloomed.

Investment Potential

Index funds are normally purchased for the long term. Their primary attraction is the potential for capital gains. They usually pay only small dividends.

The stock market has become increasingly volatile in recent years. This volatility is naturally reflected in the prices of index funds. A properly managed index fund will closely track the performance of the stock market on a daily basis. You would have a very good

idea how your fund did on any particular day by just checking the performance of the stock indexes.

Index funds are very liquid. Most will execute sell orders over the telephone. Your money will be sent to you within seven days after the sale has taken place. Index funds are designed to do one thing: replicate the performance of a particular stock market index, usually the S&P 500. Not much flexibility is offered in terms of investment approach.

Index funds are as safe as the stock market as a whole. Long-term bear markets, such as the one from 1966 to 1975, saw price losses as much as 50 to 80% in major companies' stocks. The most recent bull market, which began in 1982, was up nearly 350% by the first quarter of 1987.

 All mutual funds must register with the SEC. Securities law requires a fund to provide prospective investors with a prospectus detailing the funds objectives, philosophy, management team, past track record, and all financial details. There is no federal insurance. Many of the periodicals mentioned earlier publish performance rankings and relative safety ratings. Index mutual funds are suitable for most retirement plans.

Strengths

 Index funds are liquid investments. Many index funds offer flexible withdrawal options. For example, you may opt for periodic automatic payments. Index funds minimize the risk of a poor investment advisor underperforming the market. Index funds afford some protection from inflation. They offer good capital growth potential. The stock market is considered the best long-term growth investment in the United States.

Weaknesses

 Index funds offer little current income. They do not offer the chance to significantly outperform the stock market averages. They do not offer downside protection in bear markets.

Tax Considerations

 The 1986 Tax Reform Act eliminated the preferential tax treatment of long-term capital gains. Gains and dividend income are taxed at your ordinary income rate. Capital losses offset other capital gains. Losses are carried forward.

Summing Up

In 1982, the stock market was deeply undervalued by most commonly used fundamental valuation methods. A high number of stocks were trading below book value. Price-to-earnings ratios were very low. Dividend yields were 5 to 6%, an historically high rate. By 1987 most stocks were much more fairly valued by these same measures.

The potential for future gains is closely tied to the potential for increasing corporate profits. Many companies recently have restructured into much more efficient, cost-effective organizations. Earnings for the first quarter of 1987 were at the highest levels in over three years. As earnings increase, stock prices will probably follow, despite such major setbacks as the October market collapse.

Low inflation, low interest rates, and moderate economic growth are ideal for stock prices. Index funds thrive in such an environment. However, changes signaled by a different, more restrictive Federal Reserve policy as well as hidden after shocks of the October collapse could finally stem the bull market.

Closed-end Funds

CLOSED-END
FUNDS

Fair income

Good safety

Good liquidity

Good inflation
hedge

No tax benefits

Good growth

Closed-end funds are companies organized for the specific purpose of investing their shareholders' funds in select portfolios. These portfolios range from diversified stocks, specialized stocks, bonds, or a combination. Typically, closed-end funds specialize in one area such as the stocks of an individual country (the Korea Fund) or a specific investment area (ASA in gold or Bancroft Convertible Fund in convertible securities).

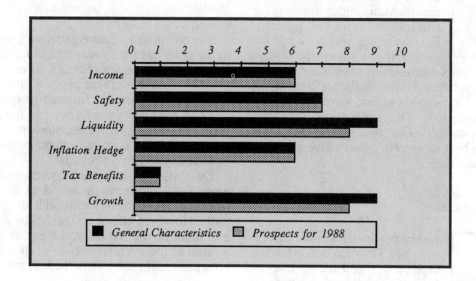

They differ from the more numerous open-end mutual funds in that they do not continually sell new shares nor redeem outstanding shares for investors. Their shares are bought and sold on stock exchanges or over the counter, just like individual stocks. Thus their price is determined by supply and demand at any particular time.

Since their price is determined by the marketplace, rather than by the net asset value of the portfolios they manage, that price can trade at a premium or discount to the asset value. This feature contrasts sharply with how prices are determined for open-end mutual funds. The price of open-end funds is determined by the net asset value of their portfolios.

Closed-end funds present an opportunity for investors to buy assets at a discount from their market value. Although a number of theories seek to explain why most closed-end

funds trade at discounts to their net asset value, the most prevalent theory states that the fixed capitalization of a closed-end fund restricts its ability to take advantage of opportunities that may arise—a limitation that is reflected in a lower price.

Yet a closed-end fund need not keep capital on hand to handle redemptions, which may actually give them an advantage by keeping more money fully employed. Even so, there is no clear evidence that the type of fund—open or closed-end—affects its performance.

Dual-purpose funds are a unique form of closed-end fund. Two classes of stock are issued: preferred and common. Preferred stock holders receive all income from dividends and interest. The common stock holders receive all the capital gains realized through stock sales in the portfolio. Dual-purpose funds have a finite life (typically 10 years). On expiration, the preferred shares are redeemed at a predetermined price and the common shareholders receive the balance left after sale of the assets.

Investment Potential

Closed-end funds are suitable for a variety of investment objectives. For example, if you seek capital gains, select a closed fund with the same objective, not one that concentrates on income-making bonds. Since closed-end funds usually trade at discounts to net asset value, they offer the potential of capital gains through a rise in their stock price quite apart from appreciation of the portfolio under management.

Closed-end funds specializing in bonds or preferred stock are appropriate when income is your goal.

Some closed-end funds that concentrate on gold or investment in foreign countries offer substantial protection from inflation. However, the market price may not reflect a rise in the value of the underlying portfolio. That is the key difference with open-end funds. On the other hand, closed-end funds may trade at a premium. ASA, the South African gold fund, traded at substantial premiums in the 1970s.

Strengths

 Closed-end funds trade like stocks and offer the same liquidity. Liquidation should only be a problem in unusual market conditions or for thinly traded issues. There are about 70 closed-end funds, offering a wide variety of portfolios to meet many investment objectives. You can borrow against your closed-end shares subject to current Federal Reserve margin requirements. The interest is tax deductible. Closed-end funds offer substantial diversification, which lowers risk.

Weaknesses

 Market volatility can mean wide swings in price. Poor management of the portfolio can be costly in two ways: lower asset value and bigger discount to asset value. Liquidity depends on market conditions, not the financial resources of the fund. Brokerage commissions and management fees may diminish your net return.

Tax Considerations

 Tax treatment is the same as that afforded common stock. Preferential capital gains treatment is phased out in 1987. Margin interest paid on loans secured by closed-end shares is tax deductible up to the amount of investment income earned. Check with your tax advisor for your specific situation.

Summing Up

Closed-end funds offer a good diversified approach for stock and bond investors. They are appropriate vehicles for retirement plans, especially when purchased at discounts. Investors seeking international diversification should certainly investigate these funds.

THE 1988 OUTLOOK FOR DOMESTIC STOCKS

 The consensus economic forecast for 1988 calls for continued slow growth, low inflation, and low interest rates. Despite the shock of "Black Monday," many investment advisors expect the Dow Jones Industrial Average to resume its gradual, if more erratic, climb in 1988 or 1989.

The bull market that began in the summer of 1982 has been led by well-known large capitalization stocks. This has been a "bluechip" market from the beginning. Analysts attribute this to two factors:

1. Foreign investors have participated heavily, and they tend to buy issues with international name recognition.
2. Many institutional money managers use stock index futures to hedge their portfolios. Since these indexes (like the Major

Market Index or the S&P) are tied to larger, better-known companies, institutions concentrate their buying on these issues.

As you will see in chapter 19, these two factors also contributed to the "internationalization" of the October collapse and the role that special investing techniques (such as futures hedging and computerized "program trading") played in magnifying its effects. Different industries will be favored in 1988. While the bull market before the October collapse had featured leadership by consumer-oriented companies, some signs of change are in the offing. Improving trade deficit figures indicate that export-oriented, capital goods, and basic industry stocks should benefit.

Three fundamental factors bear watching for early warning of a change in any resumed bull market.

1. Rising inflation. Watch four major indicators:

- The Consumer Price and Producer Price indexes are the most widely followed inflation indicators. Three consecutive months of rising price trends of over 6% per year will signal dangerous resurgent inflation.
- You should also monitor the price of gold. A move over $500 per ounce in 1988 would have very bearish long-term implications for stocks.
- The Commodity Research Bureau or the Dow Jones commodity price indexes give early warnings for rises in raw mateirals. The trend is more important than an absolute number. Key levels to watch are 250 on the CRB and 135 on the DJ.
- Oil prices. In June 1986 OPEC (Organization of Petroleum Exporting Countries) finally agreed on a floor price for oil at $18. The price surged to over $22 on heightened Middle East tensions. Steadily rising oil prices will drive U.S. production costs higher and eventually hurt the economy. Remember the 1974–1975 recession! Monitor the semiannual OPEC meetings carefully for indications of oil price increases.

2. Rising interest rates. The Federal Reserve is the key player to watch. In September 1987, the Fed raised the discount rate from 5.5 to 6%. That was the first raise since April 1984. There had been seven consecutive discount rate increases previously. Two more consecutive increases in the discount rate would have an important negative effect on stocks, although the Fed has stated it will not hinder a resumed bull market with contractionary interest rate hikes.

3. Falling dollar. Since 1985 the U.S. dollar has fallen over 40% against the currencies of our major trading partners. A weak dollar means that U.S. goods will be less expensive for foreign purchasers. However, it also means that foreign goods are more expensive for Americans. There are intense international pressures to maintain stable currency markets. A falling dollar hurts the bond markets and may lead to increasing inflation.

A continuaton of the current low inflation (under 5%) and slow GNP growth (under 4%) is bullish for equities, despite the October collapse. Deviations from these trends should be carefully watched for the effect on stocks. A major advantage of stocks is liquidity. The ability to move quickly means you do not have to be totally committed. Move to a more conservative position if post-collapse indicators appear to be deteriorating. Keep in mind that bull markets tend to run much higher—and often longer—than even the most optimistic believe. Many undervalued stocks are now available at bargain prices.

Other equity types will be affected differently from common stock. Convertible preferred stock has been a major beneficiary of the declining interest rate, and rising stock market since 1982. Inflation represents the major risk since higher inflation inevitably brings higher interest rates.

Preferreds will remain attractive investments unless the low interest rate, low inflation, and moderate growth falter. Watch inflation indexes such as the Consumer Price Index for early warnings of a return to double-digit inflation. Preferred stocks will react much more quickly to increasing inflation or rising interest rates than will the common. This is because they trade like fixed-income securities.

Many equity mutual funds have profited handsomely in the bull market that began in 1982, although the necessity for fund managers to sell stock to raise cash for panic redemptions in October put a considerable crimp in their operations. A resumption of the upward move in the market bodes well for growth funds. They do offer some protection from the ravages of inflation.

Of course, recent history shows that as stock prices move higher, volatility and risk increase. By 1987 it was not uncommon to see one hundred point upward or downward moves in the DJIA in a single day. It is very tempting to try to pick the market tops. However, very few professionals are able to do that consistently. Rather than wait for the last possible dollar of profit in a renewed, election year bull market, consider bailing out of stock positions if you see the danger signs described above. They reveal lasting, rather than transitory, trends in market prices. As we've seen, price drops occur with alarming speed and force. Conservative investors—those at the lower end of our equity allocation range—do indeed sleep well as seen on October 19 when the market fell 508 points.

TOP PERFORMING AGGRESSIVE GROWTH FUNDS - LOAD

1. Fidelity Magellan Fund
2. Weingarten Equity Fund
3. Quasar Associates
4. AMEV Growth Fund
5. IDS Growth Fund
6. New England Growth Fund
7. Massachusetts Capital Development Fund
8. Kemper Summit Fund
9. 44 Wall Street
10. Oppenheimer Time Fund

TOP PERFORMING GROWTH FUNDS - CLOSED END

1. Claremont Capital
2. General American Investors
3. Niagara Share Coporation
4. Spectra Fund
5. Engex
6. Central Securities
7. Niagara Share Coporation
8. Petroleum & Resources Corporation
9. Tri-Continental Corporation
10. Lehman Corporation

TOP PERFORMING BALANCED FUNDS
(RANKED BY 10-YEAR AVERAGE RETURN)

1. Windsor (Vanguard)
2. New England Retirement Equity
3. Merrill Lynch Capital
4. Investment Company of America (American Funds)
5. FPA Paramount
6. Putnam Fund for Growth & Income
7. Washington Mutual (American Funds)
8. Dodge & Cox
9. Smith Barney Income & Growth
10. Sentinel Common Stock

TOP PERFORMING NO LOAD BALANCED FUNDS
(RANKED BY 10-YEAR AVERAGE RETURN)

1. Windsor (Vanguard)
2. Dodge & Cox Stock
3. Fidelity
4. SAFECO Equity
5. Vanguard Index
6. Selected American
7. Pine Street (Wood Struthers)
8. Unified Mutual Shares
9. Founders Mutual
10. Lepercq-Istel

CHAPTER 11

DOMESTIC FIXED INCOME INSTRUMENTS

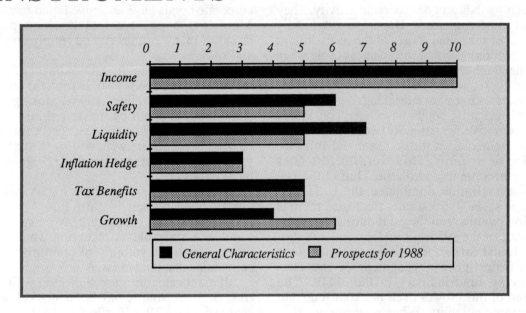

Chart showing values 0 through 10 for: Income, Safety, Liquidity, Inflation Hedge, Tax Benefits, Growth. Legend: ■ General Characteristics ▒ Prospects for 1988

Income deflation

Interest rate inflation

Ordinary income, tax exempt

A GLANCE AHEAD

In this chapter you'll discover the wide variety of debt instruments available to the public. You'll learn

- *How bonds differ from stock*
- *The relationship between bond values and interest rates*
- *How to minimize risk to principal in bond investments*
- *Why bonds are an integral part of a well-diversified portfolio*

Although the total dollar volume of the bond market dwarfs that of the stock market and bonds play a critical role in business, stocks get the front-page press. Through the issuance of debt instruments, many corporations have been able to raise capital for expansion that would have been impossible through selling stock. Treasury bond sales finance virtually the whole current federal budget deficit. The state of the bond market is critical to the economy and other investment markets.

In April 1987, the bond market began one of the sharpest collapses in its history. Oil prices were climbing as Middle East tension mounted and OPEC (Organization of Petroleum Exporting Countries) once again began to flex its muscles. The Consumer and Producer Price indexes both jumped to annual rates above 5% from 1986's lowly 1.1% level. Unfortunately, interest rates are ultimately a function of inflationary expectations and bonds trade inversely with interest rates.

OUTLOOK FOR 1988

High volatility

Rising market if:

Slow GNP growth or recession

Low inflation

Stable dollar

Falling rates

Warning signs:

Rates rise

Inflation picks up

Economy booms

Weak dollar

After a discouraging start, the course of the bond market in 1988 may tell the tale for most other investment markets.

Bonds

Whether we like it or not, the U.S. economy depends on debt. Moreover, many analysts warn that the current historically high debt levels for government, corporations, and individuals bodes ill for the future.

When interest rates rise, bond prices fall, and vice versa. Unlike stocks, bonds are not a leading indicator of economic activity. They tend to be coincident. Bond prices typically fall after the initial stages of the recession (or contraction) phase of the business cycle when demand for credit falls off. During the expansion phase, when credit demand climbs, interest rates rise after a brief lag.

Historically, bonds have been considered conservative investments because the buyer was assured a set interest rate and full face value at maturity. However, interest rates have become more volatile. During the late 1970s, inflation dominated the U.S. economic scene. Interest rates fluctuated more in a few months than they did during the entire decade of the 1950s.

Mutual funds specializing in bonds were the fastest-growing segment of the fast-growing fund industry in the 1980s. The speed of this growth itself has contributed to increased volatility. When interest rates rise, bond fund values decline. Bond fund shareholders then move to sell their shares, forcing the fund managers to sell more bonds to raise capital to meet the redemptions. This additional selling forces bond values even lower, extending the vicious cycle.

Risks

Bonds are subject to a variety of risks. Only U.S. Treasury issues are immune from business risk. Corporate bond prices will fluctuate with interest rates and/or with the fortunes of the issuing company. Many investors have learned to their chagrin that municipal bonds are not immune from business risk. New York City and Cleveland bond holders have both been hurt by financial difficulties experienced by those municipalities.

Higher inflation leads inevitably to higher interest rates, which lower bond prices. As bond investors learned in 1987, inflationary expectations are far more important for bond prices than the actual inflation rate iteslf. By August 1987 bond prices had collapsed in one of the sharpest falls in history, yet inflation as measured by the Consumer Price Index was under 4%.

Liquidity varies widely for bonds. U.S. Treasury issues are by far the most liquid. Investment-grade (lower risk, lower return) corporate bonds have an active liquid market. Municipal bonds are less liquid, though issues of many entities can be readily bought and sold.

The world economic environment affects the liquidity of bonds also. During the recent times of heightened international banking tensions brought about by massive third world debt, only U.S. Treasury issues benefitted because bond traders were willing to sacrifice yield for the greater safety of U.S. government issues.

Although the lower-quality, high-yielding "junk" bond market is quite liquid as this book is written, a recession may make them virtually unsaleable. A recession would put into question the viability of often-marginal companies that tend to issue junk bonds.

All asset categories are subject to political risk, and the municipal bond market was changed by the 1986 Tax Reform Act. Unanticipated political developments can always affect—favorable or unfavorably—the economics of any debt market.

Ratings, Insurance, and Government Regulation

 The largest single demand for independent investment rating services is in rating bonds. There are a number of such services, including Fitch's, Moody's, and Standard & Poor's. You should match your bond purchases with these ratings and your own risk tolerance. A very conservative investor, for example, will be uncomfortable holding B-rated bonds, regardless of their yield, compared to the peace of mind he or she would enjoy with A-rated issues.

Private insurance has become a major player in the municipal market. Many state and local governments contract with an insurance company to insure the interest and principal of their issues. This insurance enables them to get better ratings (usually AAA), which entitles them to pay lower interest. Insured munis, therefore, are only as secure as the financial strength of the insurance company. They certainly do not qualify as virtually risk-free investments, such as U.S. Treasuries.

The corporate and municipal bond markets are regulated by the SEC (Securities and Exchange Commission). Investors' accounts are protected by SIPC (Securities Investor Protection Corporation), coverage the same as stocks.

Bonds Compared to Other Assets

Experienced investors watch the relationship between stock and bonds prices very carefully. Typically the bond market cycle will peak before the stock market cycle. The lag time can be ten months or more.

Bond prices run contracyclically with gold prices. Inflation will push gold higher while knocking bond prices down.

It is no longer necessary to confine your bond trading to individual bonds or even bond funds. It is possible now to speculate on bonds through options and futures.

Fixed-income instruments include U.S. Treasury, corporate, and municipal issues. In addition, federal agency issues such as Ginnie Maes and Fannie Maes have become very popular. Wall Street is also busily "securitizing" mortgages on both single-family homes and business buildings.

Lasser's Recommended Allocation Range for 1988 Domestic Fixed-income Instruments: 20% to 40%

 Allocate as much as 40% in 1988.

 Allocate as little as 20% in 1988.

U.S. Treasury Securities

TREASURY SECURITIES

Good income

Best safety

Best liquidity

Poor inflation hedge

State tax benefits

Moderate growth

U.S. Treasury securities are debt instruments that are issued with set maturities paying fixed interest rates. Treasury bills have maturities from 91 days to one year, Treasury notes run from one to seven years, and Treasury bonds run from over seven years to thirty years.

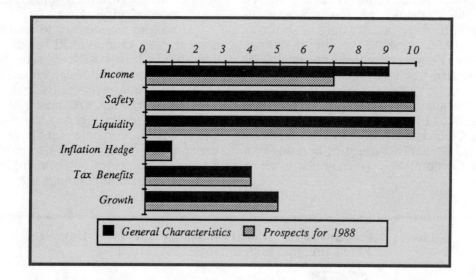

U.S. Treasury securities—bonds, notes, and bills—constitute the safest (if held to maturity) and one of the most liquid investment markets in the world. When you buy a U.S. Treasury issue, you are loaning money to the federal government with the full faith and credit (including the taxing power) of the U.S. government guaranteeing both interest and principal. There has never been a default on a U.S. debt. Even debt issued during the Revolutionary War was redeemed after Alexander Hamilton pushed hard for the fledgling government to demonstrate its creditworthiness to the world.

The U.S. Treasury market has expanded greatly in recent years as the federal government continues to run up huge budget deficits. Like anybody who spends more than he or she takes in, the government must finance the gap by borrowing. The U.S. Treasury debt is held by many foreign investors as well as U.S. citizens. In fact, Japanese purchases have accounted for as much as 30% of the debt issued in recent years.

T-bills are sold on a "discount basis." This means that you buy a $10,000 bill for less than the face value. When it matures, you receive the full face value of $10,000. The difference you receive is the interest paid to you for your loan.

T-notes and T-bonds are sold on the more common "coupon" basis. You receive interest twice a year at the fixed rate—as if you were redeeming the coupon's rate of return. If you buy a T-note or T-bond in the secondary market (that is, from a third party after it has already been sold through a Treasury auction), the price you pay may be at a discount or premium to the par or face value of the bond. If interest rates have gone up since the note or bond was originally issued, making new bonds more valuable, the old bond price will be lower making the effective yield competitive with current interest rate. If rates have fallen in the interim, you'll pay a higher price than the discounted price of the original issue.

Treasury notes can be purchased through full-service brokers, banks, specialty brokers, or even direct from the Federal Reserve. Fees are normally very low. The minimum investment for T-bills is $10,000, with multiples of $5,000 thereafter. T-notes and bonds trade in $5,000 face value lots.

Prices are regularly quoted in major financial media. Many other loans such as adjustable-rate mortgages are tied to U.S. Treasury interest rates.

Investment Potential

U.S. Treasury securities are purchased primarily for income. They can be purchased for short-term reasons (T-bills) or for as long as 30 years (T-bonds).

Like all bonds, Treasury issues fluctuate inversely with interest rates. Rising rates will drive prices down, while falling rates will push prices higher. This fluctuation offers investors the chance to earn capital gains on a secondary market transaction.

As interest rates become more volatile, so too do the prices of Treasury issues. The longer the maturity of the issue, the more volatile price changes will be.

Because U.S. Treasury obligations are backed by the full faith and credit of the federal government, they are considered very safe investments. It is possible to borrow up to 90% of the market value of your Treasury securities. This flexibility affords great capital gains potential if interest rates fall. However, fully leveraged positions are subject to large losses if interest rates rise.

The wide variety of maturities and the active "affiliated" markets (such as futures and options) offer great flexibility. Because they are the safest debt instruments you can buy, Treasury obligations are appropriate for all retirement plans.

Strengths

 Treasury obligations are very liquid. Treasury obligations offer the safest guarantee of both interest and principal of any debt instrument. They pay secure current income. They offer a wide variety of maturities that can be used to closely suit your individual needs. They are universally accepted as collateral for loans. Transaction fees are nominal. Pricing information is widely available. They offer the chance to earn good capital gains on accurate interest rate speculations.

Weaknesses

 Treasury yields are lower than other similar debt instruments due to their greater safety. Like all bonds, T-bonds will fall in price and result in losses if sold before maturity in rising interest rate environments. Highly leveraged positions can be costly if interest rates rise. Longer-term maturities offer no inflation protection.

Tax Considerations

 All interest paid by U.S. Treasury obligations is exempt from state and local taxes. Interest is subject to federal taxation level at your ordinary income rates.

Summing Up

 U.S. Treasury debt securities consitute the largest and safest single investment market in the world. Risk-averse investors should concentrate their debt investments in Treasury obligations. Keep in mind that lower interest rates are the tradeoff for the lower risk.

Remember too that before maturity Treasury bonds are subject to the same market forces that affect all bond resale values. Rising interest rates will push down the principal of the underlying bond. Rising interest rates in the late 1970s resulted in substantial losses for bond buyers who chose to sell their bonds before maturity.

 Experienced bond investors help ensure continuous income by staggering the maturities of the bonds in their portfolios. The longer the maturity, the greater the risk to principal.

Just as you should always maintain diversification throughout your investment portfolio, you should diversify within a selected investment area whenever possible. For example, you should keep a portion of your Treasury investments in short-term (91- or 180-day Treasury bills). These short-term instruments provide a measure of inflation protection since new T-bill interest rates will rise as rates rise in the marketplace. Since they mature every three or six months, there is minimal risk to principal if you must sell before maturity. At maturity, you will be able to roll over to new bills paying the higher, current market rate.

Keep a portion in Treasury notes and a portion in long-term bonds. More conservative investors should keep the average maturity of their Treasury portfolios shorter. This is especially important if you may need to sell the securities before maturity.

Mortgage-backed Certificates or Pass-throughs

A mortgage-backed certificate is a security that is issued by government agencies and is backed by home mortgages. Such certificates have become an increasingly popular investment for investors seeking income with relative security. Three main government agencies package and sell mortgage-backed securities. They are the Federal Home Loan Bank (FHLB), the Federal National Mortgage Association (FNMA), and the Government National Mortgage Association (GNMA). The securities they issue are called Freddie Macs, Fannie Maes, and Ginnie Maes, respectively.

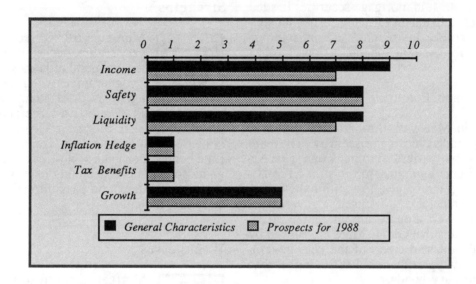

These agencies act as intermediaries acquiring a large supply of mortgage loans from savings institutions. The volatile interest rates that accompanied the inflationary 1970s has prompted many savings institutions to sell their mortgage loans immediately, rather than hold them to maturity.

The agencies then sell pieces of the packaged loans to individual and institutional investors. Investors receive a proportionate share of the interest and principal paid by the "pool" of securities.

Most mortgage securities are "pass-throughs," that is, interest and principal payments pass through directly to investors on a monthly basis. A variation called "collateralized mortgage obligations" are corporate bonds backed by mortgages that make interest payments semiannually. Pass-throughs are by far the most common form of mortgage-backed securities.

Mortgage-backed securities trade like bonds (they are debt instruments) with one major exception. Bonds trade with a fixed maturity date. Mortgage-backed securities are sold with "average" maturity dates (typically 12 years), because in an environment of falling interest rates, it is often in the interest of the mortgagee to refinance his or her mortgage ahead of schedule. The old mortgage is paid off, and a new mortgage with more favorable interest rates is taken. If you purchase a Ginnie Mae and substantial prepayments are made on the mortgages in the pool, you'd receive a return of principal as well as the expected interest on the balance of the mortgages in the pool.

Mortgage-backed securities have long been the domain of the professional and institutional investors. However, this market experienced sharp growth beginning in the early 1980s when interest rates began to fall. Money market fund yields started to drop off, and many investors who had come to expect the higher-income payouts searched out other avenues to achieve the same goal.

There is a large and active secondary market for mortgage securities. They are purchased through brokerage firms. The sharp rise in interest in mortgage securities has led to the establishment of many firms that specialize solely in them. A commission is charged for handling the transaction.

Investment Potential

Ginnie Mae pass-throughs are the most widely traded mortgage security. They are backed by Federal Home Loan (FHA)-insured and Veterans Administration (VA)-guaranteed mortgages. In addition they carry the guarantee of GNMA itself, a government agency. Even though this guarantee effectively means that Ginnie Maes are backed by the full faith and credit of the U.S. government, they typically yield 1 to 2% higher than U.S. Treasury bonds.

Freddie Macs are backed by FHA, VA, and privately guaranteed mortgages. They carry the general guarantee of the Federal Home Loan Mortgage Corporation, a privately managed public institution.

Fannie Maes are backed by VHA, VA, and conventional mortgages. They are issued and guaranteed by the Federal national Mortgage Association, a government-sponsored, publicly held corporation. Fannie Maes and Freddie Maes generally yield up to 1/2% more than Ginnie Maes, because they are not backed by the full faith and credit of the U.S. government.

Mortgage securities are income-producing investments. Capital gains are possible if interest rates fall, resulting in appreciation of the security. The primary risk of mortgage securities is early payoff of the mortgages. You would receive principal payments for those mortgages that are paid off early and a reduced income paid by the balance of the securities that have not been prepaid. This risk may be a problem if you hope to lock in a specific yield for a long-term investment.

Mortgage-backed securities are secure, because they are backed not only by the mortgage collateral but also by guarantees of various government agencies.

The 1986 Tax Reform Act created yet another entity, the real estate mortgage investment conduit (REMIC) for multiclass mortgage pools.

Strengths

Mortgage-backed securities are very secure, backed by not only the collateral of homes, but also by guarantees of government agencies. Mortgage securities are very liquid. There is a large and active secondary market. Mortgage security income is higher than that paid by Treasury bonds. Like bonds, mortgage securities offer capital gains potential in a declining interest rate environment. Interest on pass-throughs is typically paid monthly.

Weaknesses

Mortgage-backed securities offer no inflation protection. Rising interest rates cause declining principal values. Monthly income may fluctuate since early payment of mortgages will lower the principal value of the mortgage pool. It is impossible to ascertain in advance what will be the full maturity term of the security, because of the potential for early payoffs. As a mortgage pass-through pool matures, principal payments will be an ever larger part of the monthly payments.

Tax Considerations

No special tax preferences apply to mortgage securities. Interest income and capital gains (if any) are taxed at ordinary income levels. Since monthly payments are a mix of interest payments and principal repayments "passed through" to the security holder, taxes are assessed only on the interest portion of the monthly payments.

Summing Up

Mortgage-backed securities have enjoyed explosive growth in recent years. The low-inflation, low-interest-rate environment has resulted in increased interest in longer-term, secure income-producing investments to replace ever shrinking money market yields.

Investors who need an assured monthly income should concentrate on low-rate mortgage pools because the risk of refinancing is much lower. Of course such pools should only be purchased when their yield is competitive with those available in the marketplace.

Recent years have witnessed many innovations in the mortgage-backed security market. More private issuers have entered the market. The widespread interest assures good liquidity for most mortgage securities.

Stable interest rates are the most favorable condition for mortgage securities. Dropping interest rates result in heavy prepayment ratios, which cause widely fluctuating monthly interest payments. Rising interest rates depress the principal value of the securities since they must compete with other fixed-income instruments for available cash.

Government Agencies

AGENCIES

Good income

Excellent safety

Good liquidity

Poor inflation hedge

Few tax benefits

Moderate growth

The term "government agencies" refer to debt obligations issued by agencies of the federal government. Although usually not specifically backed by the full faith and credit of the U.S. government, they are guaranteed by the issuing agencies with implied backing by Congress. It is highly unlikely that Congress would let any agency bond be defaulted, although that theoretical possibility has led the market to place a slight (usually about a 0.5% premium) on their yields over equivalent U.S. Treasury issues. Many federal government agencies issue their own securities to raise funds within guidelines set by Congress.

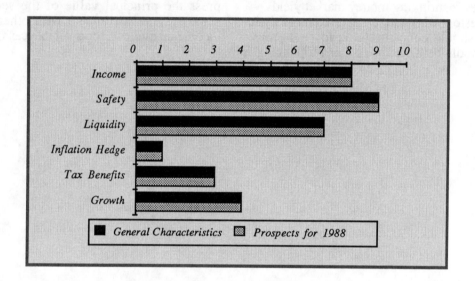

Unlike U.S. Treasury notes and bonds, which are initially marketed through auctions (usually quarterly), government agencies are sold by the Federal Reserve Bank of New York through its network of dealers. They are sold on a "best yield possible" basis.

The government agencies that issue debt securities include the Asian Development Bank, the Export-Import Bank of the United States, Farmers Home Administration, Federal Housing Administration, Federal National Mortgage Association (FNMA), Government National Mortgage Association (GNMA), Interamerican Development Bank, International Bank for Reconstruction and Development (commonly known as the World Bank), Small Business Administration, Student Loan Marketing Association (SLMA), Tennessee Valley Authority, United States Postal Service, Federal Home Loan banks, and others.

Agencies can be purchased through major securities brokerage firms, from dealer commercial banks, or direct from the New York Federal Reserve on new issues. A commission or retail markup is charged for the transaction.

There is an active liquid secondary market for most agencies. A wide variety of agencies exist, ranging from maturities of 30 days to twenty-five years. Minimum denominations range from as little as $1,000 to as much as $25,000. Unusually structured agencies may result in a large spread between the bid and offer prices. Agencies in general are liquid, though generally less so than Treasuries.

As debt instruments, government agencies fluctuate directly with swings in interest rates.

The increasing volatility of interest rates is directly reflected in wider oscillations in the prices of agencies.

Investment Potential

Government agencies are bonds that provide good current income. Capital gain is possible if interest rates drop subsequent to your agencies purchase because bond values vary inversely to interest rates. Their chief attraction for most investors is the secure, government-backed income paid.

 Agencies generally are exempt from state and local taxes, as are Treasuries. The most notable exceptions are the mortgage-backed securities issued by GNMA, FNMA, and the Federal Home Loan Mortgage Corporation (FHLMC). If this consideration is important for you, be sure to check with your broker prior to purchase.

Agencies provide no protection from inflation. As is the case with Treasuries and corporate bonds, the shorter the maturity the less inflation risk.

Because of their high relative safety, agencies are appropriate for long-term retirement programs that allow accumulation of interest on a tax-deferred basis. They offer excellent flexibility through the wide variety of denominations and maturities available.

Short-term speculators trading on interest rate expectations often borrow against their agencies. Lenders may lend up to 90% of their market value. This strategy is not appropriate for long-term investors.

Strengths

 Income and principal (if held to maturity) are very secure. Income is slightly higher than equivalent U.S. Treasury issues. Most agencies are exempt from state and local taxes. Agencies are generally very liquid, with a large and active secondary market for most issues.

Weaknesses

 Principal is subject to wide fluctuations due to changes in interest rates. Agencies provide no protection from inflation. Income, while higher than Treasuries, is less than for high-grade corporate issues.

Tax Considerations

 Interest income paid by agencies is fully taxable on the federal level at ordinary income rates. Interest income from most agencies is exempt from state and local taxes.

Capital gains resulting from sales prior to maturity is taxable as ordinary income. Capital losses can be used to offset other capital gains. Unused losses can be carried forward.

Summing Up

Government agencies are secure fixed-income instruments offering slightly higher yields than straight Treasury obligations. Trade is quite active, and most are liquid. They should be investigated by serious fixed-income investors who require very safe investments.

Municipal Bonds

Municipal bonds are debt securities issued by state or local governments. All municipal bonds issued prior to August 7, 1986, pay interest that is exempt from federal taxation. Municipal securities issued by states or their political subdivisions pay "dual-exempt" interest—interest that is exempt from state tax as well—to residents of their own state.

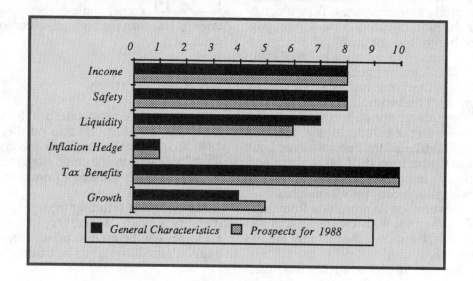

The 1986 Tax Reform Act muddied the previously clear distinction between tax-free municipals and other bonds. Municipal obligations are now divided into two groups: public-purpose bonds and private-purpose bonds. Public-purpose bonds are those securities issued by state and local government to raise funds for direct "governmental purposes."

 Private-purpose bonds are those bonds issued by state and local governments in which more than 10% of the revenues go to benefit private parties. For example, bonds issued to help finance construction of an industrial plant would be a private-purpose bond. Private-purpose bonds are fully taxable, but there are some exceptions. Your broker should advise you on many intricate distinctions imposed by the new tax law and the tax status of the interest paid by municipal bonds you may be interested in purchasing.

Municipals pay lower rates than do taxable securities. It is important to calculate your after-tax returns by comparing the yields of comparable taxable and tax-free bonds.

All municipal bonds issued prior to August 7, 1986, qualify for full tax exemption. Each state may issue only a limited amount of tax-exempt private-purpose bonds (those that meet certain criteria).

Like all bonds, municipal bonds are subject to fluctuations in principal value as interest rates change. Higher interest rates depress principal, while lower rates can yield capital gains as well as tax-free income.

The major bond-rating services cover municipals. Ratings reflect the relative financial stability of the issuing governments. Some municipal bonds are insured by private companies. As a result, their yields are lower.

Municipal bonds are sold by full-service brokerage firms and a number of firms that specialize in tax exempts. Commissions or "dealer markups" are assessed by the firms. Normally commissions are low relative to equivalent investments in stocks. However, high markups are often not fully disclosed. Make sure you know what fees you are paying before investing.

Investment Potential

The primary attraction of municipal bonds is the tax-free income they pay. Declining interest rates will result in some capital gains.

The municipal bond market is quite liquid. It is not as liquid as the Treasuries market, though. Obscure or unpopular issues (for example, New York City's securities for a period in the 1970s) can be very difficult to sell. If you stick with investment-grade bonds rated A or better, you should have no liquidity problem.

Historically, bonds have been considered safe, nonvolatile investments. The volatile interest rates of the past 10 years have changed that perception. Bonds are directly influenced by interest rates, and higher rates mean lower bond prices and vice versa.

Municipal bonds are secured in one of two ways. General-obligation bonds are backed by the full faith and credit (that is, the taxing power) of the issuing government. Revenue bonds are used to finance specific public projects. They are repaid by the revenues generated by the facilities they finance. For example, revenue bonds may be issued to build a hospital or bridge. The security of the bonds depends on the economic viability of the project.

Like all bonds, municipal bonds are hurt by inflation. Inflation brings higher interest rates, which lower bond prices.

In addition, the financial condition of the issuing government body may deteriorate after you've purchased the bond. If a rating is lowered on a bond, it will drop in price. The lower price produces a higher yield, which is intended to compensate the buyer for the perceived additional risk.

Minimum investment in municipals is typically $5,000 or higher. Professionally managed bond mutual funds or unit investment trusts offer the average investor the chance to diversify.

Recent years have seen a wide variety of features tacked onto municipals. These include floating-rate bonds and notes, bonds with "put" options, and enhanced security issues. The drive to obtain sufficient financing at the lowest possible cost will no doubt result in even more innovations.

Many municipal bonds are issued with "call" provisions. A call provision enables the issuer to redeem outstanding bonds prior to maturity at the issuer's discretion. Usually, during a minimum time period of three to five years after issue the bonds are "safe" from being called.

 Call provisions should be carefully watched by investors who want a secure income for living expenses. A bond would be called only when the issuing body could refinance the bond at lower interest rates. If you had planned on the income from a bond that was called, you could not replace the income with an equivalently rated bond. Just when you were planning on a tax-free 8% yield for the next ten years, the bond gets called—and the market yield on the same type of bond is only 6%. That's the unique danger with call provisions.

Strengths

 Public-purpose municipal bonds pay tax-exempt income. Investment-grade municipals (those rated A or better) are quite safe from default. They are also more liquid than lower-rated bonds. Municipals can generate capital gains in declining interest-rate environments. Many municipals carry privately issued insurance on both interest and principal.

Weaknesses

 Rising interest rates depress bond prices. Call provisions may limit how long you can lock in high relative yields. Inflation is devastating to municipals. Revenue bonds are not backed by the taxing power of the issuing entity. Adverse business developments in the project could affect both interest payments and principal value. Liquidity is limited in some issues.

Tax Considerations

 The interest paid by public-purpose and previously issued municipals bonds is exempt from federal taxes. The 1986 Tax Reform Act eliminated the tax-free feature of municipal private-activity bonds in many cases. And to confuse the issue even more, the interest paid on certain qualified private-activity bonds is subject to the Alternative Minimum Tax even though totally exempt for regular tax calculations.

Gains from capital appreciation due to interest rate declines or other events are taxable at ordinary income rates.

 The complexity of the tax law changes created by the 1986 Tax Reform Act make it prudent to check with your tax advisor. Each individual's situation is unique.

Summing Up

Public-purpose municipal bonds are the most widely used vehicle for obtaining tax-free cash flow. While the 1986 Tax Reform Act tightened things somewhat, carefully selected municipals remain the single best option for tax-free income.

Historically, the municipal bond market has been the domain of institutional investors. However, this began to change in the 1980s. By 1987, the presence of many loss-sensitive individual investors holding their bonds for a shorter time resulted in a highly volatile market. As a result, they buy and sell much more actively than do institutional investors.

When the bond market deteriorated in April 1987, the municipal market fell more sharply than the Treasury market. The larger drop by municipals was attributed to the big influence of the mutual fund market. As bond values dropped, bond mutual fund investors sold their shares, forcing many of the funds to sell more municipal bonds to meet redemptions. This chain of events forced the market lower than would have otherwise been the case.

As a result, municipal bond investments should be made with money you are able to commit for long periods of time. Remember, if you hold a bond to maturity, price fluctuations resulting from interest rate changes will not affect you.

Discounted Municipal Bonds

Municipal bonds are debt instruments issued by state or local governments. When interest rates move higher, the price of bonds with lower coupons (periodic interest payments) falls to bring their yield into line with the market.

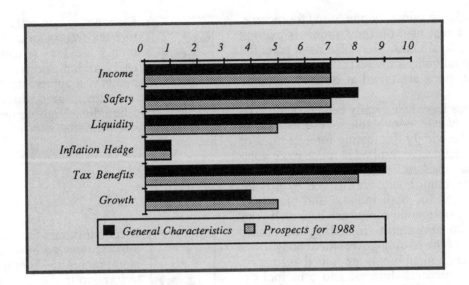

 Discounted municipal bonds (munis) are popular with investors who want to lock in yields for the long term. Since many munis have call provisions that could result in early redemptions, savvy investors who want to lock in a yield will buy discounted munis that carry low coupons. The yield will be comparable to the market, but because the bonds carry a low coupon they are less likely to be called prior to maturity.

Bonds are called early when the coupon yield is higher than the going market rate. Issuers are able to save money in interest payments by redeeming their high-coupon issues and selling new lower-coupon bonds. Since discounted bonds by definition carry lower coupons, they are less susceptible to being called before they mature.

For example, assume that a 20-year muni bond issued in 1972 carries a coupon of 5%. The face value would be $5,000 per bond. A buyer would receive $250 per year. If market rates moved to 8% for the same class of muni

in 1980, the price of the 5% bond would fall to $625. At that price the 5% bond would yield a competitive 8%. You wouldn't buy a bond with a 5% coupon at full face value, when you could get a bond yielding 8% for the same price.

Discounted munis can be purchased through major full-service brokerage firms or through smaller firms that specialize in munis. The fee for buying the bond is assessed either as a commission or as a "dealer markup" from the price at which the dealer obtained the bond. The latter practice may hide the actual costs of the transaction. You should find out in advance what the fees will be.

Prices of actively traded muni bonds are reported in the *Wall Street Journal.* You can also check a number of other sources for price information, including your broker for munis that are not carried in the *Wall Street Journal.*

Professional management of muni portfolios is available for individuals who maintain large (usually over $1 million) portfolios. Smaller investors can obtain professional management through mutual funds specializing in muni bonds. This approach offers the additional advantage of diversification.

Investment Potential

Munis are primarily purchased for income. The interest paid on most munis is exempt from federal taxes. They also have potential for capital gains if interest rates fall, although capital gains are taxed at ordinary income rates.

Bonds have historically been considered a relatively safe, nonvolatile investment. However, the widely fluctuating interest rates of recent years have resulted in much more volatile bond markets.

Many muni bonds are insured by private companies for both income and principal. General-obligation munis are backed by the full faith and credit (including the taxing power) of the issuing government body.

Revenue muni bonds are issued to finance specific projects. Interest and principal on maturity are paid out of revenues generated by the project. Revenue bonds carry slightly higher yields due to this increased risk.

Municipal bonds are rated by independent services. Two of the most prominent services are Standard & Poor's and Moody's Investor Services. Bonds rated A or higher are considered "investment grade." Lower-rated bonds carry higher risk, and carry higher yields as a result.

There is an active secondary market for most muni issues. This market ensures good liquidity for investment-grade munis and those of major issuers. Obscure munis from less well known issuers are less liquid. You may have to accept steep discounts from market prices to sell these bonds quickly.

Muni bonds are generally long-term investments. Speculators trading on interest rate expectations trade them for short-term profits.

Muni bonds are subject to market price risk if interest rates rise. They are also subject to price falls if the financial condition of the issuer deteriorates. If a rating is downgraded due to this deterioration, the bond price will fall. The yields on higher-rated bonds are lower due to the greater safety such bonds offer.

Municipals are not good inflation hedges. Higher inflation brings higher interest rates, which depress prices.

Strengths

Discount munis offer competitive tax-free income. Discount munis are less susceptible to early redemptions. Discount munis will appreciate if interest rates decline. Investment-grade discount munis have good liquidity. Highly rated munis offer security of principal and interest payments.

Weaknesses

Discount munis fall in price if interest rates go up. Many discount munis are not liquid. Deterioration in the financial condition of the issuing party may result in falling prices even if other munis are appreciating. A diversified portfolio of discount munis requires substantial capital. Discount munis that are "revenue issues" are subject to price risk if the underlying project fails to generate sufficient money to pay interest and principal when due.

Tax Considerations

Before the 1986 Tax Reform Act, all interest paid by munis was exempt from federal taxes. All munis issued before August 7, 1986, are still exempt from federal taxes.

However, municipal bonds issued to finance "private activities" after that date are fully taxable on the federal level. Certain exceptions depend on exactly what the money is used for and how many such private-purpose bonds have been sold by the issuing body.

Interest paid by munis is usually exempt from state and local taxes for residents of the issuing state.

The 1986 tax law eliminated preferential treatment for capital gains. Capital gains are taxed at ordinary income rates.

Summing Up

Municipal bonds appreciated substantially under the falling interest rates and low inflation since 1980. In the first half of 1987, the fear of inflation knocked prices down.

Because bond prices depend on interest rates, you should monitor the trend of Federal Reserve's discount rate. Consecutive increases in the discount rate will signal higher interest rates.

A rise in inflation will also depress munis, discounted or not, because higher interest rates inevitably follow increased inflation.

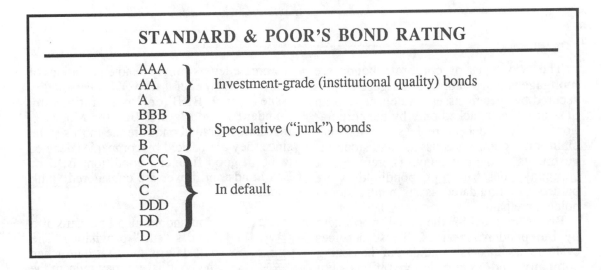

MOODY'S BOND RATING

Aaa Aa A	Investment-grade (institutional quality) bonds
Baa Ba B	Speculative ("junk") bonds
Caa Ca C	In default

STANDARD & POOR'S BOND RATING

AAA AA A	Investment-grade (institutional quality) bonds
BBB BB B	Speculative ("junk") bonds
CCC CC C DDD DD D	In default

Corporate Bonds

Corporate bonds are debt securities issued by companies for a set amount (the "par value") and maturity. Most corporate bonds specify a fixed interest rate to be paid at specified time intervals (usually semiannually). During the late 1970s when inflation was a dominant concern for investors, "variable rate" bonds were introduced. These bonds feature a flexible interest rate according to a preset formula (for example, tied to the Federal Reserve's discount rate). Variable-rate bonds generally sell for a lower current yield because they provide some measure of protection against loss of purchasing power due to inflation.

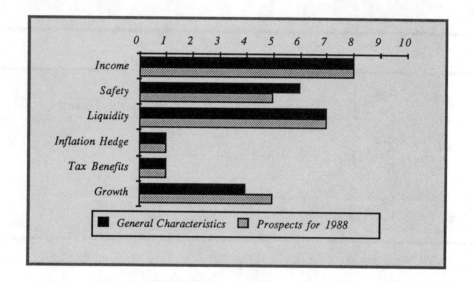

The two types of corporate bonds are mortgage and debenture. A mortgage bond is secured by specific assets. A debenture is an unsecured loan backed only by the corporation's credit. A debenture does have a higher claim on a company's assets than stock investments in the company. Therefore, if a company goes bankrupt, bondholders are paid out of liquidated assets before stockholders are paid.

Bonds are rated for their creditworthiness by independent services. These services evaluate the financial condition of the issuing company and assign letter ratings. For example, Standard & Poor's ratings for the best investment-grade bonds are AAA, AA, or A. Moody's Investor Services' equivalent ratings are Aaa, Aa, and A. (The capital and lowercase letters simply denote gradations of risk, or degree of safety.) Lower-quality issues carry BBB or lower ratings by Standard & Poor's and Baa for Moody's. Investment-grade bonds are the most secure, since they are backed by companies deemed to be in good financial condition. BBB or Baa bonds and lower are considered "junk bonds."

 You should also be aware of a bond's "call" provisions. The call date is the first date when the bond issuer may redeem the bond *before* maturity. Call provisions are spelled out in the bond's prospectus. Routinely, the issuer must pay a premium to the bondholder to call a bond. It is in

CALCULATING A BOND'S CURRENT MARKET VALUE

A bond's current market value can be calculated by comparing the bond's yield with the yield of a hypothetical bond under prevailing market interest rates, as follows:

$$\text{Yield} = \text{bond's par value} \times \text{stated interest rate}$$

$$= \text{bond's current market value} \times \text{new interest rate}$$

Therefore,

$$\text{bond's current market value} = \frac{\text{bond's par value} \times \text{stated interest rate}}{\text{new interest rate}}$$

Thus the market value of a $1,000 bond paying 10% would fall to $833 if interest rates rose to 12%, but would go up in value to $1,250 if interest rates declined to 8%:

$$\$833 = \$1,000 \times \frac{10\%}{12\%}$$

$$\$1,230 = \$1,000 \times \frac{10\%}{8\%}$$

the interest of a company to "call" a bond early if interest rates have dropped significantly after the time of issue. The company could then call in bonds requiring high-interest payments and reissue lower-yielding bonds. This is similar to refinancing your home mortgage to lower your monthly payments.

Much like stocks, bonds of major corporations are traded on the exchanges. They are also traded over the counter. They are generally purchased through brokers who assess a commission for the transaction, although normally at lower commission rates than for equivalent amounts invested in stocks.

Investment Potential

Par (or face) value of most bonds is $1,000. They are normally sold in "5-lots" (for example, 5 bonds at $5,000 par value).

"Baby" bonds have a par value of $500 or less.

Bond prices vary inversely with interest rates. For example, if the current interest rate for AAA 20-year bonds is 10%, you would receive interest payments of $100 per bond each year. If interest rates rose to 12%, the market value of your 10% bond would drop to about $833:

$$\$833 = \$1,000 \times \frac{10\%}{12\%}$$

This is so because a buyer could then earn $120 on a $1,000 par value bond in the higher interest rate environment.

No one would pay you $1,000 to receive $100 per year, when he or she could pay the same amount for the same-quality bond and get $120 per year in interest. Since bonds are purchased primarily for the income they pay, the underlying principal will fluctuate. Of course, it works in your favor if interest rates drop. For example, if market rates dropped to 8%, your bond would appreciate to about $1,225 ($100 ÷ $1,225 = 8%).

Bonds are primarily purchased for the income they pay. Capital appreciation is possible, though, if interest rates fall. Yields are lower on higher-rated bonds of the same maturity due to their greater safety. They should generally be considered long-term vehicles because if you hold to maturity (and if the company does not go under), the company pays you the full par value.

They are suitable for retirement plans such as IRAs where interest accrues on a tax-deferred basis.

Strengths

Bonds pay high current income. Investment-grade bonds have little principal risk if held to maturity. Bonds issued by major corporations are liquid. Bonds appreciate in falling interest rate environments.

Weaknesses

Security of income depends on stability of underlying company. The value of bonds falls when interest rates rise. A callable bond may be redeemed

before maturity, limiting the time you receive your expected income. The secondary market for bonds is less liquid than that for stocks. High volatility in interest rates translates into high volatility in bond prices. Bonds provide no protection from inflation.

Tax Considerations

Bond interest is taxed as ordinary income. Capital appreciation is also taxed as ordinary income since the 1986 Tax Reform Act eliminated capital gains preference.

Summing Up

Corporate bonds pay higher interest than other fixed-income instruments such as Treasuries and municipal bonds. That higher return is the tradeoff you must take for the higher risk inherent in issues not guaranteed by the government. Risk-averse investors should buy only investment-grade (A rated and above). See the next section for discussion of speculative trading of bonds.

Junk Bonds

Junk bonds are debt securities issued by companies for a set amount (the "par value") and maturity. Most junk bonds specify a fixed interest rate to be paid at specified time intervals (usually semiannually).

JUNK BONDS

High income

Poor safety

Fair liquidity

Poor inflation hedge

No tax benefits

Moderate growth

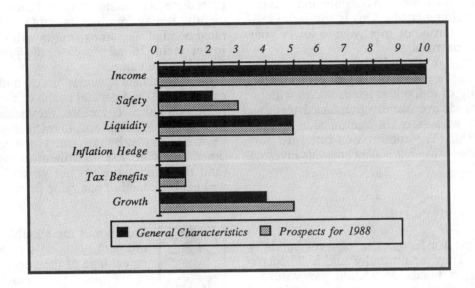

Junk bonds are unsecured debt instruments called *debentures.* A debenture is an unsecured loan backed only by the corporation's credit. A debenture does have a higher claim on a company's assets than stock (equity) investments. If a company goes bankrupt, bondholders are paid out of liquidated assets before stockholders. While even junk bonds are backed by the assets of a company, payment of interest requires ready liquid assets. Capital assets such as buildings, land and machines may not be readily saleable (or only saleable at steep discounts) to meet corporate obligations to bondholders.

"Junk bonds" have been widely used to finance corporate takeovers in the 1980s. These takeovers are usually highly leveraged transactions—credit rather than cash is used to finance the deal. As a result, corporate assets are stretched to the breaking point and corporate liquidity is impaired. Junk bonds carry much higher risk since corporate liabilities are sharply increased.

Junk bonds are rated for their creditworthiness by independent services. These services evaluate the financial condition of the issuing company and assign letter ratings. For example, Standard & Poor's ratings for junk bonds are BBB, BB, B, CCC, or lower. Moody's Investor Services equivalent ratings are Baa, Ba, B, Caa, or lower. Compare with investment-grade ratings of AAA, AA, and A for Standard & Poor's (or Aaa, Aa, or A for Moody's).

A market exists for even lower-rated junk bonds. Low C ratings indicate a bond that is not paying current interest. D ratings are reserved for bonds that are in arrears on interest and/or principal payments. These bonds have value solely as speculations since they pay no current income.

Junk bonds occasionally have "call provisions." A call proviso specifies the conditions under which an issuer can redeem a bond prior to its maturity. Call provisions are spelled out in the bond's prospectus. Routinely, the issuer must pay a premium to the bondholder to call a bond. It is in the interest of a company to "call" a bond early if interest rates dropped significantly from the time of issue. The company can then call in bonds requiring high interest payments and reissue lower-yielding bonds. This is similar to refinancing your home mortgage to lower your monthly payments.

The high relative yield paid by junk bonds in the 1980s attracted a significant market. Liquidity of individual issues varies widely. Junk bonds are usually purchased through brokers who assess a commission for the transaction. The commission rates are normally lower than equivalent amounts invested in stock.

Investment Potential

The par (or face) value of most bonds is $1,000. They are normally sold in "5-lots" (that is, 5 bonds or $5,000 par value). "Baby" bonds have a par value of $500 or less. Junk bonds are normally issued at par value. The current price of any individual issue will vary in the secondary market, depending on the general level of interest rates, the company's prospects, the industry's prospects, and even the political environment.

Junk bond prices (like all bond prices) vary inversely with interest rates. For example, if the current interest rate for AAA 20-year bonds is 10%, you'd receive interest payments of $100 per bond each year. If interest rates rise to 12% for this class of bond, the market value of your bond would drop to about $833 ($100 ÷ 833 = 12%) because a buyer could obtain $120 for a $1,000 par value bond, given the higher interest rate.

No one would pay you $1,000 to receive $100 per year, when they could pay the same amount for the same-quality bond and get $120 per year in interest. Since bonds are purchased primarily for the income they pay, the underlying principal will fluctuate. Of course, lower interest rates work in your favor. For example, if market rates dropped to

8%, your bond would appreciate to about $1,250 ($100 ÷ $1,250 = 8%).

Junk bonds are speculative vehicles offering relatively high current yields and capital gains potential. The capital gains potential is tied to the general level of interest rates, the business prospects and financial condition of the issuer. If an issuer of junk bonds is able to reduce its outstanding liabilities sufficiently, it may improve its rating. A higher-rated bond of the same maturity will sell for a lower yield. In such a case, the junk bond would rise in value.

Junk bonds are speculations on both interest rates and the financial health of the underlying company. Therefore, they should not be considered long-term investments, as investment-grade bonds are. However, like other bonds, if you hold them to maturity (and the company does not go under) you will get back the full par value from the company.

 Junk bonds are suitable for retirement plans only as a small percentage of the overall assets of the plan. They should only be considered for inclusion in a portfolio able to undertake substantial risk.

Strengths

 Junk bonds pay very high current income. Junk bonds appreciate when interest rates fall. Junk bonds appreciate if the financial conditions of the underlying company improves.

Weaknesses

 Junk bonds are highly speculative. Both interest and principal are at risk if the issuer's financial condition deteriorates further. Junk bond prices will fall if interest rates rise. Junk bonds are volatile. The secondary market for junk bonds depends on widespread confidence in business and the economy. The value of junk bonds is subject to interest rate, political, economic, and market risk. Junk bonds offer no protection from inflation.

Tax Considerations

 Junk bond interest is taxed as ordinary income. Capital appreciation is also taxed as ordinary income since the 1986 Tax Reform Act eliminated capital gains preference.

Summing Up

Junk bonds have played a major role in the merger and acquisition mania of the 1980s. The 1987 insider trading scandals have cast a pall over the takeover market, but junk bonds continue to be very big business for Wall Street.

Junk bonds should be viewed as speculative vehicles. Many investors have turned to junk bonds to get higher yields as interest rates dropped from 1982 through 1986. However, don't be lulled into complacency by the good economic times.

 In times of economic growth defaults on bonds are minimal. However, if the tide turned to recession or inflation picked up the change could devastate the junk bond market quickly. Most investors should restrict their junk bond exposure to less than 15% of their total bond portfolio.

Convertible Bonds

CONVERTIBLE
BONDS

Good income

Fair safety

Fair liquidity

Fair inflation
hedge

No tax benefits

Moderate growth

Convertible bonds are a hybrid investment combining features of both common stocks and bonds. They are initially sold as debentures (bonds issued against a company's credit) with the right to convert to a fixed amount of common stock at a set price—usually, though not always, the stock of the underlying company. In cases where the issuing company holds a large interest in another company, the bonds may be convertible into shares of the other company.

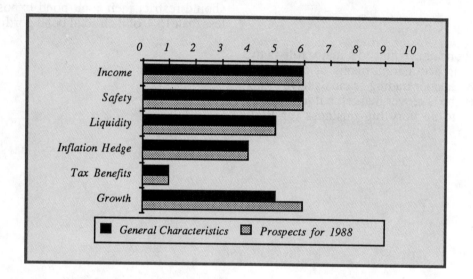

Convertibles offer the investor a higher, more secure income with the opportunity to participate in the growth of the underlying company. At first glance, it might appear that convertibles are the best of both worlds, but first glances can be deceiving. The interest paid is lower than is offered by comparable but unconvertible instruments. In other words, the price of the conversion feature is the lower interest you receive. In addition, the potential growth is also less than that offered by outright purchase of the common stock. The premium paid for the conversion privilege again mitigates potential gain.

Convertible bonds have a priority claim on the assets of the corporation over both its preferred and common stock in liquidation. Income from bonds is more secure than dividends because bond interest is a legal obligation of the company. Dividends are paid at the discretion of the directors of the corporation.

Because of their dual nature, convertible bonds have two aspects of value that must be considered: investment value and conversion value. The investment value is the price the bond would have without the conversion privilege. For example, to determine the investment value of an XYZ Corporation convertible bond compare it to a straight bond with the same coupon yield (for example, 8%) and same maturity.

An 8% convertible bond due in 20 years will sell for a higher price than a straight bond because of the conversion privilege. In adverse market conditions when the value of the common stock is negligible, the investment value of the convertible offers downside protection.

In normal markets, convertible bonds trade primarily on their conversion value. Conversion value is the current price of the underlying common stock multiplied by the number of shares into which the bond is convertible. For example, if XYZ Corporation's common stock is trading at $30 per share, and its 8% bond is convertible into 30 shares, the conversion value is $900 per bond.

When the convertible bond is trading for less than the conversion value (during a recession, for example), the convertible will trade like a bond rather than fluctuating with moves in the underlying stock. If the convertible is trading equal to or above the conversion value, it will trade like the underlying common stock.

Investment Potential

Convertible bonds provide you with higher income than the dividends of the underlying stock. Convertibles also offer capital gains potential if the value of the underlying common stock rises. The tradeoff is that you receive a lower current income than would be paid by an straight bond. Moreover, the potential capital gain is less than you would earn from purchase of the common stock.

Convertible bonds offer downside protection from a dropping stock market because they will never trade below their investment value. The tradeoff for the lower risk is lower returns than if you bought only a straight bond or common stock.

 Convertible bonds are well suited for conservative investors willing to forgo top returns in exchange for less risk. They are most appropriate for long-term objectives. They reduce the need for precise timing of the stock market since they pay good income while you wait for the common stock to rise. As such, they are excellent vehicles for retirement plans.

The capital gains potential affords you inflation protection that straight bonds do not. The biggest risk is an environment in which the stock market declines and interest rates rise. When interest rates rise bonds fall. Without the underlying common rising to support the price, a convertible will trade like a bond.

Convertibles are suitable for most retirement plans, including IRAs.

Strengths

 Convertibles offer higher income than provided by common stock. Potential exists for capital gains. There is a lower risk than with outright bonds or common stock. Convertible bonds have a priority claim on company assets in case of bankruptcy or other liquidation. Convertible bonds of major corporations are quite liquid. You also have the right to convert to the common stock at your option. Convertibles are rated by independent services such as Standard & Poor's and Moody's.

Weaknesses

 Income is lower than equivalent straight bonds. Capital gains are lower than would be realized by the underlying common stock. Most convertibles have "call" provisions that allow the company to redeem them after a specified time period. In addition to the market risk of falling prices, convertible bonds are subject to risk from adverse developments in the issuing company's business.

Tax Considerations

 Interest and dividends are taxed as ordinary income. The 1986 Tax Reform Act eliminates preferential tax treatment for long-term capital gains. As of 1988, all capital gains regardless of holding period are taxed as ordinary income.

One benefit is that gains resulting from conversion to common stock are not taxable unless the common stock is not that of the company that issued the convertible. Convertibles are suitable for most retirement plans, including IRAs.

Summing Up

Convertible securities offer a viable alternative for conservative risk-averse long-term investors. Foregoing some profit potential for greater safety makes good sense to many investors. Price information is widely available. There is extensive information and professional advice on convertibles. Professional management can be obtained through closed-end funds and mutual funds.

Convertible bonds have been the beneficiaries of the best of worlds: declining interest rates and rising stock prices. A decline in interest rates pushes up bond prices. A bull market in stock, raises the value of the underlying common stock.

With the continuation of low inflation, and low interest rates, a moderate growth environment will be very favorable to convertible bonds. It will be important to watch inflation indexes such as the Consumer Price Index. An annualized rate of 8–10% would be very negative. Federal Reserve policy is critical. The "easy money" environment is beneficial. Watch for increases in the discount rate as a negative.

Mutual Funds Bonds

Bond investing has historically been the domain of institutional investors. Proper bond investing is more difficult for the average investor than stocks. There is considerably less coverage of the intricacies of bond investing in the mass media. Even financial publications like Forbes, Business Week, *or* Money *devote more space to stocks than bonds. Perhaps most importantly though, it takes more money to purchase a well-diversified portfolio of individual bonds.*

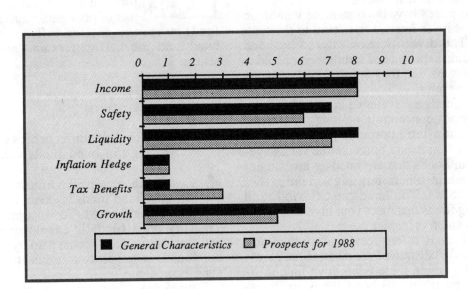

The high interest rates paid by bonds in the late 1970s and early 1980s generated increased interest in bonds by individual investors. Bond funds have enjoyed rapid growth in the rush to meet investor needs.

Bond funds are professionally managed pools of bonds that sell proportionate shares to the public. Net asset value is calculated at the end of each business day by totaling the market value of all bonds owned plus all other assets, such as cash, and subtracting all liabilities. This figure is then divided by the total number of shares outstanding.

You buy a no-load bond mutual fund (or any other type of no-load fund) at net asset value (NAV). A load fund is purchased at net asset value plus the sales charge, which may range from 2 to 8%. Some funds that call themselves "no load" assess a fee when you sell the fund (or even part of your holdings). Be sure to clarify what fees are charged prior to investing in any fund.

The largest bond mutual fund prices are covered in the *Wall Street Journal*. A number of computer databases carry up-to-date prices for most bond prices. These can be accessed with a personal computer. There is usually a charge for the time you are connected to the database.

The popularity of bond investing has led to the publication of investment advisory newsletters devoted exclusively to bonds and bond mutual funds. Both *Fortune* and *Money* magazines publish annual volumes listing the names and addresses of investment advisory newsletters.

Investment Potential

Bond funds are usually purchased for income. They are generally considered long-term investments. However, there is an increasing interest in trading bond funds as speculations on short-term changes in interest rate. Bond funds, like bonds, trade inversely to interest rates. When rates move higher, bond fund prices go down. When rates move lower, fund prices rise. The high front-end charges of load funds makes short-term trading impracticable for them.

Bond prices have become more volatile in recent years as interest rates tend to fluctuate more. The diversification offered by bond funds adds a measure of stability compared to single issues, but they won't move contrary to interest rates.

Bond funds are available in a wide variety. Some funds concentrate on long, intermediate, or short-term corporate, municipal, or Treasury bonds and notes. Some funds specialize in bonds that are rated as investment grade, while others buy high-yielding or "junk" bonds. You have great flexibility in selecting funds that meet your investment objectives and risk tolerance.

Bond funds offer greater safety than any single issue because of the diversification offered. However, there is no government insurance on them. All bond funds are registered with the SEC. They must meet strict financial and reporting requirements. Each fund must provide prospective investors with a prospectus that details information about the fund and its management.

Bond funds are appropriate investments for most retirement plans.

Strengths

Bonds funds offer professionally managed diversified portfolios to small investors. Many large investors also take advantage of this professional management. The variety of bond funds enables you to tailor your investment to meet your unique objectives and risk tolerance. Bond funds offer competitive current income. The

funds offer the potential for capital gains if interest rates fall. No-load funds can be traded for short-term capital gains on your expectations for the direction of interest rates. Bond funds are liquid investments.

Weaknesses

Bond funds are subject to market risk. If interest rates rise, fund prices will fall. Bond funds are also subject to the risk of poor performance by the funds investment advisor. Inflation will hurt bond fund prices. High fees may affect your return.

Tax Considerations

The tax consequences of investing in bond funds varies with the type of fund selected. The income paid by most municipal bond funds is exempt from federal taxes. The income paid by Treasury bond funds is exempt from state and local taxes. The income paid by corporate bond funds is subject to taxation at your ordinary income rate.

Capital gains from any type of bond fund is taxed at ordinary income rates. Capital losses offset capital gains. Excess capital losses can be carried forward.

Summing Up

Bond funds invested in long-term issues are more vulnerable to interest rate rises than funds concentrating on shorter maturities. The sharp bond market decline beginning in April 1987 demonstrated the additional risks that mutual fund investors face. When bond prices fell, the asset values of bond funds fell concomitantly. Investors moved to liquidate their bond funds. Many funds were forced to sell some of the bonds in their portfolios to raise sufficient cash to redeem their shares.

Mutual bond investors were actually hurting their own cause by selling so quickly.

The additional selling by the funds themselves pushed bonds lower faster than they might have otherwise have gone.

You should view mutual fund bond investing as a long-term proposition. Short-term selling on weakness becomes a self-defeating proposition.

Zero-Coupon Securities

Zero-coupon securities are fixed-income debt securities that sell at steep discount from face value and pay no interest at fixed intervals like most bonds. They pay full face value at maturity. You receive your return from the gradual appreciation of the security as it approaches maturity.

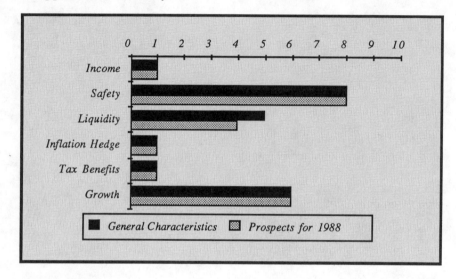

The market for zero-coupon bonds began in 1983 when Merrill Lynch introduced TIGRs (Treasury Investment Growth Certificates). Merrill stripped the interest coupons from the principal portion of the underlying Treasury bonds and sold each piece separately. Since then other brokerage firms have introduced competing products with acronyms like CAT or LION. Despite the various names, they are all essentially the same product.

In February 1985 the U.S. government stepped into the market with its own STRIPS (Separate Trading of Registered Interest and Principal of Securities). STRIPS are the safest zero-coupon security since they are backed directly by the U.S. government.

Zero-coupon securities issued by brokerage firms are also safe, but there is some risk. Typically the issuing brokerage firm places the underlying bonds in an escrow account with a major bank such as Manufacturer's Hanover or Morgan Guaranty—two big players in this market. It then sells certificates of varying maturities to investors. When the underlying bonds pay their interest, the brokers use those funds to pay off the certificates as they mature. Those certificates issued with the longest maturities are paid off when the underlying bond matures.

There are many types of zero-coupon issues:

- Corporate zeros are bonds backed solely by the credit of the underlying corporate issuer.
- Municipal zeros are based on underlying municipal bonds. Unlike other zeros, the interest is not taxable each year.
- Certificate of deposit zeros are issued by banks and savings and loans.
- Convertible zeros come in several varieties. The most common are those issued with a "put" option that enables the buyer

to convert the zero into common stock. Some convertible zeros are based on municipal bonds and are convertible into interest-paying bonds.

- Mortgage-backed zeros are secured by Fannie Maes, Ginnie Maes, and Freddie Macs. Just as straight mortgage-backed pass-throughs have the unique risk of early prepayments, so do these zeros. Therefore they tend to carry higher returns to compensate for the potential risk of early redemption.
- STRIPS are secured by Treasury bonds but are issued by brokers who place the bonds in escrow.
- STRIPS are issued directly by the U.S. Treasury Department and are the safest of all zeros. They therefore pay the lowest returns.

Zero-coupon issues are sold by leading full-service brokerage firms. Many banks and savings institutions now sell them also. Fees vary widely. In fact, the high fees associated with zeros when they were first introduced were the source of widespread complaints. As the market has grown and competition intensified, fees have dropped from as high as 5% to around 2% or less.

The fees are typically assessed as either dealer markup (the difference between what the dealer pays and what it sells to you for) or commissions. If you are buying in the secondary market, the zeros have been issued previously and commissions are typically assessed. New issues are usually sold on a markup basis.

Prices are quoted in major business dailies like the *Wall Street Journal* or *Investor's Daily*. The popularity of this device has resulted in coverage by large-circulation financial publications like *Money* and *Changing Times*.

Investment Potential

The chief attraction of zero-coupon issues is the ability to lock in a fixed compounding rate of return for a specific period of time. When you buy an interest-paying bond, you're never sure what return you will be able to earn when you reinvest the interest you receive. Interest rates fluctuate widely and may be lower or higher than the rate paid by the bond itself.

The low initial investment and known return make zeros popular vehicles for people who need a specific sum of money at some point in the future. For example, suppose that zero munis are available today at $10 with a maturity date of 30 years. Each bond has a face value of $1,000. That means that for $10,000 invested today, you know that your child, your company, or anyone else you select (even yourself at retirement) will hold tax-free bonds that can be cashed in for $1 million in precisely 30 years.

Zeros enable investors to lock in the power of compounding for their savings.

While the gains on zeros appear to be from growth, it is considered interest income for tax purposes. In fact, the IRS requires you to pay taxes on the "imputed interest" (the theoretical income) earned each year on a zero-coupon bond, *even though you don't receive interest from the bond itself!* Imputation is the IRS's tool for converting capital gain to ordinary income that can be taxed at a higher rate.

Zero coupons should be viewed primarily as long-term investments. Because they pay no current interest, every change in interest rates greatly affects a zero's future value because of the compounding that is (or is not) achieved. This makes their price highly volatile when they are traded on the secondary market. If interest rates fall after purchase, the zeros will appreciate, Although zeros are not usually bought for capital gains potential.

This inherent volatility is increased when you buy zeros "on the margin"—using borrowed money. This strategy would only be viable for someone looking to trade the bonds for capital gains. Even so, better trading vehicles are available.

Since most buyers of zeros plan to hold them to maturity, the active secondary market is small. Treasury-based zeros are somewhat more liquid than corporate and municipals.

Zeros vary widely in degree of safety. STRIPS are of course the safest since they are issued and backed by the U.S. Treasury Department directly. Other zeros secured by

Treasuries are held in escrow accounts. The small additional risk of problems developing with the issuer or the escrow bank results in slightly higher yields.

Corporate zeros carry a substantial extra premium since the buyer is subject to risk of total loss in the case of default by the issuer. A buyer of a 20-year interest-paying bond will at least have received interest for 10 years if the issuer defaults after that time. The holder of a zero issued by the same company however will lose the entire investment.

 Municipal zeros that have "call" features present the peculiar case of a zero that defeats the whole purpose of zero investing. If you need a specific amount of money at a set date in the future, you would not want to buy a zero that can be "called" earlier.

Municipal and corporate zeros are rated by independent services such as Standard & Poor's or Moody's. Since the risk of total loss is possible through zero investing, credit ratings are particularly important.

Inflation represents substantial risk for zeros. Once you've purchased a zero, its potential return for you will not change regardless of the underlying inflation rate. Inflation will diminish the purchasing power of the money you receive on maturity.

Zero-coupon securities are very popular with retirement programs that enable you to defer taxes on income. Buying zeros in this manner enable you to avoid paying taxes on "phantom income" until you elect to withdraw the funds.

Strengths

 Low initial investment is required. A $1,000 twenty-year bond paying 12% would only cost about $100. Yield to maturity is locked in. This takes the guesswork out of potential return from reinvestment of interest. Investor knows the exact cashout value of investment on maturity date.

Zeros offer convenient automatic compounding of interest.

Weaknesses

 Taxes are due annually on interest as it accrues even though interest is not paid out to zero bond holder. Zeros are more volatile than interest-paying bonds because the return on future compounded interest increases more with an interest rate rise and decreases more on an interest rate fall. Purchasing power of bonds may be impaired by inflation during holding years. Corporate zeros have greater risk than interest-paying bonds because you never receive any money until maturity. If the company goes bankrupt the day before your bond matures, you stand to lose your investment plus all accumulated interest. There is a less liquid secondary market for zeros than regular bonds.

Tax Considerations

 Zero-coupon securities present an investor with a unique tax situation. You are required to pay tax annually on the interest that has accrued to your bond even though you have not actually received payment. This "imputed" interest payment is a major drawback to zeros.

Interest from municipal zeros is exempt from federal taxes. Interest on Treasury zeros is exempt from state and local taxes.

Interest is taxed at ordinary income rates. The 1986 Tax Reform Act eliminated the preferential capital gains treatment. Capital gains are taxed at ordinary income rates.

Summing Up

Zero-coupon securities have grown rapidly since their recent introduction. Issuers have developed a number of innovative products, and even more will be introduced in the future.

Zeros are bonds that are not appropriate for investors who need current income. They are ideal vehicles for setting aside money to grow at a compounded rate for some purpose in the future. Many financial planners include zeros in programs designed to cover future college costs or other substantial fixed costs in the future.

Because the interest is taxable as accrued, zeros are best suited for retirement accounts where taxes are deferred.

Commercial Mortgage Securities (CMSs)

COMMERCIAL
MORTGAGE
SECURITIES

Good income

Fair safety

Poor liquidity

Poor inflation
hedge

No tax benefits

Moderate growth

Commercial mortgage securities (CMSs) are debt instruments secured by commercial real estate. Commercial mortgage securities are very similar to the more common residential mortgage securities. Syndicators pool a group of commercial mortgages to back securities sold to the public. For example, in April 1987 the brokerage firm Salomon Brothers sold $250 million worth of 12-year notes backed by the Chrysler Building in New York City.

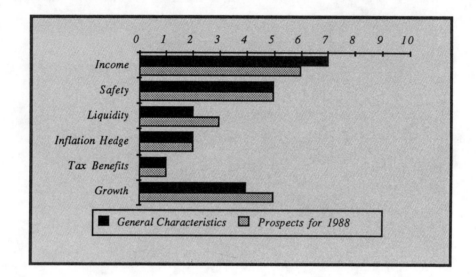

Over 30% of the $1.7 billion in outstanding residential mortgages have been converted into securities for sale to the public. Most fixed-income investors are well aware of the alternatives to bonds that mortgage-backed securities such as Ginnie Maes or Fannie Maes offer. Its only been recently that Wall Street has turned to the commercial real estate market in an attempt to create another product of interest to individual investors.

The residential mortgage market has experienced rapid growth over the past 10 years. The ability to "securitize" (package a pool of mortgages to back securities sold directly to the public) is much easier with residential mortgages because they are fairly standard and often guaranteed by an agency of the federal government. Commercial mortgages are much more individualized and are without federal guarantees.

As a result it is more difficult to put together a marketable product. Many commercial mortgage securities sold to date have been offered to private investors who meet stringent financial requirements. More public offerings can be expected in the future as the market becomes more established. The market for residential mortgages has been one of the fastest-growing financial markets in history. Although financial experts do not foresee the same explosive growth for commercial mortgages, they do look for substantial growth from this sector over the next five years.

 You buy CMSs through a licensed broker. The market at this point in time is small (only about 4% of the $800 billion of commercial mortgages outstanding are securitized). In light of the thin market, CMSs should be viewed as long-term investments. Major independent financial services like Standard & Poor's and Moody's have started rating CMSs so it's wise to check these sources or ask your advisor's opinion on CMS quality before investing.

Investment Potential

CMSs offer good current income. They are mortgage-backed securities that trade like bonds. Thus the principal value of the underlying security will fluctuate inversely with interest rates. When interest rates rise, CMSs will fall in value. Capital growth, therefore, is derived when interest rates decline. High volatility in interest rates results in wide price swings for fixed-income securities like CMSs. This relatively new market is quite thin. Their illiquidity increases risk.

Conventional mortgage-backed securities are considered relatively safe investments. Most CMSs have been issued with a third party guaranteeing payment of principal and interest. For example, the Chrysler Building offering mentioned earlier was guaranteed by Fuji Bank.

In addition, any offering to the general public will carry a rating by one of the independent services such as Standard and Poor's or Moody's. These organizations evaluate the financial strength of the issuers. You can minimize the risk of CMSs to your portfolio by buying only those issues that meet high-quality (investment-grade) rating requirements. Investment-grade CMSs will pay lower current income in exchange for greater safety. CMSs offered to the general public must be registered with the SEC and meet government regulations for such offerings.

In addition to the risk engendered by interest rate fluctuations, CMSs are subject to other risk factors. For example, business problems of major tenants of commercial rental property may drive down the principal value. Political and economic factors germaine to the property backing a CMS may adversely affect its price. CMSs provide no protection against inflation.

Strengths

 Commercial mortgage securities offer a higher yield than equivalent residential mortgages or bonds with similar maturities. Most CMSs are secured by third-party guarantees of principal and interest. The underlying property serves as collateral for CMSs. CMSs yield capital gains in a falling interest rate environment.

Weaknesses

 Commercial mortgage securities offer no inflation protection. There is no government insurance or guarantees for CMSs. CMSs are relatively new securities, and the market is illiquid. Some mortgages in the pool may mature before others as a result of refinancing. As a result you may receive a return of principal earlier than expected, lowering your monthly interest payments.

Tax Considerations

 There are no special tax preferences for commercial mortgage securities. Interest and capital gains are taxed at your ordinary income levels. Since regular payments may represent a mix of interest and "return of principal," taxes are assessed only on that portion representing the interest payment.

Summing Up

Wall Street is enthusiastic about the potential for commercial mortgage securities. That enthusiasm has not be shared by the investing public to date. Major problems still need to be resolved before CMSs take their place alongside the residential "pass-through" mortgage securities described earlier.

However, that very "newness" offers you the chance to obtain excellent yields with moderate risk. Yields relative to competitive products will come down as CMSs become more widely accepted as good-quality alternatives to bonds.

Commercial mortgage securities are a good income-paying investment. They offer capital gains potential in a declining interest rate environment.

Top High-grade Tax-exempt Funds

1. Stein Roe Managed Muni
2. DMC Tax-free Income—USA Series
3. United Municipal Bond
4. Hutton National Muni Bond
5. Mutual of Omaha Tax-free Income
6. Financial Tax-free Income Shares
7. Seligman Tax-exempt—National
8. New England Tax-exempt Income
9. National Securities Tax-exempt
10. Cigna Municipal Bond

Top High-yield Tax-exempt Funds

1. Vanguard Muni Bond—High Yield
2. Fidelity High-yield Muni Bond
3. Stein Roe High-yield Muni Bond
4. Pru-Bache High-yield Muni Bond
5. IDS High-yield Tax-exempt
6. Merrill Lynch Muni—High Yield
7. GIT Tax-free—High Yield
8. Alliance Tax-free Shares
9. Value Line Tax-exempt—High Yield
10. Massachusetts Financial Managed High-yield Muni Bond

Top High-grade Bond Funds

 1. Bond Fund of America
 2. United Bond
 3. Axe-Houghton Income
 4. Hutton Bond and Income
 5. Sigma Income Shares
 6. Alliance Bond—Monthly Income Portfolio
 7. Massachusetts Financial Bond
 8. Hancock Bond
 9. Investment Quality Interest
10. IDS Select

Top High-yield Bond Funds

 1. Financial Bond Shares—High Yield
 2. Fidelity High Income
 3. Pacific Horizon High Yield
 4. Kemper High Yield
 5. Delchester Bond
 6. Investment Portfolio—High Yield
 7. IDS Bond
 8. United High Income
 9. High Yield
10. Boston Managed Income

CHAPTER 12

REAL ESTATE

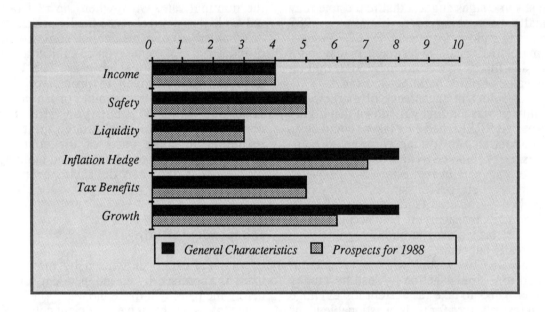

A GLANCE AHEAD

Real estate represents a secure, solid conservative investment for most Americans. Although its fortunes have fluctuated over the years, the long-term trend in prices has been up. And unlike the stock, bond, or gold markets, periods of price weakness in real estate are not cause for concern, because there are always areas that seem to buck the trend.

This perception of real estate as a bastion of value is at least partially due to the fact that there is no central auction market where prices are set daily. Each piece of real estate is unique. When you want to sell a share of IBM, you know what price you can get today. When you go to sell your house or another piece of real estate, the selling price is not sure. Even after getting a professional appraisal, there may be no one who wants to buy at the adjudged "fair price."

In this chapter, you'll discover the many types of real estate and the ways you can invest in it. You'll learn:

- How the 1986 Tax Reform Act has changed real estate limited partnerships
- About real estate investment trusts (REITs)
- Why you should treat your home as an investment
- The pros and cons of owning rental property
- The varying degrees of liquidity offered by different types of real estate investments

209

REAL ESTATE IS A LONG-TERM INVESTMENT

The advertising slogan "Buy land—they're not making any more of it" sums up the "can't lose" attitude that many real estate investors had in the 1970s. But as happens with all "perfect" investments at some point, the early 1980s proved that even real estate is subject to sharp downdrafts.

Analysts have identified a number of cycles in real estate. The most widely accepted one is the 18-year cycle. It peaked in 1979. The ideal trough would be in 1988. At least some signs suggest that real estate may finally be probing for a bottom as 1987 draws to a close. In August, RREEF Fund—a major real estate investment manager for pension funds—wrote down by $100 million the value of office buildings it owns.

This reluctant acceptance of marketplace reality (it was the first writedown that highly respected RREEF had ever taken) could be an important step in forcing widespread reappraisals of bloated real estate portfolios. Since managers in real estate don't have to compare their performance to an easily watched barometer (such as the S&P) to which stock managers are held accountable, it has been far too easy to blithely ignore what was really happening to prices.

The RREEF writedown has been compared to a similar action by leading money center banks to take (as current losses) huge loan loss reserves for their questionable loans to third world countries. Painful at first, but certainly much healthier for the long pull.

Risks

Most real estate investments suffer from liquidity problems. While certainly not impossible, it is rare to be able to sell a piece of real estate and get your cash out quickly.

Real estate investments are more subject to regional influences than are many other types of investment. For example, from 1984 through 1986 oil prices collapsed, devastating many heretofore rapid-growth metropolitan areas such as Dallas and Houston. The situation got so bad in Houston that thousands of apartment units were actually plowed under! Oil companies in the area were also hurt, but many had already diversified into other businesses, which helped stem stock price falls.

Real estate is very sensitive to the real interest rate. The real rate is the nominal rate (the published or announced rate minus the rate of inflation). Higher real rates depress real estate prices. It is important to note the significance of the distinction between real and nominal rates. In the late 1970s, nominal rates went well into double digits. Real estate continued to boom right along, however, because the inflation rate was rising faster than the nominal rate. Only when the real rate moved higher did real estate finally peak.

Whether you own residential, commercial, or industrial real estate, you're subject to the whims of the political process. The U.S. Supreme Court moved to protect private landowners' rights in a number of landmark decisions in 1987, but you still run considerable risk of loss through arbitrary rezoning. In some parts of the country, anti-development forces have forced building moratoriums that can devastate property values for years.

Independent Ratings

Any real estate purchased by mortgage loans is appraised by an independent source before the bank will make the loan. The bank wants to ensure that it has sufficient collateral in the property. It is a good idea to have any property appraised before entering any binding purchase agreement. You may lose your deposit if you haven't protected yourself in advance.

Compared to Other Assets

In November 1985, *Money* magazine published the results of a study showing that stocks and bonds are top-performing assets when inflation is 4% or less. Not surprisingly, gold is the best performer in double-digit inflation. Real estate also outperforms financial assets during very high inflation, but really shines during moderate inflation of 7% to 9%.

Portfolio for Real Estate: 10 to 20%

 Allocate as much as 20% in 1988.

 Allocate as little as 10% in 1988.

Rental Real Estate

RENTAL REAL ESTATE

Fair income

Fair safety

Poor liquidity

Excellent inflation hedge

Good tax benefits

Good growth

The most common type of real estate investment, other than one's private residence, is the purchase of developed property to earn income through rentals. Such rentals can be either single- or multiple-family residences, office buildings, or even industrial property.

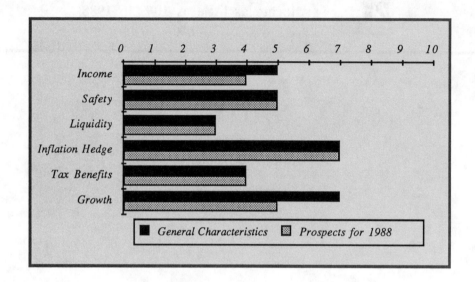

Historically, real estate has been valued for the cash flow returns that can be achieved. The fundamental value of any given real estate project was considered a function of the cash flow that could be earned from rentals. This conservative valuation approach was lost in the high-flying inflation of the 1970s. Rather than carefully assess the future value of cash flows, investors bid prices steadily higher, betting that prices would continue to rise.

By the late 1970s, most real estate deals offered negative cash flows for years into the future. The idea was that appreciation of the property combined with preferential tax treatment featuring substantial writeoffs against your ordinary income would yield above-average returns. To their chagrin, many smaller investors discovered that nothing, not even real estate, goes straight up in price.

When land prices began to flatten out and even fall after 1980, mortgage defaults rose to record highs. No longer did it seem like such a great idea to buy a rental property in which the rents did not even cover the costs of the mortgage.

This mania to buy at any price was largely "tax driven." The limited partnership industry was based on passing through the great tax benefits to individual investors. You could write off unlimited interest expenses and negative cash flows, and accelerate depreciation to offset other income. Far too many investors focused on the tax benefits rather than on the economic value of the properties.

Tax law changes, beginning in 1984 and culminating in the major 1986 reform, curtailed these tax advantages while encouraging income and growth investing through lower tax rates. Real estate is once again beginning to appeal to investors for solid economic value reasons.

The massive overbuilding that accompanied the real estate mania of the late 1970s has left some types of real estate, such as office buildings, severely depressed. However, some undervalued, conservatively financed projects are being marketed. In fact, the limited partnership industry has turned from tax shelter selling to emphasizing positive cash flows and conservative financing.

Income-producing real estate is widely marketed by the industry. Your real estate agent or full-service broker can provide plenty of information on current deals. A commission is charged for handling the transaction. This fee can be substantial. If you are a regular customer or large investor, the fee is usually negotiable.

Investment Potential

Investing in income-producing real estate is a long-term project. Capitalization rates comparable to the yields offered by competitive income-producing investments are available if you are patient and willing to search out undervalued situations.

Real estate prices tend to be less volatile than more liquid markets such as bonds or stocks. You can use leverage in buying real estate to just about any level that is comfortable for you. Keep in mind, though, that the new tax law limits the amount of interest that can be deducted. The more highly leveraged the deal, the greater the risk.

Income-producing real estate is illiquid. Occasionally you'll be able to find a buyer in a matter of days, but it is not unusual for properties to remain on the market for months before a buyer is found.

Many different types of income-producing properties are available. Most individual investors concentrate on rental housing, but commercial properties such as shopping centers, or industrial sites can also offer good income.

Capital growth in real estate has been much less dynamic in the 1980s than the 1970s. However, over the long term real estate has historically proven an excellent vehicle for

growth. Combined with a good income, it is an excellent inflation hedge.

Strengths

Rental real estate provides good current income and also offers good capital growth potential. Prices tend to be less volatile than in auction markets such as bonds or stocks. In addition, the wide variety of rental projects offers great flexibility in finding one that fits your financial needs and risk tolerance. Finally, you can leverage your real estate investment, and real estate is an excellent inflation hedge.

Weaknesses

Rental real estate does have weaknesses. It is illiquid, and rental real estate investors are subject to political risks such as the imposition of rent controls, zoning changes, or tax increases. Finally, being a landlord can be costly and time consuming.

Tax Considerations

A major goal of the 1986 Tax Reform Act is to return real estate investment decisions to considerations based on economic value rather than tax avoidance. If you are an active manager of your property (as opposed to buying it through limited partnerships or other arrangements) there are still some tax advantages. For example, an active participant in the management of his or her real estate rental properties can deduct up to $25,000 in losses from other income. This amount diminishes, however, if your annual income is above $100,000.

The tax law is complex in this area. You should consult with your tax advisor for full details for your particular situation.

Summing Up

Over the long term, the return to value-driven real estate investing will provide a safer, less volatile haven for investors. The low interest rates bode well for real estate's prospects over the next few years. However, the heady days of buying virtually anything and making huge profits in a matter of months are gone. Tax law changes, a booming stock market, and the still very depressed state of many real estate syndicates have put a cap on the unrealistic real estate speculative euphoria of the 1970s.

Carefully researched, conservatively financed, positive cash flow projects should appreciate in value as well as pay competitive current income.

Raw Land Real Estate

Investing in raw, undeveloped land received a boost from the 1986 Tax Reform Act. Now many national syndicators are putting together partnerships to buy undeveloped land that may be ripe of commercial development in the near future. The very fact that raw land is often the least expensive way to buy real estate has triggered increased interest among individual investors.

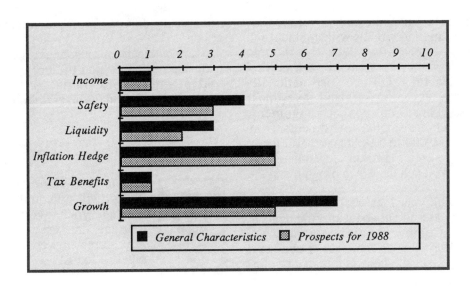

For many years real estate appeared to many investors to be the only investment without downside risk. Then the boom of the 1970s gave way to the reality of the 1980s. Real estate values, which had climbed steadily for years, suddenly plummeted across the country. High interest rates, disinflation, and illiquidity combined to make real estate much less attractive. With the passage of the 1986 Tax Reform Act, many pundits predicted further weakness.

 Few areas came in for more pessimistic assessment than raw land. In the high-flying 1970s, everything seemed a good investment. Investors bought land in Hawaii sight unseen. Only later did they learn that large patches of barren lava were not such hot investments. Thousands of investors still own acres of desert or swamp-land that had been marketed as future vacation spots.

Raw land has typically been the domain of developers. They would buy prospective land sites and set them aside ("bank them") until they could move ahead with their projects. The high interest rates of the 1970s made this approach very expensive.

Developers then approached syndicators to package raw land and sell it to individual investors, as a method for "banking it" for later use. However, before 1986 no improvements could be made on the land after it was purchased or investors would lose the favorable capital gains tax treatment. They could only wait for the price to move up through inflation or until demand from expanding communities pushed the price higher.

Paradoxically, the elimination of preferential tax treatment for capital gains has generated renewed interest in raw land investing. Now syndicators buy raw land and sell it to investors with the prospect that improvements will be made to increase its value more quickly. Rather than waiting for the market to come to them, syndicators work to increase the land value through subdividing it, bringing in utilities, building access roads, and arranging building permits with local governments. The raw land is thus converted into made-to-order residential, industrial, or commercial sites.

Syndication deals are typically local arrangements financed and developed by companies and individuals with contacts and knowledge in the area. Recently, though, some large syndicators have begun putting together deals that are marketed nationally through real estate brokers and investment advisors. These national arrangements generally require smaller investments, from as little as $1,000 to $10,000 to participate. Some full-service brokerage houses are preparing to launch their own programs in the near future.

Check with your local real estate agent or your broker to find out about specific deals in your area. Commissions are normally assessed to pay the salespeople. Local real estate agents are the best source of price information on respective properties.

Investment Potential

Raw land is a long-term investment. Even the new syndication deals suggest you plan on a minimum holding period of five to seven years. If the economy slows down or local regulations change, that wait could be much longer.

Raw land offers the opportunity for capital gains. Normally it pays no income. In fact, because you usually put down only a fraction of the purchase price, there is a cash outflow for interest payments until the property is sold. This leverage adds to the potential return.

Land prices are not quoted in an active daily auction market so it is difficult to ascertain the true price in the short term. Many factors can affect the desirability of the property in any one area. The general national economy, local economic developments, political

events, and pending tax law changes all affect land prices.

Real estate, and especially raw land, is an illiquid investment. It may take months to sell even attractive parcels. Raw land is more flexible than other types of real estate because it can be put to a variety of uses, from residential to industrial and commercial, depending on demand.

You can obtain an independent appraisal of the value of any property by hiring a professional real estate appraiser. However, getting an appraised value does not necessarily ensure finding a buyer at that price.

Most syndications must be registered either with the state in which the project is being sold, or with the SEC for interstate projects. A prospectus is usually available for review prior to investing.

Strengths

Raw land offers substantial capital growth potential. You can leverage your investment, and mortgage interest rates are usually much lower than other types of loans.

Weaknesses

Raw land has some weaknesses. First, it is illiquid. It is also subject to political vagaries. For example, the land could be rezoned to much less lucrative uses after your purchase. Moreover, investment in syndications risks poor judgment by the syndicator. And it may take years for the project to become economically viable.

Tax Considerations

No special tax benefits apply to raw land investments. Capital gains are taxed at your ordinary income rates. Limited partnership raw land investments generate passive income or losses that offset other passive income or losses.

Summing Up

Many people are boosting the investment potential of raw land. Many of the same people were behind the "vacation home in a resort area" boomlet that cost many investors thousands. Keep in mind that developers and salespeople put the best face on the potential for their projects. And even the best-sounding project may be held up in the courts for years before getting off the ground.

Raw land is the riskiest type of real estate investment. There is little downside protection if anticipated growth does not develop in the region of the project. Liquidity is always a problem.

Raw land is attracting more interest now that capital gains have been eliminated. You're no longer stuck with the dilemma of having to give up preferential tax treatment if improvements are made. Sometimes even minor improvements can enhance a property's value.

Residential Real Estate

The largest and most important purchase in the lives of many people is their home. In years past, such purchases were not thought of as investments as much as just a secure place to live. However, times are changing. High inflation and the resultant explosion in real estate prices propelled many people's homes into becoming the major asset of their personal wealth.

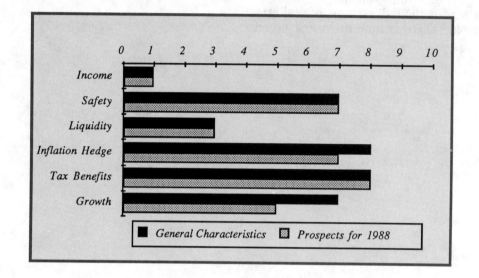

The 1986 Tax Reform Act further enhances the value of your personal residence as an investment. Because consumer interest is no longer deductible, home equity loans are becoming a major force in consumer spending habits. If you own your home and have sufficient equity in it, you can borrow at far lower interest rates than you pay for credit card and personal loans and use that money to pay off those loans. The interest on your equity loan is also tax deductible, giving you a double benefit as a homeowner.

Many investment "gurus" got their start with purchases of their own homes. As the price of their house rose, they were able to parlay the additional equity into other investments.

Most financial advisors quantify all investment returns in terms of capital gains and yields. But homeownership affords a psychic profit to many people that is more important than all the potential monetary profits! Homeownership affords a sense of security, a fixed known monthly payment (unless your mortgage has an adjustable interest rate), and an opportunity to increase its value and your potential profit through your efforts.

Homeownership gives you a way to begin to accumulate wealth at an early stage in your life. The demand for housing is increasing as the "baby boomers" become adults and start their own families. The supply of housing is not meeting this demand, though, because government red tape and other factors are slowing growth.

The housing market is very flexible. There are numerous financing options; different types of housing, from single-family homes to condominiums and cooperatives; and a wide range of prices, depending on location. Although you have no guarantee that residential real estate prices will continue to move higher, ownership itself conveys certain advantages that don't show up on your financial balance sheet. For example, many banks consider homeownership a sign of stability and are more likely to make consumer loans or approve credit card applications.

Although you can buy a home yourself, the complex laws of different localities make it far more prudent to go through a licensed real estate agent. There will be a commission charge. The fee is often negotiable. Using an agent will prevent unpleasant, time-consuming and costly problems that may crop up later over incorrectly completed paperwork.

Investment Potential

Homeownership is a long-term proposition. Your first objective should be securing comfortable, convenient living quarters. That goal does not conflict with the chance for long-term capital growth. Buying a home in a growing, dynamic community affords a good opportunity for future growth.

Every community is different. Some areas are declining for various reasons. Others, which may be just as convenient, may be attracting people. Your real estate agent should be able to tell you about growth patterns in the locales that are of interest.

Residential home prices are not usually volatile. The expenses involved in buying a home make short-term investing impractical. Also residential real estate suffers the same liquidity problems that investment real estate has. You simply cannot be assured of a quick sale at market prices.

Homes have been a very good store of value in virtually all economic environments. Homes have become one of the very best inflation hedges.

Strengths

Residential real estate offers secure long-term capital growth potential, and fulfills one of the basic requirements of life: shelter. Moreover, the interest on home equity loans is still tax deductible. Your ability to borrow against your home equity affords great flexibility for undertaking other investments. And residential real estate is an excellent inflation hedge.

Weaknesses

Residential real estate is illiquid. In addition, you are subject to substantial economic risk if your area is rezoned or other areas are favored for growth.

Tax Considerations

The 1986 Tax Reform Act confirmed the importance of homeownership in the United States. Although many deductions were eliminated, homeownership maintained the deductibility of mortgage interest and property taxes. You can avoid taxes on capital gains by reinvesting in a home of equal or greater worth. If you are over 55, you are eligible for a one-time exemption for the profits realized on the sale of your principal residence. Homeownership itself is a valuable retirement vehicle. You cannot buy a home through retirement plans, however.

Summing Up

There is little likelihood that the American dream of homeownership will fade. Although there are no guarantees of future performance, homeownership should continue to provide an excellent store of value for most people.

REITs

The beneficial tax treatment of homeownership will enhance the attractiveness of real estate investment trusts (REITs). REITs are companies that pool investor money to invest in real estate properties or loans. They are required to pay out nearly all income received in the form of dividends to shareholders. They resemble mutual funds as they invest in a diversified portfolio and distribute income as dividends. Their structure is similar to closed-end funds because they do not stand ready to redeem shares at net asset value.

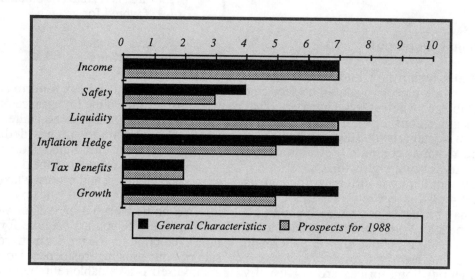

Investing in real estate presents two main problems for the average investors: illiquidity and the need for substantial capital for most multifamily or commercial properties. Wall Street's answer to these problems is the real estate investment trust (REIT).

Prices of REITs fluctuate like common stock and are determined by supply and demand rather than by net asset value. Many investors consider this a key favorable attribute because it is possible to buy REITs at a discount to the value of the underlying portfolio of properties.

REITs were very popular in the late 1960s and early 1970s as real estate rose in price. Many REITs bid up in price to multiples that were unrealistic in retrospect. REITs were viewed as a hedge against inflation. However, in the recession of 1973–1974 REITs joined many other stocks as prices dropped sharply. Some REITs were unable to weather the storm and went into bankruptcy. The severe shakeout in REITs has taken years to overcome, though they are once again being included in the portfolios of major institutions.

Although most REITs operate indefinitely, reinvesting proceeds from one liquidated project into another, "self-liquidating" REITs have a finite life. Typically they are structured to liquidate all properties in seven to ten years (or earlier, at the discretion of the management) and to distribute the proceeds to shareholders.

REITs are purchased through licensed stock brokerage firms. Many full-service firms have analysts who specialize in the field and provide regular research updates. A commission is charged for handling the transaction.

Investment Potential

REITs invest either directly in real estate properties or in mortgages. Some specialize in one or the other while others divide their portfolios between the two types. REITs that invest solely in loans pay higher dividend yields. Those invested primarily in real estate equity offer greater capital growth potential.

Since REITs are liquid investments, they can be long- or short-term investments. Keep in mind that short-term trading incurs higher transaction costs that will affect your return. Also, the underlying asset, real estate, takes time to realize its full investment potential.

REITs have had a very volatile history. During periods of inflation, they tend to outperform the market as a whole, providing a good hedge. However, volatile interest rates and the economy can cause wide price swings. The high dividend yields offer some downside protection. Those yields, though, depend on the stability of the underlying portfolio. Defaults in the portfolio can deal you a double whammy because the income drops as well as the price.

REITs offer you good flexibility in choosing the type of real estate to invest in. For example, different REITs tend to specialize in different types of real estate. If you are interested in commercial real estate, look to those REITs that concentrate in that area. Others specialize in industrial properties, multifamily rental dwellings, or even geographical areas.

All REITs must register with the SEC and provide annual financial reports. Most full-service brokerage firms provide research opinions on the prospects for individual REITs, but no widely accepted service rates their financial condition.

It is important to remember that when you buy an REIT you are not making a direct investment in real estate. You are buying real estate investment expertise, in the form of the company's management. Therefore, even if real estate in general is appreciating, poor management could limit your profits. However, good management can provide protection when the market is falling.

Strengths

 REITs provide a liquid method for investing in real estate. The minimum required investment is small, and dividend income is high. REITs give you a diversified real estate portfolio that minimizes the risk from any one property. And REITs are not required to pay corporate taxes. Therefore, you avoid double taxation of dividends. Finally, REITs provide a good hedge against inflation.

Weaknesses

 The management of REITs may be poor or inefficient, hurting your profit potential. A poor real estate market will knock down REIT prices even if the stock market in general is moving higher. Also, the underlying portfolio is illiquid. It may take months to sell troubled properties. In addition, the dividend yield varies, and in a negative environment REITs may sell at a sharp discount to the value of the underlying assets.

Tax Considerations

 Dividends and capital gains are taxed at your ordinary income rates. However, part of the dividend may be considered return of capital and therefore not taxable.

REITs are appropriate investments for most retirement plans.

Summing Up

After living under the dark cloud of poor and volatile performance for many years, REITs are gaining wider acceptance once again. The 1986 Tax Reform Act eliminated the benefits of most tax shelter limited partnerships that had competed with REITs in bidding for properties.

It is important to understand the type of REIT you are considering. Brokers too often sell all REITs as plays on real estate itself. Yet some REITs specialize in making loans. Others buy properties directly. The latter type, called *equity REITs*, are more direct investments in the direction of real estate prices. Since inflation often boosts real estate prices but also pushes up interest rates, a mortgage REIT will tend to drop in price even though land prices are rising. The loans they make are just like bonds. When interest rates rise, the value of the loan goes down.

Real Estate Limited Partnerships

Before the 1986 Tax Reform Act, the business form known as limited partnership *was widely used for tax shelter investments. Although there are many types of tax shelters, the most common was organized around real estate investment.*

RELPS

Good income

Fair safety

Poor liquidity

Good inflation hedge

Some tax benefits

Moderate growth

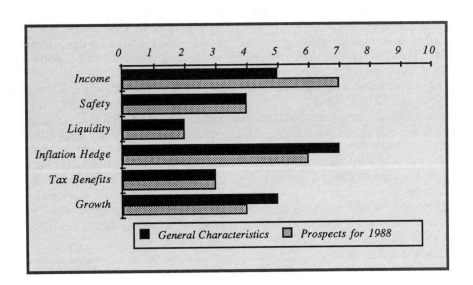

There are two major ways to organize joint business projects. Corporations are legal entities registered with state governments. They have their own legal identity, pay taxes, and assume a wide range of legal and financial responsibilities.

The other major form is the partnership. In a partnership, many legal obligations pass through to the individual owners of the enterprise. The most important difference is that losses that exceed the financial means of the partnership become the liability of the individual owners.

This liability exposure deters most investors from participating in various ventures in which they do not have direct expertise or involvement. The form of business organization called the *limited partnership* arose as an answer to this problem.

Many ventures require capital far beyond the resources of a single investor. For example, many apartment buildings, office buildings, and industrial projects are too expensive or risky for an entrepreneur to fund.

A general partner will organize a partnership to fund a project. To convince outside investors to contribute capital, the general partner exempts the limited partners from some of the risks and liabilities involved in the business. In return, the limited partners entrust the actual day-to-day operations to the general partner.

Before the 1986 Tax Reform Act, the most popular limited partnership was one that invested in real estate. Previously, real estate investment had many tax advantages that were not available to other investments. For example, accelerated depreciation, investment tax credits, and interest deductibility over and above the amount of investment were given favorable tax treatment. Multiple writeoffs were common features of real estate partnerships. The deductions generated by these tax shelters could be used to offset earned or investment income.

This has changed with the new tax law. Now real estate limited partnerships (RELPs) are geared to producing "passive" income that can be offset with the passive losses produced by previous tax shelter investments!

Passive income-generating real estate partnerships are called PIGs. They've become big business.

Real estate limited partnerships are either private or public offerings. Private offerings are not registered with the Securities and Exchange Commission (SEC). They are restricted in the number of investors who may participate. In addition, strict income and wealth requirements must be met.

Public limited partnerships are registered with the SEC. They are subject to stringent financial and disclosure rules. A prospectus that has been filed with the SEC must be provided to all prospective investors.

Limited partnerships are sold by major full-service brokerage firms as well as by smaller specialty firms. Normally the salespeople are compensated by the general partner out of revenues generated by the sales. You are still paying a sales fee, it is just paid indirectly. After all, the assets of the partnership are yours on a proportionate basis. These fees can be quite high. They should be carefully checked out in advance.

Investment Potential

Real estate limited partnerships offer the average investor a chance to participate in very large real estate projects that he or she might not otherwise be able to afford. The objectives are twofold: (1) generation of current passive income and (2) potential capital gains stemming from property appreciation.

Many conservatively financed deals (less than 50% of the partnerships assets are financed with borrowed money) offer good income that can be offset by other limited partnership income (such as previous tax shelter-oriented real estate partnerships). They also offer good protection from inflation. Real estate has historically been a good hedge against the ravages of inflation.

More highly leveraged deals promise income with at least some portion sheltered from taxation. The new tax law eliminated the multiple writeoff deals of years past. In these investments the chief attraction was the tax benefits rather than the economic prospects of the property.

There are a wide variety of real estate limited partnerships. You can invest in apartment buildings, industrial property, farm land, or commercial real estate. Some partnerships specialize in a single type of real estate or even a single project, while others diversify over different types.

Partnerships can also be used to invest in disparate geographical areas. Some general partners restrict their investments to particular areas, states, or even cities. Others search out what they consider to be good values anywhere.

Limited partnerships are notoriously illiquid. They should be considered long-term investments. Although it is possible to sell partnership shares, usually such sales are only at steep discounts from net asset values. Many partnership agreements include restrictive clauses on selling shares.

Typically real estate partnerships are structured to liquidate their assets in seven to ten years. The proceeds are distributed to shareholders.

Strengths

 Limited partnerships offer the chance to invest in large real estate projects by spreading the risk with other investors, and the chance to take advantage of a good general manager's expertise in finding undervalued real estate. You can get good diversification and hence run less risk in real estate investing through partnerships. Moreover, income generated through real estate partnerships is passive income. You may use passive losses from previous investments to shelter gains. Well-managed, properly structured deals still offer good current income, which may be partially tax sheltered. And, of course, real estate provides a good hedge against inflation.

Weaknesses

 Lack of liquidity is a major drawback. In addition, partnership investors run not only market risk but also the risk of poor management. Transaction fees are often high.

Independent verification of asset values is difficult. Usually you must obtain that information from the general partner who has a vested interest in making things look as good as possible. Furthermore, there is no widely accepted rating service, and there is no government or substantial private insurance in case of defaults.

Tax Considerations

The 1986 Tax Reform Act made fundamental changes in how real estate partnerships are taxed. Any losses that are generated are passive losses and can only offset other passive gains. The use of passive losses to offset earned or investment income is being phased out over a five-year period. Only 65% of total passive losses can be used to offset earned or investment income in 1987, 40% in 1980, 20% in 1989, and 10% in 1990. Unused losses may be carried forward.

A number of changes have taken place in tax treatment of gains and losses from limited partnerships. When combined with substantial tightening of the Alternative Minimum Tax, these changes make it crucial for you to check with your tax advisor before investing in any limited partnership.

Summing Up

In the 1980s real estate has fallen on hard times in many areas. The elimination of favored tax treatment for leveraged real estate transactions will result in more sensible real estate investment. The days of buying purely for tax reasons are gone.

The severely depressed real estate market in many areas of the country offers the chance to buy truly undervalued real estate for the first time in years.

Although the emphasis has changed from selling tax benefits to selling income, the real estate limited partnership industry continues to be a viable alternative for investing in land.

REAL ESTATE OUTLOOK FOR 1988

Real estate of virtually all types has been under pressure for the past few years. National office vacancy rates have been as high as 20% (some areas such as the "oil patch" states have seen vacancies at twice that rate!). Even apartment dwellings have been under pressure from high vacancy rates over the past few years.

Literally hundreds of real estate limited partnerships have been forced into bankruptcy in recent years. Rather than stemming the flow of partnerships, though, the industry has performed an abrupt change. No longer are RELPs sold as tax shelters for earned income. Rather, they're being recast as passive income generators (PIGs) to produce passive income that can be offset by those tax shelter partnerships you bought a few years ago!

The fall from grace, however, has positive implications for investors. Fees have dropped as much as 50% for most partnerships. When real estate was skyrocketing and tax benefits were plentiful, investors were paying as much as 20% to buy into RELPs. The collapse of so many of these highly touted programs has resulted in stiffened resistance to the exorbitant fees being charged.

Another development has been the rise of lightly leveraged and nonleveraged deals. The collapse came in those RELPs so heavily leveraged that even minor vacancy increases created cash flow crunches.

One major beneficiary of the changed tax law is raw land investment, as can be readily seen in the scramble by syndicators into this previously ignored area. In 1985 only three companies were selling undeveloped RELPs nationally. By 1987 that number had risen to over 54! Since preferential capital gains treatment has been eliminated, these raw land RELPs run the gamut from doing nothing to the land to making substantial improvements.

WHAT TO EXPECT

During 1987 fixed long-term mortgage rates rose to over 11%. Variable-rate mortgages did not rise as much. However, the rise in rates substantially slowed in housing construction.

The outlook for real estate hinges on interest rates. Dropping rates will boost single-family home construction first. Multiple-unit residences will also be aided.

Rapidly rising inflation would also be favorable for real estate. Inflation will cause investors to turn from financial assets to tangibles.

Office space is still substantially overbuilt. The outlook for this segment of the industry in 1988 is bleak regardless of interest rates and inflation.

A strong stock market will pull money from real estate investments. It would be very unlikely to see a resurgent real estate market with the very strong stock market. Some exposure to real estate is called for, however, as a hedge against a topping stock market and against resurgent inflation. Consider carefully selected REITs as a proxy for your real estate allocation if you are unable to find a conservatively structured RELP that invests in property you are familiar with.

Stick with equity REITs for the best real estate play. Mortgage REITs will tend to act more like fixed-income securities.

Growth

Volatility
Business failure

IRS

Ordinary income
Capital gain

CHAPTER 13

INTERNATIONAL SECURITIES

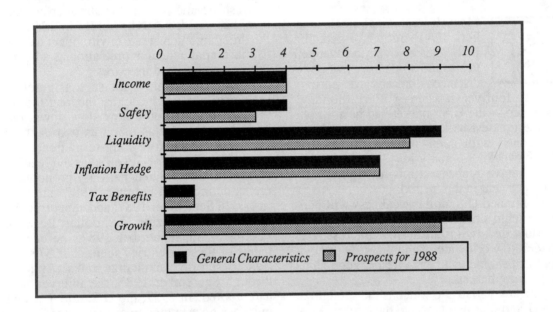

OUTLOOK FOR
1988

Rising trend

Be select on
markets

Twofold returns:

Price rise

Currency gains

High volatility

Positives:

Weak dollar

Low US
interest
rates

Vibrant
international
trade

Warning signs:

Strong dollar

Booming US
GNP

Falling
inflation

Rising US
interest rates

Protectionism

A GLANCE AHEAD

In this chapter you'll discover the increasing importance of foreign investment markets to the world's economy. You'll learn

- Different ways you can invest in foreign companies
- How international investing offers your portfolio important inflation protection
- The many ways you can invest in foreign securities

- Which foreign markets are viable alternatives to the U.S. market
- The important differences between foreign markets and U.S. markets
- Why international securities should play an important part in any well-managed diversified portfolio

The times are certainly changing. In the 1960s and 1970s the international trend was toward greater government involvement in all aspects of the economy. The idea was that the government was needed to direct economic affairs away from individual greed to enhance the "public good." The failure of government direction to substantially improve economic conditions became widely recognized by the early 1980s.

Now countries that were in the forefront of the campaign to nationalize industries have backpedaled sharply. Britain, Japan, and even France have either sold or are planning to sell major state-owned industries to the private sector. Such important companies as British Airways, Nippon Telegraph & Telephone, and Banque Paribas of France have been put on the public auction block.

PROSPECTS FOR INTERNATIONAL MARKETS IN 1988

 Many international stock markets have outperformed the U.S. market over the last ten years, and some have even outdistanced domestic markets over the last four years, when—"Black Monday" excepted— the U.S. market had been in one of the greatest bull moves in history. When combined with gains resulting from U.S. dollar weakness, many investors in foreign stocks have reaped returns as high as 30–50% per year in this period.

Continued U.S. dollar weakness will benefit foreign stock holdings. A continuation of worldwide low inflation, low interest rate, moderate worldwide economic growth environment should yield even further good gains in foreign markets.

The key variable to watch is the strength of the U.S. dollar in relation to the currencies of our major trading partners: Japan, West Germany, Switzerland, Canada, and the United Kingdom. A rise in U.S. inflation not matched in other countries should translate into even further gains for foreign currencies. A position in international stocks will provide a purer hedge against domestic inflation than even South African gold stocks. The South Africans are buffeted as much by day-to-day political developments as they are undersigned by the fortunes of gold bullion.

On the cautionary side, monitor Federal Reserve policy. An aggressive money-tightening stance signaled by consecutive increases in the discount rate would bode well for the U.S. dollar. Sustained dollar strength would knock out the double benefit that holders of foreign stock have achieved in 1985 and 1986.

Without the cushion of a 20% currency gain, you need to become much more selective in 1988 and 1989. For example, given a world increasingly beset by protectionist sentiment, companies that have strong domestic markets may prove better investments. Retrenching might be especially relevant for countries such as Japan, which has been running huge trade surpluses. European legislatures as well as U.S. Congress are threatening to trim Japan's bulging surpluses.

Investors in international bonds have profited handsomely over 1985 and 1986. The drop in the U.S. dollar, combined with the interest income paid in the stronger currencies, has yielded good returns. In addition, the dropping interest rate environment has led to substantial capital appreciation as a bonus for income-oriented investors.

Fundamental valuations such as purchasing power parity indicate that the long slide of the U.S. dollar should now slow down. Often a lead time of as much as two or three years appears before long-term trends reverse. The Group of Seven's (seven leading western industrialized nations) pronouncements dating from February 1987, and confirmed in September 1987, add support to the notion of a stabilizing U.S. dollar. Between February and September 1987, the central banks of these countries spent over $70 billion to stabilize exchange rates. At least through September 1987, the interventions had worked. In 1987, the U.S. dollar traded in its narrowest range in over five years.

For bonds as well as equities, it's important to closely monitor relative interest rates. If U.S. rates gain on other governments' rates, look for a rise of the U.S. dollar. Higher U.S. inflation, though, would have a negative impact on the dollar.

Improvement in the U.S. trade balance would be favorable for the dollar. Every cycle has its own peculiar aspects. This downtrend in the dollar has been closely related to the trade balance. A turn in the trade figures will be presaged by a rise in the GNP. Two consecutive quarters of over 4% growth in the GNP should signal a healthy U.S. economy and a stronger U.S. dollar.

International bonds are most attractive on a total-return basis for U.S. investors if the dollar is weak, international interest rates are falling, and the issuing countries are politically stable. By most fundamental measures, the U.S. dollar has slipped enough. Purchasing power parity measures indicate that the dollar is fundamentally undervalued. Domestic developments concerning the economy, inflation, and the trade deficit are the major concerns for this market.

A strong economic recovery, lower trade deficit figures, a declining budget deficit, or receding inflation (or preferably a combination of all four factors, would boost the U.S. dollarmaking dollar-denominated assets most preferred.

The current trends and momentum for Japan, other Pacific Rim markets, and the United Kingdom are strongly higher. Aggressive investors who monitor short-term trends should invest at the upper end of our recommended allocation. More conservative investors may want to trim exposure to such explosive markets as Japan where the average P/E (price-to-earnings) ratio is running over 50. That figure compares to a ratio of 20–30 for U.S. stocks, and they are at the upper end of their historical ranges.

INTERNATIONAL SECURITIES

Foreign markets returned an average of over 60% per year to U.S. investors in both 1985 and 1986. The declining U.S. dollar contributed about 20% of those gains.

According to a study of mutual fund performance conducted by *Changing Times* (published in their October 1987 issue), the top-performing mutual fund over the past five years was an international fund: Merrill Lynch Pacific. In fact, four of the top ten funds in this survey were international funds. The others were Putnam International Securities, T. Rowe Price International Stock, and Scudder International.

Despite many warnings that such performance could not continue, many markets posted excellent returns for the 12 months ending July 31, 1987:

- Hong Kong   +89.1%
- Australia   +81.0%
- Britain   +46.1%
- Canada   +39.0%
- Japan   +33.3%

Only once in the last 10 years has the United States been the top-performing market! Even 1986's outstanding 27.1% gain was only good enough for fifteenth place worldwide.

Many Americans do not realize the substantial inroads that foreign securities markets have made over the last 10 years. In 1970 the United States accounted for 47% of the world's GNP. At that time U.S. markets capitalized 66% of the world's equity markets.

By 1986 the U.S. economy accounted for only 39% of the world's GNP. At the same time, U.S. equity market's share of world capitalization had dropped to 39%!

The international bond market is larger than the equity markets. Total capitalization of the world's major bond markets in 1985 was $5,850 billion. That compares to equity market capitalization of $5,642 billion. As of 1985 the U.S. bond market accounted for 52% of the total world bond market capitalization.

Many bond markets were devastated by the inflationary experience of the 1970s. Once confidence is lost, it takes a long time to recover. The U.S. market still actively trades bonds that have 20- and 30-year maturities. The average long-term foreign bond has 8 to 12 years maturity.

Over the last 10 years total returns for government bonds of Japan, West Germany, Britain, Switzerland, and Holland have been comparable to that of U.S. bonds. Total returns for each country (including the effect of currency changes) were:

- Japan   14.0%
- West Germany   9.5%
- Britain   9.4%
- Switzerland   9.3%
- Holland   9.3%

Total return for U.S. Treasury bonds was 10.1%.

RISKS

International securities markets present substantial risks. Just as the U.S. market has become more volatile in recent years, so have foreign markets. When markets trade at unprecedentedly high levels, it is only natural for volatility and risk to increase.

An investor in international securities faces unique risks in addition to price volatility. Each country has different regulations for the disclosure of financial information. The whole industry of stock and bond research is relatively new in Europe. Historical records for comparison purposes are certainly not as complete as in the United States.

 Political risks play a large part in foreign stocks. It would be unwise to concentrate all your money in any one country, especially if that country has a history of nationalizing industries. As mentioned earlier, a number of countries are now selling state-owned companies to the private sector—at public auction—but that trend can always change with the next election.

While worldwide developments affect all markets, the effects may be different for each one. For example, when the Iran-Iraq war broke out, the U.S. market rallied in the belief that the United States would have the strongest, most stable economy in times of international turmoil.

The frequent oil crises affect markets differently. Japan depends more heavily on imported oil than do most other industrialized countries. When oil prices go up or OPEC discusses an embargo, Japan's markets usually suffer more than most others.

The worldwide inflationary experience of the 1970s has resulted in much more careful monetary policies for many countries. For example, the United States tried to push West Germany into expansionist economic policies in 1987. West Germans resisted these pressures, fearing that expansive monetary policies would reignite the inflationary fires. They believed that inflation would be far worse than sluggish economic growth.

1987 was the year of the bond bear market internationally. Interest rates rose in West Germany, Japan, Britain, and of course the United States. Bond markets fell sharply. Although the equity markets were able to resist the downward momentum in 1987, the decline is a major concern for the future.

Liquidity varies widely in foreign markets. Listed issues in major markets such as Japan, Britain, and West Germany are quite liquid.

 One problem with investing in foreign securities is that there is no SEC regulation to give you uniform information. Each country has its own regulatory body. Some practices, such as insider trading, are considered more reprehensible in the United States, than in other jurisdictions. However, most countries do have regulations against fraud and similar abuses.

Your securities are insured to $100,000 of their value in the case of failure by the brokerage firm. This coverage applies whether they are U.S. securities or foreign ones.

Compared to Other Assets

International securities can play a vital role in reducing overall portfolio risk, while enhancing total return potential. This benefit is perhaps best seen in a comparison of returns over the past ten years. According to a study by Morgan Stanley Capital International (published in the August 6, 1987, *Investor's Daily*) the U.S. market over the past 10 years has risen 194%.

This falls far short of returns achieved by the following major markets:

- Hong Kong   +2435%
- Japan   +1084%
- Britain   +591%
- Canada   +352%
- Australia   +288%

When you want to ascertain whether diversification into another asset category will provide any net benefit, it is important to establish the level of correlation between markets. For example, if foreign equity markets are to reduce risk, their performance must not be closely correlated with that of the U.S. market. In other words, when the U.S. market goes up, the other markets should not usually rise proportionately. When the U.S. market falls, the other markets should offer some downside protection for the equity portion of your portfolio.

That pattern is exactly what international equity markets show. The average correlation between the U.S. market and the markets of other leading countries—including West Germany, the United Kingdom, Hong Kong, Japan, and Indonesia—is less than 40% over the last 10 years.

just noted, such diversification has enhanced returns over the last 10 years.

Low correlation also appears among international bond markets and the U.S. bond market. International bonds offer excellent risk reduction diversification for the fixed-income portion of your portfolio.

 Diversification to include international markets offers you a prudent method for reducing overall portfolio risk. As you can see by the average returns

---

**Lasser's Recommended Allocation Range for 1988
International Securities**

   Allocate as little as 15% in 1988.

   Allocate as much as 40% in 1988.

Foreign Currencies

Foreign currencies are legal tender issued by foreign governments. In today's highly interdependent world, the value of currency in the country that manufactures the product you want is a key variable in its price. For example, during 1985 and 1986 the Japanese yen climbed over 60% against the U.S. dollar. This meant that Japanese products became more expensive for Americans (reflected in higher prices for Japanese-made cars, for example). At the same time, U.S. products became less expensive for the Japanese (reflected in Japanese investors' investment in U.S. real estate more than doubling in 1986).

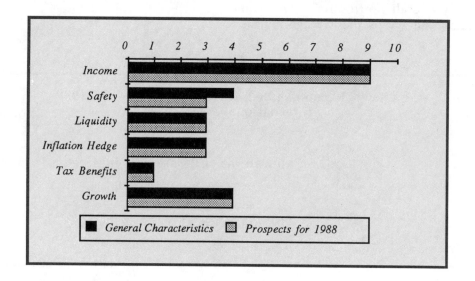

Although all currencies fluctuate, the primary market for foreign currencies in the United States has been concentrated in the Japanese yen, the Swiss franc, the West German mark (Deutschmark), the British pound, and the Canadian dollar. To a lesser extent, the Mexican peso, the French franc, and the Italian lira are traded. The high inflation of the 1970s increased interest in foreign currencies as investments, as people scrambled to find ways to protect their assets from the ravages of inflation.

Following World War II, the world's currencies were fixed in relation to each other and the dollar by the Bretton Woods agreement, whereby the United States agreed to convert foreign dollar claims into gold on demand. However, as inflation depressed the value of the dollar, the United States was forced to close the "gold window" in 1971. Thereafter, currencies began to "float." Basically, the open marketplace replaced government fiat in determining the value of respective currencies.

Foreign currencies can be bought and sold in a variety of ways. Physical possession can be taken by exchanging dollars for the desired currency at currency brokers or at most major banks. In addition, travelers checks can be purchased in denominations of the major currencies. Savings or checking accounts can be opened foreign countries. Foreign currencies are actively traded in the futures and options markets both in the United States and elsewhere (see Chapter 15 for more detail on these alternatives).

The fees for exchanging currencies can be steep. Normally, dealers maintain a current bid/ask spread. The bid is the price they are willing to pay for the currency. The ask (or offer) is the price at which they are willing to sell the currency. The spread can vary from less than 1 to 5% or more, depending on the currency, on the market's current interest in the currency, and on the dealer's normal profit margin.

Once you have purchased the currency at the offered price, it must appreciate enough to cover the spread before you can make money. Some dealers also assess a "transaction fee" or commission.

Investment Potential

Investing in currencies is highly speculative. Income is not guaranteed, nor are capital gains assured. Many nonquantifiable factors may influence the day-to-day price fluctuation of any currency. For example, some factors that are considered important in determining relative currency values are interest rates, inflation rates, political environment (government stability, upcoming elections, and so on), trade and budget deficits, war and weather, monetary and fiscal policy, purchasing power parity, and investor confidence— to name only a few!

Currencies can be highly volatile. Several times in the first quarter of 1987, the yen appreciated over 5% in one day against the U.S. dollar. From 1981 to 1985, the U.S. dollar enjoyed a rise against other currencies.

The primary motivation for currency speculation is capital gains. In the 1970s the U.S. dollar was losing value both domestically and relative to foreign currencies due to high inflation. Americans bought foreign currencies to protect themselves from inflation.

Foreign currency speculation is highly flexible. A broad variety of currencies exist, and a plethora of methods for investing in them. In addition to the methods already listed, professional money managers will trade currencies for you individually. Also, some mutual funds specialize in currency speculation.

Currency speculation is a short-term business. The vagaries and ever changing conditions make long-term positions treacherous at best.

Strengths

 The many different currencies and methods of investing offer maximum flexibility. Major currencies have active highly liquid markets. The short-term capital gains potential is substantial. Foreign currencies offer considerable protection from inflation.

Weaknesses

 Currency markets are very volatile. Transaction costs are high for cash buyers. Risk is not limited to market considerations. Political uncertainties play a major part. Accurate timing is vital, because of high volatility. No current income protects against wrong timing.

Tax Considerations

 The 1986 Tax Reform Act eliminated the favorable treatment of long-term capital gains. All gains from currency speculation are taxed at ordinary income rates.

Foreign currency speculation is not suitable for most retirement plans.

Summing Up

The weakness of the U.S. dollar has become a fact of life since 1985. The rapid fall of the U.S. dollar in early 1987 has resulted in significant inflation fears and even rising interest rates.

Yet only a few short years ago the U.S. dollar was criticized as being too high! Since the end of the Bretton Woods fixed-exchange agreement for currencies, volatility has increased substantially. The erratic behavior of the U.S. dollar in relation to the currencies of our major trading partners has become on going front-page news. For most of 1987, the gyrations of the U.S. dollar were the single most important events in the fate of the U.S. bond market.

Foreign currency trading has grown explosively in the past 10 years. You can now hedge your bets in many ways. But make no mistake—it is important to know what the U.S. dollar is doing and why.

In Chapter 15 we discuss some of the most common methods for investing in currencies other than simple cash purchase. The options and futures markets offer highly liquid—and very risky—ways to profit (or lose) from dollar volatility.

TOP-PERFORMING INTERNATIONAL MUTUAL FUNDS (RANKD BY 10-YEAR AVERAGE RETURN)

1. Merrill Lynch Pacific
2. Putnam International Equities
3. Oppenheimer Global
4. New Perspective (American Funds)
5. Sogen International
6. United International Growth
7. Templeton Growth
8. Scudder International
9. Transatlantic Growth
10. G.T. Global Growth—Pacific

International Stocks

International stocks are equities issued by foreign companies denominated in foreign currencies. You acquire an equity interest in the foreign company, much the same as you would when buying U.S. stocks.

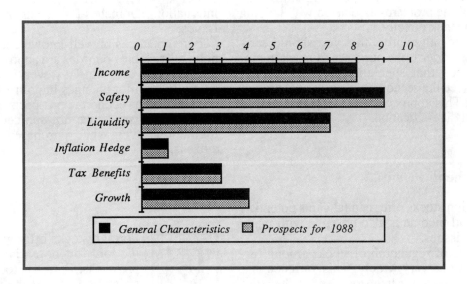

International stock markets have experienced substantial growth over the past 20 years. In 1970 the U.S. stock market constituted 66% of the world's stock market capitalization. That share had shrunk to 39% in 1986. In fact, the Japanese market, with a capitalization of $2.7 trillion, surpassed the U.S. market as the single largest market.

The increasing interest in stocks of foreign countries is yet another indication of the internationalization of the world's economy. Economic growth of major western countries is closely tied to trade flows between each other and eastern and western Nations. Even Peking launched its own stock market in 1986!

The attraction of international stocks is not hard to understand. The ready liquid access to many different companies in many different countries offers investors even more opportunity to seek out fast-growing concerns that are not matched in the United States.

The floating currency exchange rates afford investors the chance to profit not only from internal growth of a disparate selection of companies but also from currency exchange fluctuations. For example, a stock purchased in Japan may appreciate only 10% in a year. But if the U.S. dollar falls an additional 10–15% or more, a U.S. stockholder earns that extra increased purchasing power.

International stocks are purchased in a number of ways. Larger multinational brokerage firms are only one source. International banks, especially banks in countries such as Switzerland or Luxembourg, buy and sell stocks around the world for their clients.

Substantial risks are involved in purchasing international stocks. These risks include differing regulatory requirements for each country, high transaction costs, widely varying tax treatment, and substantial political risk in addition to market risk. Substantial investors, willing and able to take greater risks, can purchase foreign equities directly through their brokers or foreign-based banks.

 One alternative to direct purchase on foreign exchanges is the American Depository Receipt (ADR). These negotiable receipts, issued by U.S. banks, represent actual shares held by the bank's foreign branches. ADRs are actively traded on major U.S. exchanges and on the over-the-counter (OTC) market. For example, Sony is traded on U.S. exchanges as an ADR. Dividends, stock splits, and other changes are handled by the bank. Dividends are converted into U.S. dollars. This agreement eliminates many of the problems associated with holding foreign stock directly.

Another alternative that you should seriously consider is the purchase of stock in mutual funds that specialize in international stocks (see the section on international mutual funds). This approach affords you the chance of good diversification.

Investment Potential

Foreign stocks offer capital gains potential. Dividend income is also possible with many foreign issues.

Levels of regulation of stocks among foreign nations vary widely. This variance is a major problem for investors used to the strict U.S. regulations. Moreover, financial information is usually not as widely disseminated as for U.S. stocks. Only in the past 10 years have independent investment analysis firms become established for many markets such as those in West Germany, Denmark, Sweden, and Spain.

 Volatility is also a problem in some of the newer markets. It is important to have access to a specialist for the market in which you intend to invest. The specialist can advise you on matters such as liquidity, potential political risks, and other factors that may be different for U.S. investors. Although liquidity can be assured for most exchange-listed U.S. stocks, that is not necessarily the case with foreign exchange-listed issues.

Minimum purchase requirements may also be quite high. Given a maze of transaction costs, including commissions, transfer fees, transfer taxes, custodial fees, and currency conversion fees, direct investment in foreign

stocks is usually only within the purview of wealthy investors.

Leverage through purchase on margin is available for foreign stocks traded on U.S. exchanges and some ADRs. The Federal Reserve Bank decides which stocks are marginable. Regulations elsewhere vary widely. Check with a broker with international branches for details on specific issues.

Foreign stocks of well-known concerns in politically stable countries are appropriate for long-term investment. However, you should carefully monitor changes in political conditions as well as economic prospects. Remember, foreign issues are not subject to SEC regulations even when purchased by U.S. citizens.

Strengths

 Foreign stocks offer greater selection for potential growth prospects. Foreign stocks offer protection against the inflation that causes U.S. dollar weakness. Income potential is enhanced in times of U.S. dollar weakness. International diversification spreads risk.

Weaknesses

 Currency fluctuations can hurt potential returns if the U.S. dollar appreciates against the currency in which the stock is denominated. Foreign stocks are not subject to SEC financial reporting requirements. Reliable financial information is more difficult to obtain. Different accounting procedures are used in many countries. These problems makes direct comparison with U.S. reports more difficult. Many foreign stocks are less liquid than equivalent U.S. exchanges-listed issues due to large holdings by foreign governments, which are rarely traded. Price information is not as widely available as that for U.S. stocks.

Tax Considerations

 Gains and losses on foreign stocks are treated the same as domestic stocks for U.S. tax purposes. Capital gains and dividend income are taxed at ordinary income rates. Capital losses can be used to offset other capital losses. Unused losses can be carried forward.

However, it is important to learn the tax policies of respective foreign countries. Many countries assess withholding taxes of 20 to 30% on interest paid to foreign investors. Numerous tax treaties have been made between the United States and other countries. You should investigate many possible tax consequences before you invest in foreign securities of any type. Some taxes may be so heavy as to negate the value of the investment for U.S. citizens.

Summing Up

Foreign stock markets have outperformed the U.S. market for the past four years. Combining with gains resulting from U.S. dollar weakness, many investors in foreign stocks have reaped returns as high as 30 to 50% per year during this period.

Given the increasing interdependence of industrialized economies around the world, diversification with foreign investment markets adds value to your portfolio. In the 1950s the U.S. dollar did not fluctuate widely in value. Investors had little need for protection from the complex vagaries of international markets.

Most professional managers now consider it prudent to diversify internationally. In addition to the potential for excellent returns in many foreign markets, as in 1985 and 1986, such diversification also helps to minimize risk. When bouts of dollar weakness depress U.S. equities, stocks in foreign countries often appreciate.

Although inflation has not been a problem here since 1982, the threat of a resurgence is always present. In August 1987, the Consumer Price Index rose at an annual compounded rate of 5.8%, the highest level in over a year. Inflation fears push interest rates higher, which often hurts stocks. International diversification minimizes the effects of adverse developments in a single country.

International Bonds

**INTERNATION-
AL BONDS**

Good income

Moderate safety

Moderate
liquidity

Good inflation
hedge

No tax benefits

Moderate growth

*International bonds are debt instruments issued by foreign governments and compa-
nies denominated in currencies other than the U.S. dollar. Just like U.S. Treasuries and
corporate bonds, they have set maturities and "coupon" yields. For example, 10-year
Japanese government bonds in April 1986 yielded 3.35% compared to 8.5% on equivalent U.S. bonds. Both the principal at maturity and the interest are paid in yen. These
bonds would be attractive to U.S. investors if the U.S. dollar dropped enough relative
to the yen to make up the difference.*

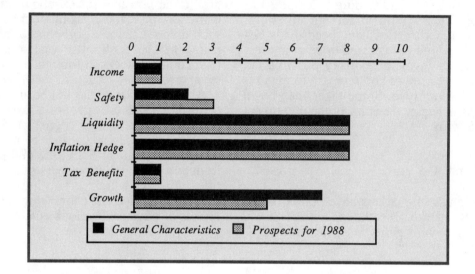

The large gyrations in both interest rates
and currency values have stimulated substantial interest in international bonds.

Even though the interest rates paid by
bonds issued by foreign governments and
corporations in Japan, Switzerland, and West
Germany have generally been lower than the
rates paid by equivalent U.S. bonds, their returns, plus the appreciation of their respective
currencies, paid off handsomely in 1985 and
1986.

Like international stocks, international
bonds must be evaluated for many different
factors. Fluctuations in the interest rates in
the issuing country and the United States may
affect relative value. Fluctuations in currency
values among countries also contribute relative value.

Because of the myriad price factors, investing in international bonds is a difficult
undertaking for the average investor. Although an investor may be able to get a fairly
accurate picture of the earnings prospects of a
foreign concern for purchasing its stock,
evaluating the many factors that affect interest
rates is certainly no easier in a foreign country than it is in the United States.

Few analysts have been able to forecast
U.S. interest rates with any accuracy for the
short term (3 to 18 months). Many factors
must be evaluated. For example, monetary
and fiscal policies, trade balances, economic
growth, and relative inflation are only a few
necessary considerations. Of course, this
tangle is even more complicated for foreign
countries.

International bonds are bought and sold
through international brokerage firms and
banks that have branches in various countries. Many foreign banks, such as Swiss
banks that have U.S. branches, are specifically set up to handle such transactions.

Transaction fees typically are higher than fees for equivalent bond purchases in the United States. Banks generally assess steeper fees than United States-based brokers.

Investment Potential

International bonds offer a variety of investment returns. They are primarily income producers. The income is paid in the currency in which the bond is denominated. This arrangement allows additional gains through currency appreciation. Finally, capital gains are earned when interest rates fall (see the section on corporate bonds).

The volatility of bonds depends on the political and economic environment of the issuing country. The interest rates of stable low-inflation countries such as Switzerland fluctuate much less than in the United States. However, government regulations and registration requirements vary widely. Do not make the mistake of assuming that foreign-issued bonds have met requirements similar to those imposed by the SEC in the United States. Evaluating foreign bonds through independent rating services is considerably more difficult than for U.S. bonds.

Although foreign banks often will make loans for purchases of foreign bonds, the costs tend to be quite high. Swiss banks, for example, tend to charge for many services that Americans take for granted. Custodial fees can be high. However, full-service bank customers can generally negotiate fees.

Both domestic or international bonds should be viewed as long-term investments. Interest rate fluctuations can create short-term opportunities.

Strengths

 International bonds offer investors the opportunity to play currency exchange rate swings, with downside protection provided by the income paid by the bonds. High-risk investors can earn higher-than-average returns on bonds issued by countries that have high-risk economies. International bonds offer good diversification for income-oriented portfolios. International bonds provide a hedge against U.S. inflation through their connection to foreign currency exchange rates.

Weaknesses

 Liquidity may present a problem for many international bonds. Timely pricing information is not as uniformly available abroad as in the United States. International bonds are sensitive to adverse political developments. A country's decision to devalue its currency can devastate international bonds. Worldwide inflation drives bond prices down. And different foreign accounting practices make direct comparison to U.S. bonds difficult.

Tax Considerations

 Tax treatment of foreign bonds is complex. Not only U.S. tax authorities, but also many countries, assess withholding taxes on foreign investors. Generally, tax treatment on capital gains and interest income is the same as for equivalent U.S. securities. The United States makes tax treaties with many foreign countries, and you should check the details before investing. Adverse tax decisions made after you invest may substantially erode your returns.

Although foreign bonds *can* be used for retirement plans, the complexities rule them out for all but the very largest investors. As an alternative, therefore, to get proper diversification and professional management consider mutual funds that invest in foreign securities.

Summing Up

Investors in international bonds profited handsomely in 1985 and 1986. The drop in the U.S. dollar, combined with the interest income paid in the stronger currencies, has yielded good returns. In addition, the dropping interest rate has produced substantial capital appreciation as a bonus for income-oriented investors.

Investing in international bonds is a complex undertaking. When you purchase U.S. bonds, you can get a pretty good understanding of the financial strength of the underlying company through the ratings of independent agencies. Then the primary consideration is the direction of interest rates. If rates go up, bonds will fall in price.

 International bonds offer sophisticated investors a good method for diversifying the risk in their fixed-income portfolios. For example, a weak U.S. dollar usually has a negative effect on U.S. bonds. However, if you own foreign bonds, depreciation in the dollar yields a currency exchange profit to U.S. citizens who hold bonds denominated in foreign currency.

Investing in international bonds is very complex. As we've seen, over the past 10 years it has been virtually impossible to forecast U.S. interest rates with any real degree of accuracy. Imagine the additional problems of forecasting rates in a foreign country!

Moreover, different countries' currencies move at different rates relative to the U.S. dollar. By mid-1987 the U.S. dollar had declined over 40% since 1985 against the yen and the mark. Yet the trade deficit showed little real improvement, because the currencies of other important trading partners—including Taiwan and South Korea—showed little appreciation.

International Mutual Funds

Sophisticated investors can appreciably improve the returns on their fixed-income portfolios through diversification with international bonds. However, as noted repeatedly, the complexities make it difficult for the average investor to participate directly. Yet 1987 shows an increase in the number of mutual funds that provide professional management in this area. The 1980s have begun the internationalization of security markets. International bonds will play an increasingly important role in the future. International mutual funds allow you to invest in foreign stocks with less trouble. A mutual fund is a pool of professionally managed securities. You buy into a fund and receive a proportionate share of the funds assets. International mutual funds trade like stocks, with fluctuating prices determining your profit or loss. Most international funds invest only in foreign stocks, but some funds also buy foreign bonds. An even smaller number invests in both.

MUTUAL FUNDS INTERNATIONAL

Low income

Moderate safety

Good liquidity

Good inflation hedge

No tax benefits

Good growth

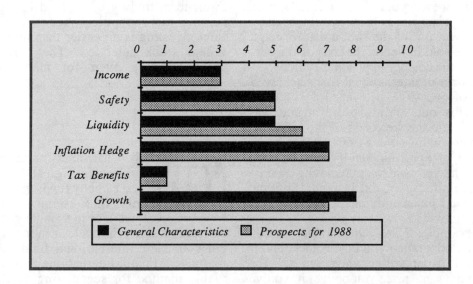

■ General Characteristics   ▨ Prospects for 1988

The world's economies are steadily becoming more interdependent. The prosperity of the U.S., Japanese, and other economies is no longer only a factor of each country's own domestic demand. The profitability of major companies in the industrialized world is closely tied to their export business.

This "internationalization" of the world's economies is reflected in the rise of stock markets around the world. Investing in foreign markets is a difficult procedure. Different regulations apply to each country's markets. This red tape is further complicated by the differing currencies of each country.

The net asset value of a fund is the market value of the fund. There are two primary types of international mutual funds. A no-load fund assesses no sales fees. Such funds are usually purchased direct from the fund itself through the mail. When you purchase a no-load fund, you buy it at its current net asset value on the day of your purchase. Net asset value is calculated at the end of every business day.

A load fund charges a sales fee. The fee ranges from 2 to 8% of your investment. This fee is added to the net asset value when you purchase a load fund. Some funds call themselves "no-load," yet assess a fee when you sell all or part of your shares. Investigate a fund's fee structure before you invest. Fees may significantly affect your total return.

Most large mutual fund groups have at least one international fund. You can follow prices of the larger funds in the *Wall Street Journal*. Financial magazines such as *Money* and *Changing Times* periodically feature detailed reports on the performance of most international funds.

Investment Potential

The primary attraction of international funds is the capital gains potential. The potential and risks, though, are unique. International funds offer capital gains and losses resulting from the price action of the selected stocks. However, your "bottom-line" return, though, is often just as heavily influenced by the relative value of the U.S. dollar. Foreign stocks are sold in denominations of the currencies of the country in which they trade.

A number of international funds achieved returns of over 50% per year for 1985 and 1986. This outstanding performance was largely due to the weakness of the U.S. dollar. When you invest in a stock on the Tokyo exchange, you profit in yen if the stock price rises. If the yen is also appreciating against the U.S. dollar (as it did in both 1985 and 1986), you gain an additional profit from the currency move!

For example, if the yen is trading at 200 per U.S. dollar when you buy a stock, and it rises to 150 per dollar when you sell the stock at the same price you bought it, you've earned 33% despite the flat stock price!

The volatility of foreign markets varies. A international fund's diversification tempers this factor somewhat. But a fund invested in only one foreign market that goes through a cycle of wide swinging prices, will reflect that volatility in its own prices.

International mutual funds, like most funds, are liquid investments. However, political changes in foreign countries can cause some liquidity problems. For example, in the 1970s Mexico suspended market trade temporarily after it announced its first devaluation in many years.

All United States-based mutual funds must register with the SEC. They are required to meet stringent financial and disclosure regulations. A prospectus must be provided to prospective buyers before they buy the fund. Some international funds are based off the United States shore, in places such as the Cayman Islands, the Bahamas, and the Antilles. These funds often do not register with the SEC. They do not always follow the strict disclosure requirements that govern domestic funds. Many off-shore funds have fraudulent dealings. Although some are legitimate, off-shore funds cannot be considered as safe as domestic registered funds.

Mutual fund investing, especially in load funds, is generally a long-term proposition. Short-term trading of no-load funds is becoming more popular. Accurately timing fund investing is no easier than timing individual stock selection. That ability has proven elusive even for many professionals.

Strengths

The wide variety of international funds offers great flexibility. You can buy funds that invest in only one country (such as Japan), or in a single geographical area (such as Europe), or in many different countries. International funds are normally very liquid. International funds offer a viable method for speculating on the U.S. dollar. International funds offer capital gains potential. The funds simplify investing in foreign markets. They offer good protection from inflation.

Weaknesses

Foreign stock markets operate under very different regulations. Abuses may occur that U.S. markets guard against. Currency speculation works both ways. If the U.S. dollar strengthens while your investment is denominated in a foreign currency because it is invested in foreign markets, you may lose money even if the stock goes up! Foreign currency markets have been very volatile over the past 10 years. Foreign political developments may result in liquidity problems.

Tax Considerations

 No special tax advantages attach to investing in international funds. The 1986 Tax Reform Act eliminated preferential treatment of capital gains. Capital gains and gains from currency changes are taxed at your ordinary income rate. Capital losses offset capital gains. Excess losses are carried forward.

Some foreign countries assess withholding taxes on foreign purchases of their securities. Your fund takes care of those matters. If you are entitled to a credit for such transactions, the fund will advise you on an annual basis.

Summing Up

International investing is here to stay. International funds will attract ever larger amounts of U.S. investors' funds. Investors are recognizing interdependencies among the industrial countries.

The complexities of directly investing in foreign markets rule it out for most investors. International funds, however, give you the global diversification that many professional investment advisors recommend.

A weak U.S. dollar enhances the attraction of foreign markets. It can bail out investors who do poorly in selecting stocks, yet who are buying in the correct currency. A reversal of the dollar's slide will require greater care in selecting of foreign issues. The stocks will then have to rise enough to offset gains in the dollar as well as to yield capital gains in their own currency.

Inflation
Liquidity

Volatility
Business failure

IRS

Ordinary income

CHAPTER 14

PRECIOUS METALS AND COMMODITIES

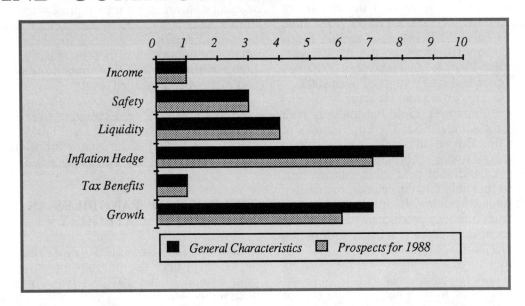

| | General Characteristics | Prospects for 1988 |

OUTLOOK FOR
1988

Neutral trend

Stocks strongest

Gold is leader

Silver lagging

Chief value as
hedge

Positives:

Rising
inflation

International
unrest

Chaotic
markets

High money
growth

Strong GNP
growth

Rising oil
prices

Warning signs:

Recession

Falling
interest rates

Falling oil
prices

Calmer
markets

Falling CPI

A GLANCE AHEAD

Wall Street gurus generally do a better job coming up with catchy phrases to describe market developments than they do explaining those events. By 1983 and 1984 it had become obvious to even the most convinced "gold bug" that momentum had switched from "tangibles" (commodities) to "financial assets." In this game of words, the term commodities *is often confused with* futures. *Smart investors, however, refer to* commodities *interchangeably with* tangibles, *but as distinct from* futures. *Precious metals are the most prominent class of tangibles.*

In this chapter you'll learn

- *The many different ways to own gold*
- *The role that gold plays in even the most conservative investor's portfolio*

- *How "tangibles" differ from "financial assets" The connections among gold, oil, and inflation*

PROSPECTS FOR 1988

After falling for the larger part of six years, precious metals prices began to recover in late 1986. This rise carried over in 1987 as the first signs of a return to moderate inflation began to make itself felt, although this trend is far from certain.

The Consumer Price Index for 1986 rose only 1.1%. However, the sharp collapse in oil prices accounted for much of that weak-

245

ness. When you exclude the volatile energy and food sectors, prices rose at a 4% compounded rate.

The Consumer Price and Producer Price indexes both jumped sharply in early 1987, then settled back. However, the August CPI came out at +0.5%, an annual compounded rate of 5.8%. The fear of inflation contributed to weak bond prices and buoyant commodity prices.

Interestingly, the prices of gold stocks and mutual funds significantly outperformed the price rise in the bullion itself. *Changing Times* tracks over 900 funds annually. The October 1987 issue carried the results of funds for the 12-month period from June 1986 to July 1987. Precious metals funds took the top 16 places on the list of best-performing funds for that time period! Eleven of the funds had total returns of over 100%!

The strong performance is actually a warning signal, however. Gold bullion only rose 30% in the same period. The huge amount of money that flowed onto gold funds distorted the prices of many gold issues. Because only a relative handful of gold-mining properties, the mad rush into this thin market has caused some unusual pricing. In one case, a marginal North American producer with estimated reserves of only eight years was selling at a P/E (price/earnings ratio) of over 40!

Many analysts see signs that the markets may be undergoing another shift from financial assets back to commodities. We do not believe that there is strong evidence of a return to the inflationary markets of the 1970s. Therefore, we recommend that most investors treat the gold portion of their portfolios as inflation insurance. Maintain the lower allocation levels for the moment.

However, we do list the key areas that should be monitored. Changes in these items would dictate an increase in your precious metals holdings.

If U.S. economic growth surges above the 3–4% range of recent years, inflationary pressures may be aggravated. Watch particularly the level of factory use. If this level goes over 85%, it means the country's industrial plant is being fully employed. If production cannot be quickly increased without buying new capital goods, prices will rise as the marketplace adjusts to distribute materials to those uses with the best potential returns.

Monitor both the Consumer Price and Producer Price indexes. Steady increases over a three- or four-month span would indicate a return to inflation. If annual rates hit 7% for more than three consecutive months, increase your precious metals allocation by 3 or 4%.

Oil prices have played a central role in the direction of the CPI over the past few years. In early 1987, oil prices nudged over $22 a barrel at the height of Middle East tension. When matters settled down, and massive stockpiling by consumers had moderated, the oil price dropped back to OPEC's official $18 a barrel. With the huge overhang of supply, it would be surprising if the oil price were held above $22. However, if the average price does hold above $22 a barrel for three consecutive months, consider increasing your precious metals allocation toward the upper end of the recommended levels.

Finally, watch key price levels for both gold and silver. If gold closes at over $500 and can stay over that level for 30 days, that signals the potential for major inflationary problems. Silver's key upside price is $10.

THE ROLE OF TANGIBLES AS A BASIC ASSET CATEGORY

Investing in commodities is motivated by a desire to protect the purchasing power of your assets. In the 1970s it was common wisdom to "Buy now—it will only get more expensive later." Financial assets, however, are certificates representing ownership or a loan relationship. Gold bugs sneeringly refer to financial assets as "paper" claims. A true investor in tangibles expects to take delivery of an actual commodity such as gold.

You would turn to tangibles in times of great uncertainty. Rather than "trust" in the fortunes of a company, of which you may be partial owner through stock shares, or even in the banking system, extreme advocates of tangible investing much prefer physical possession of gold: you don't have to trust anyone then.

Although "gold fever" has cooled off in recent years, you'll discover in this chapter a wide variety of products that are still tied to gold.

Gold has served as a final, inviolable refuge of value for all history. The Pharoahs of ancient Egypt were adorned with gold. The Aztecs offered gold as tribute to their sacred ruler, Montezuma. More recently, gold has surfaced as the only sure medium for the purchase of personal freedom from communist regimes such as in Vietnam and the People's Republic of China.

The 1960s and 1970s were difficult years. The Vietnam War tore the country apart. U.S. inflation ran to levels unprecedented in modern times. Interest rates on short-term money market instruments such as Treasury bills went to double digits.

Many accepted academic economic theories were being disproven in the most important laboratory of all—reality. The so-called Phillips curve had postulated a connection between employment and inflation. The idea was that increased inflation would raise employment by boosting the economy. Its limitations became evident when the marketplace began to factor increasing inflation into future decisions.

Now the country was burdened with increasing unemployment *and* rising inflation. The Keynesian economists (disciples of John Maynard Keynes) had long held that proper government stimulation could level out the sharp rises and falls of the business cycle. Yet increased fiscal stimulation through heavy spending by the federal government did little to alleviate the economic crisis.

People began to turn to the historic "chaos hedges": gold, silver, and physical commodities. When you purchase a stock, you are far removed from actual possession and control over what you own. Trust in management and the marketplace plays a strong role in your investment decisions. When this confidence is shaken, investors turn to those investments that are much less removed from actual possession and control. The price of an ounce of gold is pretty clear-cut. It has very little variance worldwide. The same could be said for most physical commodities.

The price of a financial asset such as stocks or even bonds, however, depends on a whole panorama of subjective factors. How good is the management of the company? How good and competitive are its products? Does the marketplace recognize its true value? Many considerations make up the price of a financial asset, and they vary daily.

Characteristics

Europeans have been inflation conscious for centuries, as the result of many bouts with runaway inflation. Americans have become conscious of inflation over the last 20 years. Value was confiscated by fixed passbook interest rates of 5.25% when inflation ran 10%. Investor and consumer resistance to such confiscation resulted in the rise of a major new financial industry: money market funds.

Most Americans were not able to participate in the sophisticated high-priced money market instruments used by the rich. But they did know they were losing money by saving the old way. When first one, and then many entrepreneurs offered the average saver the chance to at least "stay even," there was a rush of money to money market funds.

As Americans became more used to active money management, many vehicles became more volatile. Gold and silver prices rose to unprecedented levels, and then (in early 1980) fell even more sharply. Commodity prices in the late 1970s ran to all-time highs, boosted by raging inflation and investor rejection of traditional "paper" investments.

Make no mistake: investing in tangibles—whether gold, silver, wheat, oil, diamonds, or whatever—is a very risky game. Heavy participation in the financial markets by long-term institutional investors offers these markets some stability over the long haul. But there is no such institutional support in precious metals and straight commodity investing. As a result, these markets are more volatile.

Risks

Commodities are highly vulnerable to political risk. For example, in the 1970s President Carter, without warning, declared an embargo on U.S. grain shipments to the Soviet Union. Since the Soviet Union was one of the largest buyers of our grain, that announcement devastated the markets overnight.

In 1933, President Roosevelt decreed that ownership of gold was illegal for U.S. citizens. That ban lasted until 1975! True, gold held during that time may have had value as determined by demand in other countries. But its value for Americans was diminished by the criminal penalties attached to its ownership.

A prominent risk for holders of financial assets is business risk. What if a company is mismanaged or overlooked by the market? Investors in precious metals and commodities do not have to worry about that risk if they own the actual commodity. Owners of gold stocks, though, may not benefit from a rise in the gold price because of business problems. A mine may be poorly managed. Or, as has often been the case, individual mines may have suffered disasters such as floods or cave-ins that rendered the mine less valuable.

A sidelight to the business and political risk consideration is the political situation in the Union of South Africa. Further political upheavals there would be "bullish for gold"—that is, the supply would be smaller. However, owners of South African gold stocks would lose substantially. Most gold mutual funds have at least some connection to South Africa, and so they would also be hurt.

Contrary to conventional wisdom, rising interest rates are not usually a negative for gold prices. Since rising rates are often caused by increased inflation, gold and commodity prices will also be lifted by the same concerns. Only at the top of the inflation cycle, when inflation begins to turn down, would rising rates hurt gold prices.

Keep in mind that the last inflation cycle peaked in 1980, but interest rates continued to rise for two more years. They lagged behind the rise in inflation, and significantly lagged behind the turn.

The worldwide inflation of the 1980s spawned a vibrant "inflation hedge" industry. Gold and silver in their many forms are quite liquid. However, some forms, such as coins or futures, are considerably more liquid than others.

Compared to Other Assets

Gold and physical commodities play an important part in any well-designed portfolio. They tend to trade contracyclically with the stock market: the main trend and gains from price appreciation for precious metals appear during those times when the stock market is moving down.

This is not to say that gold and the stock market always trade opposite one another. For example, the last stages of a bull market are often the most exciting and rewarding for investors who have the capital, knowledge, and fortitude to persevere.

During those last stages, gold usually reverses its downward slide, or awakens from a long sideways trading range. Thus they may both go up together for a while.

As you can see from the charts of investment characteristics, stocks do offer some inflation protection. However, as the experience of the 1970s showed, prolonged inflation so distorts the market processes that eventually stock prices decline. Then precious metals and other raw commodities offer the best returns. Their appreciation can offset losses incurred by financial assets.

How to Invest

You can purchase gold, silver, and platinum in bullion or coin form and store them yourself. However, such direct possession is not practical for most commodities or even for sizable amounts in the precious metals.

 Stocks are available for companies that produce most raw commodities. We've mentioned gold mining stocks, but many companies exist whose primary business is the production of natural resorces. Ask your broker for a list of companies in that industry group. Or investigate mutual funds that specialize in precious metals, natural resource, or energy stocks.

Highly leveraged futures trading is the most liquid method for direct investment in a wide range of raw commodities and precious metals. This market is really only suitable for investors willing and able to risk substantial sums for substantial earning potential. It is very high risk!

Lasser's Recommended Allocation Range for 1988
Precious Metals and Commodities Allocation:

 Allocate as much as 15% in 1988.

 Allocate as little as 5% in 1988.

Precious Metals

PRECIOUS
METALS

No income

Moderate safety

Good liquidity

Best inflation
hedge

No tax benefits

Moderate growth

The label "precious metals" is the most widely used label for metals valued for their monetary role as hedges against inflation. Precious metals are primarily gold and silver. (In recent years, platinum and even palladium have been included. Although the latter two are now usually included, it is difficult to see any monetary role played by either.)

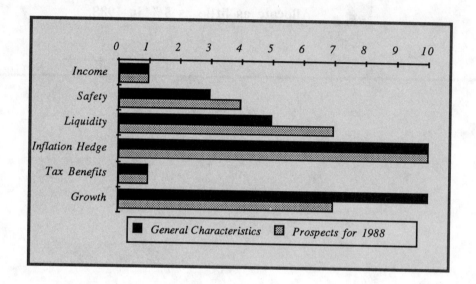

As already noted, before January 1, 1975 it was illegal for Americans to own gold in any form other than numismatic coins. Gold ownership had been declared illegal during the Great Depression. For many years, the huge U.S. gold bullion reserves were used to "fix" gold at $35 per ounce (actually, that rate was the final exchange rate prior to gold legalization). The Bretton Woods agreement between the major political powers after World War II, set the U.S. dollar as the world's reserve currency. The United States stood ready to redeem dollars for gold.

In the early 1970s, inflation began to pick up around the world. Some countries, most notably France, began to exchange large quantities of U.S. dollars for gold. Rather than allow this continued outflow of gold ("the great gold drain"), President Nixon closed the gold window in August 1971.

Gold has been the classic inflation hedge throughout history. While countries throughout history (including the United States) have

tried to "demonetize" gold, individuals have ultimately turned to it rather than to government-issued currency. Before 1975, Americans either bought gold coins that were recognized as numismatic (having collector's value) or silver coins (the "poor man's gold") to hedge against inflation.

There are now many ways to buy precious metals. Gold and silver stocks are freely and actively traded. Gold and silver are traded on futures and even option exchanges. You can buy gold and silver coins, numismatics and bullion (having no value other than their gold or silver content). You can "warehouse receipts" for gold held by a third party. The third party may be a Swiss bank or a domestic storage facility. Some mutual funds even offer "shares" in gold bullion stockpiles.

You can buy gold in any one of many different forms from full-service brokerage firms, many banks, and independent metal dealers. Some forms of gold investing are closely regulated by the federal government, such as stocks, mutual funds, options, or futures. Coin and bullion dealers are not always subject to government regulation. There have been many scandals involving nonregulated precious metals dealers who have not bought and stored the gold or silver for which they sold warehouse receipts, and fraudulent coin dealers are always a threat to the naive investor.

Fees can vary widely. Commissions are assessed for stocks, options, and futures. Coins are usually sold with an undisclosed dealer markup. Bullion, such as bars, must be assayed before resale.

The precious metals industry has generated many independent investment advisory newsletters covering everything from penny stocks to futures, to coin and bullion. Gold prices are quoted daily in the *Wall Street Journal*.

Investment Potential

Gold, silver, and platinum are the three most commonly traded precious metals. The purchase and sale of precious metals produce capital gains (or losses). The chief drawback to precious metals investing is the lack of income (except for dividend-paying gold stocks).

Inflation-wary investors hold gold as long-term protection from the ravages of inflation. Investors in gold and silver options and futures tend to be oriented toward short-term holdings.

The most popular bullion gold coin is the American Eagle. These coins can be purchased in a variety of sizes from 1 ounce to 0.1 of an ounce. There is usually a 5 to 10% premium. Other popular bullion gold coins include the Canadian Maple Leaf, the Krugerrand, the Mexican 50 Peso, and the Austrian Corona.

 Numismatic gold coins share the appreciation potential of gold bullion, with the added factor of "collector value." Popular numismatic gold coins include the U.S. $20, $10, and $5 gold pieces and the British sovereign. This highly specialized market is crucially dependent on "grading." A numismatic coin is graded for its condition. A change in grade can mean a substantial change in the value of a coin. For example, if you buy a coin graded BU ("brilliant uncirculated") from one dealer, and another grades the same coin AU ("almost uncirculated") you can lose as much as 50% of your investment, with no change in the price of gold!

Silver coins also have an active market. Silver dollars were once traded primarily for their silver content. However, now most silver dollars trade for significant premiums over their silver content. Even bags (usually $1,000 face value) of "junk" silver coins (worn, well-circulated) trade at premiums over their silver content.

Precious metals prices are quite volatile. Since they do not pay any income, there is little protection from sharp drops in price. Do not overlook this volatile nature when buying gold. If you stick with popular bullion coins or have a good working relationship with a gold bullion dealer, your investment should be quite liquid.

Fees vary widely. Some dealers assess a commission in addition to a price markup. Even if you buy bullion or coins at a small premium of 3 to 8% over gold value, when you sell you will lose that premium. Most gold and silver coins and bullion are quoted with a bid (the price the dealer is willing to pay) and an ask (the price at which they are willing to sell). This spread between bid and ask is your cost of the transaction.

No federal insurance protects bullion or coin purchases. Nor is there a widely recognized rating service for precious metals dealers.

Strengths

Precious metals provide an excellent hedge against inflation. Carefully selected precious metals investments are liquid. Numismatic gold and silver coins provide downside protection from price weakness in the metals themselves. Some banks will loan money against gold or silver collateral.

Weaknesses

No government regulation oversees precious metal coin and bullion dealers. Numismatic coins are subject to wide variances in "grading," which can significantly affect the resale value of the coins. Precious metals (except for dividend-paying stocks in precious metals) pay no income. Bullion must be assayed before resale. Fees may be very high, limiting profit potential. Precious metals prices are volatile. Owners run a business risk of unscrupulous dealers as well as market price risk.

Tax Considerations

No special tax benefits apply to precious metals investments. All gains are capital gains. Gains are taxed at your ordinary income rates.

Until 1987, gold coins and bullion were not legal for IRAs. Some coins such as the American Gold Eagle are now legal for IRAs.

Summing Up

Precious metals serve a twofold economic purpose. First, they have some value through their industrial uses. For example, silver is very important in photography. Gold is critical in high-technology uses. Both are valued for their beauty in jewelry.

Gold (primarily), and silver (to a smaller extent) also serve an important monetary role, Throughout history, people have opted for gold (or silver) rather than for government-issued money if they have reason to suspect fraud in the issuance of a government's legal tender.

This protective role as a hedge against financial instability survives to this day. When U.S. inflation moved to double digits in the late 1970s, it was obvious to most consumers that the traditional havens for savings—stocks, bonds, and bank savings plans—were losers. Many investors turned to gold, silver, and platinum as the last resort for protecting their purchasing power.

Despite the long bull market in stocks that started in 1982, savvy investors continue to monitor the gold markets for early signs of resurgent inflation. Just as the stock market tends to "discount" (predict) the economic future (the market will typically peak before the economy does), so does gold discount the future of inflation, as seen in government indexes such as the Consumer Price Index.

Strategic Metals

Strategic metals are rare metals such as titanium, chromium, and cobalt that have crucial high-technology uses. Usually these metals are mined as by-products of gold and silver. The major supplies of these metals are in Zimbabwe, the Union of South Africa, and the Soviet Union. Advocates of strategic metals investing argue that the metals are crucial for U.S. defense and that the unstable political situation in the major supplying countries could create shortages.

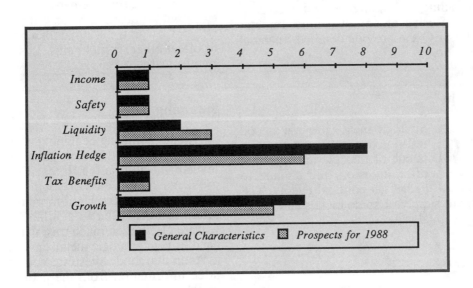

Many of the same investment advisors who correctly identified the fundamental factors that led to the great precious metals bull market of the late 1970s, began to tout strategic metals as the next great growth market in the late 1970s and early 1980s. Initial interest and activity was high, fueled by inflation and political fears.

Prices boomed initially as inflation-wary investors sought to diversify their portfolios. When the precious metals bull market peaked in early 1980, the strategic metals market also was hurt. After an enthusiastic beginning—including the launching of a mutual fund, numerous warehouse certificate programs, and even the minting of bars for physical possession—interest fell off dramatically.

Strategic metals now have a very thin, hard-to-follow market with only a few sources of reliable information for the average investor. Prices are very difficult to follow, because no real, active auction market exists for many of the metals.

Most major precious metals dealers can provide information on investing in strategic metals. Fees vary widely and are a major problem with investing in this esoteric market. The best alternative for most investors is a mutual fund that offers some liquidity.

Investment Potential

Like precious metals, strategic metals offer capital gains potential. No income is paid. This market is a long-term investment. Given the erratic pricing caused by the thin, closely controlled market, bid/ask ranges are very wide. Substantial appreciation is needed just to cover such a spread.

Prices are very volatile. The lack of easily accessible prices and market information limits your potential for leveraging your investment.

Strategic metals are very illiquid. Gaining access is a problem even for an average investor. The paucity of investment vehicles limits flexibility. A few investment advisory newsletters are on the market, but they are usually produced by interested parties who want to sell their particular investment vehicle.

The government does not regulate strategic metals trading. A mutual fund or limited partnership offering of any size must register with the SEC and provide detailed financial information.

Strengths

 Strategic metals provide a good inflation hedge. Strategic metals is one of the few markets that offer investors the chance to hedge geopolitical events. The very small supply of some metals can result in large capital gains.

Weaknesses

 Strategic metals are very illiquid. They are not an accepted asset class in the investment community, and therefore accurate information is difficult to obtain. Flexibility is limited by the fact that very few outlets are available. They pay no income. The very thin markets can result in large losses overnight. You have no way to hedge your exposure with other markets. The trading history is too short to make reliable forecasts of future price action.

Tax Considerations

 There no special tax benefits for strategic metals investing. All gains are capital gains and are taxed at your ordinary income rates. Capital losses can be used to offset other capital gains. Losses are carried forward.

Summing Up

After a promising beginning, strategic metals have not fulfilled their potential as a real investment alternative. Intensified political problems in the Union of South Africa could reignite this market. Until more independent pricing information is available, however, you are placing too much trust in the firm that handles your strategic metals investments.

As in diamond investing, you have to get price information from the people who sell you the product, who tend to interpret all developments in the very best light. Also the problem of buying retail and selling wholesale has certainly not been resolved. This market is best left to adventurous, risk-oriented souls willing and able to risk and lose their entire investments in exchange for the potential of large profits.

Gold and Silver Mutual Funds

Precious metals funds invest in a diversified pool of gold- and silver-related stocks. Some funds also invest directly in the bullion. Gold stocks provide substantial leverage for precious metals investors.

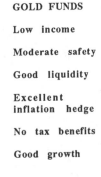
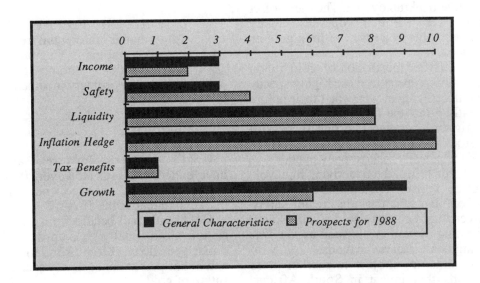

Gold and silver are classic inflation hedge investments. They tend to be very volatile though. The major gold-producing mines are in South Africa, and the tenuous political situation there inflames price volatility.

The stocks tend to outperform the bullion because costs of production are relatively fixed. It costs $300 per ounce to mine gold, and price increases above that amount dramatically enhance a mine's profitability. For example, from January 1, 1987, through April 15, 1987, gold rose 9.7%. Many individual gold stocks rose more than 60% in the same time period. The *average* gold mutual fund appreciated 62.6% in that same time period!

The universe of gold stocks is small compared to common stock issues. Only about fifteen mutual funds are oriented toward gold, compared to hundreds of stock funds. Only one fund invests strictly in silver stocks and bullion. You have considerably less flexibility in finding funds that closely match your investment objectives and risk tolerance.

The gold bull market in the 1970s led to an explosion in the investment advisory newsletter field. Many advisory letters still specialize in precious metals. Most major financial periodicals cover the precious metals markets. Most gold fund prices are listed in the *Wall Street Journal*.

Both load and no-load gold mutual funds are available. Load funds assess an up-front charge of 2 to 8%. No-load funds have no sales fees. No difference in performance is discernible between the two types of funds.

Investment Potential

The chief attraction of gold funds is large potential capital gains. However, many funds also offer attractive income. Many South African gold stocks pay relatively high dividends. Since gold is a depleting asset (once the reserves are mined, more gold cannot be created), high dividend payouts enable investors to recoup their investment.

Some gold funds invest a small portion of their assets in "penny stocks." Penny stocks are issues that trade for less than $1 per share. They are new untried companies that trade more on future promises than on actual present-day results. Penny stocks carry very high risk. They have a very high relative bankruptcy rate. They also offer very high leverage if their properties actually do become viable as a result of high gold or silver prices.

The diversified portfolios of gold funds enables them to invest in these highly speculative ventures without worry that their failure will greatly affect the funds assets. Yet they are so highly leveraged that one successful penny stock venture out of a hundred can be sufficient to actually make money overall.

Gold funds reflect the underlying high volatility of gold prices. The funds are liquid and diversified, and thus provide greater safety than investing in a single gold stock. No accepted rating system exists such as the system rating bond issuers for funds.

Gold funds are subject to market price risk. Funds that invest in South African stocks are subject to substantial political risk. Gold and silver funds provide excellent protection from inflation.

Gold funds are suitable investments for well-diversified retirement plans. They would not be appropriate as the only asset in such plans.

Strengths

 Gold and silver funds are liquid investments. The funds provide greater safety through diversification than investing in single stocks. Gold funds offer potential for excellent capital gains. Gold funds provide excellent protection from inflation. Gold share investments usually outperform bullion. Gold funds offer professional management in a high-risk area.

Weaknesses

 Gold fund prices are volatile. They substantially underperform the stock market in noninflationary times. Funds that invest in South African shares are subject to the political uncertainty surrounding that country. Poor management may result in high fees and bad performance.

Tax Considerations

 The 1986 Tax Reform Act eliminated preferential treatment for capital gains. Capital gains and dividend income are taxed at your ordinary income bracket.

Summing Up

Gold's long-term downtrend appears to have ended in 1986. However, it is highly unlikely that gold will experience a superbull market like that of the 1970s.

Gold funds will benefit from a surge in inflation. Gold usually goes up when the U.S. dollar goes down. Monitor inflation indexes and dollar performance as key factors for the future of gold.

Many investment advisors believe that gold and gold funds should be a small part, 5 to 10%, of a diversified investment portfolio. The variety of gold funds offers you good flexibility in selecting a fund that meets your objectives and risk tolerance. Funds investing solely in South African shares would run higher risk than funds investing in North American and Australian gold shares. Funds that invest a portion of their assets in bullion will be less volatile than share-only funds.

CONCLUSION

We do not expect inflation to be a major problem in 1988. While inflation levels as seen in the CPI or PPI may be slightly higher, we expect continued low inflation. However, you should have at least the minimum 5% invested in precious metals. If any of the warning signals move higher, incease your allocation. We do not foresee the need to invest more than the upper end of the allocation levels.

CHAPTER 15

OPTIONS, FUTURES, AND SPECIAL INVESTING TECHNIQUES

A GLANCE AHEAD

Many analysts believe that the margins, high leverage, and general speculative fervor were responsible for the severity of the Great Depression. In 1929 you could buy stock from full-service brokerage firms for only 10%. When prices started to fall, the heavily margined public couldn't come up with the money necessary to prevent liquidation.

Since those heady days, the Federal Reserve Board has controlled margin requirements. Today you must put up a minimum of 50% of the value of the stock you want to buy. Certainly that's far more conservative than 60 years ago.

But some advisors worry that the market has moved ahead of the regulators and ahead of the desire for control over speculation. At the peak of the last inflationary surge, President Carter went so far as to blame inflation on speculators who were bidding prices to what he felt were unconscionable prices. All this has inflamed the desire many investors feel to add quick profits to their portfolios by betting on the dynamics of the market itself, as well as on the soundness of the underlying companies.

In this chapter, you'll learn

- *How put-and-call options can help you cash in on short-term market changes, but*

at *considerable risk to your principal—and more money as well!*
- *How futures help investors share business risks—and profits—with commodity producers and other investment companies.*
- *How special trading techniques such as short selling and leveraged contracts can help to hedge your market bets.*

THE HOW AND WHY OF ADVANCED TRADING TECHNIQUES

In the 1920s, the futures market was called the *commodity market*. Agricultural commodities dominated the trade. Now agricultural commodities play a minor role in futures.

The rise of the listed stock options market has made highly leveraged speculation easily accessible to anyone with a few thousand dollars. Most option premiums are less than 10% of the value of the underlying stock.

However, there is one significant difference. Option buyers don't have to come up with additional money if their stocks fall. Your loss is limited to the amount you paid for the option. And you can't buy options on margin!

Although there will always be "doom-and-gloomers" decrying every innovation, every

257

change of any sort, no real evidence supports the notion that the rise of stock options and financial futures has resulted in widespread speculative excesses. In fact, one of the reasons for the huge volumes in both these vehicles has been their widespread acceptance by institutions, from mutual funds to banks to international corporations.

Many mutual funds hedge downside risk with stock index futures. Savings institutions use financial futures to hedge their portfolios. This hedge helps them even out the wide swings in earnings that plagued the industry during the 1970s.

Risks

Concomitant with the higher returns possible with options and futures is the higher risk. The fact is that the vast majority of option and future traders lose money. You have to decide whether or not you are smarter and more disciplined than 75% of the other speculators.

Don't confuse option buying with investing in stock. You have no ownership interest in the underlying company. A well-managed company should show appreciation over time. But time is one thing an option buyer does not have. Stock buyers earn money from the growth of a company's assets even if it is not reflected immediately in the price. They may also receive dividends. Option buyers earn money only when the price of the stock appreciates more than the time value of the option depreciates. It does option buyers no good to have an option on an undervalued company if the market doesn't recognize it immediately!

In the past, much attention was directed to ferreting out undervalued stocks on the assumption that "you can't buy the market." That is no longer true. Both stock and future index options afford individuals the chance to "buy the market."

Some advisors would have you believe that timing the whole market is easier than selecting individual stocks, but the evidence certainly doesn't support that contention. Ac-

curate timing has proven as elusive in today's high-tech environment as it was 50 years ago.

Futures trading is very high risk. The money you are required to deposit represents only about 5–10% of your total exposure.

Futures trading is dominated by short-term trading. Holding a position for more than two months is the exception for most traders. It requires close daily contact with your broker. Because of the leverage involved, you must track prices every day or risk substantial losses. This kind of trading is for risk takers, willing and able to sustain intense activity and sizable losses.

Options are hyped as a "safe" alternative to futures. But beware of the glossy language. Do you *really* feel all that much safer knowing that your total investment becomes worthless on a set day in the near future? We've said that "time heals all." Obviously, that proverb doesn't apply to trade options! It cannot be emphasized too strongly that *of all investments, option buying requires the best timing*.

Conclusions

We don't mean to discourage all interest in option or futures trading. We do mean to emphasize that both endeavors may be suitable for many investors. Most readers of this book have full-time jobs that occupy their primary attention. The speculative tactics we are about to discuss in this chapter are not to be engaged in part time, casually. The stakes are high.

If you are willing to take the greater risk but still do not have the time to devote, consider professional management. However, just as you shouldn't believe everything a securities salesperson tells you, neither should you take a manager's claims at face value. Get a manager whose philosophy most closely fits your own outlook. An intense, short-term, big risk taker may perform well over time. But are you willing to sit through the bad spells? If not, select a manager with more consistent results, if less spectacular.

Keep in mind that compounding power will ensure that a steady performance of 10 to 15% per year will yield huge returns over ten or fifteen years. Many advisors who can show spectacular performance for a short time; but no one makes 50% a year consistently.

Buying Stock Options

BUYING
OPTIONS

No income

Low safety

Good liquidity

Good inflation
hedge

No tax benefits

Good growth

The two types of listed stock options are: calls and puts. A call option gives the buyer right to buy 100 shares of a specified stock at a specified price within a specified time period. A put option is the reverse. A put option gives the buyer the right to sell 100 shares of a specified stock at a specified price within a specified time period.

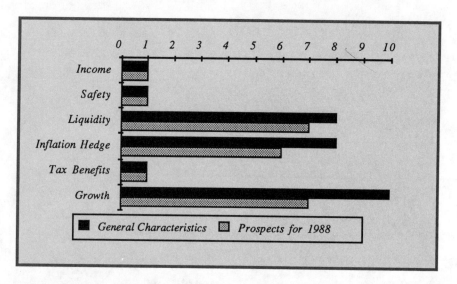

Options offer investors an opportunity to leverage their investments. For example, an investor who buys an IBM July 150 call has purchased the *right* to buy 100 shares of IBM from the seller of the option at $150 per share up to the third week in July (see the section on stock options income). On March 23, 1987, the July 150 call was $8 when the price of IBM on the New York Stock Exchange (NYSE) was $150. Since each option is for 100 shares, multiply 100 by $8 to get the day's price of $800 for the option.

Puts are the exact opposite. For example, on March 23, 1987, the IBM July 150 put sold for $7 per share, or $700 for the option. Its expiration is the same day as the call.

A combined example can help sort out these complexities. On March 23, 1987, IBM sold for $150 per share on the NYSE. If you felt that IBM had a good chance to rise to $160 or more by the end of July, you could have profited in two ways:

- You could buy 100 shares of IBM stock for $15,000 (plus commission).

- Or you could buy a July 150 call option for $800 (plus commission).

If you believed that the price of IBM will go *down* by the end of July, you again would have had two alternatives:

- Sell short 100 shares of IBM for $15,000 (plus commission)
- Buy a July 150 put option for $700 (plus commission)

Investment Potential

The difference between stock and option investing is *leverage*. Options enable investors to control stock with an investment of only 5 to 10% of the value of the underlying stock. However, an options buyer has one important consideration that a stock buyer doesn't: time. Time works against the options buyer because the option loses value every day up to expiration.

On March 23, 1987, the May 150 call option was worth only $550 compared to $800 for the July contract because only eight weeks were left before the call expired. The July option had an *additional* eight weeks for IBM to make its anticipated move, and therefore commanded a higher price.

Options buying offers capital gains potential only. Options pay no income (see the later section on stock options income).

Options trading is a very high risk, highly volatile investment. Most options trading is now done via the major exchanges. The uniform contract specifications and active markets make them very liquid.

As mentioned earlier, options run the unique risk of time. An option buyer always has time working against him or her. Therefore timing expertise is at a premium. In addition, of course, options are subject to the same business, political, and economic risks as are the underlying stocks.

Strengths

Exchange-listed options are very liquid. Options offer significant leverage. Option investing requires less capital than do stock purchases. Losses are limited to the amount of the premium.

Weaknesses

Options are very high risk. On expiration date, the option value drops to zero! If your timing is off by even a few weeks, you can lose your whole investment. Options pay no income. (Most stocks pay at least some dividends.) Option trading requires close attention to market action, as options are time related. Option traders must meet stringent suitability requirements.

The example of the call option assumes that IBM appreciated from $150 to $160 per share between March 23, 1987, and Friday, July 17, 1987, when the option expired. If the stock rises to $160 *before* the third week of July, the option usually trades with some premium for the time left before expiration as well as "intrinsic value." Intrinsic value of a call option is determined by subtracting the strike price of the option from the current price of the stock. For example, when IBM is trading at $155, the intrinsic value of the call 150 options (any expiration month) is $5. In other words, the minimum value of the option would be $5.

The put option example assumes that IBM falls from $150 to $140 per share between March 23, 1987, and Friday, July 17, 1987, when the option expired. As with the call option, the more time left before expiration, the more valuable the option will be. Calculate the intrinsic value of a put by subtracting the price of the underlying stock from the strike price. For example, if IBM is selling at $145, the intrinsic value of the 150 put options will be $5.

Summing Up

The bull market in stocks that commenced in the summer of 1982 has resulted in increased interest in options trading, although the danger of that have been revealed in the October 19 collapse. Many analysts have forecast a further rise in the market as measured by the Dow Jones Industrial Average, to as much as 3,500. Astute call buyers can profit handsomely in such an environment.

This is not, however, an area for neophyte traders. Experienced traders who can devote considerable time to the market have a distinct edge.

Option buying is highly speculative. You should use only funds you can afford to lose. Never invest more than 10% of your liquid assets in option-buying strategies. Remember, a call will profit *only* when the underlying stock rises quickly. A put is profitable *only* when the underlying stock drops quickly. "Trading range" (flat) markets and contrary markets (that is, contrary to the anticipated direction) will result in losses!

Selling Stock Options

SELLING
OPTIONS
——

Good income

Low safety

Good liquidity

Poor inflation
hedge

No tax benefits

Moderate growth

As noted, there are two types of listed stock options: calls and puts. A call option is a contract between a seller and buyer that gives a buyer the right to buy 100 shares of a specified stock at a specified price within a specified time period. A put option gives the buyer the right to sell 100 shares of a specified stock at a specified price within a specified time period.

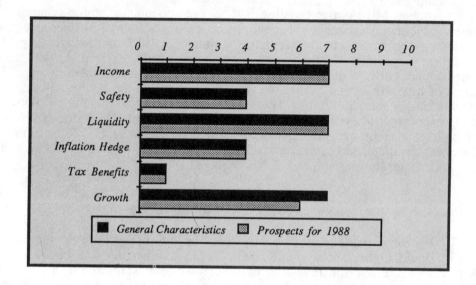

Options are most commonly thought of as a leveraged short-term approach to stock investing. Many professionals find, however, that over the long haul it is more profitable to be on the selling side of an options contract. When you are the seller, you receive the option premium (minus commission) paid by the option buyer.

To better understand how this works, look at an example. Let's say that on March 23, 1987, IBM sold for $150 per share on the NYSE. If at the time you felt the stock may rise, you could

• Buy 100 shares of IBM stock for $15,000 (plus commission)
• Buy a July 150 call option for $800 (plus commission)

Or you could

• Sell a July 150 put option for $700 (you needed to post margin funds, a portion of which could be Treasury bills)

If you bought the stock or the call option, you'd make money only if the stock rose (not counting the dividend paid by the stock). However, if you elected to sell the put option, you'd pocket the premium if the stock (1) rose, or (2) stayed flat. This is because the "time value" of the premium deteriorates with every passing day. If the stock price was still $150 on June 15, only a few weeks were left before expiration. The put option would be much less valuable to an investor than if he or she had bought it in March.

This "selling" or "writing" of options works both ways. To profit from flat or dull markets, you can sell either puts or calls or both!

Investment Potential

If you believed that the price of IBM would go *down* by the end of July, you could

- Sell short 100 shares of IBM for $15,000 (plus commission)
- Buy a July 150 put option for $700 (plus commission)

Or you could

- Sell a July 150 IBM call option for $800 (minus commission)

If you sold the stock short or bought an option, you'd only make money if the stock actually falls. If you sold the call option, you'd make money (1) if the stock price fell, or (2) if the stock stayed flat. The time value of the option deteriorates every day the price does not go up!

Contrary to popular belief, the stock market spends most of the time in flat "trading ranges." The option-selling strategy is an ideal method for capitalizing on flat markets.

Unlike the situation when you are buying options, when you write (sell) options time works for you because the option loses value every day up to expiration. On March 23, 1987, the May 150 call option was worth only $550 compared to $800 for the July contract, because only eight weeks were left before the call expired. As mentioned earlier, the July option had an *additional* eight weeks for IBM stock to make its anticipated move and therefore commanded a higher price.

There are two ways to approach writing options. If you already own 100 shares (or multiples) of the underlying stock, you can sell a call option without having to post additional margin funds. For example, if you had bought IBM at $130 per share, you could have sold the July 150 call options as in the preceding example, for no additional money. You'd have received the premium income immediately.

If the stock moved above 150 by the third week in July, you could have bought the option back and kept your stock. You might decide to let your stock be "called" away at the $150-per-share price. Your profit on the transaction would be the $20-per-share profit you made on the stock, plus the $800 premium you received for the option.

A more aggressive approach is to sell call options on stock you do not own. This is another method of selling short. It is very high risk. If the underlying stock shoots much higher in price, you could lose far more than your original investment. To sell naked options, most firms require that you have a minimum of $10,000 or more in your account. Margin money must be posted and is adjusted daily depending on the price movement of the stock. If you sell a call option and the price of the stock moves higher, you are required to deposit additional capital.

Strengths

 Exchange-listed options are very liquid. An option writer has time on his or her side. Option writing generally requires less capital than equivalent stock transactions. An option writer receives income up front. That income can earn interest immediately.

Weaknesses

 Options are very high risk. Because they are leveraged plays on the underlying stock, their price movements are even more volatile than the stock's movements. Option writing requires close attention to market action, because they are time related. Option traders must meet stringent suitability requirements. Option writing, particularly naked writing, requires substantial money. An options writer is liable for losses that could exceed his or her investment.

Tax Considerations

 Income earned from options writing is taxed as ordinary income. No special tax advantages apply to options writing.

Summing Up

Option writing is highly speculative. You should use only funds you can afford to lose. Never risk more than 10% of your liquid assets in option-writing positions. Unlike option buying, option writing offers the potential to profit in "trading range" (flat) markets. However, unlike the situation in option buying, your loss is not limited to your initial investment if the market moves contrary to your expectations.

Option writing can significantly increase your income on a portfolio of stocks but must be closely monitored. If you cannot devote full time to watching your investments, consider retaining a professional manager or investigate option-writing mutual funds.

COMPARISONS BETWEEN STOCKS AND OPTIONS

Stock Purchase

1. 100 IBM at $150 = $15,000
2. Sell IBM at $160 = $16,000
3. Profit = $1,000 (before commissions)
4. Return = 6.66% (profit ÷ purchase price)

Call Option Purchase

1. 1 IBM July 150 at $8 = $800
2. Sell July 160 at $10 = $1,000 (minimum value with IBM at $160)
3. Profit = $200 (less commissions)
4. Return = 25% (profit ÷ purchase price)

Stock Short Sale

1. Sell 100 IBM at $150 = $15,000
2. Buy back IBM at $140 = $14,000
3. Profit = $1,000 (less commissions)
4. Percent return = 6.66% (profit ÷ sale price)

Put Option Purchase

1. Buy IBM July $150 put at $7 = $700
2. Sell 150 put at $150 = $1,000 (minimum value when IBM is at $140)
3. Profit = $300 (less commissions)
4. Percent return = 43% (profit ÷ purchase price)

Stock Index Options

Index options are contracts between buyers and sellers just like stock puts and calls. However, instead of trading on an individual stock's rise or fall, index options are tied to broadbased indexes such as the S&P 500, the Major Market Index (which closely follows the Dow Jones Industrial Average, the NYSE Composite, and others). Unlike options on individual stocks, buyers of index options settle for cash because it would be impossible to deliver stocks that exactly fit the indexes. Many new index options are being added all the time. The latest group has been for industry sector indexes such as technology.

STOCK INDEX
OPTIONS

Income possible

Low safety

Good Liquidity

Good inflation hedge

No tax benefits

Good growth

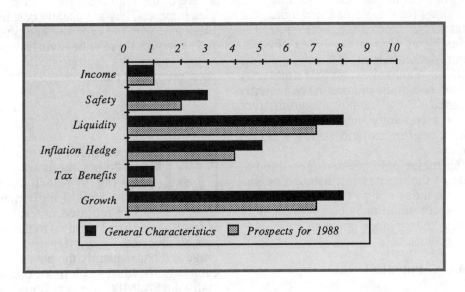

General Characteristics ▨ Prospects for 1988

Most investors have had the frustrating experience of being right on stock market direction but wrong in the individual stocks they bought. On Wall Street, there used to be a saying that "It's not a stock market, but a market of stocks." In other words, the stocks you select are more important than the direction of the market. But that's no longer true.

There are now a number of ways to bet on the direction of the market as a whole without having to select individual stocks. There are stock index futures, options on stock index futures, and stock options on market indexes. The most heavily traded option in history is the S&P 100 option traded on the Chicago Board of Trade. The market is so well known that it is often merely referred to by its ticker symbol—OEX.

As with all stock options, stock index options are either call or put. Stock index options have one major difference from options on individual stocks: they settle for cash. It is impossible to deliver "the S&P 100 Index." Instead, you figure the prices—and your profit and loss—by multiplying the quoted price of the option by $100.

For example, on May 29, 1987, the S&P 100 Index closed at 284.96. The July 285 OEX call option closed that day at 9. To buy the July 285 you'd pay $900 ($100 x 9) plus the commission. If the market rallied before the third Friday in July, and your option went to 12, you would make $300 minus commissions if you sold.

Like other stock options, there is a nonquantifiable "time value" in each option. This merely means that the more time left in the option before expiration, the more valuable it is. For example, on May 29, the June 285 OEX call option was selling for only 5 1/4 ($525).

Put options are also available stock index options. Just like their counterpart for individual stocks, a put option appreciates if the market goes down. The value is calculated the same way. Multiply the price times $100 to get the value. You'd buy a put if you felt the stock market was going to go down.

Index options have become so popular as trading vehicles that the *Wall Street Journal* carries their prices in a separate section every day. In addition to the S&P 100, there are index options for the Value Line Index, the National OTC Index, the S&P 500, the Financial News Composite Index (FNCI), the Major Market Index (MMI), and the New York Stock Exchange (NYSE) Index. A number of subgroup indexes have recently been started. These include the gold/silver index, the technology index, the oil index, the institutional index, and even the NYSE Beta index.

All the major option exchanges trade at least one of the indexes just listed. You can buy a stock index option through a licensed broker. A commission is charged for both buying and selling index options.

Investment Potential

Index options have been called "the ultimate speculation." You are not buying the right to real entity such as stock ownership in a company. You are speculating purely and simply on the direction of the stock market as a whole.

Stock index options are short-term (remember that there is an expiration date) capital gains speculations. They produce no income.

Stock index options are highly leveraged investments. In our preceding example, a $900 investment actually controls almost $28,500! As a result, minor changes in the underlying indexes can mean great profits or losses. However, unlike futures indexes, your loss is limited to the amount of money you have invested.

Index options are very volatile investments. They are very high risk. It is possible to lose your entire investment in a

short time. S&P 100 options are very liquid. Most other index options are liquid in varying degrees. It is important to check the average daily volume of the index option you wish to trade to ensure that there is an active liquid market.

 Investment professionals have developed a number of sophisticated strategies for trading options. These include spreads, straddles, and numerous other concoctions. Neophyte traders should be aware of the high costs many of these strategies impose. They are usually best left to professionals with the expertise and time to carefully monitor these wide-swinging markets.

Options are not appropriate investments for most retirement plans.

Strengths

 Stock index options allow you to "trade the market" without having to select from among over 50,000 individual issues. The required initial investment is small. Your loss is limited to the amount of money invested. They offer tremendous leverage and consequently the potential for large capital gains. Most stock index options, especially the S&P 100, are very liquid. You have great flexibility to profit from both up and down markets.

Weaknesses

 Stock index options are very volatile. You can lose 100% of your investment on expiration day. You are subject to both market and timing risk. Commission costs are high relative to the amount of invested capital. They pay no income.

Tax Considerations

 Stock index options generate capital gains and losses. Gains are taxed at your ordinary income rates. Losses offset other capital gains. Excess losses are carried forward.

Summing Up

Stock index options are one of the fastest-growing markets in the financial arena. The volatile nature and time element limit the market to those investors with time necessary to carefully monitor them. They should only be traded with risk capital that you could lose entirely without affecting your lifestyle.

No more than 10% of your investment funds should ever be devoted to buying stock index options. Selling (or writing) index options is a very high risk venture that should be tried only by experienced investors.

Agriculture Futures

**AGRICULTURE
FUTURES**

No income

Low safety

Good liquidity

Good inflation
hedge

No tax benefits

Good growth

A futures contract is a binding contract between a buyer and a seller that specifies the commodity, the amount of the commodity, and the delivery date when the seller must deliver the commodity. Futures originally arose as a method to enable producers, principally farmers, the ability to shift some of their business risk to speculators.

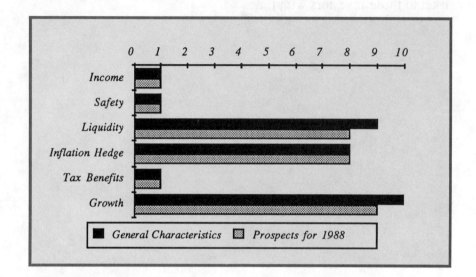

It seems only fitting that the most dramatic changes in the financial markets over the past 10 years have occurred in the most dramatic marketplace—futures. Originally called *commodities*, as noted earlier, the futures markets have evolved so much that the agricultural commodities that once formed the foundation for industry now play a much smaller role. Over the last 20 years, futures markets have expanded to bonds, T-bills, Eurodollars, crude oil, and even the stock market.

Farmers' decisions to "hedge" their risk is made at planting time. They know how much corn they will have at harvest. They have two choices. They can wait until they harvest their corn and sell it at the price available at that time. Or they can sell the future, yet-to-be-harvested crop at planting time, for physical delivery after harvest. The decision depends on the prevailing price and the expectations for the future.

For example, assume that when farmers plant corn in the spring they know that costs will be $2.00 per bushel if all goes well by harvest. If corn for December delivery is selling at $2.50 per bushel, farmers may elect to lock in the $0.50 profit by selling the in-the-ground crop in the spring. One contract of corn on the Chicago Board of Trade is fixed at 5,000 bushels. A single contract at $2.50 per bushel would be worth $12,500.

In order to sell one contract of corn, farmers would have to post a margin "good-faith" deposit of $600. Someone would buy the contract, expecting the price to go higher than $2.50 per bushel. Since each contract is 5,000 bushels, a $0.01 move is worth $50. If December corn's price goes up $0.05, buyers would make $250 (5 cents x $50) per contract. Farmers would lose $250 in potential profit they would have received if they had waited to sell. If the price goes down $0.05, speculators would lose $250 per contract. The farmers would gain because they locked in the higher price.

The speculator is motivated by profit. The farmers' motivations are more complex, since they must choose whether to take a set profit margin and to forgo additional potential profit by selling in the future. If they guess wrong and sell early to lock in a fixed profit, if they meet no other surprises such as a drought, the worst that will happen is that they will not make as much money as they could have. They have shifted the price risk to the speculator.

On delivery day—which is always specified for each commodity—the seller must deliver the specified amount to the buyer. The buyer is obligated to pay the full value of the contracted price to the seller. In the preceding example, the buyer would pay the seller $12,500.

In actual practice, less than 2% of all futures contracts are settled by delivery. What actually happens is that the buyers and sellers "offset" their positions before delivery date. If you *sell* the December corn contract, you'd merely *buy* a December corn contract to offset your obligation to deliver 5,000 bushels. If you are a buyer, you sell an equivalent contract to offset your obligation to pay the full $12,500 value of the contract.

Agricultural futures contracts are actively sold on exchanges around the world. The most popular agricultural commodities include wheat, corn, soybeans, soybean oil and meal, cotton, sugar, coffee, cocoa, and the meats—live cattle, hogs, and pork bellies (bacon). The largest exchanges trading agricultural commodities are the Chicago Board of Trade (CBT), the Chicago Mercantile Exchange (CME), the New York Cotton Exchange, and the Coffee, Sugar & Cocoa Exchange. Buyers and sellers do not actually know who is on the other side of their contracts. Just remember that for every seller there is a buyer, and the reverse. Someone is always on the other side of the contract, hoping it moves against you and for him or her.

Investment Potential

Futures offer great capital gains potential. They pay no income. Futures trading is a "zero-sum" business. That means for every winner there is a loser. This situation differs markedly from stocks, where everyone can win in a rising market. Even more than in stock trading, you are competing with other traders for available profits.

The greatest attraction, and greatest danger, to futures is the leverage. As we detailed in the preceding example, a deposit of $600 can control a $12,500 contract. That's putting up only 5% of your total liability. A futures investor is liable for the full value of the contract, not just the deposit.

Leverage works both ways. A 6% rise in price from $2.50 per bushel to $2.65 means a profit of $750 (before commissions) for a $600 investment. That's a 125% return!

But remember, the seller loses $750. He or she would get a "margin call" once the corn rose $0.06 ($300) against him or her. The initial deposit is merely a good-faith deposit required by the exchanges to ensure that the contracts are fulfilled. If price movement causes a "paper loss" of 50% of the initial margin, the broker will require additional money to ensure the seller can still meet his or her obligations. If you posted the minimum of $600 and the price of corn went against you $0.06, the "equity" in your account would drop to $300 ($600 minus the $300 loss from adverse price action). You would be required to either post an additional $300 to bring your equity back to initial levels, or you'd be forced to liquidate your position if you refused to commit further money.

In other words, leverage—which looks so attractive if you are correct on the direction of the market—can be devastating if you are wrong. In the case of corn at $2.50 per bushel, if you guess wrong a price move of only 2.4% ($.06) will wipe out 50% of your initial $600 deposit!

Futures are not appropriate for most retirement plans.

Strengths

 Leverage offers the chance for tremendous profits. Actively traded futures contracts are usually very liquid. You do not pay interest on the balance between your margin deposit and the full value of the contract. Commodities offer excellent protection from inflation. There are no "insider" (merger, acquisition, or takeover) rumors to distort the market price. Much flexibility can be achieved through various strategies such as spreads. Traders have equal capability to sell short (profit from price drops) or to buy long (profit from price rises).

Weaknesses

 Leverage can be devastating if you are wrong on price direction. The short-term nature of futures puts a premium on accurate timing. News events may cause adverse price reactions, which reach exchange-specified "limits" that make it impossible to get out of a position. Futures are characterized by high volatility. Futures are high-risk investing by any definition.

Tax Considerations

 The previous preferential capital gains treatment accorded futures is eliminated in the 1986 Tax Reform Act. All capital gains are taxed as ordinary income for speculators. Loss carried forward is limited to $3,000 per year.

Summing Up

The agricultural futures market is a highly leveraged, very risky investment arena. This market is not for casual investors. Over 80% of futures traders lose money.

Agricultural futures do offer you a direct play on tangible assets. During the inflationary blowoff in the 1970s, agricultural futures were big gainers.

The futures market offers good liquidity for most commodities. Many professional advisors will manage your funds for a fee.

Stock Futures

Most futures contracts are binding contracts between a buyer and a seller that specify the commodity, the amount of the commodity, and the delivery date when the seller must deliver the commodity at the price at which the contract was entered. However, stock index futures are unique in the futures world. Rather than settling in terms of a specific quantity of a specific commodity, stock index futures are settled in cash on delivery day.

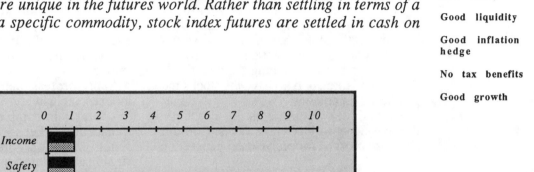

The newest development in the ever changing world of futures has been the incorporation of stock trading. When the S&P Index futures first began trading on the Chicago Mercantile Exchange, it quickly became the most popular futures market of all time. It quickly displaced U.S. Treasury bond trading, which had replaced gold and silver, which had superseded the traditional agricultural commodities.

The S&P Index traded on the Chicago Mercantile Exchange (CME), the New York Composite Index on the New York Financial Exchange (NYFE), and the Value Line Index on the Kansas City Board of Trade. They all are priced by multiplying $500 times the index. For example, if the June S&P contract was selling at 260, the value of the contract would be $130,000. The Major Market Index (MMI) is designed to emulate the Dow Jones Industrial Average and is traded on the Chicago Board of Trade. Its value is calculated by multiplying $250 times the index.

Stock index futures have been blamed for much of the volatility of the stock market in recent years. Large institutional traders use index futures to hedge their stock positions. For example, if the S&P 500 cash index in May was selling at a significant discount to the June S&P futures index, institutional investors (especially arbitragers, who seek to profit from price differentials) would buy a basket of stocks closely related to the makeup of the cash index and sell the futures index. On settlement day, the futures index will come down to the cash index, or the cash index (and the basket of stocks) will move up to what the futures index sold for. Either way, the institutional investor makes money.

Also the concept of "portfolio insurance" is closely related to the use of futures indexes to hedge money managers' stock portfolios. Once managers have a profit in their portfolios, they may elect to sell futures contracts in anticipation of a market drop rather than sell out their stocks.

Stock index futures contracts offer the individual investor the chance to literally trade "the market" rather than individual stocks. Many investors have experienced the frustration of correctly anticipating the direction of the stock market, only to have the stocks they purchased do nothing!

Stock index futures can be purchased through licensed brokerage firms. Commissions are charged for each closed transaction.

Investment Potential

Stock index futures trading is a zero-sum game. For every winner, there is a loser. When you purchase an index contract in anticipation of a market rise, the other half of the contract is filled by someone who believes the market is going down!

Like other futures contracts, index futures are highly leveraged. Initial margin deposit requirements run approximately 10% of the value of the contract. In addition to the initial deposit requirements, most brokerage firms require that futures traders have substantial incomes and net worth.

Stock index futures are very high risk investments. The markets are very volatile. The high leverage results in even greater volatility for your account's equity.

The very high interest in index trading provides very good liquidity. Stock index futures do not have exchange established limits like other futures contracts. You cannot get "locked" into a position with no escape, as in other futures markets. However, large price movements can and do occur frequently.

In addition to market risk, index futures are very sensitive to economic and political news. Unforeseen developments can result in rapid price changes.

The availability of cash stocks and varying delivery months has resulted in numerous investment strategies. This enhanced flexibility enables astute investors to devise strategies to fit their investment objectives and risk tolerance.

Index trading generates capital gains. There is no income.

Stocks historically provide some measure of protection from inflation. Index futures can be sold short (can profit from price drops) as easily as being bought for price rises. This flexibility differs from stock trading, which has various rules that limit short selling.

Many professional managers trade stock indexes exclusively. Other managers use index futures in combination with cash stock transactions. Fees vary widely, and you should thoroughly understand them before signing any contracts. Active trading in index futures can result in large commission charges.

Strengths

Index futures offer very high leverage and consequently the potential for large profits. Index futures give investors the chance to trade the market without having to select from over 50,000 individual stocks. Index futures offer large investors the opportunity to hedge their cash stock portfolios. As the most heavily traded of all futures contracts, index futures are very liquid. Cash settlements are paid 24 hours after the close of a transaction. Exchanges set no "limits" on daily price movements, further enhancing their liquidity.

Weaknesses

High leverage means high risk. Index futures are very volatile, making for substantial risk. Index futures tend to exaggerate stock market movement caused by unanticipated news. Index futures may diverge from cash index movements. The large dollar value of daily price moves places a premium on accurate short-term timing. Losses may significantly exceed your initial investment.

Tax Considerations

 Index profits are taxed as ordinary income. Paper profits on December 31 are taxed as though the gain has been taken on that day. Losses can be used to offset other capital gains. Losses not used in one year may be carried forward.

Summing Up

Stock index futures have already found a permanent place in the investment world. Not only are they widely used by individuals who like high risks, but they are also being increasingly employed by large institutions to hedge their portfolios' performance.

Daily volume in the S&P futures alone far exceeds that of traditional commodity markets such as wheat or corn.

This is a very high risk market. Only investors well schooled in the risks and rewards should venture into this market. The high leverage is a very attractive feature when you are right about market direction. However, that leverage works both ways. You are at risk for the entire value of the contract, not just the amount of your margin deposit.

Interest Rates Futures

INTEREST RATE
FUTURES

No income

Low safety

Excellent
liquidity

Poor inflation
hedge

No tax benefits

Good growth

A futures contract is a binding contract between a buyer and a seller that specifies the commodity, the amount of the commodity, and the delivery date when the seller must deliver the commodity. Futures originally arose as a method to enable producers, principally farmers, to shift some of their business risk to speculators.

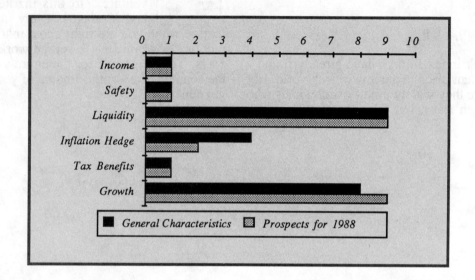

The face of commodity futures markets was changed forever with the introduction of interest rate futures in the early 1970s. Trading volume in Treasury bond futures quickly became the heaviest of all futures markets. Although the subsequent introduction of S&P Index futures supplanted T-bonds as the most widely traded, they still command substantial interest from individual and institutional traders.

Interest rate futures were introduced at a time when interest rates were nearing all-time highs as a result of prolonged inflation. Many banks and thrift institutions were in deep trouble for having committed the grave error of borrowing short term while lending long term. Typically a savings institution would secure deposits for three months, six months, or one, two, or three years through its certificates of deposit. Its liabilities, however, were often for much longer time periods. Thrifts at that time were pretty much limited to mortgage loans.

What happened was that their long-term obligations, such as mortgage loans, were lent out at a fixed rate, say 8%. This was fine when they only had to pay depositors 5 or 6%. But when inflation turned higher, many depositors shopped around for better yields. The money market mutual fund industry played a very large part in making consumers aware of alternatives to the low interest rates paid by banks.

Just as grain, metals, stock index, and foreign currency futures are used by commercial interests to hedge their risks, so do savings institutions make use of futures to lock in a profitable spread between their assets (deposits) and liabilities (loans). The risk is shifted to speculators in the futures market.

Four main interest rate future contracts are actively traded: Treasury bills (91 days), Eurodollars (91 days), Treasury notes (7 years) and Treasury bonds (20 years). T-bills and Eurodollars trade on the International Monetary Market (IMM) in Chicago. T-notes and T-bonds trade on the Chicago Board of Trade.

Interest rates futures are bought and sold through licensed futures brokers. All brokers must be members of the National Futures Association, a self-regulating body. A commission of $25 to $100, depending on type of service required, is charged on closing out a transaction.

Investment Potential

Interest rate futures are very highly leveraged. Margin deposits of $3,000–$5,000 control $1 million face value in both T-bills and Eurodollars. T-note and T-bond contracts are $100,000.

Trading in interest rates puts you into very volatile markets. Small changes in interest rates mean large dollar-amount fluctuations. For example, T-bonds and T-notes minimum price movement is 1/32 of a point. A 1/32-point move is worth $31.25.

Interest rate futures trade inversely to interest rates. This feature often confuses neophyte traders. When interest rates move higher, the futures move lower. If a newspaper headline reads "T-bond Futures Rally," you know that long-term interest rates have dropped.

Investing in interest rate futures offers tremendous flexibility. The different maturities from 91 days to twenty years makes it possible to take advantage of the yield curve with a variety of sophisticated strategies. The complexity of interest rates and the various strategies used makes it a difficult area for inexperienced traders. A number of professional management programs are available. Fees vary widely, and you should fully understand them before you enter into any contract with a manager.

Interest rate futures are not appropriate for most retirement programs.

Strengths

 Tremendous leverage (often the initial required margin is less than 5% of the value of the contract) offers great capital gains profit potential. High liquidity is a feature of interest rate futures. Even though exchange-specified limits exist, the market for

Treasury bonds is so huge that there is little risk of being locked by the limits for more than one or two trading sessions. Traders expecting rising interest rates can sell short as easily as buying. No special provisions limit short selling. No interest is charged on the balance between the value of the contract and the margin deposit. By short-selling interest rate futures, you gain protection against the ravages of inflation.

Weaknesses

 Great leverage means that small adverse moves in interest rates can mean large losses. Markets are very sensitive to news and therefore are very volatile. A premium attaches to short-term timing since expiration dates normally run out only one or two years. Interest rate futures are a very high risk investment.

Tax Considerations

 Profits or losses from interest rate futures are capital gains or losses. The 1986 Tax Reform Act eliminated preferential capital gains treatment. All gains are taxed at ordinary income levels. Losses can be used to offset other capital gains. Losses can be carried forward.

Summing Up

Interest rate futures have become the most heavily traded of all futures markets. Financial institutions now play an active role in this market. They use futures as one way of hedging their interest rate risks.

The high leverage inherent in interest rate futures makes this field very dangerous for part-time investors. If you do not have the time or expertise to devote to careful detailed monitoring of these treacherous markets, consider professional management.

Metals Futures

A futures contract is a binding contract between a buyer and a seller, that specifies the commodity, the amount of the commodity, and the delivery date when the seller must deliver the commodity to the buyer for the set price. For example, the most widely traded type of gold contract is for 100 ounces of gold for delivery in February, April, June, August, October, and December. While you can buy and sell gold contracts for as much as a two-year delivery "future," most trading involves contracts for delivery within 12 months.

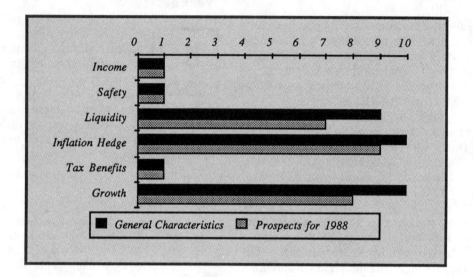

The first futures product to gain widespread trader interest after the agricultural commodities was the metals markets. Specifically, the inflationary 1970s saw the rise of interest in the precious metals—gold and silver. Gold bullion was illegal for Americans to own from 1933 until 1975. Silver—"poor man's gold"—served as a proxy for inflation-conscious investors until 1975. By the late 1970s, gold and silver became the most actively traded futures markets, far outstripping the traditional agricultural commodities.

Futures developed as a method for producers or consumers to hedge their risk by shifting it to speculators. For example, mine owners know what it costs to produce one ounce of gold. They have customers such as jewelry manufacturers who require certain amounts of gold for their products. Once a mine owner knows how much gold will be needed by customers, he or she works out an agreement for delivery of the gold. Since jewelry makers will need their biggest supply in December, for the holiday season, the mine owner can hedge the risk by "pre selling" the predetermined amount of gold for December delivery in the futures market.

For example, the mine owner may sell 10 contracts (1,000 ounces) of gold at $400 for December delivery in March. He or she knows the cost (say it's $350 per ounce). By selling the gold when the deal with the jewelry maker is completed, the mine owner locks in the profit. Of course, there is a trade-off for this security. If gold goes to $450 in the interim, the mine owner has given up the potential additional profit of $50 per ounce in exchange for protection from a drop in price.

The buyer of the contract may be a speculator who believes that the gold price will go higher. Since each contract is for 100 ounces, each $1 move in gold will mean a $100 profit (if the price goes up) or loss (if the price drops). The speculator's motivation is purely one of profit. The hedger also wants to make a profit of course, but is willing to forgo some profit potential to ensure a profit in the business of gold production. The price the mine pays for this "insurance" is the loss it takes on the transaction. It's merely a cost of business, like insurance for any other industry.

Gold, silver (5,000-ounce contracts), and copper are traded on the New York Commodity Exchange (called the Comex). Platinum and palladium are traded on the New York Mercantile Exchange. Silver (1,000-ounce contracts) and gold (to a much smaller extent) are traded on the Chicago Board of Trade.

You buy or sell futures contracts through licensed brokerage firms. A commission is charged for the transaction. Unlike stocks, commissions for futures are usually charged when the transaction is closed out. (Stock and bond commissions are charged on each purchase and sale.)

The futures business is closely regulated by the Commodity Futures Trading Commission (CFTC), a government agency. The National Futures Association (NFA) is a self-regulating entity that handles most of the regulatory procedures such as registration. All futures brokers must be members of the NFA and registered with the CFTC.

Investment Potential

The greatest attraction of futures for speculators is the leverage. For example, a contract of gold at $400 per ounce is worth $40,000. To buy or sell one contract, though, the trader must post a deposit called *margin*. The amount of the margin is set by the respective exchanges. The margin for gold is typically about $3,500.

In other words, you can control $40,000 with less than 10% of the full value of the contract. If you buy a contract of gold for December delivery at $400 per ounce, you'll need to post the $3,500 margin. If gold goes to $450 in the interim, you can sell the contract and pocket $5,000 profit ($50 x 100 ounces) before commissions. That's 43% profit on a price move of only a 12.5%!

Keep in mind, though, that you are legally bound for the full value of the future contract. Even though only $3,500 is required as initial deposit, a drop in price would mean that you would have to post more money to hang onto the contract. Typically, if the price drops so that 50% of the initial deposit is lost ($17.50 in this case), the brokerage firm will issue a "margin call" requiring you to post an additional $1,750. If you do not post the additional margin in 24 hours, the brokerage firm will sell your position.

Because of this leverage, futures markets are highly volatile. They are very high risk. Any number of economic or political developments can dramatically affect prices overnight.

Futures investing generates capital gains. There is no current income. Historically, precious metals offer an excellent inflation hedge.

A wide variety of trading techniques is available to precious metals futures traders. For example, spread trading involves the simultaneous buying of one delivery month and the selling of another in the same metals. Sophisticated traders even do spread trading between related commodities such as gold and silver. This flexibility means there are many different ways to trade precious metals futures, with varying degrees of risk. However, even the "safest" approach carries substantial risk exposure.

The late 1970s precious metals futures markets revealed a risk unique to futures trading. Each exchange specifies "limit" ranges that a price of a specific commodity can trade each day. For example, if the limit for gold is $10, the price can only go $10 higher or lower than the previous day's closing price. Once it reaches that limit, no further trade can take place unless additional buyers or sellers decide to enter the market.

In January 1980 the long bull market rises in gold and silver were reversed. Many traders who had bought contracts were unable to get out of their positions because the price dropped the daily limit very quickly. Large profits turned into huge losses with no chance for escape. The Hunt brothers, famed precious metals traders, suffered losses totaling hundred of millions of dollars in only a few short weeks.

Strengths

Under normal circumstances, futures contracts are very liquid. Settlement is made in 24 hours. Gold bullion and coins are subject to fraudulent valuations. Closely regulated futures markets avoid these subjective valuations. High leverage can yield excellent profit potential. No interest is charged on the difference between the value of the contract and your margin deposit. Precious metals futures can be sold short (that is, profit is gained from price drops) as easily as they can be bought. Commissions are low, relative to the value of each contract.

Weaknesses

High leverage and high volatility make for very high risk investments. Exchange-set "limits" may hamper liquidity. The short-term nature of trading puts a premium on accurate timing. Precious metals are very sensitive to political news (such as developments in South Africa). Potential loss substantially exceeds required minimum investment.

Tax Considerations

All futures profits are taxed as ordinary income. Open positions are "marked to the market" as of December 31 each year. In other words, open, unrealized profits are taxed as though the position were closed on that day. Losses are capital losses and can offset other capital gains or be carried forward.

Summing Up

Precious metals dropped very sharply from January 1980 to 1986. A surge in inflation will be immediately reflected in large rises in gold and silver prices. The long bear market is probably over, but a return to the runaway inflation of the 1970s is not likely at this time.

The futures market gives well-capitalized, sophisticated investors the chance for high returns. If you do not have the time or experience to follow these markets closely on a daily basis, consider retaining a professional manager. This area is high risk. You should limit your exposure to no more than 10–15% of your investment funds.

Foreign Currencies Futures

A currency futures contract is a binding contract between a buyer and a seller that specifies the currency, the quantity of the currency, and the delivery date when the seller must deliver the currency for the transaction price.

CURRENCY FUTURES

No income

Low safety

Good liquidity

Good inflation hedge

No tax benefits

Good growth

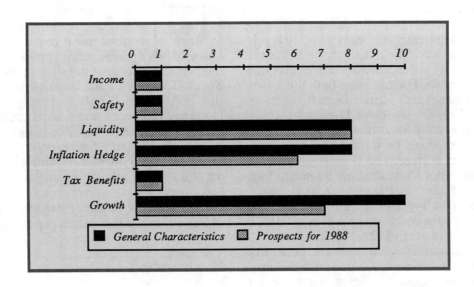

After the final abrogation in 1971 of the Bretton Woods agreement, which had fixed currency exchange rates, foreign currencies have been a volatile market. Futures in foreign currencies arose to give businesses a method for hedging the risks inherent in international trade.

When a U.S. business concludes a business agreement with a foreign company or government to supply a particular product or service in the future, both sides to the transaction have a substantial risk of loss if the currencies of their respective countries vary relative to each other.

For example, assume a U.S. business agrees to sell a set supply of equipment to a West German manufacturer for delivery in six months, for $1 million. At the time of the transaction, the exchange rate is 2 Deutschmarks per U.S. dollar. If the exchange rates drops to 3 marks per dollar in interim, the German manufacturer's costs will have increased 33% even though nothing changed in the contract. If the exchange rate rises to 1 mark per dollar, however, the U.S. supplier will receive 50% fewer marks for the same product.

This risk can be hedged in the futures market. Futures offers a liquid active market for shifting the exchange risk to speculators.

Foreign currencies are traded on the International Monetary Market (IMM) in Chicago. The most active markets are in West German Deutschmarks (D-marks), Japanese yen, Swiss francs, British pounds, and the Canadian dollar. Other currencies, such as the Mexican peso and the French franc, have much less active markets.

Foreign currency futures are bought or sold through government-licensed brokers. As mentioned earlier, all futures brokers must be members of the National Futures Association, a self-regulatory body of the futures industry. The NFA is charged with ensuring compliance with federal regulations.

Commissions ranging from $25 to $125 per contract are typically charged for handling the transaction. Although initial margin deposits of \$3,000 to \$6,000 are required for each contract, most brokerage firms require proof of substantial income and personal assets prior to opening an account. The initial margin deposit is only a small portion of the potential liability of the investor.

Investment Potential

Foreign currency futures is a highly leveraged investment. The initial margin deposit is typically only about 5 to 10% of the full value of the contract. For example, both the Swiss franc (S-franc) and German D-mark contracts are for 125,000 francs or D-marks respectively. If each S-franc is worth \$0.50, a single contract would be worth \$62,500.

The yen, S-franc, and D-mark are quoted in dollar terms. Currencies are quoted to four decimal places. A quote of 0.5000 would mean \$1 can buy 2 of the quoted currency. To give you a better perspective, a 0.0001 point move is worth \$12.50 per contract.

Foreign currency futures are generally short-term investments—liquid contracts usually only run about 6 months. They are not appropriate for most retirement plans. The high volatility of the markets requires close attention by investors.

Foreign currency futures offer capital gains (and loss) potential. There is no income on futures.

Foreign currency futures offers great flexibility. Many different strategies can be used, involving buying and selling of related currencies (such as the S-franc and D-mark). "Spread" trading (the simultaneous buying and selling of different contract months of the same currency or different currencies) is a common tactic.

Your initial margin deposit is only a small portion of your total liability. In the preceding example, a S-franc trader is liable for the full \$62,500 value of the contract even though the margin deposit may have only been \$6,000. If you buy a S-franc contract and the franc drops 0.0250 (a loss of \$3,125), your brokerage firm will issue a "margin call" for additional money to bring your account equity back to the initial deposit level. You have 24 hours to meet a margin call, before the brokerage firm sells out your position. You are liable for any additional loss that may have been incurred in the interim.

Strengths

High leverage offers above-average capital gains potential. A small amount of money can control much larger sums. Foreign currencies provide substantial protection against inflation in the United States. The Swiss franc is considered a inflation hedge second only to precious metals. Currency futures of major U.S. trading partners are liquid. It is possible to ascertain the relative liquidity of a futures contract by looking at the "open interest" figures. Open interest is a total of all outstanding contracts for that currency and delivery month. No interest is charged on the balance between the amount of a contract and the margin deposit.

Weaknesses

Leverage works both ways. A small adverse move can wipe out your equity very quickly. Potential risk is substantially greater than your required initial margin deposit. Foreign currency futures are characterized by very high volatility. Foreign currencies are very sensitive to news developments. A multitude of factors influence currency values. Sometimes relative interest rates are the most important factor. At other times, each country's relative trade balances prove crucial. There are many other potential determinants of relative value, which change all the time. Direct government intervention is a much greater factor in currency trading than in any other market.

Tax Considerations

Gains and losses from foreign currency futures are capital gains and losses. They are taxed at ordinary income levels.

Losses can be used to offset other capital gains. Losses can be carried forward.

Summing Up

The flexibility of either buying or selling short with equal facility makes foreign currency futures a viable alternative in any market environment. After four years of dollar strength, 1986 witnessed a reversal. In the past two years, the U.S. dollar has fallen sharply.

 This market is highly volatile, very risky. It takes considerable time and expertise to trade with any degree of success. If you can't devote substantial time to learning the intricacies of foreign currencies, consider hiring professional management.

Options on Futures

Income possible

Low safety

Fair liquidity

Good inflation
hedge

No tax benefits

Good growth

A futures call option is a contract giving the buyer the right to buy the underlying futures contract for a specified price within a specified time period. A put option is the opposite. It gives the buyer the right to sell the underlying futures contract at a specified price within a specified time period.

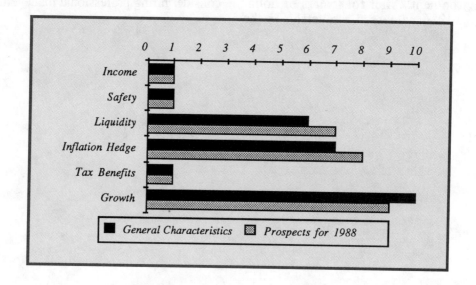

The futures market, with its promise of large profits with relatively small investments, has attracted many investors. Yet this promise has turned into nightmares for inexperienced traders who learned too late that small investments may also turn into large losses! When you make an initial margin deposit on a futures contract, you are legally obligated for the full value of the contract, regardless of the amount of money invested. The initial deposit is usually only 5 to 10% of the value of the contract.

An option has the advantage of limiting the potential loss to the amount of your investment. If you pay $1,000 to buy a call option on a futures contract of gold, the most you can lose, even if gold falls to zero, is $1,000. In contrast, if you put up $1,000 to buy a gold futures contract, you are liable for the full value of the contract. If you buy a gold contract at $500 per ounce, you're liable for up to $50,000!

Future options are relatively new. The most heavily traded futures options at the mo-ment are the S&P 500 index, T-bonds, Euro-dollars, the D-mark, the yen, gold, silver, crude oil, and soybeans. Interest is picking up in copper, sugar, corn, live cattle, the British pound, the Swiss franc, T-notes, and the NYSE Composite.

 Futures options can be purchased through specialized licensed futures brokers. Not all futures brokers are licensed to sell futures options. A commission is typically assessed when the transaction is closed.

A number of independent advisory newsletters serve this market. Prices are quoted daily in the *Wall Street Journal*.

Investment Potential

Futures options are short-term, highly volatile investments. They generate capital gains (and losses!). They pay no income. Because their underlying instrument—futures contracts—are highly leveraged investments, the options reflect their volatility.

Professional traders have developed a number of highly sophisticated trading strategies combining different expirations, commodities, and both puts and calls in spread and straddles. These complex tactics are beyond the reach of most part-time investors.

The increased popularity of many different markets, as listed earlier, make futures options very flexible investments. Most are also very liquid. However, it is critical to check the average daily volume and the open interest (the number of outstanding contracts) in those futures options you are interested in trading. Low average volume, or an open interest of less than 8,000 contracts, may mean problems with liquidity on occasion.

Futures trading is very high risk. Futures options are also very high risk. The primary difference is that a futures option investor cannot lose more than his or her initial investment. However, he or she also has to contend with the potential for completely losing the premium on expiration day.

Futures options are not appropriate for most retirement plans.

Strengths

Losses are limited to the amount of investment. Futures options are highly leveraged investments offering the potential for large capital gains. Most options are liquid. Futures options, especially on gold and silver, offer good inflation protection. Futures options offer the opportunity for substantial short-term gains.

Weaknesses

Futures options are very volatile. You can lose 100% of your investment on expiration day. Time works against you, since the option loses value every day that the underlying futures contract does not move in the anticipated direction. Futures option premiums are high relative to stock options. The trading history of futures options is too short to provide accurate historical precedents.

Tax Considerations

The 1986 Tax Reform Act eliminated preferential tax treatment for capital gains. All gains from futures options are taxed at your ordinary income rates. No special tax benefits apply.

Summing Up

Futures options have quickly established themselves as a viable market for speculators and hedgers. Many financial institutions and large stock managers use futures options to hedge interest rate and portfolio risks.

You should only speculate in futures options with risk capital you can afford to lose. Never risk more than 10% of your investment capital in buying futures options.

Investors who do not have the time to devote to careful research of these markets should consider professional management.

Futures options, especially gold and silver, will rise in an inflationary environment. Investors with substantial interest rate exposure should investigate futures options on T-bonds for hedging potential.

Short Selling

Everyone knows that the secret to successful investing is to buy low and sell higher. But it does not always have to go in that order! To profit from down moves in prices, you can sell high and then buy lower. This technique is called short selling.

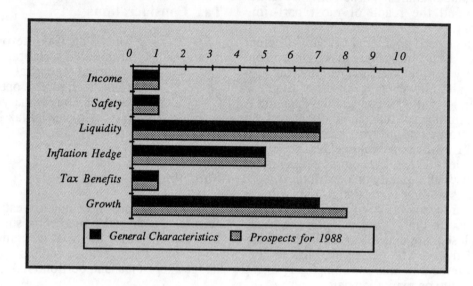

While everyone is encouraged to "buy a piece of America" and profit from stock market rises, most investors are discouraged from short selling. Government regulations make it more difficult to do than simply buying stock. For example, in order to sell a stock short it has to have an increase in price first. In other words, before you can sell it short it has to move contrary to your expectations! Brokerage firms usually require more stringent financial requirements for short sellers.

It is not hard to understand corporate America's negative attitude toward short selling. No one wants to see the price of his or her stock go lower.

Yet the very same people who make it difficult for the average investor to sell short, major brokerage firms and exchange members sell short as a regular practice.

Short selling is riskier than buying stock for the simple reason that a stock can move infinitely higher, but can only fall to zero. However, intelligent professional investors know ways to protect against unlimited losses (for example, using stop loss orders).

And at least so far, no stock has risen to infinity, while many stocks have gone to zero.

When you sell a stock short, you enter an order with your broker that he or she has to specify clearly on the order ticket. Your brokerage firm takes the stock from its inventory of stock held in "street name" (in the broker's account on behalf of its clients) and sells it. Since the stock held in street name belongs to someone, it must be replaced on demand. In practice, however, you won't be forced to replace the stock by the owner. However, you may be forced to buy the stock back by adverse price action.

To sell stock short, you must open a margin account. A minimum of 50% of the value of the stock to be sold must be deposited as initial margin. If the stock rises after you've sold it, the value of your account drops. If the equity in your account drops to 30%, a margin call will be issued requiring you to deposit additional money if you want to keep your short position. If you do not deposit the additional funds within 24 hours, your brokerage firm can buy the stock back. You are liable for any loss that has been incurred.

On the brighter side, if the stock drops your account equity increases. You can buy the stock back to return it to whomever you borrowed it from. If the stock price is lower when you buy than when you sold, you've made a profit.

For example, if XYZ Corporation stock is selling for $60 per share, you can sell short 100 shares for $3,000. If you later buy it back at $40 per share, you will have made a profit of $2,000 before commissions.

Fees are an important consideration for short selling. You must pay a brokerage commission for each buy and sell, just as when you are buying stock. Also, an interest charge must be paid on your margin account. And finally, if the stock you sold short pays a dividend during the time you've sold it, you must pay the dividend amount to the stockholder from whom you borrowed the stock.

Stocks can only be sold short through licensed stock brokers. A monthly report is issued on the extent of short selling in individual stocks for the New York Stock Exchange, the American Stock Exchange, and the NASDAQ over-the-counter market. The extent of short selling is called "short interest." If the short interest is high for the market as a whole, that is a negative, because all that stock will have to be bought back at some time.

Investment Potential

Price falls tend to occur quicker and more dramatically than price rises. Short selling is a short-term business. Time works against a short seller because he or she must pay interest and dividends in the interim.

Short selling is a high-risk venture. The increasing price volatility in stock prices offers opportunity and danger for short sellers.

Short selling is a leveraged transaction because you borrow to effect the trade. Short selling offers the potential for capital gains. There is no income from short selling.

Short selling is a high-risk, short-term venture. The long-term trend of stock prices is up, so short sellers are bucking tradition.

Alternatives to direct short selling now offer the chance to profit from price drops while limiting your risk. The purchase of put options limits your risk to your investment while enabling you to profit from price falls. Other option strategies are employed by professionals to achieve the same goals.

Strengths

Short selling offers the potential for capital gains. Short selling enables you to profit from price declines. In combination with options, short selling offers wide flexibility in structuring trades to meet your objectives. Short selling is quite liquid if confined to large-volume, actively traded stocks.

Weaknesses

Short selling offers no income. Fees are high and require substantial price moves to cover. Potential losses are unlimited. Time works against you in flat trading range markets.

Tax Considerations

Even before the 1986 Tax Reform Act, short selling was denied preferential long-term capital gains treatment. All gains are taxed at your ordinary income rates.

Summing Up

Short selling is generally discouraged by most brokerage firms. They prefer that you buy a piece of America rather than sell it before you own it! The regulations themselves discourage shorts because a stock must tick up before a short sale can be executed. And finally, history shows that the market has a definite bias to rise over time.

Nevertheless, short selling plays an integral part in the investment strategies of many professionals. The current market is very broadbased even when the price collapse of October 19 is considered. However, every bull market in history has given way to bear markets eventually.

 Short selling is a high-risk tactic. It is not appropriate for most investors. However, if you are willing and able to undertake substantial financial risks, short selling will yield good profits when the bear market finally begins in earnest.

Leveraged Contracts

A leveraged contract is a form of forward investment in which the buyer makes an initial margin deposit on an amount of the underlying precious metal. Monthly interest charges are assessed on the balance between the initial margin and the full value of the contract.

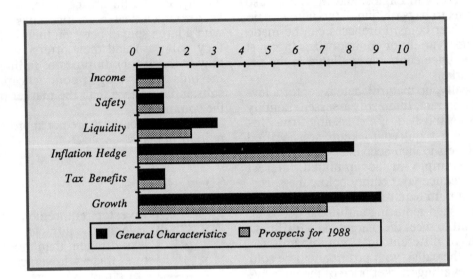

Leveraged contracts are a hybrid investment that gained a wide market in the precious metals boom in the 1970s. Subsequent widespread fraud and business failures among many "leveraged contract" dealers resulted in the imposition of stringent federal registration requirements in the early 1980s.

Leveraged contracts developed as an alternative to futures contracts. Typically firms selling leveraged contract investments set less stringent requirements for investors than firms dealing in futures. Initial deposits of as little as 10% are used to control substantial amounts of precious metals.

For example, a $1,000 deposit may control $10,000 worth of gold at the price prevailing on the transaction day. If gold is trading at $500 on the transaction day, 20 ounces of gold would be controlled by the $1,000 deposit. Theoretically, the issuing firm would buy the gold and store it for the purchaser. Once the contract is paid off, the buyer can either take delivery of the gold or let the issuing firm "warehouse" it for a custodial fee until the buyer elects to sell.

Many shady firms entered the business in the heyday of the inflationary bull markets of the 1970s. These firms often failed to purchase the gold to back the full value of the leveraged contracts they had sold. When the precious metals bull market reversed, many investors were left holding worthless paper when the firms went under. Some of the failed firms went under owing investors millions of dollars. Only a handful of legally registered leverage contract merchants are active today.

Investment Potential

Leveraged contracts offer capital gains potential. No income is paid.

Leveraged contracts are attractive to many investors because of the high degree of flexibility offered. Unlike futures contracts, which have uniform sizes and maturities, leveraged contracts are often tailored to meet specific the specific desires of their investors.

Leveraged contracts are sold for bullion and various coins ranging from Krugerrands, American Eagles, and Mexican Peso gold coins to bags of "junk" (no numismatic value) silver coins. Purchases can be made for a wide variety of contract sizes, not just the 100-ounce contracts available in the futures markets.

Typically, no maturity date is set for a leveraged contract. Interest is assessed monthly at rates established by the issuing firms. Investors are required to keep prespecified equity levels in their accounts.

For example, if accumulated interest charges reduce your equity below the specified minimum requirements, a "margin call" will be issued requiring additional deposits. If you fail to meet the margin calls (different firms have different time requirements for meeting the calls), your position will be sold at the prevailing market price of the underlying commodity. You are liable for any losses that exceed your equity at the time.

In this way, leveraged contracts are similar to futures contracts. You are liable for the full value of the contract. Your potential loss is not limited to your initial investment.

Leveraged contracts are very high risk investments. High-interest charges may not be offset by appreciation of the underlying commodity. This factor alone can result in losses in flat markets. Interest rate charges are typically tied to some independent market interest rate. If interest rates rise and the underlying commodity stays flat or rises more slowly, your equity again can be lost.

With passage of the 1986 Tax Reform Act, investment interest is deductible only up to the amount of investment income. Previously the interest charges of leveraged contracts were fully deductible against your gross income.

The most prominent markets for leveraged contracts are precious metals: gold, silver, and platinum. These markets are classic inflation hedges. They provide little return in non-inflationary times. Historically, these markets are very volatile.

 A key problem with leveraged contracts is liquidity. There is no secondary market. If you want or need to sell your position, you are at the mercy of the issuing firm for the selling price. Some leveraged contract dealers maintain market prices with a large spread between their bids (what they will pay) and their offers (what price they will sell for). In times of falling prices, the bids for leveraged contracts may drop substantially more than the market price for the commodity.

Leveraged contracts are not appropriate for retirement plans.

Strengths

 Investor requirements to trade leveraged contracts are usually less stringent than those for futures traders. Leverage contracts are typically offered in a wide variety of sizes. Leveraged contracts are one of the few ways an investor can purchase gold or silver coins with leverage.

Weaknesses

 Liquidity is dependent on the good graces of the issuing firm. There is no secondary market. Interest charges are generally high. Precious metals markets are volatile. No government or well-established private insurance exists for leveraged contract accounts. Prices of leveraged contracts are set by the issuing firm and may vary widely from market prices for the underlying commodity. Transaction costs typically are very high relative to costs for competitive products. Investors are subject to the risk of the business of the issuing firm as well as to market risk. The high built-in costs may mean that even if you are right on market direction, you may lose money by the time you close out your position. Your potential loss is not necessarily limited to your initial investment.

Tax Considerations

 Gains and losses from leveraged contracts are capital gains and losses. Gains are taxed as ordinary income. Losses may be used to offset other capital gains. Unused capital losses may be carried forward. Interest charges are deductible up to the amount of investment income. Interest charges may also be carried forward.

Summing Up

Leveraged contract dealers have shrunk from hundreds to only a few federally registered firms. If inflation turns higher, you can expect to see increased advertising and public exposure on the part of the remaining firms.

Investors interested in leveraged investments in precious metals should investigate the futures and futures options markets. The transaction fees are usually considerably lower, and the market is more liquid and less subject to manipulation.

If you do not qualify for futures trading, you probably should restrict your investments to precious metals mutual funds or cash coin purchases. Only very savvy experienced traders who recognize the high fees and can afford the risks should trade leveraged forward contracts.

Option-Buying Mutual Funds

The mutual fund industry was slow to capitalize on the popularity of the options market for a number of reasons. Mutual fund investments are sizable, and the fledgling options market simply couldn't handle the volume. Without sufficient track records, it was difficult even for professional traders to develop consistent usable trading systems. And finally, few investors will place money with an untried trading advisor. Once actual track records began to develop, the mutual fund industry began to offer aggressive investors the chance to have professional management in the high-flying options market.

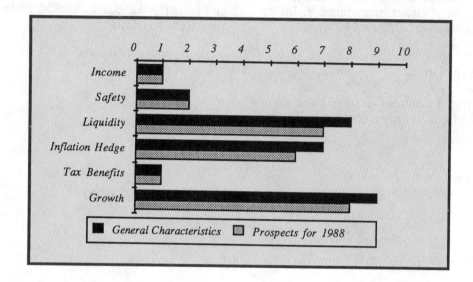

Options have developed into a very large, very liquid, and very popular market since the inception of exchange-listed options in 1974. At first only a few stocks had options, and for years only call options were traded. Now there are five major options exchanges: the Chicago Board Options Exchange (CBOE), the PBW, the Pacific, and the American and New York option exchanges.

A call option gives the buyer the right to buy 100 shares of a specified stock at a specified price for a specified time period. For example, assume that XYZ stock is selling at 50 in January. The March 50 XYZ call option is selling for $5 ($5 x 100 shares ÷ option = a total premium of $500).

For an investment of $500, you have the right to buy 100 shares of XYZ from the seller (or writer) of the option at $50 per share until the third Friday in March. If the stock goes to $60 per share before the end of March, your option would go to at least $10 ($1,000 total value per option). In other words, a 20% move in the stock price translates into a 100% move in the price of the option!

A put option is just the opposite. A put option is a contract that gives the buyer the right to sell 100 shares of a specified stock at a specified price for a specified time period. You'd buy a put if you thought the price of a stock were going to go down. For example, assume that XYZ stock in January was selling for $50 per share. The XYZ March 50 put option sells for $4 ($4 per share x 100 shares = total value of option $400). Put options generally trade for a smaller premium than do call options. If XYZ fell to $0 per share, your put gives you the right to sell 100 shares at $50 per share to the seller of the put option. You've profited from a fall in price.

Mutual funds that concentrate in option buying are usually structured so that 80 to 90% of the funds on hand are used to buy Treasury bills. Because options expire worthless, it would not be prudent to invest everything in vehicles that may expire worthless! The balance of funds are used to speculate in calls and puts. The tremendous leverage that options provide make this strategy viable. Small percentage price moves in the underlying stocks can translate into very large profits by the options.

Option mutual funds are either load or no-load. A load fund assesses a sales charge that is added to the fund's net asset value (NAV) when you purchase the fund. A no-load fund sells at its NAV without any sales charges. A load fund is usually purchased through a broker. A no-load fund is purchased direct from the fund.

Investment Potential

Option funds generate capital gains. Generally they pay no income since interest earned from Treasury bills is reinvested in the option-buying portfolio.

Aggressive option funds trade as very short-term vehicles. There is much activity in the funds' portfolio because options are short-term investments. An advantage of using a mutual fund rather than trading options yourself is that a fund can be viewed as a long-term investment. If you buy a load fund, it is impractical to trade the fund in the short term because of the large up-front fees you paid.

 The stock market has become increasingly volatile in recent years, culminating in the "Crash of '87" and its aftershocks. As leveraged plays on stocks, options are even more volatile. A mutual fund that is structured to buy options is a high-risk investment. Investors run market risk, timing risk, high fees from high portfolio turnover, and management risk.

Option mutual funds are very liquid. They keep a large portion of their assets in Treasury bills to ensure that liquidity. However, no federal insurance is available on mutual funds. Mutual funds that specialize in option buying are more apropriate for retirement plans than direct purchase of options because of the professional management and diversification. Even then, only a very small portion of your money should be invested in this type of fund.

Strengths

 Option-buying mutual funds offer the potential for very large capital gains. They trade broadly diversified portfolios that minimizes the damage of any one position. Professional management fees of mutual funds are generally less than the fees you'd pay for a manager to trade your account. Option funds are very liquid. Option funds offer inflation protection.

Weaknesses

 Options are very volatile and high risk. Their mutual funds are less risky than outright positions but still high risk. The high management and commission fees that accompany active trading may hurt your bottom-line return. No income cushions adverse market moves. Option-buying funds have generally underperformed other growth-oriented mutual funds.

Tax Considerations

 The 1986 Tax Reform Act eliminated preferential tax treatment for capital gains. All gains from option mutual funds are capital gains. Capital losses offset other capital gains. Excess losses are carried forward. Capital gains are taxed at your ordinary income tax bracket.

Summing Up

Surprisingly, option funds have not been sterling performers in the bull market prior to

October, 1987. Many explanations are possible, but the bottom line is that the funds have not done the job commensurate with the higher risk inherent in options trading.

Given the expectations of further rises in the stock market, option funds should be checked. The relatively short track records of these funds may be misleading. For the present, though, aggressive growth stock funds appear to offer better performance.

Option Income Mutual Funds

A mutual fund pools the money of a number of individual investors to invest in se- curities through professional management. An option income fund sells put and call options in accord with some plan in order to generate current income from the premi- ums received.

OPTION FUNDS
—INCOME

Good income

Low safety

Good liquidity

Poor inflation hedge

No tax benefits

Low growth

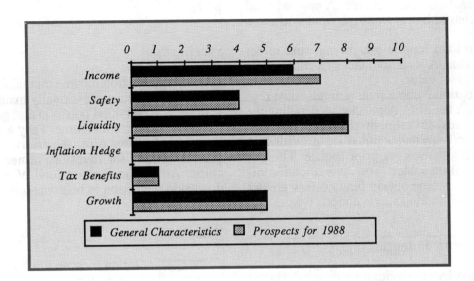

The stock option market began to receive widespread investor interest in 1974 and 1975 after the Chicago Board Options Exchange (CBOE) was launched. For the first time, option contracts were standardized and listed on a central exchange. Previously, stock options had traded on the over-the-counter (OTC) market but a lack of uniformity in contract specifications limited their use primarily to professionals. Now stock options are traded on the CBOE, the PBW Options Exchange, the Pacific Options Exchange, and the American and New York options exchanges.

A call option gives the buyer the right to buy 100 shares of a specified stock at a specified price for a specified time period. A put option gives the buyer the right to sell 100 shares of the specified stock, at the specified price, within a specified time. Every option contract has both a buyer and a seller.

A buyer is motivated by the potential for growth. A seller earns income because he or she receives the premium minus commission.

For example, a three-month call option with a strike price of $50 on XYZ stock is selling for $400. A buyer who thinks XYZ will move significantly above $50 would pay the $400 for obtain the right to buy 100 shares for the next three months at $50 per share regardless of what the market price is. The seller of the option, receives the $400 immediately. This is payment for undertaking the risk of guaranteeing that the seller will deliver the stock if "called" by the buyer.

The seller is called the "writer" of the option. Investors "write" options in two ways. A covered option means that the seller owns the stock he or she may be forced to deliver. A "naked" option means that the seller of the option does not own the underlying stock. Naked writing is very high risk. If the stock price jumps sharply higher, the seller may be forced to buy it at a much higher price than he or she has to sell it to the call buyer.

Professional options traders use many sophisticated option strategies. A mutual fund that specializes in generating income from its option trading, undertakes writing strategies. An income program would not be involved in outright buying of options, although it may buy options as one part of a spread. A spread is the simultaneous buying and selling of options with different strike prices or expiration dates.

Option income mutual funds are purchased through brokers direct from the fund. A load fund assesses a sales charge. A no-load fund is purchased direct from the fund without a sales fee.

A no load fund is bought and sold at net asset value. A load fund tacks its charge onto the net asset value.

All option income mutual funds must register with the SEC. A prospectus detailing the fund's fees, investment philosophy, objectives, and strategies must be provided to prospective investors prior to sale. There is no federal insurance. The diversification offered by income option funds offers greater safety than writing single options would.

Investment Potential

Option income mutual funds are designed to generate good current income. They should be thought of as long-term investments, though options themselves are short-term vehicles. A fund that engages in "covered writing" may also earn some capital gains.

The stock market has become increasingly volatile in recent years. Options, which are leveraged stock market investments, are even more volatile and risky. In addition to the market risk of adverse price movement, there is a timing risk. Options expire totally worthless on specified days. An option buyer can lose 100% of his or her investment through deterioration of the time value in the option, if the underlying stock price stays flat.

This withering of the time premium pays a crucial favorable part in the option writer's strategy. However, the option writer can also be badly hurt by bad timing. If a stock price explodes upward before expiration, the writer will lose money. Option trading, both writing and buying is a high-risk proposition.

Option income mutual funds are liquid investments. Most funds allow you to sell

shares over the telephone. Most funds also offer a variety of payout options for shareholders. You can elect to have a fixed amount paid out periodically, or have interest or dividends paid out. Read a fund's prospectus for full details.

Option income mutual funds are appropriate for retirement plans. They should not be the only investment in most retirement plans.

Strengths

Option income mutual funds offer a professionally managed diversified portfolio that generates current income. They are liquid. They offer a variety of withdrawal options for investors in need of income. An option income fund offers some downside protection in bear markets.

Weaknesses

Option income funds do not offer significant capital gains potential. Options trading is a very high risk, highly leveraged investment. Options trading includes the unique risk of time deterioration. Since options expire at set times, their value shrinks as the expiration date gets closer. Option income funds have generally underperformed the market since their inception.

Tax Considerations

Income generated in options trading is taxed as ordinary income. Capital gains are also taxed at your ordinary income levels. Capital losses offset other capital gains. Losses are carried forward.

Summing Up

Option income mutual funds do best in flat sideways markets when premium time value deterioration becomes an important factor. In the strong bull market of the past five years, these funds are at a distinct disadvantage.

The prospects for a continuing bull market limit the appeal of option income mutual funds for the present. They should be considered as a good alternative or diversification with bond funds for current income.

CONCLUSIONS

These sophisticated investing tools and tactives afford investors a myriad of ways to achieve enhanced returns, hedge portfolios, or even to profit from price drops. However, the risk is high and all too often misunderstood.

Don't dismiss these vehicles without giving them careful thought. However, limit your exposure to theses speculative instruments to no more than 15% of your portfolio in any case.

---

10 TOP PERFORMING OPTION INCOME FUNDS

1. Putnam Option Income
2. Franklin Option
3. Colonial Diversified Income
4. Analytic Optioned Income
5. Oppenheimer Premium Income
6. Kemper Option Income
7. Gateway Option Income
8. First Investors Option
9. Industrial Series—Option Income
10. ABT Security Income

CHAPTER 16

EXOTICS AND SPECIAL SITUATION INVESTMENTS

A GLANCE AHEAD

Many investors like to venture beyond the basics into the realms of the so-called exotics, the limited partnerships and tangible assets that can add zest and personality to a well-balanced portfolio. In this chapter you'll explore the possibilities of

- *Limited partnerships that get you into big-time programs for very sensible dollars*
- *Coins, stamps, and other collectibles that combine the pleasures of ownership with the advantages of investing*
- *How and when each should and should not be used*

SPECIAL INVESTMENTS AND SPECIAL INVESTORS

Colin (Ben) Coombs, a well-known financial planner from Woodland Hills, California, likes to say, "If it eats, grows or glitters, I don't touch it." That attitude reflects the way a number of respected planning professionals think, but a growing number are coming to recognize the investment value of the so-called exotics: the special limited partnerships and collectibles that offer great potential and varying degrees of risk. Coombs and those who agree with him remember all too well various rabbit-breeding programs and diamond deals that either failed to produce or

were pure fraud from the outset. But today's exotics include many outstanding programs that have enhanced the portfolios of many careful investors.

As good money managers will, George and Betty had cultivated their financial plan as carefully as they had their vegetable garden. Their defensive strategies were in place to safeguard them against potential losses, and every month they added to a portfolio that was quietly building up assets for their retirement.

As their incomes continued to grow, George and Betty decided to have a little fun with their money. Betty had a friend at work who had done quite well with an investment in a limited partnership that owned a jojoba bean operation. They didn't know jojoba beans from limas, but George and Betty started to learn about limited partnerships and other alternatives to traditional investment products. Betty's interest in old buildings also led them to invest in a limited partnership that bought and rehabilitated historical buildings. They had entered the world of the so-called exotics.

Exotics are the limited partnerships and hard-asset categories generally considered too risky for pension planning and core portfolio building. Many of them, such as coin, stamp, and gemstone collecting, are as old as investing itself. Others, like leveraged-buyout (LBO) limited partnerships and cable TV partnerships, are fresh, new concepts.

297

For many products, the term *exotic* implies far too harsh a judgment on their stability—they are "plain vanilla" safe. For others, the term fits just right. Clearly, the word *exotic,* although widely accepted, can be misleading: a better choice is "special situation investments," which more accurately describes the opportunities of nontraditional investing.

Special situation investments are for seasoned investors who have made their cash equivalent investments, who are well positioned in cash and mutual funds, who have done their defensive planning, who own their homes and have structured retirement plans. Such people have protected their long-term security and own balanced portfolios. Special-situation investments are for people who can afford to have fun with non-essential investment dollars that they are willing to put at greater risk than the body of their portfolio. And these investments are for people who don't need a lot of extra liquidity.

Sometimes, investors like George and Betty are attracted to exotics because they're fun. Such investments have the potential to earn higher returns than more traditional products. Exotics often are imaginative and have some sizzle—some "sex appeal." Some people have a feel for certain industries—as with Betty's appreciation for old buildings—and others get pleasure out of owning objects they enjoy tangibly. Many people own collections of cars or art or china that are as valuable for their esthetic appeal as for the investment they represent. Often, tangible assets are favored by people who have controlling personalities—they need to have investments that they can get their hands on.

Exotics can be good inflationary hedges, too, but they are more speculative than core investments and can be highly illiquid.

LIMITED PARTNERSHIPS

A limited partnership is a form of business organization that enables small investors to pool their funds and participate in programs otherwise available only to investors with much larger sums. Normally, the partnership diversifies its investments within an industry such as real estate, oil and gas, agriculture, or equipment leasing. Limited partnerships are set up to be self-liquidating, usually within 5 to 12 years.

A limited partnership consists of (1) a general partner (or partners), who organizes and manages the ongoing affairs of the partnership, and (2) a number of limited partners, who contribute capital but have no role in the day-to-day management of the partnership. Limited partners are liable for nothing beyond their original investment. The general partner—who should be a professional in the targeted field—receives a management fee for organizing and running the business.

Originally, some limited partnerships were structured as tax shelters to create "passive," or paper losses. Such losses could be used by the limited partners to offset at tax time any kind of income they had received during the year. Changes in the tax laws—beginning in 1984 and culminating in the 1986 Tax Reform Act severely restricted the tax advantages of passive losses, and prompted many people to predict the death of limited partnerships. But the concepts that underlie limited partnerships are still sound and have survived, primarily as income-producing tools. In many cases, the income produced by a contemporary limited partnership can be sheltered by passive losses of the type incurred by the old loss-generating partnerships. In addition, some of the older, loss-oriented partnerships still have value to some—mainly wealthy—investors who need to generate passive losses.

Unlike flow in the corporate structure, profits and losses in a limited partnership flow through directly to the limited partners. This path eliminates the double taxation of dividends that occurs when the corporation is taxed on its profits and then shareholders are taxed on their dividend income.

Historically, some limited partnerships have been structured as highly leveraged operations to take full advantage of tax provisions. More than 50% of a leveraged partnership's assets may be financed with borrowed money. Unleveraged partnerships are more conservative. They operate almost entirely on invested cash and place capital at significantly less risk. The new limitations on deductibility of interest and depreciation from passive investments make many of the unleveraged partnerships increasingly attractive.

Limited partnerships are sold in a variety of ways, chiefly through major full-service brokerage firms and small, specialized broker/dealers. Sales fees are normally paid by the general partner out of capital generated through the sales. As partners, the investors pay the fees indirectly. Sales fees can vary considerably and should be considered when evaluating a limited partnership offering. The reputation and track record of the sponsor or general partner also should be a major consideration for the investor. Major brokerages and most broker/dealers maintain "due diligence" departments that carefully evaluate limited partnership offerings, determine risk levels, and establish criteria to help protect investors from getting into partnerships that are too risky for their means.

The two types of limited partnership offerings are private and public. Public offerings are registered with the SEC and must meet strict disclosure requirements; prospective buyers must be provided with a prospectus. Private offerings are not registered with the SEC. They may sell only to (1) "accredited" investors with annual incomes of $200,000 or a net worth of $1 million and (2) to a limited number (usually 35) of "unaccredited" investors with smaller incomes and net worth. The minimum investment usually is much higher in private offerings, so smaller investors should avoid private offerings in favor of less risky public partnerships.

Investment Potential

Most current limited partnerships are now sold as income-producing instruments. There may be capital gains potential, but typically such gains are realized when the partnership is closed out. The capital gains are dictated by the amount of money raised when the assets are liquidated. Most partnerships are structured to sell or refinance their assets in 5 to 12 years. The proceeds are then distributed to the limited partners.

There isn't a significant secondary market for limited partnerships yet, so a partner who needs to get out early may take a loss. Thus, limited partnerships must be considered an illiquid investment. Considerable demand is developing, however, for successful partnerships in their third or fourth year of maturity.

It's difficult to judge the volatility of limited partnerships because no central marketplace exists with current prices for outstanding shares. Also, there are no widely recognized rating systems for limited partnerships, although the Robert Stanger organization has begun a ratings system for subscribers to the Stanger Register.

Limited partnerships are subject to a variety of risks. One risk is that the investments may simply turn out poorly, owing to sagging markets or poor management. Do not invest in a limited partnership unless you are entirely confident in the management abilities of the general partners.

Strengths

Most limited partnerships offer passive income that can be offset by the passive losses of leveraged tax shelter credits. Limited partnerships offer investors the chance to invest relatively small amounts without assuming full financial risk for the success or failure of the enterprise. And limited partnerships allow for almost unlimited diversification with the chosen area of investment. For relatively small investments, investors can increase diversity by sampling a variety of partnerships in different asset areas. Some limited partnerships have produced outstanding capital gains in new investment areas. And finally, some limited partnerships may provide a good hedge against inflation.

Weaknesses

Limited partnerships offer poor liquidity, and no insurance is available for them. It is difficult to independently ascertain the value of a partnership share. The ability and integrity of the general partner is a key factor in success. If market or political conditions (such as the tax laws) change, a limited partnership that began well may start to fail and offer little chance for escape. Limited partnerships are long-term investments.

Tax Considerations

The 1986 Tax Reform Act dramatically changed the tax treatment of partnership income and losses. Passive losses can be used only to offset passive gains—not earned or investment income. In effect, the TRA traps portfolio income, such as dividends and interest from investments, and makes it wholly taxable. This provision is being phased in over a 5-year period. In 1987, 65% of passive losses can be used to offset other types of income. This percentage dwindles to 40% in 1988, 20% in 1989, and 10% in 1990.

In a partnership, income may build up as a cash fund that can be sheltered and the gains may be offset by other passive losses. This passive-income, passive-loss provision becomes increasingly attractive with higher incomes and bigger net worths.

Summing Up

Limited partnerships are expected to perform well in 1988 and into the foreseeable future. They were sluggish in 1986 when the TRA undermined the value of the old loss-oriented partnerships, but the fundamental concept survived and flourished, and partnerships rebounded in 1987. The basic concepts of the limited partnership are sound and can be applied to almost any investment category, so most experts expect to see partnerships proliferate. Also, shrewd investors will watch for seasoned partnership interests as they become available on the secondary market at attractive prices.

MASTER LIMITED PARTNERSHIPS (MLPs)

In the late 1970s and 1980s, a new type of organization came into being that combined the benefits of a limited partnership with the liquidity of corporate stocks. These *master limited partnerships* (MLPs), as they are called, were originated by a realty and construction company that spun off its real estate division by issuing partnership "shares." The firm assumed the responsibility of a general partner, which limited the liability of the limited partners, just as in a standard limited partnership. This structure also qualified the limited partners for passive income tax advantages. (Note: Legislation is being considered that would reclassify this income as portfolio income.)

The oil and gas industry quickly perceived the possibilities for immediate cash infusion and jumped into the field. Until 1985, almost all MLPs were in the energy field, but since then the opportunities have proliferated. In 1986, the owners of the Boston Celtics raised $48 million through the sale of partnership interests.

Other tradeable limited partnerships are formed by "rolling up" several standard limited partnerships to offer greater diversity and the liquidity of public trading. In all cases, MLPs currently offer the same "passive income" benefits of untraded limited partnerships, and limit the liability of the limited partners to their original investment.

MLPs are bought and sold through licensed securities brokers just like stocks and are registered as securities by the SEC. They may be disguised as "no-load" products, but in fact the commission and management fee structure is essentially the same as that of an untraded limited partnership. However, fees may be more difficult to detect, due to the way shares are marketed. Because they are buried in complex acquisition costs, unnecessarily high management fees may be made invisible. MLP prices are listed in the financial pages of major newspapers and the financial press.

Because MLPs are publicly traded, they are more liquid than untraded partnerships. The investor who must sell during the first few years is not as likely to take a substantial loss. However, the value of MLP shares will vary according to a variety of market influences, so investors must determine the "right time to sell."

Two significant warnings should be stated. First, since the major marketing benefit of an MLP is liquidity, general partners may employ a number of techniques to maintain artificially high yields and thus ensure a healthy secondary market. Before investing in an MLP, investors should familiarize themselves with the yield on equity as well as the advertised yield, and determine which yield support technique is being used to close any gap between true yields and advertised yields.

Second, considerable discussion is taking place in Washington, D.C., about the wisdom of reclassifying income from MLPs as "portfolio income." This reclassification would diminish the tax advantages that now accrue from an MLP. If you're trying to offset MLP taxable income with tax shelter losses, you might wind up a loser.

Investment Potential

MLPs meet a number of investment objectives. Some are specifically designed to provide current income, while others are primarily oriented to the growth of capital. MLPs should be considered long-term investments.

MLPs are available in a wide variety of industries and price volatility closely reflects the volatility of the underlying business.

Some MLPs qualify for margin and can be leveraged. The investor posts a minimum of 50% of the value of the desired MLP and is loaned the balance by the brokerage firm. Margin purchases are inherently a more speculative investment: the investor pays interest on the loan balance, and adverse price moves may result in "margin calls" that require an immediate deposit of capital.

Exchange-listed MLPs may be sold short to profit from price declines. The availability of options on some MLPs increases investment flexibility.

The safety of MLPs depends on good business management and economic conditions, not on their organizational structure. Some are much safer than others. MLPs must be registered with the SEC and provide annual audited financial information.

Strengths

 MLPs offer good liquidity and capital gains potential. They avoid double taxation of dividends, and some MLPs pay income that is nontaxable as a return of capital or is partly sheltered from taxation. MLPs in such industries as real estate and energy are good hedges against inflation.

Weaknesses

 Management fees for MLPs vary widely. High fees adversely affect performance. Moreover, since partnerships typically pay out cash flow, reinvestment allocations may be limited. In addition to the market risk of price fluctuations, poor managment also poses a risk. Finally, uncertainty about future tax treatment creates political risk.

Tax Considerations

 Some MLPs are designed to pay tax-exempt income as a return of capital. However, this design means that the assets of the MLP are being diminished. Other income and capital gains are taxed at ordinary income rates.

MLPs are appropriate for most retirement plans, provided they meet the specific investment objective being sought.

Summing Up

 The 1986 Tax Reform Act was thought to be the death knell for master limited partnerships, but that didn't happen. In fact, many corporations are marketing MLPs structured around specific company assets. Barring another change in the tax laws, MLPs will become an even more attractive way for companies to raise capital. They also should continue to provide growth potential comparable to common stocks and the tax and limited liability benefits of untraded limited partnerships.

SOME TYPES OF LIMITED PARTNERSHIPS

The variety of limited partnerships is as wide as the economic activities they are designed to support.

Oil and Gas

OIL AND GAS

Moderate income

Low safety

Low liquidity

Good inflation hedge

Good tax benefits

Good growth

The oil embargo sponsored in the 1970s by the Organization of Petroleum Exporting Countries (OPEC) shook U.S. complacency as no other economic event since World War II. "Energy independence" became the accepted political slogan of the decade. Predictably, investors began to seek out energy investment plays. Domestic oil companies with substantial reserves were the darlings of Wall Street. Oil and gas investments—many structured as tax shelters—had been around for many years, but suddenly the demand for further exploration and development expanded the market.

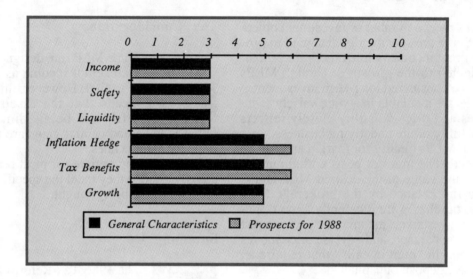

Limited partnerships quickly formed to get in on the potential profits. Another, more important feature was the development of the domestic energy industry as a national priority. Huge tax credits were allowed for investments in energy issues. Oil and gas programs commonly offered writeoffs of 90 to over 100% of the initial investments and the potential for large capital gains. They became the hottest tax shelters on the market.

The 1986 TRA eliminated the investment tax credits previously enjoyed by the energy industry, but left intact the depletion, intangible drilling costs, and equipment depreciation allowances.

Investment Potential

Oil and gas partnerships offer both income and the potential for capital gain. They are long-term invesmtents, usually scheduled for liquidation within 7 to 10 years. Income is paid when the project begins earning money, and capital gains are normally achieved when the partnership is liquidated.

Partnership investors are subject to market and business risk. The price of oil is quite volatile, and fluctuations of oil prices directly affect the value of partnership shares.

The two types of oil and gas drilling partnerships are *exploratory* and *development*. Development projects bring known reserves to the market. They normally begin to pay income relatively quickly. They generate fewer losses to offset income payouts. Since the reserves are already known, the risk is lower and capital gain potential is less.

Exploratory projects are devoted to locating new reserves. Initial expenses are great and risk is high, because no guarantee exists that oil or gas will be found. The odds of success are minimal for any given well; most partnerships expect to drill a number of wells to increase the odds for success. The potential for capital gains is substantially higher than for a development project.

Some oil and gas partnerships are combinations of the two types, and many partnerships of this sort opt to direct some earnings back into development to maintain or boost the partnership income stream. This approach offers greater capital gains potential than do straight development projects and less than do exploratory projects.

This flexibility is enhanced by the wide range of leverage possible, enabling investors to search out those projects that most closely fit their own investment profiles.

Strengths

 Oil and gas partnerships are good hedges against inflation. A successful exploration project offers large income and capital gains potential. And development projects pay current income that usually is sheltered to some degree.

Weaknesses

 Exploration projects are very high risk. Oil prices are volatile and directly affect the value of a partnership share. Initial costs tend to be very high.

Tax Considerations

 The 1986 Tax Reform Act changed much of the treatment for limited partnerships—the chief form of investing in oil and gas for most individuals. How-ever, the beleaguered oil and gas industry did manage to keep favored treatment for some things. Unlike virtually all other limited partnerships, losses generated through intangible drilling costs can still be used to offset ordinary income. As discussed earlier, most other limited partnerships' losses are considered "passive" and can be used only to offset passive income. There are, of course, some changes in details. Check with your tax advisor *before* investing.

Summing Up

 In 1974, people widely believed that oil prices would never go down again, because of OPEC's obvious muscle, but history and the marketplace proved that forecast shortsighted. After moving as high as $40 per barrel in the early 1980s oil prices entered a long downward slide that finally ended late in 1986, when oil briefly sold for around $9 per barrel. OPEC agreed to cut production, and the price per barrel had risen to $18 by late 1987. Whether this agreement is sustained depends in part on the willingness and ability of Saudi Arabia to bear the brunt of the cutback.

The longer oil holds near the $18 mark, the more likely it is that the bottom has been seen. If inflation rises, oil and gas prices will benefit. Americans can now more easily monitor oil prices by watching the crude oil futures contracts traded on the New York Mercantile Exchange. There is much talk of imposing a high tax on imported oil; such a measure would have a short-term negative impact on oil prices.

Agriculture

Agriculture is the world's largest industry. Food consumption naturally increases as more children are born and life expectancies increase. Worldwide, the agricultural industry is so vast that its scope defies casual discussion. It is enough simply to observe that in every country in the world, food and related issues—food production, processing and distribution—have become key concerns. Keeping up with food demand is changing the way the world looks at a variety of economic, political, and technological issues. As usual, where a need exists an economic solution is in the making. Some solutions are old, and some are new, and almost all hold out potential for wise investors.

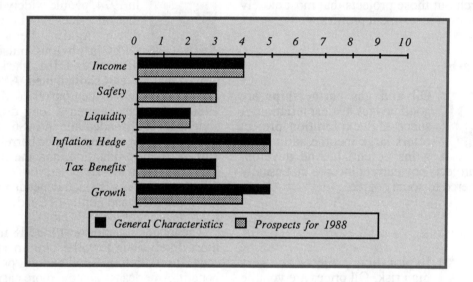

Land use is one consideration. As farmers in the powerhouse agricultural states of the U.S. West and Midwest have discovered, financing the farm through mortgage payments can be a dead end. Fixed mortgage payments continue despite erratic production and uncontrollable prices and demand. One solution is the recent development of limited partnerships that take over land in default and create joint ventures with the farmer to produce crops. The farmer is paid a management fee, shares in the profits, and has the option of buying back the land on a lease-back basis. This strategy is being called "the new share cropping."

But the truly important developments are in food production, processing, and distribution. Limited partnerships developed by Granada Corporation (Houston, Texas) are scaling their operations to control the entire process. The "green revolution" of the 1960s and 1970s turned many "second world" countries into agricultural producers, crowding markets for traditional products. Companies such as Granada are responding by developing important new technologies to increase yields in traditional product areas and to create breakthroughs in new areas. Genetic engineering, for example, is creating new products such as the Lite Beef (trademark) breed, which is lower in fat and carcinogens than are standard beef cattle.

Aquaculture is another example. In the U.S. South, wornout cotton fields are being flooded to become catfish farms. Catfish, shrimp, trout, oysters, striped bass, and salmon are all under active production.

USDA experiments with jojoba beans hold exciting promise, as does USDA's work with a new plant called *knauf,* which produces both long and short fibers for paper products.

Progressive partnerships also are working to establish vertical market penetration. Traditionally, farmers have had no control over the market value of their products. Limited partnerships have the resources to produce, process, and market the product. Partnerships have created important marketing breakthroughs that create demand and market price stability. Examples are turkey hams from the dark meat of the turkey, which retail for $2.29 a pound, (not $0.29 a pound as for the unprocessed meat); gourmet food products; and convenient restaurant packaging. These offerings are known as "niche" products. The profits increase as value is added through processing and specialized marketing.

Some currently productive agricultural areas for limited partnerships include livestock and poultry breeding, processing, and distribution; timber; aquaculture; basic food crops; orchards (including citrus), walnuts, pistachio nuts, avocados; and row crops such as beans, corn, and peas.

Investment Potential

Like all limited partnerships, agricultural opportunities are long-term investments. Some partnerships are offering exceptional cash returns: held for at least 10 to 12 years, some jojoba bean operations may provide returns as high as 80% per year. And after three years of operation, Imperial's aquaculture farms estimate cash flow at 13 to 20%.

Strengths

 The decreasing value of the U.S. dollar has reinvigorated the agricultural sector. In addition, value-added processing entices profits away from com-

modity price dependency. Biotechnology holds a promise for breakthroughs in food production and quality. And professional management and off-balance-sheet financing limit business risks.

Weaknesses

 Agricultural limited partnerships are subject to worldwide price volatility and to supply and demand competition in markets. Government price support and policies are uncertain. In disinflationary times leverage is dangerous. Farmers risk loss of property if debt can't be serviced.

Tax Considerations

 The tax treatment of agriculture-related partnerships is complex. A number of changes made by the Tax Reform Act tightened the rules for obtaining write-offs. It is particularly important to check with your tax advisor in this area.

Summing Up

 Many factors combine to make modern agriculture an exciting investment arena for progressive limited partnerships. The earth's ever-increasing population, the ongoing concern over the cost of financing a family farm, the potentials inherent in creating a vertical marketing structure that takes into account all aspects of production, process, and distribution—all contribute to a healthy picture.

Of course, food production is closely linked to uncontrollable factors such as the weather, political and social upheaval, and the availability of resources. But careful and creative partnerships are uncovering new ways to make agricultural production and marketing profitable.

Equipment Leasing

EQUIPMENT
LEASING

Good income

Low safety

Low liquidity

Good inflation
hedge

Good tax
benefits

Moderate growth

Equipment leasing is one of the great success stories of limited partnerships. Properly administered, leasing programs are profitable both for the lessor (the owner of the property) and the lessee (the user of the property).

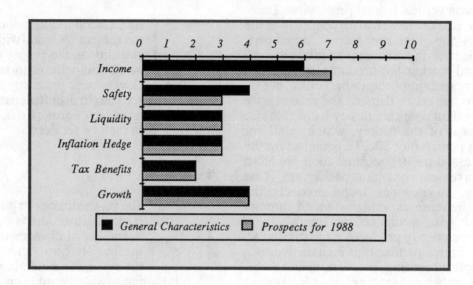

The lessor—in this case, a limited partnership—buys equipment from the manufacturer and leases it for a substantial portion of its useful life span. At the end of the lease, the lessee may purchase the equipment or return it to the lessor, which in turns sells it as used equipment.

Commonly leased equipment includes steel shipping containers, airplanes, truck fleets, copy equipment, and vending machines. The demand for leased equipment has grown since the 1986 TRA introduced the Alternative Corporate Minimum Tax, which in many cases penalizes businesses that buy large amounts of equipment. Leasing allows companies to conserve capital for use in more profitable areas than equipment. Northwest Airlines leases its DC-10s and uses capital in customer services. Corporations no longer consider off-balance-sheet financing a liability; from a net worth standpoint, leasing improves the balance sheet.

In 1984, U.S. businesses spent $84 billion to lease equipment; in 1985, they spent $93 billion; in 1986, $100 billion; and they are expected to have spent $120 billion in 1987.

That kind of activity has made equipment leasing one of the most attractive investments of the decade.

The two types of leases are (1) full payout leases and (2) operating leases. Full payout leases require the lessee to pay off the full value of the equipment over the duration of the lease. Full payout leases are a "do-or-die" proposition backed by the credit of the lessee. Operating leases are short-term leases in which the equipment is leased more than once during its useful life span—clearly, a riskier position than the one assumed in a full payout lease.

Investment Potential

Leasing partnerships generate revenues in two ways: through the lease payments and through the subsequent sale of the equipment. In some cases, the lessor's original purchase is highly leveraged, so during the early years of the partnership the lease payments may be used to amortize the purchase costs. Of course, the returns paid to the partners are passive income and may be used to offset the passive losses of tax shelters purchased before the 1986 TRA.

The major U.S. leasing companies lease only to highly rated corporations. In addition, equipment leases hold a position senior to that of corporate bonds, so the holdings of the partnership are secured by the value of the equipment. Depending on the creditworthiness of the lessees and assuming equipment with a long useful life span, leasing partnerships are among the most stable and conservative partnerships available.

Leasing partnerships provide excellent current income and growth of capital when the equipment is liquidated. In inflationary scenarios, the value of the equipment increases for higher residual worth at the lease's end. Residual values also are sustained in recessionary markets since corporations are likely either to re-lease or buy used equipment. However, the danger exists that in a recession the value of the equipment will be seriously compromised.

Strengths

 Leasing partnerships provide higher current income than does real estate and they also provide growth on assets. They generally are regarded as a conservative investment if the lessee is a high-quality company and the equipment is long-lived. The holding is collateralized by the equipment; a lease has a senior position to that of corporate bonds. And leasing partnerships are an excellent complement to municipal bond investments under zero to moderate inflation.

Weaknesses

 In a deflationary scenario, the residual value of a leasing partnership may not be profitable. Leasing partnerships are also vulnerable to the failure of the lessee's business. And high-tech equipment may become obsolete by the end of the lease period, destroying residual value.

Tax Considerations

 Highly leveraged leasing deals were formerly the darlings of the tax shelter industry. Losses can only be used to offset passive income, not ordinary income. The death blow to the tax shelter aspect of these programs, though, was the elimination of the investment tax credit. There are no particular tax advantages for leasing deals now.

Summing Up

 Every indication suggests that equipment leasing will continue to offer significant returns to limited partnerships. The desire of major corporations to lease so that capital is freed for other uses should result in an increase in leasing activity.

Potential profits depend on the value of the equipment on the resale market at the end of the lease and on the ability of the lessee to maintain lease payments. High-tech equipment—including computers—is especially vulnerable to obsolescence.

Leveraged Buyouts

LBOs

Low income

Low safety

Poor liquidity

Good inflation hedge

No tax benefits

Moderate growth

Everyone knows the story of Victor Kiam, "the man who liked the razor so much he bought the company." Buy you may not know that Kiam didn't buy the company with his own money—not much of it, anyway.

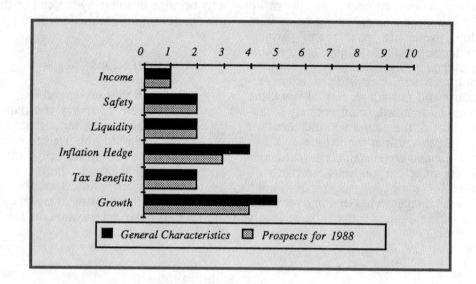

When Kiam bought Remington, he used a financing mechanism known as a *leveraged buyout* (LBO), which enabled him to buy a multimillion-dollar company with less than $1 million down. A lending institution provided the balance.

How can so little buy so much? It's quite simple: in a leveraged buyout, the assets and anticipated future cash flow of the acquired business are used as collateral. Of course, the acquisition target must be profitable and relatively debt-free, to be attractive to the lender.

In the last few years, the financial press has been full of tales of leveraged buyouts, and great amounts of wealth have been generated by the strategy. But until recently the game was open only to the big players— investors with between $10 million and $25 million to invest at one time. Companies such as Kohlberg Kravis Roberts and Forstmann Little generate revenues as high as $5 billion a month with their LBO acquisitions.

Now, however, the LBO game can be played even by average investors with stable portfolios who want to add some sizzle to the mix. Pioneered by Equus Capital Corporation (Houston, Texas), limited partnerships are now getting into the LBO hunt—and they have been paying off handsomely.

Equus specializes in the friendly acquisition of healthy, middle-sized companies in fragmented industries. These may be niche businesses, operations that have learned to use a specialized technique or product to succeed in a competitive environment.

Once a business has been located and identified as a potential target for acquisition, it is carefully analyzed by both Equus and prospective lending institutions for fundamental soundness. This double-check by both Equus and an understandably wary lending institution gives the program stability. Once a business qualifies for acquisition, a financing package is structured in which assets and future cash flow are used to support borrowing; the partnership may put up only from 10 to 25% of the total purchase price. To assure that the business is managed properly, existing management is maintained and brought into an ownership position. The tactic is especially valuable for businesses in which the owner wishes to retire or restructure the organization. In some cases, ownership wants to take a public company private or go public with a private company—in which case the partnership will sell the business back after the financing package has been consolidated by the partnership. The goals of a leveraged buyout are to restructure the business for increased profitability, quickly reduce the debt, and ultimately dispose of the assets or refinance.

Investment Potential

Because they are highly leveraged, LBO partnerships aren't structured for immediate income. They may begin to produce some income within three or four years, but the real goal is growth of capital. They are long-term investments.

Strengths

 LBOs have a higher-than-average profit expectation. Moreover, the partnership invests in a diversified portfolio of companies. The value of corporation stocks are not necessarily tied to the public markets. Equity buildup is expected through debt reduction from the company's cash flow. Finally, participation by present management creates added incentive for increased productivity and performance.

Weaknesses

 The offering corporation could falter if cash flow expectations don't materialize or if general economic conditions deteriorate.

Tax Considerations

 As we go to press, a significant amount of legislation is being proposed concerning tax treatment of leveraged buyouts. Limitations on the deductibility of interest and other changes are being considered. It is likely that a significant tightening of tax laws concerning leveraged buyouts will be passed. Check with your tax advisor for the current treatment of this area.

Summing Up

 The limited partnership LBO is a different animal altogether from the hostile corporate takeovers that have occurred with uncommon frequency in the 1980s. Acquired companies are cooperative participants, and the existing management usually assumes a leadership role under the new corporate structure. Barring unforeseeable problems in the fundamental structure of the U.S. economy, limited partnership LBOs promise to continue to be an effective way for a company to undergo a financial restructuring and to provide investors with significant benefits.

Cable Television

CABLE
TELEVISION

Low income

Low safety

Poor liquidity

Good inflation hedge

Some tax benefits

Good growth

Cable television has surprised everyone. In 1976, the Arthur D. Little Company predicted that by 1980 3.4 million Americans would subscribe to a pay television service, and that by 1985 the number would be up to 5.7 million. In fact, those numbers fell far short of the mark, and the industry continues to grow.

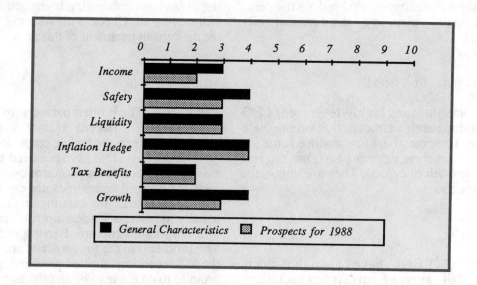

Cable originally was attractive primarily in remote areas where normal television signals were weak or unavailable. But now cable franchisers can offer their subscribers a wide variety of programming unavailable on standard UHF and VHF frequencies, and cable penetration in urban areas has grown substantially.

Cable systems are franchised by the communities where they market their services. The cable company receives TV signals via satellite and distributes the signal throughout its service area via coaxial cable. After the initial costs of installing a service grid are paid, maintenance costs are generally very low. Because the system is franchised to service an area, it can operate much like a utility, with stable revenues and predictable expenses. Cable TV is sometimes called the "unregulated monopoly."

Although the costs of establishing cable are high, the stability of the industry has encouraged lending institutions to provide financing that is leveraged against the assets of the fu-

ture company. Cable television has proved sensitive to inflation, so investors can position their cable investments as inflationary hedges.

The 1986 Tax Reform Act was a boon to cable TV partnerships. Most cable equipment is depreciable over five years, compared with 27.5 to 31.5 for real estate, and income is fully or almost fully sheltered during the early years of the partnership.

Investment Potential

Originally, cable partnerships were growth oriented, but income partnerships have come on strong recently. Growth partnerships are heavily leveraged—usually from 50 to 75%—and thus produce very little cash flow, if any. Revenue left over after debt service usually is plowed back into the system for maintenance and expansion.

Income-oriented cable TV partnerships use leverage ranging from 25 to 35% to buy profitable existing systems. Aside from maintenance of the service (which can be expensive if the system is outdated), overhead is minimal, so revenues can pass directly through to partners, although long-term gains may fall short of those produced by growth funds.

Strengths

 Cable TV systems are an "unregulated monopoly"; existing systems are virtually immune from competitive pressures. Traditionally, cable systems produce high operating margins. Cable partnerships are "recession-proof," since cheap entertainment is a priority in hard times. New technologies keep cable fresh, ensuring long-range viability. Most cable TV equipment is depreciable over five years, so income is fully or almost fully sheltered during the partnership's early years.

Weaknesses

 As in any equipment-heavy partnership, management qualification is a crucial issue. An increasing demand exists for a limited number of cable franchises in good locations; management might be tempted to pay too much for a system. Finally in a rapidly changing industry, partnerships need to be wary of the costs of necessary equipment upgrades.

Tax Considerations

 Cable television partnerships are no longer being marketed for their tax benefits. Losses can only be used to offset passive income.

Summing Up

 After some industry-wide shakeups, cable TV partnerships now are generally recognized as offering a combination of safety plus growth, or income. The industry has proved to be stable and highly profitable. Conservative investors can choose income funds, with their purchases of proven systems, for immediate payback. Investors who want growth can turn to a number of reputable programs that are now expanding their existing systems and buying new ones.

Historic Rehabs

HISTORIC REHABS

Low income

Moderate safety

Poor liquidity

Good inflation hedge

Good tax benefits

Moderate growth

Perhaps no other investment product meets with more universal favor than "historical rehab" (rehabilitation), a subcategory of the real estate market. Virtually every community in the country boasts an important, yet fragile, architectural tradition that gives the community character and provides a link with the past. But time takes a toll on old buildings, and historical properties can be kept alive only with the infusion of new capital.

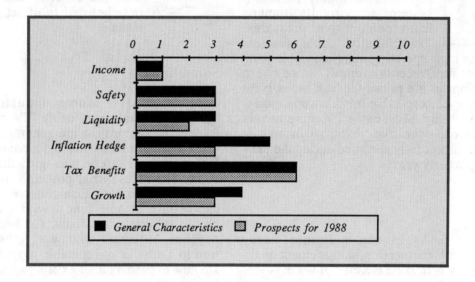

These realities were recognized by Congress when it passed the 1986 Tax Reform Act. Although Congress eliminated investment tax credits in almost every other investment area, it maintained a 20% investment tax credit for certified historical rehabilitation. Now some very successful limited partnerships are taking advantage of the opportunity by structuring historic rehab programs in accordance with the standards of the U.S. Department of the Interior.

The rehab market got off the ground in 1982, following the 1981 Economic Recovery Tax Act (ERTA), which first allowed tax credits for rehab investments. Under the provisions of the 1981 law, most rehab programs were structured as private placement partnerships. They were highly tax oriented and were sold only to accredited investors with annual incomes of at least $200,000 and net worths in excess of $1 million.

The 1986 TRA eliminated the tax credits for individuals with adjusted gross incomes of over $200,000. So the rehab programs were restructured as niche products to satisfy the needs of investors with incomes of less than $200,000. Unit sizes are as low as $3,000. The 20% investment tax credit is more favorable to taxpayers in lower brackets. Historical rehab is an exception to the passive loss rules of the 1986 TRA; investors can shelter writeoffs against other income up to $25,000 per year regardless of passive loss limitations.

Strengths

Outstanding demand exists for historical buildings, yet there is a finite supply of qualified buildings. Historical rehab is an excellent inflation hedge and excellent tax favors exist after the 1986 TRA.

Weaknesses

 Historic rehab is subject to the same economic and market influences that affect real estate in general. The success of an historic rehab program is largely dependent of the capabilities of the management. Moreover, certification must be granted by the government. And historic rehab is highly illiquid; the IRS imposes a five-year recapture rule.

Tax Considerations

 The 1986 Tax Reform Act did provide continued tax-favored treatment for investment in rehabilition projects. Investors get 20% credit for "qualified" expenditures incurred in the rehab of certified historic structures. A 10% credit is given for nonresidential buildings that are *not* certified historic structures. Definitions that have been changed include that of "qualified rehabilitation housing." As always in these more complex matters, be sure to check with your tax advisor.

Summing Up

 Great tax advantages and a diminishing stock of old buildings are certain to increase the demand for qualified partnerships. Also investors can know that their money has contributed to the well-being of a community.

Self-Storage

A number of national trends have given rise to self-storage, one of the most important new subcategories of the real estate industry. The most obvious trend is the reduced size of the U.S. home: many more Americans are living in apartments and condominiums than ever before, and the size of the average home continues to shrink. There's less storage space in these new dwellings, at a time when people are buying more possessions. Factor in the increasing cost of commercial space, and you have fertile ground for self-storage. Over 12,000 self-storage facilities are now scattered across the country. Self-storage began in Texas and spread throughout the South and the West; it is not yet well established in the Northeast.

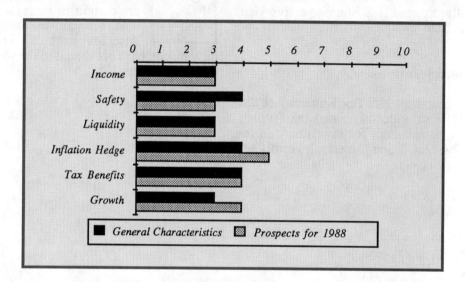

Self-storage units are owned primarily by individuals, by joint ventures of a few people, or by limited partnerships. An industry-wide analysis shows the importance of small ownership in the self-storage industry:

Public Storage (limited partnership)	700 Facilities
U-Haul (private ownership)	200
Shurgard, Inc. (limited partnership)	125
Balcor Colonial (limited partnership)	100
Others: (includes individual ownership, corporations and small partnerships)	10,875

Strengths

Self-storage offers a chance of increasing cash flow. All-cash ownership reduces risk. Self-storage combines low operating expenses and high demand. When they are unleveraged, self-storage partnerships are a hedge against inflation and deflation hedge.

Weaknesses

Self-storage is illiquid. Highly leveraged properties cut cash flow. Self-storage requires geographic diversification; locating too many facilities in a single area makes the partnership vulnerable to local economic downturn. In addition, larger syndicators can hurt small operators through price wars and national marketing efforts. Low occupancy affects cash flow and market value. And development partnerships take on market risk.

Tax Considerations

There are no special tax benefits for self-storage investments. Sole proprietors may be able to structure fianancing to take advantage of the writeoff allowed for business interest. However, limited partnership participation limits the use of any losses to offsetting passive income. See your tax advisor.

Summing Up

The huge number of small operators in this field create a healthy takeover market for limited partnerships. In addition, this market is not near its saturation point.

There also appears to be considerable potential for new ideas in self-storage. The newest idea is record retrieval centers, which store records for downtown offices and provide pickup and delivery services. Companies such as Shurgard are moving into city centers with high-rise storage facilities. Freeway storage facilities are being tagged for later sale and potential development for higher and better use. Self-storage firms are augmenting their business with auxiliary sales in areas such as shelf sales, support materials, and other related services.

Collectibles

COLLECTIBLES

No income

Low safety

Poor liquidity

Good inflation hedge

No tax benefits

Moderate growth

Collectibles attracted much attention from investors in the inflation-torn 1970s. Although experts and neophytes alike profited in those years, 1982 marked a reversal for inflation and resulted in a severe shakeout in these markets.

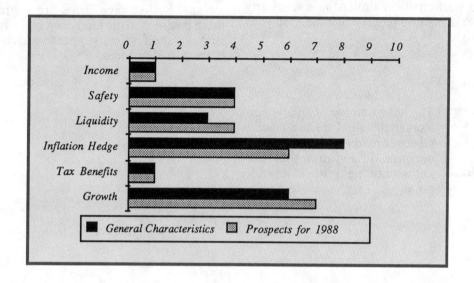

The term *collectibles* encompasses a wide variety of items. The most popular markets, include stamps, antiques, art, and photography (see also the section on rare coins). Collectibles are nonfinancial physical assets found in limited supply that provide esthetic, psychological, or practical value to the owner. They are expected to appreciate as a result of inlation or through increased recognition of their rarity.

Unlike financial assets, collectibles are not traded in a central auction arena. Rather, they are bought and sold through loose networks of dealers, collectors, and even flea markets. Prices fluctuate widely from transation to transaction.

Experts recommend that investing in collectibles should only be undertaken by those with an abiding interest in the particular item.

The collectible market is susceptible to fraud and even to well-intentioned but mistaken valuations.

Because no uniform method is used for valuing collectible assets, there is a wide range for legitimate differences of opinion.

This variability makes the market particularly treacherous for amateur investors.

Costs are a two-edged sword: Not only is a price paid for an item, there is also the cost of lost opportunity for the money invested. *Opportunity cost* is merely the return that is given up in order to hold the collectible. For example, to figure opportunity cost calculate how much interest would have been paid by an equivalent investment in Treasury bills over the same time period. That is the cost of holding an investment such as a collectible that pays no income.

The profit acquired when the item is sold is the return *over and above* what could have been earned in the safest financial vehicle.

Investment Potential

Investing in collectibles is a long-term project because rarely can short-term profits be made. Often, nonprofessional investors wind up paying retail prices, but can sell only at wholesale levels. For many investors the psychic benefit is well worth the aggravation. This is a decision only you can make.

Collectibles provide capital gains when buying at one price and selling at a higher price. There is no income.

Strengths

 Collectibles have an outstanding record in protecting your assets from the ravages of inflation.

Weaknesses

 Liquidity varies greatly. Some collectibles can only be sold through auction houses, via consignment or with dealers. Even "fairly" priced assets may take a long time to sell in depressed economic environments. Because prices are not listed regularly in daily papers, as are stocks or bonds, accurate valuations are difficult to ascertain. Many factors go into determining the value of collectibles, including such subjective details as their condition. There is no current income, and costs vary greatly. Also, collectibles are not eligible for IRAs. And, finally, each collectible carries its own unique risks, including potential loss of value due to deterioration, widespread fraud, changing interest in "fads," or even a large increase in supply.

Tax Considerations

 Beginning in 1988, no tax advantages apply to collectibles. In fact, because the IRS may determine that your collectible investing is a "hobby" rather than a business, associated costs may not be deductible. However, tax on gains is due regardless of whether your collectible investing is deemed a hobby or an investment.

Summing Up

 The widespread popularity of collectible investing has decreased considerably. If you have a real interest in a specific area and have the time to pursue detailed study, it can certainly be very profitable. However, for most investors the prime consideration should be whether the enjoyment derived from the activity is sufficient to offset the potential financial drawbacks.

Rare Coins

Rare coins are coins, issued by governments as legal tender, that have collector's value over and above the face value of the coin.

No income

Moderate safety

Moderate liquidity

Excellent inflation hedge

No tax benefits

Good growth

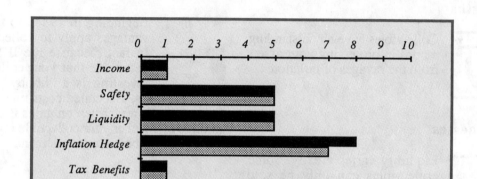

According to Salomon Brothers, the major investment banking firm, rare (numismatic) coins have been one of the best investments for the past 20 years. The Salomon Brothers numismatic coin index has outperformed the stock market, bonds, and gold. The Salomon Rare Coin Index is based on the performance of a 20–coin portfolio.

The numismatic value of coins was recognized by the U.S. government in the 1943 Gold Reserve Act. That law made it illegal for U.S. citizens to own gold but it specifically exempted gold coins of "recognized special value to collectors." Numismatic coins are not limited to gold and silver. Coins minted in other metals, such as copper, are also actively sought by rare coin investors.

The rare coin market is loosely organized. Sales are made through coin dealers in shops and through the mail. The most common method for the sale of highly valued coins is through auctions. Often investors bid for coins through "mail auctions." Another popular marketplace is coin shows that convene in major cities around the country.

The rare coin investment community is well served by many periodicals, including weekly newspapers such as *Coin World* and *Numismatic News*. One national teletype service provides up-to-date price information for dealers. Most dealers subscribe to the *Coin Dealers Gray Sheet* newsletter, a weekly update of price information and market trends. Also, many investment advisory newsletters ferret out good values in rare coins for their subscribers.

The loosely knit organization provides fair liquidity for more actively traded coins, including most U.S.-issued gold coins. U.S. silver dollars also offer a very popular market. More obscure coins are less actively traded and hence provide substantially less liquidity. Fees vary widely. Most pricing is done on a "markup" basis whereby the dealer purchases a coin through its resources and then resells that coin at a higher price. This markup is usually not disclosed to the buyer. The best way to tell if you are being charged excessive fees is to comparison-shop with a number of dealers before buying. Competition serves to limit abuses for actively involved investors.

The most troublesome area for rare coin buyers is the grading of individual coins. A coin's grade is a rating of its condition. A coin sold as BU (brilliant uncirculated) is supposed to be in mint condition. A lesser grade is AU (almost uncirculated). A widely accepted numerical rating now accompanies these letter designations.

Regardless of the numerous enhancements that grading has gone through over the years, evaluation of individual coins remains largely subjective. Experienced coin investors and dealers detect the subtle nuances that make the difference between grades. Neophyte investors must rely on the dealer's integrity. Brown and Dunn's *Guide to Grading of United States Coins* is the classic book on grading and evaluating coins.

Investment Potential

Rare coin investing is a long-term proposition for most investors. Most investors buy coins at retail prices but can only sell them wholesale. It takes time for the appreciation to cover transaction costs. Coin experts suggest that an investor should expect to hold coins for at least five to seven years.

Rare coin investing generates capital gains. No income is paid. Coin prices are generally not volatile. The coin market in normal circumstances unfolds in a stable, slow-growth manner. However, times of great volatility do occur. The high inflation in the late 1970s and the subsequent disinflation resulted in wide price swings for many coins, especially gold and silver issues.

As mentioned earlier, liquidity is a factor in the decision of which coins to buy. Some coins have quite liquid markets and can be sold quickly. However, even widely traded gold coins can suffer large overnight price movements. A buyer can always be found but the investor may be forced to take steep discounts if the coins must be sold quickly.

Rare coin investing is straightforward. Coins are bought, held and sold. Only a limited number of strategies are available. Some dealers offer leveraged investments where a fraction of the cost of a portfolio of coins is paid. The dealer holds the coins for the investor who makes periodic interest and/or principal payments. Rare coins are also accepted by some banks as collateral for loans.

A central coin-grading service is offered by an industry trade group, the ANA (American Numismatic Association). For a fee, they will grade the coin and issue a certificate of authenticity. However, the federal government does not regulate the rare coin industry. This freedom may change in the near future as a result of scandals involving overgrading of coins by large national dealers.

Strengths

 Rare coins offer good potential for long-term capital growth, and they are an excellent inflation hedge. Most rare coin investors are motivated by the esthetic satisfaction of putting together beautiful collections as well as by the potential profit. Most U.S. gold and silver coins are quite liquid.

Weaknesses

 A coin's condition is the most important factor in determining that coin's price. Grading is a subjective art with valid disparities of opinion. A change in grade of only one level may mean the reduction of a coin's value by as much as 50%. Moreover, no central, easily accessible source standardizes coin prices. And high-value coins are often counterfeited. Some counterfeits are so good they can be detected only with expensive, high-tech procedures.

Fees are not usually disclosed. They can be very high and consequently hurt your potential return. In addition, rare coins pay no current income.

Finally, rare coins can be stolen or misplaced.

Tax Considerations

 No special tax benefits apply to rare coin investments. The 1986 Tax Reform Act eliminated the preferential treatment of long-term capital gains. All gains are taxed at your ordinary income rates.

Summing Up

 Rare coin investing is a rapidly growing industry. As more investors participate, disparities in pricing will even out. Market information will increase. Rare coins are excellent inflation hedges.

Supply and demand ultimately determine all prices. The supply of rare coins is fixed.

As the interest in them increases, their prices should continue to rise.

It is vital to do business with reputable, established coin dealers. The potential for fraud is high, and the investor must be careful. Never rush to buy a coin. Verify the price with independent sources to ensure you are not paying more than the market price. A coin that is a good value today will still be a good value in the two or three days it takes to evaluate its worth.

---

10 Popular "Exotic" Investments

1. Rare coins
2. Collectibles
3. Raw land real estate
4. Limited partnerships in mini-warehouses (self-storage)
5. Strategic metals
6. Venture capital
7. Wines
8. Scotch whiskey
9. Forward contracts
10. Repurchase agreements

CHAPTER 17

ANNUITIES AND INSURANCE

A GLANCE AHEAD

Although the 1986 Tax Reform Act dealt a death blow to many tax shelter schemes featuring limited partnerships and multiple writeoffs, the life insurance industry managed to come out virtually unscathed. You can still earn money on a tax-deferred basis on cash value insurance. You can still borrow on your cash value insurance policies tax free. The latter loophole is already coming under close scrutiny in Congress but the insurance company lobby has proven formidable to date.

It's increasingly likely that your stock broker will be approached about your life insurance needs. Many insurance products now appeal more to your investment needs than your protection needs. The proliferation of complex products makes the arcane world of life insurance even more difficult to understand.

This chapter introduces the most important of these new insurance/investment products. You'll learn

- *The difference between term and cash value insurance*
- *Why life insurance may be the right product for deferring taxes on part of your investment portfolio*
- *How life insurance can increase your protection with wise investment decisions*
- *Why life insurance products are not appropriate for short-term investing*
- *Two important indexes you should use in evaluating policies*

THE WORLD OF LIFE INSURANCE

The 1986 Tax Reform Act did not so much bestow new benefits on the life insurance industry as preserve elements that have existed since 1913. The 1986 act decimated the competition by virtually eliminating multiple real estate-based writeoffs and most other shelter techniques.

Life insurance products have maintained their favored status, because they are seen as providing private alternatives to public finance. Three main tax-favored benefits have been with us since income tax began in 1913:

1. Earnings on the cash value of a policy accrue tax free.
2. Loans taken against the cash value of a policy are tax free.
3. The death benefit proceeds are tax free to your beneficiaries.

Recent years have seen a veritable flood of new products. No longer is life insurance merely a contract providing your dependents with financial protection in the case of your death. In fact, that is one of the real dangers that the complex new products present. The heavy emphasis on them as investment products (stock brokers are becoming an increasingly important segment of the market) tends to obscure the real reason for having life insurance in the first place: protection for your dependents.

The insurance market has undergone dramatic changes in recent years. In 1982 term insurance accounted for 60% of all life insurance policies. Today that figure has dropped below 40%. Insurance companies (with a few exceptions) have put their advertising money in programs emphasizing tax shelter investing and high-yield returns—with protection almost as an afterthought!

Risks

Those products that enable you to tie part of your return to the stocks or bonds subject you to the same risks as outright investing in those markets. Rest assured, the one time you need to borrow will be the time when your selected investment option is performing at its worst!

Historically the insurance industry has been conservatively managed and quite safe. However, in the early 1980s a major issuer of annuities, Baldwin-United went bankrupt. Their products had been heavily marketed by leading brokerage firms including Merrill Lynch and E. F. Hutton. It is obviously vital to do business with only the most financially secure companies.

Remember, insurance-related investment products are very long term. Typically you must hold a cash value product for a minimum of 10 years before you can expect to achieve a competitive return. It takes that long for the policy's investment income to exceed commissions and fees.

 It is now possible to protect yourself to at least some extent from inflation by selecting products that fluctuate with market prices. A policy tied to money market interest rates will rise in times of inflation offering at least nominal inflation protection. Because of the long-term nature of the investment, you should discuss this factor with your agent, broker, or financial planner.

You can always cash in your cash value policy for something. However, you'll take a substantial loss for redemptions in the first years of the policy. You are able to borrow tax free from most policies. You take a big risk, though, if you borrow too much against your policy's value. If you do not repay the loan, your policy could lapse (be canceled). If that happens, the IRS will assess a massive

tax bill on the basis that the unpaid loans are investment income.

While the life insurance industry has enjoyed a favored tax status, we now face significant risk of political changes. Members of Congress are already directing their attention to the tax-free status of policy loans. This large loophole (no other investment lets you withdraw funds from tax-deferred plans at anytime without penalty) may be closed. It is doubtful whether any penalty would be assessed against outstanding loans. But there may be changes in the tax treatment of loans, especially on single-premium policies.

Purchasers of insurance products do run risks that are unique to the product. Fitting the right coverage with each individual's singular circumstances leaves much room for abuse. Regardless of how the various products are touted to the public, the main reason for buying life insurance is protection, not investment. While many families are underinsured, many others are overinsured with the wrong type of coverages.

For example, a common sales pitch against term insurance is that the premiums are "wasted" money because no cash value accrues (insurance agents receive much higher commissions for selling cash value insurance than for term insurance). However, since term premiums may amount to as little as 20% of a comparable whole-life policy, the money saved may yield a far greater return if wisely invested. Insurance companies gladly offer to manage your money for you but they inevitably charge you for the service.

Many life insurance products, especially single-premium items, are being sold by investment specialists rather than by life insurance agents. While such specialists are often well versed in the *investment* aspects of the products, they are not usually conversant with the best information about the necessary *protection* aspects for you.

Independent Ratings

All life insurance companies are rated by A. M. Best & Company annually. Best's Insurance Reports are available from most libraries. The National Insurance Consumer Organization (121 North Payne Street, Alexandria, VA 22314) offers numerous publications to help consumers sort through the complexities and hype of insurance sales. For example, their booklet "Taking the Bite Out of Insurance" ($8.25) features a list of the maximum rates they recommend paying for renewable term policies.

 The National Association of Insurance Commissioners is an organization of state insurance regulators. They've developed two indexes to give you a method for comparing equivalent policies. While the indexes won't tell you whether a term policy is better than a whole-life policy, they are good guides for comparing two policies of the same type.

The interest-adjusted net payment cost index measures the present value of the premiums you pay for the next 10 years. This index takes into consideration the fact that you could earn interest on the premium money. The index number represents the cost of insurance per each $1,000 of death benefit. The lower the number, the cheaper the policy.

The other index is called the *surrender cost index*. It measures the present cost of cash value policies if you cancel them to take your cash in 10 years.

Most state regulations require insurance agents to provide you with these numbers on request. Since insurance policies are increasingly complex, with fees varying widely even for the same type of coverage, it is important that you do your own comparison shopping.

FIXED DEFERRED ANNUITIES

A fixed deferred annuity is a contract between an insurance company and the purchaser of the annuity (called the *annuitant*) that specifies the premium and the payout options. In exchange for a premium paid by the annuitant (the premium can be either a single lump sum or can be paid over time in installments), the insurance company guarantees a minimum rate of return. Usually, a return substantially higher than the contract minimum is guaranteed for one year. The interest rate then is adjusted according to a specified formula annually but can never be set below the contract minimum.

Although you can buy an annuity with a single premium that begins monthly payments immediately, the more common form is a "deferred" annuity. With a deferred annuity, the buyer pays either a single or installment premium, which earns income until the buyer (the annuitant) elects to start taking payments, at age 59 1/2 or later. The amount of monthly payments will be determined by the size of the cash value that has built up in the interim "accumulation" period.

Annuities have gained new life with the 1986 Tax Reform Act. They are now being aggressively marketed as an alternative to the recently changed IRAs for investors who want to defer taxes on income and capital appreciation investing above the $2,000 IRA limit (see Chapter 8 for further information).

Interest income is accumulated while taxes are deferred until "payout" begins at age 59 1/2 or higher. The amount of the payout is determined by the amount of money invested, the length of time invested, and of course, the rate of return. The payout schedule is specified in the annuity contract.

A basic annuity is structured to pay income for the balance of an annuitant's life. However, like many other financial products in recent years, annuities have undergone a number of changes. Many options are now available. For example, the standard annuity expires with the death of the annuitant. Some companies now offer a provision to transfer the payments to a specified beneficiary such as a spouse. Such added benefits do cost more, though. A wide variety of options are available, but investigate each carefully. It is important to balance the potential gain with the added cost. Remember, there may be other ways to accomplish the same goals for less money.

Investment Potential

Fixed annuities are long-term investments. Although early withdrawals can be made, substantial penalties usually are levied. Penalties include assessment of a charge by the insurance company (typically 7% the first year, declining 1% per year thereafter) and tax penalties.

Investment characteristics of fixed annuities include

- No capital appreciation (see section on variable deferred annuities)
- Interest income accumulated on a tax-deferred basis
- No current income
- Payout provisions specified in the contract (typical options: payout of fixed monthly amount for the life of the annuitant, for a set time period, or for a set total amount)

Strengths

 Insurance companies are strictly regulated and must maintain reserves. Annuities of established companies are very low risk, although no federal insurance is available at this time. You can borrow against your annuity's cash value. Interest accumulates on a tax-deferred basis until withdrawal. Annuities provide a secure retirement income.

Weaknesses

 You run a small risk that the issuer may go bankrupt. In the early 1980s Baldwin-United Corporation, one of the largest issues of deferred annuities filed for bankruptcy. Although arrangements were made to minimize losses, it is a risk that should be noted. There is no secondary market, which limits liquidity. Early withdrawals are subject to substantial penalties. Fixed annuities offer no protection from the ravages of inflation. Fees may be high for the benefit received.

Tax Considerations

 Deferred annuities are being aggressively marketed due to their favored tax status. Interest paid accrues on a tax-deferred basis. Taxes are paid only when pay-out begins. Presumably, your tax bracket on retirement will be lower than during your peak earning years.

A portion of the payments to annuitants are considered "return of principal" and are not taxable. This feature differs from IRA payouts, which are taxed as ordinary income.

Early withdrawal (before age 59 1/2 or within five years of purchase) is subject to a 10% tax penalty. There are exceptions, so check with your tax advisor *before* investing.

Summing Up

Annuities should be viewed as part investment and part insurance. The security of a fixed income for life should be balanced against the lower guaranteed returns you can earn. A wide variety of options are available. These include payment options, payout options, and insurance options (naming a beneficiary).

VARIABLE DEFERRED ANNUITIES

A deferred annuity is a contract between an insurance company and the purchaser (the annuitant) that specifies a premium to be paid by the annuitant in exchange for a specified payout schedule, which begins at some future date. The payout depends on how much money is invested, the length of the "accumulation" period, and the rate of return earned during the accumulation period. Historically the rate of return was a specified interest rate (a fixed annuity).

Variable annuities allow the annuitant to select from a variety of investment vehicles during the accumulation phase. For example, you may elect to invest your premium money in a stock fund, a bond fund, or a money market fund; all are managed by the insurance company. Most variable annuities allow you to switch between a variety of funds at your option. Usually limits are set on how often you can switch without being assessed additional fees. This arrangement is similar to switching between different types of funds in a mutual fund group except that the gains earned in an annuity are sheltered until payout begins.

Rather than being locked into a fixed interest rate, in a variable annuity you can earn a return tied to the stock market, gold, or some other investment. However, unlike a fixed annuity, variable annuities do not feature a guaranteed minimum return. If the investment you select goes down, you can actually lose some of your principal. The variable annuity offers the opportunity to trade a guaranteed minimum return and a set maximum return (the set interest rate) for unlimited upside potential with equivalent downside risk.

Interest in annuities has rebounded following the 1986 Tax Reform Act. The inflationary 1970s and the bankruptcy of major deferred annuity issuer Baldwin-United Corporation in the early 1980s both hurt this investment category severely. New life was breathed into annuities by the 1986 Tax Reform Act, which severely restricted competitive products for accumulating tax-deferred income. The inflationary 1970s served to limit the appeal of fixed annuities, as the purchasing power of the earnings was devastated over time. Annuitants found that payout levels that seemed adequate when the program was started, later proved inadequate due to inflation during the payout phase.

The variable deferred annuity was specifically developed to meet inflation concerns.

Investment Potential

Variable annuities are long-term investments. Although substantial penalties are levied for early withdrawals, you can remove without charge up to 10% of the principal that has been in your account for over a year. If you exceed the 10% annual limit, a 5% redemption charge is made—although withdrawal of earnings is never penalized. After seven years, any amount of principal can be withdrawn without charge. A typical penalty fee is 7% the first year, declining 1% per year thereafter. In addition, tax penalties may be assessed.

Investment characteristics of variable deferred annuities include

• Potential for capital appreciation

• Flexibility to choose from a variety of investment options
• Fluctuating returns based on your selection of investment vehicle and the management of that vehicle by the insurance company
• All gains tax sheltered until withdrawal begins
• Ability to hedge against inflation

Strengths

 Security is a major strength. Insurance companies are closely regulated and required to maintain reserves. Default is a minor risk. You can borrow against your annuity's cash value. All earnings (capital gains and interest) compound on a tax-deferred basis. You can switch between different investments in differing economic environments. And you can participate in capital growth as well as just interest income. A flexible, probate-free death benefit ensures that your beneficiary will receive the greater of two amounts: either your total contributions (less withdrawals), or the current account value.

Weaknesses

 There is always the slight risk that the issuer could go bankrupt. In the early 1980s, a major issuer of deferred annuities filed for bankruptcy. Although most investors were able to recover the majority of their investment, the event clearly demonstrated that annuities are not as secure as U.S government obligations. No secondary market limits liquidity. Annuities must be liquidated directly with the issuer who sets redemption fees. There is no guarantee of principal. If the investment you select goes down, your principal is at risk. You are dependent on the management ability of the insurance company issuing the annuity. For example, if you select a stock fund, the stock market may appreciate more than the value of your fund due to poor management. Your selection of funds is restricted to those offered and managed by the issuer.

Tax Considerations

 Deferred annuities are being aggressively marketed as tax-sheltered investments. All earnings, whether through capital appreciation or interest payments, accrue tax deferred. Taxes are assessed only when payout begins. A portion of your receipts are considered a return of principal and are not taxable. This differs from the tax treatment accorded IRA payouts, which are fully taxed as ordinary income at the time of withdrawal.

It is assumed that your tax bracket will be lower on retirement than during your peak earning years. Therefore, you would pay less tax on the earnings than you would have if taxed when earned. This is not always the case, and you should check with your tax advisor *before* investing.

Early withdrawal also triggers tax penalties. If you withdraw before age 59 1/2 or within five years of purchase, a 10% tax penalty is levied. There are exceptions, depending on the exact type of annuity.

Summing Up

Annuities are a hybrid investment. They should be viewed as part insurance and part investment. Consider a variable deferred annuity as a tax-deferred retirement savings plan. Carefully evaluate your insurance needs and status before you buy an annuity.

It is impossible to delineate all the many options that modern annuity plans offer. However, it is crucial to understand in detail the annuity's withdrawal policies. Fees vary greatly and can make a significant difference in your decisions.

VARIABLE LIFE INSURANCE

Variable life insurance is a cash value policy that provides set minimum death benefits with the potential for increased benefits and cash value if your selected investments perform well. It gives you the option of selecting different types of investments for the cash value portion of your premiums. The choices are among mutual fund-type portfolios of stocks, bonds, or money market instruments. The insurance company manages the portfolios. Usually you can switch among these options by notifying the insurance company.

Long-term fixed-return investments fell into disfavor in the 1970s as inflation ravaged the purchasing power of historically secure vehicles. Cash value insurance was one of the hardest hit areas as policyholders learned that the investment portion of their policies was lagging behind the returns that could be obtained from the safest of all investments, the 90-day Treasury bill.

The insurance industry responded by creating more flexible products to meet the needs of conservative investors. Variable life is one form of cash value life insurance that has gained widespread acceptance.

Features include the following:

- A minimum death benefit is established when you purchase the policy. It can increase depending on how your investments do.
- The premium is a fixed amount paid monthly, quarterly, or annually.
- You can take out loans against the cash value for rates that usually run between 6 and 8%.
- There is no minimum rate of return on your cash value. It fluctuates with your chosen investment.

Life insurance companies are rated by Best's Insurance Reports. Companies rated A and A+ are financially secure. There is little risk of default.

Variable life policies are sold by licensed insurance agents and brokers. Many full-service investment brokerage firms have in-house insurance specialists. Substantial fees are charged. The fees are "front loaded," which means that they are higher in the early years of the policy.

Variable life offers greater flexibility than other cash value life insurance because you can choose among three disparate investments.

Like all cash value insurance decisions, you must take certain considerations into account before buying variable life. Does it provide the necessary insurance protection for your family's needs? When buying cash value insurance, that is the most important question. The investment potential is important but secondary to the primary purpose of life insurance: protecting the insured's beneficiaries.

Investment Potential

The attraction of variable life insurance is enhanced by the tax-deferred status of accumulated earnings. Variable life is a long-term investment. Fees are very high in the first few years of the policy. It must be held for a long time (10 years) in order to amortize the front load so that the returns are competitive.

The portfolio alternatives are managed accounts, much like life mutual funds, that are managed by the issuing insurance company. The track records of variable life's portfolios are short. Some of the investment portfolios are tracked by Lipper Analytical Services, which monitors leading mutual funds.

 You should evaluate insurance company investment portfolios as you would mutual funds. Insurance company portfolios generally charge much higher fees than do competitive mutual funds. For example, one major investment portfolio assesses commissions and other expenses of up to 35% for $1,000 premium payment by a typical investor the first year. This load drops to 18% for the next three years, after which the load drops to 15%.

Such fees are very high compared to fees charged by most mutual funds. Of course, mutual funds do not provide insurance protection as part of their fees.

The stock and bond portfolios offer capital gains potential. The money market portfolio offers a lower income potential than the bonds but with less risk to principal.

A well-managed stock portfolio may offer some protection against inflation. The short maturities of a money market portfolio also offers some measure of inflation protection since yields would rise with increasing inflation.

A variable life policyholder faces a variety of risks. These include the financial condition of the issuing company, market risk for both the stock and/or bond portfolios, and the political risk that the tax benefits of life insurance may be phased out.

Strengths

 There is very little risk of default for companies rated A and A+. Minimum death benefits are provided regardless of the performance of the investment portfolios. Variable life policyholders have great flexibility to switch among the various portfolios to take advantage of current economic conditions. Earnings, both income and capital gains, accumulate on a tax-deferred basis. Both death benefits and cash value can be increased through good performance by selected investment portfo-lios. Loans against cash value are readily accessible.

Weaknesses

 Investment performance will lag behind that of straight mutual funds, due to very high fees. Your cash value principal is at risk if the investment portfolio drops. Front-end fees require long-term commitment to make competitive investment returns. No minimum return on your investment is guaranteed. Substantial penalities for cash withdrawals in the first few years of the policy are levied. The track records of most investment portfolios is very short. Since three years constitute a long track record, it is impossible to know how the portfolios will react through a full investment cycle—they've only had up markets so far!

Tax Considerations

 All earnings—whether capital gains, dividends, interest—are accumulated on a tax-deferred basis. Interest charged on policy loans is only partially deductible (60%) for 1987. This deduction is phased out over the next three years.

Summing Up

Variable life insurance has enjoyed increasing popularity over the past few years. A continuation of the bullish stock market will enhance its appeal. However, the short track records of the investment portfolio managers give little clue to what performance may be in an extended bear market.

You should purchase any life insurance policy only if you need the insurance protection. Don't be misled by the hype over their investment value. The high fees, low short-term liquidity, and moderate investment potential rules them out for serious investors looking for maximum investment returns.

Variable life offers savvy investors who need insurance protection the best alternative among cash value policies. It is important to check the track records of the investment portfolios before buying. Performance varies widely.

WHOLE-LIFE INSURANCE

Many years ago, before the proliferation of life insurance products now available, there were two main types: term and whole life. Term insurance has no direct investment value other than freeing up additional money through its much lower premiums. That "freed" money can of course then be invested. But the term policy itself provides protection only. There is no cash value buildup during the life of the policy. Typically, term premiums increase as the insured person grows older. The only payment that a term policy makes is the death benefit paid to the beneficiary.

Whole-life insurance is the classic alternative to term insurance. When the yields paid on whole life were actually less than paid on bank savings accounts, buyers began to turn to other products. Sales volume dropped sharply during the late 1970s when the yields on very safe money market funds climbed to record levels.

However, in recent years whole-life insurance has staged a comeback as the rates paid on cash value buildup have become more competitive. Typically premiums are invested in secure long-term government or high-grade corporate bonds, mortgages, and blue-chip stocks.

Whole-life insurance features include

- A fixed death benefit selected when the policy is purchased
- A fixed premium for the life of the policy, paid annually, quarterly, or monthly
- Policy loans at rates generally ranging from 6 to 9%

Whole-life insurance premiums are substantially higher than term premiums because whole life provides for guaranteed cash value buildup, fixed premiums, and ready access to loans against the cash value.

Whole-life insurance is purchased from licensed insurance agents or brokers. The sales charge is substantial. Typically, sales commissions are 50 to 100% of the first year's premium. As a result, it takes a few years for the policy to build up a positive return.

Investment Potential

A whole-life policy is a long-term investment. More favorable returns are paid the longer the policy is held. As a rule of thumb, a policy must be held about fifteen years to be earning at the maximum rates. This is because it takes about ten years for the investment income to cover the commissions and fees assessed by the insurer.

Most whole-life policies pay annual dividends. These are called *participating policies* and charge higher premiums. Over the long term, however, these policies are actually less expensive because of consistent dividend payments. Dividends can be taken in cash, or, as an offset to premiums, or as additional cash value in the policy.

Whole-life insurance is essentially a method for enforcing a savings discipline while providing death benefits protection for your family. There is limited liquidity, especially in the early years of a policy. Withdrawals are typically assessed a penalty that declines annually over a seven- to nine-year period.

The security of your investment rests with the financial stability of the insurance company. Best's Insurance Reports rate all major insurance companies. You should stick with A (+/–)-rated companies for safety and peace of mind.

One drawback to whole life is that you have no choice as to how your cash value is invested. In fact, insurers do not spell out what rate of return your cash value is earning. The policy specifies a guaranteed cash value, which accumulates each year to a new level. However, the insurer never specifies how much of your premium pays for insurance.

 A key factor to be checked prior to purchasing a participating policy is the length, consistency, and amount of the insurer's annual dividend payouts.

Whole-life insurance does not provide any protection from inflation. Investments are typically made in long-term bonds, which suffer in inflationary times.

Strengths

 Whole-life policies issued by A or A+ companies are very safe. Risk of default is negligible. Earnings accumulate on a tax-deferred basis. Irregular withdrawals are tax free. Volatility does not affect the base insurance value, which guarantees a set increase in cash value annually. Death benefits are federal tax free to the beneficiary.

Weaknesses

 Initial fees are high. Policies must be held for 10 years or longer to achieve competitive returns. Return on investment is not clearly disclosed. Early withdrawals (usually before 9 years) are sub-

ject to penalties. You have no choice about how your cash value is invested.

Tax Considerations

 Earnings paid on cash value insurance policies accumulate on a tax-deferred basis. You can borrow earnings from your policy tax free. The policy's beneficiary receives the proceeds federal tax free on the death of the insured.

Summing Up

The returns paid on whole-life policies have increased substantially in recent years. However, you should view whole life as a viable investment only if you need the insurance feature. High fees and the long-term commitment necessary to achieve a competitive return make other investment products better values in the absence of death benefits.

Single-premium whole-life insurance is heavily marketed as a tax shelter. However, investors who need current tax-sheltered income should consider municipal bonds or municipal bond funds as lower-cost alternatives.

UNIVERSAL LIFE INSURANCE

Universal life is a widely accepted form of cash value life insurance featuring a flexible premium and death benefit program that keeps the premium lower than other whole-life policies. Universal life clearly separates the cash value and the death benefits elements of the policy. The cash value is typically invested in a tax-deferred savings program tied to a specified money market rate.

Although life insurance is not usually thought of as an investment in the popular sense of "earning profits," the 1986 Tax Reform Act provides substantial tax-preferred treatment of insurance products. As a result, many insurance companies are aggressively marketing a wide variety of products. Regardless of the investment potential of tax-deferred accumulation of earnings offered by many life insurance products, the primary consideration should still be whether and how much *insurance* coverage you need. Wage earners whose families depend on their income should seriously investigate various forms of life insurance.

Term life insurance offers you pure protection (no investment "frills") for a specific amount of time. You pay only for death benefits: usually for lower premiums at first, then for higher premiums as you get older. Although term insurance is (at least initially) the most economical insurance of all, it can become the most expensive if your age is quite advanced; and some policies even exclude renewals past age 65 or 70. Younger people often favor term insurance because of the low initial premiums, sometimes calling it "mortgage insurance" because the untimely death of the insured would not result in loss of the family's often highly leveraged home.

Term insurance can be renewed in a variety of ways. At the end of the term, you may elect to extend the coverage period at a specific additional premium. If the policy is guaranteed renewable, it will specify an age at which you may receive the policy's face value. "Level" term policies are good for a specific number of years, the premiums for which are averaged into equal installments— even if the term is for 20 to 30 years. "Declining balance" term insurance features constant premiums too, but the amount of coverage decreases each year. For people who want to use term insurance as a bridge to permanent insurance, a "modified" term policy might be best. This plan converts a term to a whole-life policy after a specified period of time.

The alternative to term life insurance is variously called *cash value*, *whole life*, *straight*, or *ordinary life*. The key difference is that cash value life insurance offers the death benefits of term with the added feature of building up a cash value over the life of the policy. Some advisors refer to this feature as a "forced savings."

There are many different varieties of cash value insurance. More are being added every year as the life insurance industry develops products to meet the demands of a diverse population. We can only touch on the distin-

guishing aspects of the more popular policies here. We strongly advise that you check with an independent financial planner or insurance agent to evaluate the myriad of available options.

A very new development is variable universal life. First sold in 1985, variable universal offers the opportunity to invest in stocks, bonds, or money market portfolios rather than just a savings program for the cash value portion of your policy.

Two key features of universal life are

1. Death benefit amount is chosen at time of purchase. However, it can be changed annually.
2. Premium varies depending on what the cash value portion is earning. The cost of the insurance depends on a number of variables, including your age, sex, and health. Some policies offer a slightly higher guaranteed yield on the cash value portion of your policy if you agree to pay a fixed premium monthly, quarterly, semiannually, or annually.

This flexibility—to vary not only the death benefits but the premium (and in the case of variable universal life, your investments) is a major attraction of universal life insurance. The premiums tend to be lower than that for straight whole life with equivalent death benefits.

Investment Potential

The investment appeal of universal life insurance rests on the tax deferral of earnings on the cash value. Universal life policies typically guarantee a relatively low minimum rate of return, about 4%. Rates above the minimum are variable and fluctuate day to day. It pays to comparison-shop, as rates may differ widely among companies.

Variable universal life policies are so new that it is difficult to evaluate track records at present. However, well-managed stock or bond portfolios may significantly outperform the normal "savings" program route.

Policyholders can borrow against the cash value. Typically there is a $25 fee for partial withdrawals. Policy loans (as opposed to direct withdrawals) are usually also offered. Interest charges are competitive, ranging from 6 to 8%.

Universal life should be viewed as protection for your loved ones. An added benefit is the long-term savings program, which offers tax-deferred earnings.

Universal policies offered by companies earning an A or higher rating by the independent rating service (Best's Insurance Reports) are very secure.

Variable universal life policies may experience some volatility due to fluctuations in the stock or bond portfolios. Straight universal life will not experience volatility in the savings program.

Fees vary widely. "No-load" universal life policies charge no agents' commissions. Otherwise fees can run from 1% to more than 10%. No-load policies are sold through the mail without direct face-to-face agent contact.

Strengths

 Universal life policies offer ready access to your cash value whether for withdrawal or for loans. Income and cash value of A-rated companies is very secure. There is little volatility associated with the cash value. Universal life offers substantial flexibility in policy options.

Weaknesses

 Universal life is first and foremost life insurance. Investment returns are lower than are possible in straight investments. If you select variable universal life, you are limited to management by the insurance company's portfolio managers. Their performance may not be up to par. Fees vary widely and can be very high. No federal insurance covers company failures.

Tax Considerations

 The 1986 Tax Reform Act retained the tax-deferral feature of earnings on whole-life insurance policies. Earnings are taxed at your tax bracket at the time of withdrawal. Life insurance proceeds to beneficiaries are normally not subject to federal income taxes.

Summing Up

Cash value life insurance was a major beneficiary of the 1986 Tax Reform Act. The proliferation of insurance products will undoubtedly continue offering consumers an even wider variety of options.

The relatively new variable universal life policies offer significant flexibility and the chance to profit from stock and bond market moves.

Universal life can play an important part in the financial plans of many families. It is worth investigating.

1988 PROSPECTS FOR INSURANCE PRODUCTS

The growth of the many new insurance/ investment products now being widely touted depends on continued favored tax treatment. There is little likelihood that U.S. Congress will totally eliminate the tax-deferred growth of cash value life insurance.

The same cannot be said about all aspects of the tax treatment of the various features of cash value insurance. Specifically, the tax-free status of policy loans appears in jeopardy. Although it is highly unlikely that any penalties or changes would be incurred for loans already taken out, futures loans may come in for different tax treatment in the near future. If this consideration is important for you, watch tax law changes very closely. Your agent or broker should be able to provide up-to-date information on this aspect of the business.

If you think the industry seems confusing now, just wait! The next few years will see an even greater proliferation of products from the insurance industry. Presently less than 50 of the 100 largest insurance companies offer some type of variable policy. That will change rapidly as more and more companies move to selling investment-related products. Many experts predict that within the next ten years 50% of all life insurance products will be variable.

A number of other changes are also underway. We have mentioned the increasing presence of stock brokers in the business. Mutual funds are gearing up for a major push into the business. Charter National Life and Security National Life have both retained mutual fund managers for their portfolios. The well-known fund manager Value Line now manages portfolios for Guardian Life.

The largest fund group in the country, Fidelity Investments, has launched a fund for a single-premium variable life policy. The policy is issued by Monarch Resources but will be marketed by Fidelity.

All too often the consumer's real reason for buying life insurance is lost in the shuffle. The great flexibility offered by the range of products currently available is certainly a boon to many people. However, overselling the investment aspects tends to overshadow the real reason for buying life insurance.

Don't be fooled into buying a speculative investment vehicle when what you want is protection. The tax benefit of life insurance is the most widely touted feature since passage of the 1986 Tax Reform Act. However, the high fees are not quite so prominently mentioned. Don't hesitate to investigate alternatives.

The insurance industry is changing. Now more than ever it is crucial to your financial health to know your financial status: what you have, what you need, and what you want. Careful planning is necessary to prepare you with the facts you need to make intelligent long-term decisions. The many new insurance products offer great variety and flexibility for tailoring a program to your specific needs.

PART IV

ESTABLISHING AND EXECUTING A FINANCIAL PLAN

Your knowledge of yourself, money mechanics, and investment vehicles must come together in a coherent way if you are to maximize your net worth. In this final section, you'll learn how to gather and evaluate data about investment opportunities, allocate your resources over multiple asset categories, and implement an effective financial plan.

CHAPTER 18

EVALUATING A PROSPECTUS

A GLANCE AHEAD

Your first encounter with most securities will be the legal description of the investment—but beware, such documents are not always what they seem. In this chapter, you'll learn

- *The difference between registered and unregistered securities—and the risks involved with each*
- *How to read "between the lines" of a prospectus offering circular or private placement*
- *What to do if you suspect fraud or misinformation*

"WHAT CAN GO WRONG?"

An elderly woman was attracted to a prominent advertisement for a mutual fund sponsored by one of the largest fund managers in the country touting "high monthly income." The woman called the toll-free phone number and received the prospectus. She filled out the subscription form in the back of the thin booklet and returned it with her check for several thousand dollars.

She used no advisor. "After all," she reasoned, "this is a no-load mutual fund, and I read the legal prospectus—what can go wrong?" Three months later she had still received no income. She again used the toll-free telephone number of the fund sponsor.

She was informed that buried in the fine print of the prospectus footnotes, the fund had elected to save administrative costs by modifying its distribution policy. From now on, income would be distributed *annually,* rather than monthly.

The woman screamed at the sponsor's representative, asking how in the world he expected her to pay her rent and medical insurance for the next eight months, but even as she spoke she knew the "horse had bolted" through the "barn door" she herself had left unlocked. Reading a document, she discovered, is not the same as *understanding* it.

THE THREE CATEGORIES OF OFFERINGS

Most investors are unaware of three distinct categories of written offerings and what they mean to financial planning. You should know whether an investment has been registered as a public offering, registered within the laws of one state exclusively, or if it unregistered with any regulatory body whatsoever. The three offering types are known by the labels, which you will find in the investment materials:

1. A prospectus, or legal description of a security offered for sale to the general public nationwide

2. An offering circular, registered under the laws of a particular state
3. A private placement-offering memorandum, which is offered only to "highly qualified" or "sophisticated" investors, who theoretically do not need the protection of a legally registered security

What Is a Prospectus?

When a securities offering is made to the public under the rules of the Securities and Exchange Commission (SEC), as well as the laws of the state in which you reside, the document that discloses all relevant and material facts to the prospective investor is referred to as the *prospectus*. A registered public offering is normally used when the sponsor seeks to raise a relatively large sum of money. Public offerings are very expensive. Nationwide filing fees alone can total more than $50,000. Legal and accounting expenses often exceed a quarter of a million! Printing and marketing budgets also can be huge, and it's not unusual for total expenses of a public offering to *exceed* $1 million.

Offering Circular

An offering circular offers a security that has been registered *only* within a particular state. These securities are governed by the state in which you are a resident, so you or your advisor should be familiar with the protection they may give you.

Private Placement Offering Memorandum: Buyer Beware!

No regulator necessarily checks any portion of an offering that is solicited by means of a "private placement offering memorandum." Although the sponsor of such an investment is theoretically held to the same disclosure standards that are applied to the prospectus and offering circular, the term "private placement-offering memorandum" means that the parties involved believe they are "exempt" from registration—normally because of the smaller size of the offering, the

suitability standards of the investors solicited, or other reasons allowed by law.

 Private placements must be handled with care. No one is watching out for you as an investor when you subscribe, so the old dictum applies: Buyer beware! It is very likely that no government agency, federal or state, has reviewed the document. To avoid trouble, be certain you follow these guidelines:

1. Know the people behind the offering. Read the résumés of the key players, assess their past experience, and check up on their records if you think it's necessary.
2. Know the investment. Don't buy "a pig in a poke." Learn about the industry the security represents, and make sure its risk-return characteristics match your portfolio needs and investor attitudes.
3. Even if you think you understand the offering perfectly, get an outside opinion from a trusted professional.

The Prospectus Is Not a Sales Brochure

To understand what a prospectus *is,* it is useful to know what a prospectus is *not.* A prospectus is *not* a marketing brochure. The prospectus is not intended to help sell investments, although legal "weasel words" are often employed to confuse potentially unflattering facts, as well as clarify. Even so, the prospectus is definitely *not* oriented toward the positive elements of any deal. Therefore, the investor and the financial advisor must read, analyze, and evaluate a prospectus and then make their decision *in spite* of the negative or complex information. Good opportunities are sometimes disguised under mountains of conditional terms, while financial "black holes" can seem as innocuous as any other investment.

To understand any prospectus accurately, the reader must first consider all information presented, extract those pearls of wisdom hidden among the "boilerplate" of warnings and somehow determine what is "good" about the deal in spite of all the complex legal language and disclaimers. A seasoned investor can glean key information from most prospectuses in about 15 minutes.

Limitations on the Goal of "Full Disclosure." There is a great irony in the stated goal of both the law and its regulators in mandating "full disclosure of material facts" within offering material. Investment sponsors want to limit their liability for deals that go sour. Therefore, positive speculation about an investment is completely discouraged. People don't want to stick their necks out and paint a too-pretty picture that might be judged later as having induced an investor to put money on a too-risky venture. For this reason, among others, prospectuses tend to read very much alike—and your job is to sift the investment-related "wheat" from the defensive-minded legalese "chaff."

Think of the Prospectus as "A Letter to the Judge." When everything goes well with an investment, the language of disclosure is merely an academic curiosity. As any experienced salesperson knows, "good deals" are exempted from relevant laws. The "good deal exemption" means that as long as the deal works out, no one cares very much if full disclosure of material fact had been accomplished by the prospectus. Another way of looking at this phenomenon is "You are only as successful as your last good deal." The true test of a prospectus, then, is when an investment *doesn't* pan out. After the hand wringing and the finger pointing subside, the law normally requires that written documents be evaluated for misinformation, guarantees, warrantees, or fraud. For this purpose, the investor must think of the prospectus as "a letter to the judge" in the event the deal falls apart. Its duty is to protect the innocent and punish the wicked—and enrich more than a few attorneys in the process!

Approaching the prospectus from this consumer-oriented perspective, it is little wonder that a significant portion of the document is devoted to disclosure and discussion of pertinent risks. Provided the sale can be made in spite of all the negative and complex language, the security sponsor must attempt to minimize potential liability while accurately describing the nature of the investment—a difficult balancing act.

ANATOMY OF A PROSPECTUS

Although most prospectuses tend to look and read alike, each offering must be analyzed individually. The basic elements of a typical prospectus are as follows:

Terms of the Offering

The cover page of the prospectus often contains the gross dollar amount the sponsor seeks to raise from the public, the minimum amount of money it will take for the investment to function (often referred to as a "mini-maxi" offering), the minimum investment required, and one or more disclaimers—the first of all that boilerplate you'll encounter later.

While legal opinions may vary as to the precise language of many disclaimers, the first warning normally reads something like this:

> *These securities have not been approved or disapproved by the Securities and Exchange Commission nor has the commission passed upon the accuracy or adequacy of this prospectus. Any representation to the contrary is a criminal offense.*

In other words, you must understand that although both federal and state regulators are always willing to mandate form, they are never willing to take responsibility for the substance of any security. Similar disclaimers often follow concerning various state provisions. However, their emphasis is normally on establishing wealth as a screen for "suitability." The law presumes that people with more money need less protection from taking investment risks.

Table of Contents: Your Road Map to the Prospectus

You may have to hunt for it, but there is always a "table of contents" that lists major sections and headings within the prospectus. Look at the contents *first,* then read the sections that are most relevant to you. Remember, it does not matter if you are looking at a prospectus for a mutual fund, a real estate limited partnership, a cable television deal, an equipment-leasing offering, or a solicitation to invest in a good old-fashioned sunken treasure hunt (all of which are on the market, by the way), the order of information is almost always the same (especially important sections marked with an asterisk).

    Terms of the offering
* Summary of the offering
* Risk factors
* Estimated use of proceeds
* Management compensation
* Conflicts of interest
    Fiduciary responsibility
    Prior performance summary
* Management
* Investment objectives and policies
* Income and losses and cash distributions
* Federal income tax consequences
* Taxable versus tax-exempt entities: status considerations
    Description of units
    Reinvestment plan summary
    Summary of partnership agreement
    Plan of distribution
* Investor suitability standards
    Minimum unit purchase
    Sales materials
    Legal opinions
    Tax opinions
    Reports
    Experts
    Further information
    Glossary
    Financial information and balance sheets
    Appendix: prior performance tables
    Index to partnership agreement
    Partnership agreement
    Order form
    Reinvestment plan

Please remember—these are not *all* the categories sometimes contained within a prospectus. Even so, is it any wonder that people can be intimidated, confused, frightened, and/or hopelessly bored by all the "discussion and disclosure"? The key is in knowing what to read and how to read it. In the remainder of this chaper, we'll take a closer look at those especially important sections marked with an asterisk in the list.

Summary of the Offering

In the summary discussion, the sponsor typically provides an overview of the deal. Although in theory each investor is responsible for reading every word of the prospectus before an investment is made, the reality is far different. The summary is often read by an advisor (attorney, accountant, broker, or planner), and the structure is discussed with respect to the client's immediate tax or investment needs. In such a case, the investor may not be assured that the investment fits his or her long-range financial plan—so don't listen passively to this important information.

Normally, there will be several references within the summary of the offering to longer and more detailed sections relating to risk factors, conflicts of interest, income tax consequences, and similar concerns. These sections will spell out more specifically the various potential problems that can arise within the overall investment structure, so you will want to pay particular attention to them.

Risk Factors

Although virtually everything in a prospectus is intended to disclose factors relevant to risk, the section on "risk factors" contains specific warnings about the most common and best-known risk factors *inherent* in the type of investment under consideration. The idea is to convey at least *these* risk factors because sponsors cannot implement the investment without facing them as business and market uncertainties.

Risk factors vary greatly among different investment types. Real estate sponsors must be familiar with regional and local economies for their properties to be profitable. Cable television system operators must be familiar with the Uniform Commercial Code and its interpretation. Each type of investment requires its own special brand of expertise. Each business area carries with it certain technical knowledge that is crucial to competent management. You must understand the particular expertise that is required for successful management of the investment being considered, and must ask your advisor about the special skills and risks it may involve.

General management risks are relatively consistent from offering to offering. Competition between programs for management time and expertise, conflicts of interest, and many other risk factors are routinely discussed. Less apparent, however, are "educational" risk factors.

For example, the general experience of the sponsor is of little importance without experience in *this* type of investment. Often reputations are made in one field or particular area of expertise, then depicted as relevant to a totally different field. If the sponsor made money in real estate, there is no guarantee that same sponsor will be equally successful in equipment leasing or cable television. Avoid being a guinea pig for new investments with inexperienced sponsors. If you need more information, review the investments' annual report.

Another risk factor that sometimes lies below the surface involves technology. Suppose you are investing in a research and development partnership, and you read in the risk factor section that a competitive company has applied for a patent that, if granted, could stop the subject sponsor from fulfilling its stated business plan. This should give rise to some very pointed questions, at the very least, such as how likely is the patent to be granted, and are there alternative paths the partnership might take to retain its viability as an R&D investment? The same holds true for pending lawsuits or review of the company's operation or industry by regulatory agencies. Contact the company if any of these factors are not sufficiently explained.

Be sensitive to small differences in risk factor discussions. You can learn a great deal by reading them carefully, and comparing them from one offering to another.

 Other Risk Factors Not Discussed. Perhaps the most important point to remember about the risk factors section of a prospectus is that it can, by its very nature, *never* be complete. There are always risks that are, for various reasons,

omitted from the discussion. For example, real estate deals rarely discuss natural disasters in detail, yet a private placement in property located on the Gulf of Mexico could (and should) raise questions about hurricane potential, insurance costs, and the history of those occurrences in the area and precautions taken against them—construction standards, sea wall reinforcement, and so on. The point is, let common sense trickle down through the sometimes numbing affect of all that legalese.

Estimated Use of Proceeds

This section spells out how the money will be used from the beginning of the investment cycle until the subscribed amount is fully employed. In different public offerings, the allocation between overhead, expenses of the offering, capital reserves, investment proceeds, and related categories can vary widely, even though they may at first appear almost identical. Although it does not ensure ultimate success of the venture, an offering that places over 80% of money raised into the object of the investment (such as stocks or real estate) may have a somewhat greater likelihood of positive returns than an offering that places less, such as 70%, of the money raised into the productive, underlying asset.

Management Compensation

Investment companies don't manage assets for free, and the section that describes the compensation for the sponsor is vitally important. Because your return depends on asset performance, the sponsor must be sufficiently motivated to look after the investment carefully. Although there is no strict standard for compensation, the generally accepted practices of the industry in which you are investing are well known. For example, the sponsor of a real estate investment will have different requirements, overhead, and expenses from the sponsor of an equipment-leasing deal, and you should compare only like investments. However, it can be a mistake to choose only the cheapest sponsor—just as it may be an error to consistently choose only the least expensive tool for your workshop or the cheapest replacement parts for your car. As the old saying goes, quality doesn't cost—it pays; and a good investment manager should earn his or her fees many times over.

Conflicts of Interest

The section on conflicts of interest can be almost as interesting as a good detective story. While some dual roles and interlocking business relationships are perfectly acceptable, certain intertwining sponsor interests can cause future problems.

For example, suppose the sponsor of a real estate investment that interests you discloses that loans will be made primarily to affiliates of the general partner. You would ask yourself what safeguards are in place to ensure that rates and terms will not unfairly favor one of the parties to the transaction. If this question is not answered elsewhere in the prospectus, it might not be wise to keep on looking.

However, such a clearly disclosed potential conflict of interest is better than to the more-objective sounding sponsor who intends to make "arm's-length," disinterested third-party loans with investor capital, but has no demonstrated capability to screen potential borrowers the way professional lenders might. Such short-sighted (if well-intended) plans are sometimes a formula for bad debts and subsequent loss of investment income.

Most disclosed conflicts of interest make sense within the structure of the investment. For example, the manager of an asset will expect to receive substantial management fees over the course of the investment. However, the prospective investor must also understand that if the market for the asset is soft, the sponsor may elect to hold off on asset resale in order to retain at least some income from management fees. This type of conflict can be mitigated by well-designed performance incentives or clauses that subordinate sponsor profits to a specified investor return. The idea here is to read and understand such provisions and correlate them to other parts of the prospectus. Here are some relevant questions to ask about such conflicts:

1. How is cash flow divided between "you" and "them"?
2. How are gains, profits, and other proceeds divided between "you" and "them"?
3. How much, if any, do *you* receive *before* "they" receive proceeds from the investment?
4. Does the return in Question 3 seem equitable based on all the known circumstances?
5. If you have not fully understood the conflicts-of-interest clauses, have you consulted with someone who *did?*

The distribution of sponsor time and attention among projects is one of the most difficult arenas for conflicts of interest that you can evaluate. For the small sponsor, even one or two competing projects or partnerships can dramatically stretch resources to their limits. Management time and expertise is always a finite and valuable commodity. However, in a larger firm even a relatively large program could be given short shrift simply because the sponsor is huge and your investment means little to them in the overall scheme of things. The key is to ask how important your program is to the investment sponsor and to decide for yourself whether the resources available leave you comfortable with the stated management capacity and priorities.

Management

The organization and résumé information provided about the investment manager is sometimes overlooked. After all else is said and done, investing is about people as well as numbers. It does not matter how much money is raised, how wonderful the economy looks or how clever the investment structure appears at first glance—if the *people* who manage your money are less than competent (or less than honorable!), then you have a high probability of disappointment.

While university degrees by themselves are no guarantee of success, it is logical to look for strong academic credentials in the field of business, economics, or finance as well as strong management expertise *in* the asset areas. There is just no substitute for practical, hands-on experience. The investment sponsor who is making a first offering must be a longshot. This does not mean you should *never* invest with a manager who lacks a long and unblemished track record, but it does mean that if alternate, comparable opporunities are available with experienced sponsors, you should probably consider them first. This is true even if the object of the investment is purchased with "all cash" or "unleveraged (unencumbered by debt) funds"—theoretically a lower risk proposition. There is always the unseen "leverage" of a sponsor's and overhead learning curve expense. With a new sponsor, the risk is much greater that normal or unusual business problems may interrupt the investment program's continuity. Ask yourself, "Will this sponsor most likely stay in business throughout the full cycle of the investment program"?

Investment Objectives and Policies

Whatever the objective of the investment—be it growth, income, or tax benefits—you may be assured that the prospectus will clearly state, "There is no assurance that such objectives will be attained." Remember, the warnings we discussed earlier still apply. There is a rule to help you maintain a realistic and healthy perspective: "The prospectus does not promise." Everything is couched in conditional and qualifying language.

Typically, investment objectives may include preservation of capital (again, these are only goals *not* guarantees), maximizing income and/or capital appreciation, minimizing negative tax consequence, and similar, if commonsense, targets. The objectives will be as broad as possible to permit the sponsor as much flexibility as possible. Just be sure the objectives stated match your own.

 Of course, no single investment can be all things for all people. Some investments provide more cash flow, tax benefits, growth potential, and/or safety than others. It's likely, however, that no single deal does it all better than any other deal. As sensible as this sounds, it is amazing how many brokers sell (and how many investors buy) the concept of a single "best" investment. There simply is no such animal! If it is good for you, it is probably inappropriate for some other kinds of investors. If the salesperson, broker, or marketing organization is selling only one product for everyone, watch out! The product may be fine, but you must assume your marketer has commissions, rather than your ultimate satisfaction, on his or her mind.

Income, Loss, and Cash Distributions

If the form of the investment is a limited partnership (as many of them are), the discussion of income, loss, and cash distributions will often make several references to the limited partnership agreement that is normally an "exhibit" in the prospectus. The first mention of these factors is usually meant to direct the reader to the proper place later in the document, where a more complete description can be found—so don't think you know all about it until you've read the partnership exhibit.

Income and loss distributions should always favor the investor. If it doesn't sound "fair" (and "fairness," of course, will vary with each investor's personal needs and values) to you, then it probably isn't, and you should look elsewhere.

The distribution of benefits are among the most important paragraphs of the prospectus. Do not skim these lightly. A slight change of wording can mean the difference between receiving a good return and receiving nothing—regardless of how well the investment itself performs for the partnership.

For example, cash distributions from operations should almost always be weighted heavily in favor of the investors, not the general partners. If general partners participate, it should not be until the investors have received the equivalent of all their money back.

Adjusted Capital Accounts

One commonly used accounting device that can mislead you is the "adjusted capital account." This means that as cash distributions are made and tax benefits accrue (and as losses are passed through to investors), your principal, as measured by your "capital account", is constantly decreasing—at least from an accounting viewpoint. Therefore, when a subordination clause says you get your money back before the general partner gets a share of profits, it is common for that subordinated return to be tied to your "adjusted capital account." If an investment pays out 10% cash each year for ten years, your adjusted capital account would probably be zero at the end of that period. Hence, the profit sharing would be weighted more heavily toward the sponsor when partnership assets are finally sold.

For example, suppose the subordination clause states that cash flow will be split 99% to the limited partners and 1% to the general partners until the limited partners receive return of principal as measured by their adjusted capital accounts. Assume, too, that the limited partners have received a preferential cash flow of 10% per year for ten years. Their adjusted capital accounts are now at zero. Suppose, too, that the subordination clause also says that after return of capital on the adjusted capital account, the limited partners receive 75% of asset resale proceeds and the general partners receive 25% of such proceeds. How does this affect your investment?

First, it means that the 75%/25% split will govern the distribution of all resale dollars received—often a substantial amount. Second, it means that the 99%/1% split is rendered a minor, if not meaningless, investor benefit by its linkage to each investor's capital account. The "adjusted capital account," whatever its provisions, should raise questions in every investor's mind.

More acceptable distribution provisions will specify that reductions of a limited partner's capital account in this manner will not affect the investor's preferential right to a return of original contributions, even if they come from nonterminating asset sales or dispositions. If the sponsor does not state that intent, it might be wise to discuss the reasons.

Income Tax Consequences

The tax laws change constantly, and the biggest change in decades took place in 1986.

It is not a question of "if" tax laws will change during the investment, but rather, when, how often, and with what impact on your investment. The discussion of income tax consequences found within the prospectus will normally contain many qualifiers. This section says as little as possible because of a sponsor's conscious desire to avoid commitment. If the sponsor has paid for an opinion from tax counsel, then that opinion will be included or referenced to an exhibit that is intended to give you some assurance that tax matters have been thought out prior to the offering the security to the public. However, no sponsor controls the Congress or the Internal Revenue Service. Laws change, and interpretations of existing laws change also. This section is extremely time sensitive. The smart way to approach such tax discussions is to refrain from relying on them at all—at least until you have consulted with your own tax advisor.

Taxable Entities Versus Tax-exempt Entities. The tax status of each investment dollar is always important, both for achieving goals and for determining an investment's value for your overall financial plan.

When you invest a taxable dollar (also referred to as a *pretax dollar*), you are looking for sheltered income and/or growth whenever possible. You can then use tax deductions when and if they are passed through to you via a limited partnership or other business form.

However, when you invest a dollar in a "tax-exempt" entity, or in such tax-deferred investments as those for your IRA, Keogh, defined benefit plan, or defined contribution plan, you will normally avoid "tax shelter" and "writeoff" deals in favor of the heaviest cash flows and best current income available. This only makes common sense: no one wants or needs a "shelter within a shelter." While there may be certain exceptions, this conventional wisdom is a generally sound guideline for allocating your dollars between tax-sensitive and tax-insensitive investments.

Avoiding Risk with Tax-Exempt Dollars. When determining your risk tolerance levels, it is also relevant to first determine if the dollars being risked are taxable or tax-deferred because every tax-deferred dollar *is* ultimately taxed.

If money is to be tax deferred (by investment in your IRA, for example), then your dollars should probably be placed in less risky investments. Why? Because the tax-deferred vehicle usually permits a limited number of dollars to be invested during each tax year. In theory, the dollar "not invested" in a pension or IRA can never be replaced. You can be sure *next* year's contribution is made, but you get no credit or deduction from last year's forgone contribution. Because of this, you want those deferred dollars to *be* there when you need them. Since low-risk investments are usually the most reliable income producers, they belong in the tax-deferred segment of your portfolio.

Investor Suitability Standards

 Every investment sponsor must qualify its potential subscribers. "Investor suitability standards" will vary from state to state, and a separate paragraph will often be mandated by individual state securities laws. It is therefore important for you to find the particular paragraph, if any, that qualifies you for the investment. In general, the wealthier the investor, the fewer suitability standards apply. At the extreme, investors with a net worth in excess of $1 million (called *accredited investors* in the language of the securities laws), are generally considered "suitable" regardless of investment risk. The theory is that while widows and orphans need protection, millionaires do not. There-

fore, the wealthier investor has an even more legitimate reason to be cautious. In the absence of a trusted advisor, no one is really looking out for your best interests but you!

The Limited Partnership Agreement

The wording of the limited partnership agreement, when it appears in a prospectus, is critical to every investor's results. These provisions dictate distribution amounts and allocations when money is received from the investment. A single phrase can destroy the potential for an individual's ultimate return.

For example, when marketing the partnership, the sponsor and/or its agents may stress the potential for selling its assets in 3 to 10 years, depending on the nature of the offering. However, a close examination of the limited partnership agreement will commonly reveal that the *legal* duration of the partnership is going to be 30, 40, or even 50 years from the date of subscription! The reasons for this (as in real estate) may include requirements of mortgage holders, or other third parties, but the fact remains that the agreement signed by the partners controls the term of the offering, not the marketing summaries discussed with potential investors by salespeople. Until you dispose of your shares, you will be involved in the partnerships, even if its economic activity is nil.

The key to remember is, don't take anything for granted. If something is not in the agreement, it probably is not legally binding on the sponsor, *regardless of other assurances.*

PERSONAL FINANCE / Carole Gould

Those Tricky Mutual Fund Costs

Here are formulas to show you which of your funds have the lowest fees. The calculations are worth the trouble.

U NTIL recently, mutual fund investors faced a simple choice: They could buy no-load funds directly, or they could purchase load funds and pay a broker's commission of up to 8.5 percent. But now it requires a heavy dose of new math to compare the costs of different funds. Apart from the customary operating expensives and management fees, fund managers have devised a farrago of other charges—high or low loads imposed when you buy, exit fees when you sell and some hard-to-find fees levied while you hold the fund.

"There are too many different types of charges today, and it's getting too confusing for the investor" to sort through them all, said Kathleen Quigley Lantero, editor of Wiesenberger Investment Company Services. Of the 1,000 mutual funds the company monitors, about half impose front-end sales loads. About the same number have so-called 12b-1 plans, which were authorized by the Securities and Exchange Commission in 1980.

These plans, named for the regulation that permitted their creation, let funds deduct up to 1.25 percent of their assets to cover advertising and other marketing expenses. Investors must typically plow through the fine print of a prospectus to find out if the fund has a 12b-1 plan; then they must check the most recent accounting statement to see what percentage of assets the plan absorbed. With 12b-1 plans, mutual funds "can levy pretty much what the devil they want, and the only way you can find out is in retrospect," said Gerald W. Perritt, editor of The Mutual Fund Letter.

Norman Fosback, president of the Institute for Econometric Research, in Fort Lauderdale, Fla., dismisses 12b-1 charges of less than three-tenths of 1 percent as a "minor consideration." Charges of more than 1 percent he calls "clearly abusive."

Apart from 12b-1 charges, some funds impose redemption fees when investors sell their holdings. These may be levied as a flat percentage of the share price or on a sliding scale, ranging from 6 percent, say, if you sell in the first year, to zero if you hold your shares six years or more.

All of this leaves investors in a dilemma. They cannot rely on funds advertised as no-load to be free of sales costs. And how do the various charges and fees stack up over the long term? If you plan to keep your funds invested until you retire in six years, for example, are you paying more in expenses if you buy the fund with the 8.5 percent sales load or the fund with the .75 percent 12b-1 charge and the sliding-scale exit fee?

John Markese, director of research for the American Association of Individual Investors in Chicago. has come up with a possible solution: a series of formulas that convert the various expenses into equivalent charges. Using his formula, the investor can convert a front-end load into an equivalent annual percentage 12b-1 plan, or find the 12b-1's equivalent in a front- or back-end load. Many shareholders are surprised by the results, he said.

Mr. Markese's first formula converts front-end loads to their 12b-1 equivalents for various holding periods. Int his case, the 12b-1 charges equals the front-end load, stated as a percentage, divided by the investment holding period stated in years. For example, suppose a fund has a 3 percent front-end load and you hold it for four years; if you take .03 and divide it by 4, the answer is three-fourths of 1 percent—and that percentage would be the equivalent 12b-1 charge.

This approach also lets you compare costs of no-load funds that have 12b-1 plans with an equivalent front-end load fund. for example, a no-load fund with a one-half of 1 percent 12b-1 plan held five years is cheaper than a 4 percent load fund, which over the same time period is equivalent to an eight-tenths of 1 percent 12b-1 charge.

To compare a 12b-1 charge to its equivalent front-end load, multiply the 12b-1 annual charge, stated as a percent, by the umber of years the investment is held. so, for example, an investor who holds shares in a no-load fund with a three-fourths of 1 percent 12b-1 plan for five years has paid the equivalent of a 3.75 percent front-end load.

Investors who are not sure how long they intend to hold their mutual fund shares can compare charges by finding the break-even point at which the charges become equal: to do so, divide the front-end load by the 12b-1 annual charge, both state as percentages. For instance, a one-quarter of 1 percent 12b-1 charge becomes equals to a 3 percent front=end load after 12 years (3 divided by .25 equals 12). Because annual charges build up over time, investors who expect to hold securities for longer than the break-even point would be better off with a one-time sales charge; those who expect to sell more quickly would find a 12b-1 plan the cheaper option.

To convert a back-end load into its 12b-1 equivalent, first multiply the number of years the investment is held(n) by the sum of 1 plus a discount rate (Mr. Markese uses 10 percent), raised to the nth power. Then divide the back-end load by the result. for example, a 4 percent back=end load for fund shares held four years converts to a .68 percent 12b-1 charge (Raise 1.1 to the fourth power and multiply by 4; take the product, 5.8564, and divide it into 4 for a result of .68 percent.)

Some funds with front- or back-end loads also have 12b-1 plans, Mr. Markese pointed out. In these cases, you must add the annual 12b-1 charge to the 12b-1 equivalent for the load fees, to get the total fund expenses. Say you are considering a fund with a 3 percent back-end load plus an annual .5 percent 12b-1 charge. For a three-year holding period, the back-end load converts to a .75 percent 12b-1 equivalent; add to this the .5 percent 12b-1 charge, for a total annual cost of 1.25 percent.

There are two reasons why it is worth the trouble to compare these costs. First, when you are talking about a long-term investment, particularly an Individual Retirement Account, cumulative deductions can make a big difference.

"Small annual charges can significantly reduce your pot of retirement dollars," Mr. Perritt said. "For example, over 15 years, a one-half of 1 percent 12b-1 charge equals a front-end load of about 7.5 percent." If you move your account around and each place siphons off a fee, he added, "over time it adds up to a lot of money."

The second reason is that the tax act has made these charges more expensive for the investor. The itemized deduction for miscellaneous business expenses will be harder to obtain, since only expenses in excess of 2 percent of adjusted gross income will qualify—and this means that most investors will have to pick up the tab for investment advisory fees paid on their behalf by the funds. Beginning in 1987, mutual funds must add these fees to dividends and other payments that are considered taxable income for the shareholder.

WHAT TO DO IF YOU HAVE PROBLEMS

Timing can dramatically affect the options available to you in case of difficulty with your investment. When you are made aware of potential problems, you must first ask yourself whether or not subscription documents have been executed and accepted into the partnership or similar investment vehicle.

Before Subscription

If you find out something that bothers you *before* you invest, simply back out. Until subscription documents have been *accepted* by the general partner, there is normally a clear provision in the prospectus and/or partnership agreement providing that all bets are off if you say they are.

During Subscription

Suppose a negative newspaper article comes out on your investment sponsor while your documents are sitting at the offices of the general partner being reviewed for approval. You can still rescind your agreement under most circumstances. If you are sure you want out, wire or telefax your decision, followed by a written "election to rescind."

Immediately after Subscription

In most states and in most circumstances, even if you have discovered disturbing news *soon after* you have subscribed, you may *still* have statutory right of rescission (right to rescind), depending on your state law and on the circumstances. That means you should *immediately* consult with qualified legal counsel when you hear of negative news right after investing. The law may give you a second chance.

If you have been in the deal for a while, the discovery of misinformation, or in the worst case—outright fraud—may cause you to consider suing the sponsor. This step should not be taken lightly.

Litigation is costly, lengthy, and in most cases there are no winners. Also keep in mind that *you* assumed the risks spelled out in the prospectus and related offering materials. Do not expect any guarantees, especially with a prospectus whose sole purpose is to painstakingly describe potential risks.

Before the Attorney, Ask the Sponsor

After your own advisors, the first source you should turn to for information is the investment sponsor who accepted your money. If you have questions, ask the general partner or fund manager. Prospectuses normally provide the sponsor's legal address and phone number. The documents may also include a toll-free telephone number for investor services. Take advantages of such resources. In most cases, a sponsor will volunteer to send you additional information to clarify particular provisions or aspects of the deal. Keep in mind, however, that the explicit wording of the prospectus or partnership agreement will in most cases control the final outcome of any dispute.

There is no such thing as a completely "objective" investment advisor. The company's investor services representative will normally stick up for the sponsor, while your personal investment advisor, regardless of his or her primary profession, will probably validate the original advice given, out of professional pride. However, subjective advice is not necessarily invalid advice. Everyone has his or her own particular slant and individual perceptions. Understand them before you criticize them. Then evaluate *all* the input you receive in the best possible manner for benefitting *your* interests.

Be Skeptical of Litigation

If you suspect that laws have been violated in the information given to you (for example, if the sponsor has "guaranteed" verbally while denying such a representation in writing), then by all means seek legal advice and report such events to appropriate securities regulators. For exchange transactions, contact the securities exchange itself. For over-the-counter companies, contact the National Association of Securities Dealers (NASD). When in doubt, contact the Securities and Exchange Commission (SEC) in Washington, D.C., or the state regulators where you reside.

Checklist for Complaints

1. First contact your financial advisor, broker, or agent who represented you.
2. If the problem involves a brokerage, contact the firm's management.
3. Seek arbitration privately through your own legal counsel.
4. Seek arbitration through the exchange, if appropriate.
5. If all else fails, consult legal counsel regarding litigation.

Please note that you must first make a formal demand for what you want before you can expect someone to respond to your complaint. Be certain that you have done so before contacting the regulators indicated. If you don't know what you want, you cannot expect much help from someone else. Remember, the ultimate alternative is to walk away from the problem and cut your losses. If you have spread your portfolio over the basic asset categories, this may be the best choice. Think about your quality of life and the negative consequences of becoming involved in complex litigation before you decide to declare war over money you may or may not have coming.

CONCLUSION

The prospectus is a complicated and important document for prospective investors. You should read, analyze, evaluate, and thoroughly understand its content before you invest in any offering it represents. If you lack the time, patience, expertise, or inclination to do the reading yourself, pay someone else to do it for you. If you don't, you will be gambling or acting on blind faith—neither of which is a recognized road to riches.

CHAPTER 19

FORECAST OF THE 1988 ECONOMIC ENVIRONMENT

A GLANCE AHEAD

Forecasting isn't difficult; forecasting correctly is the problem! Certain economists and investment analysts are frequently quoted in the financial media not because of their track records, which are often dismal, but because of their accessibility, gift for a colorful phrase, and desire to be quoted.

Economic forecasting is an integral part of the investment industry. Economists research mounds of data to predict possible futures for the economy. Investment analysts pore over these statistics, charts, price histories, and qualitative assessments in an attempt to ordain the future direction of various markets.

In this chapter you'll discover that sharp differences of opinion exist between highly qualified specialists for our economy in 1988. That's where you come in. No one knows the future. Ultimately your own financial decisions rest with you. You may select a professional manager or advisor, but remember that the decision to act on thier recommendations is yours. You'll learn

- *Why multiple-asset diversification enables you to benefit from a wide variety of investment forecasts*
- *How professionals view the interrelationships among asset categories*
- *How managers view the relationship among the economy and the investment markets*

- *What investments a variety of highly qualified advisors recommend for 1988*

WHAT'S PAST IS PROLOG

The great stock market debacle of October 1987 provides a good illustration of the mechanics of the forecasting business. By early 1988 you are liable to conclude from the many claims made in advertisements that many advisors called the Great Crash. Unfortunately reality reduces this herd to a very select few. Only a handful of analysts forecast anything like the crash that actually occurred on "Black Monday," and none of those foresaw its true dimensions or effects.

Many readers will find some advisor's comments about a potential market peak or a tentative sell recommendation that was made in the six months before October. The advisors will then design public relations or advertising copy around the isolated comment to make it sound particularly insightful. This is not a condemnation of these individuals, but rather a description of how the financial advisement business really works. A touch of cynicism when examining any exorbitant sales claims is always a useful defense.

In any event, the thoughtful investor couldn't have asked for a better demonstration of the value of diversificaton over a number of asset categories than the recent stock market "collapse."

THE GREAT CRASH

On Monday, October 19, 1987, the Dow Jones Industrial Average fell 508 points for the largest single-day crash in history. This exceeded the previous single-day record of 108, set only the previous Friday, October 16. Even more significantly, the percentage drop exceeded even the crash of October 19, 1929, the infamous Black Tuesday that signaled the beginning of the Great Depression: a 22.6% drop that dwarfed the 12.8% drop in 1929.

Confirming the seriousness of the fall was similar action in other, broader based indexes such as the S&P 500, which also fell over 20%. Volume—which many analysts believe gives vital clues to the significance of price action—soared to over 600 million shares, nearly double the previous record day. Declining stocks outpaced advancing issues by a staggering 49 to 1.

What does it all mean? It will be many months and possibly years before anyone knows for sure. The significance of the 1929 crash was not recognized immediately, and its sociological impact is still being felt today. Just as in 1929, there has been much commentary on what caused the crash of 1987. Contributing factors mentioned most often by analysts include

- The continued rapid growth of the budget deficit despite five years of economic expansion.
- Excessive market valuations. Corporate earnings were not sufficient to justify the sharp price rises.
- The sharply rising interest rates in preceding months. The rate on 30-year Treasury bonds had moved from 7.5% to over 10.2%.
- The yield on stocks (under 2%), which had fallen to too much of a discount from bonds.
- Evidence that international economic cooperation was falling apart, as interest rates in West Germany and Japan edged higher, despite pleas from the United States to stimulate their economies to help the U.S. trade deficit.

- Fear of a wholesale collapse by the dollar following comments by Treasury Secretary James Baker that the United States may let the dollar slip further.
- The attack on Iranian oil installations that day, which raised war fears.
- Disgruntled foreign investors, who had poured unprecedented amounts of money into the U.S. markets in 1987.
- Loss of confidence in the Reagan Administration's ability to deal with crucial issues following the Irangate probe, the Bork nomination fiasco, and a hostile Congress impatient with a lame duck presidency.
- Uncertainty about the Federal Reserve Board policies under its new chairman, Alan Greenspan.
- The persistence of the huge trade deficit despite repeated assurances that it would show sharp improvement.

This disparate array of explanatory factors clearly demonstrates the need for diversification. Many of these factors had been evident for months. The budget deficit had actually gone down. What triggered the final collapse? No one really knows, and probably no single event was the trigger. By the summer of 1987 the market had risen 40% for one of the strongest moves on record. The economic statistics underlying the market through September remained positive. Unemployment was shrinking, incomes were on the rise, consumer confidence was at record levels, demonstrated by rising consumer spending and increased industrial production. The government's chief tool for forecasting the economy, the Commerce Department's Index of Leading Indicators, pointed to steady growth. From the short vantage point of this book's date of publication, the market seems to have become the proverbial "overinflated balloon" that was ripe—for any or all of the factors mentioned—to burst its overvalued bubble. Once the decline began, it was hastened by computerized "program trading" and panic by investors who hedged their portfolios in options, futures, and other instruments dependent on market dynamics.

So What Does It All Mean?

The *Wall Street Journal,* on October 19, 1987, noted that one stock index options trader had shrieked "It's the end of the world!" in the midst of trading on the previous Friday (when the market was deep into what proved to be the largest single-day drop up to that time). We don't know what that trader's observation was during the much bigger crash Monday, but we don't feel his prediction will be borne out any time soon.

However, once the extremes have been identified, it becomes more difficult to assess the short- and long-term implications of such movements. There are basically two schools of thought—and a large contingent of honest "I don't know's." On the one hand, some people believe that the crash was largely due to changed financial markets, including such factors as stock index options, futures, programmed trading, and portfolio insurance. As a result, proponents of this school argue that the crash is not on par with that of 1929. It doesn't foretell grave things for either the market or the economy.

On the other hand, a number of analysts point to the fact that the stock market itself is the single best (although far from infallible) leading indicator of the economy's future direction. Their argument is that the devastating fall in market value could itself lead to a recession. By some estimate, over $900 billion was lost in the market slide dating from October 6, including over $500 billion lost on October 19 alone. They argue that this loss will devastate consumer net worth, the foundation for the spending spree that has invigorated the economy since 1982. Since consumer spending constitutes two-thirds of GNP, a slowdown would be very bad for GNP growth by late 1988. Counterarguments state that rank-and-file consumers have proportionally fewer assets in equities; that the crash is not "financial" (banks remain sound); and that as a leading indicator, the stock market has predicted "eight of the nation's last four recessions."

Obviously, good cases can be made for either position. Unfortunately, no one knows which is correct, or whether the truth will even lie somewhere in between. However, a number of variables to watch can give thoughtful investors an early clue.

It's time to get very defensive in your investment allocations if

- The leading indicators turn down for three consecutive months.
- Consumer confidence drops sharply.
- Industrial production reverses its recent uptrend.
- Consumer spending turns down for three straight months.
- The trade deficit doesn't show any improvement.
- Protectionist trade legislation is passed.
- Gold rallies and stays above $500.
- The stock market is unable to stabilize above 1,700.
- Corporate earnings consistently fall below expectations.

A defensive strategy would include the following:

- Buy defensive stocks (utilities, food, tobacco, liquor) to the minimum allocation for 1988.
- Increase cash equivalents. Hold at least 50% in T-bills or in money market funds that invest solely in T-bills.
- Buy gold: coins as well as stocks.
- Pay down debt as fast as possible.
- Buy only the highest-grade bonds. Hold at least 50% U.S. Treasuries.
- Emphasize liquidity. Stay away from highly leveraged real estate or long-term commitments (over five years).

If those people are correct who believe that this whole trauma is only a reflection of changing and volatile financial markets, the market should hold well above 1,900 by December 1987 and you can trust more normal forecasting methods, as we detail in the balance of this chapter. From this perspective, the bulls may not be quite finished yet on Wall Street.

Who Won and Who Lost?

Although it's a painful lesson to many, the great October Crash offers an ideal illustration of the virtues of multiple-asset diversification. Only investors who had already diversified over a number of asset categories were able to escape the carnage. Those who thought they were diversified because they owned a number of different stocks—even income-producing blue chips—learned (as we pointed out in Chapter 21) that 90% of a portfolio's total return is due to asset allocation and not to security selection.

Owners of stocks lost money. Those who also had bonds in their portfolios (especially Treasury bonds) saw at least some of their losses offset by a sharp rally. Treasury bonds were the chief beneficiary due to a predictable "flight toward quality." When investors are unsure (and on October 19 uncertainty was the byword), they are willing to give up yield for safety.

Money also flowed heavily into cash equivalents. Three- and six-month Treasury bill yields fell sharply as investors ran from stocks to seek a safe liquid home.

Gold was the other beneficiary. It rallied $10.10 to close at $481.70, the highest level in 4 1/2 years.

International stock market also fell in sympathy with the U.S. market. London and Hong Kong set records for single-day drops. Japan was also down sharply.

Commodities other than the precious metals took a beating. Even oil—which many thought would rally, due to the increased tension in the Middle East occasioned by U.S. bombing of Iran installations—finished lower on the day.

If you only look at one day, of course, you can get a misleading picture. For example, the precious metals rallied back on Tuesday (and even the stock market rallied back a record 100 points). However, this "snapshot" lends further credence to our main thesis that today's volatile, sophisticated markets are best approached through diversification over a variety of asset categories.

OUR PANEL OF EXPERTS

To get a variety of perspectives on investment prospects for 1988, we approached a number of highly qualified advisors:

- Jeremy Black, CFP, is president of Interfinancial Corporation, a financial planning firm in Denver, Colorado.
- Charles Brandes is president of Brandes Investment Counsel, a financial planning firm in San Diego, California.
- Claire S. Longdon, CFP, is an independent financial planner in New York City.

- Ronald Kaiser is senior vice-president and director of Bailard, Biehl, & Kaiser, a money management firm in San Mateo, California.
- Luke McCarthy is president of August Financial Corporation, a financial planning firm.
- Avery Neumark, JD, LL.M, CPA, is a tax partner with Ernst & Whinney in New York City.
- Philip Wilson is president of Philip S. Wilson Associates, a financial planning firm in Woodland Hills, California.
- Judith Zabalaoui, CFP, is president of Resource Management, Inc. a financial planning firm in Metairie, Louisiana.

They were all asked for their forecasts on the various asset categories we've used: cash equivalents, U.S. stocks, U.S. bonds, real estate, international securities, and precious metals. We asked each for their own asset allocation recommendations to give you further ideas on how you may want to personalize your own portfolio. The remainder of this chapter is devoted to their conclusions.

Cash Equivalents

In today's volatile environment, it is important to maintain a liquid reserve. Charles Brandes was by far the most bearish of the group, recommending that 60% of your portfolio be invested in short-term cash equivalents for 1988.

Ronald Kaiser noted that yields have moved to more attractive levels recently, and a diversified portfolio should hold 11% in cash. Cash equivalents can give you important flexibility in these volatile markets. Not least, this portion of your portfolio offers peace of mind!

Philip Wilson takes a more aggressive stance, suggesting that by the second quarter of 1988, cash should be reduced to "only a minimal portion." Instead, he will be investing in U.S. equities and fixed income early in the year.

Both Avery Neumark and Claire Longden note that it is important for you to keep enough cash available to cover six months of expenses.

U.S. Equities

As you would expect, the outlook for U.S. stocks provoked the biggest disagreements. Zabalaoui recommends minimal positions. She fears the increasing politicization of the markets through tax legislation. She feels the Federal Reserve has failed to provide strong monetary leadership and as a result stocks are susceptible to wide swings. Rather than lead, the Fed has been a follower. The huge deficit problems must be faced soon.

Kaiser notes that his firm completed its bi-annual asset allocation review in October 1987. It reduced its U.S. stock allocation to only 24%, the lowest in many years. At one point early in the bull market the level was 36%. He is skeptical of the prospects for further growth. The market is getting fully priced. Other assets offer better value.

Neumark cautions investors to adopt a defensive posture with the equity portion of their portfolios. "Don't get heavily involved at this point." However, some stocks should always be considered. He looks for stocks with a history of stable earnings growth and says, "Stick with blue chips." While it is often difficult to resist the impulse, he cautions readers against trying to trade the short-term fluctuations in the market. Buy and hold carefully selected stocks for the long term.

Longdon believes the market may turned higher in 1988, but for the wrong reasons. Therefore, she suggests taking selective long-term (five to ten years) positions in blue-chip stocks. After you've built a foundation of blue-chip issues, she suggests a very careful search for two or three "turnaround" candidates. Carefully selected turnaround companies will probably have to be held two to three years. When selecting mutual funds, look to no-load funds that have a good record for holding up in down markets. One fund she liked was Fidelity Puritan.

McCarthy is an aggressive bull, allocating 40% to stocks. He expects continued earnings growth and high liquidity to boost prices further. He doesn't expect inflation fears to hurt the market, as he believe companies have sufficient room to raise prices without losing market share. Expect companies to raise prices when the opportunity presents itself. This raise will result in even better earnings.

Brandes recommends that 40% of your funds be put in stocks. He's buying only fundamentally undervalued issues. He cautions against chasing stocks in this environment when stocks are averaging two times book value. When the S&P 500 P/E is 22 and dividend yield is under 3%, that's a time to look for a short-term setback in the market. He likes savings and loans institutions and banks, both clearly undervalued situations. He warns that the "greater fool theory" seems operative at lofty levels. Things won't go up forever, but real values are available.

Wilson expects a good year for the market, with prices up 10–12%. He expects good corporate earnings to push the market higher, especially in the first quarter. He prefers companies that do not depend on foreign trade for a major part of their business. Foreign buying will continue to flow into U.S. markets because our markets still represent the best values.

Black does not try to forecast. Rather, he bases his portfolio recommendations on the historical performance of the asset categories (see Chapter 21). He recommends putting 25% into U.S. equities, and 10% into S&P 500 issues. With the balance, buy small capitalization issues. He suggests buying stocks from the bottom quarter of the NYSE as ranked by capitalization.

U.S. Bonds

Kaiser is the most bullish on bonds. He feels bonds are the most undervalued of the seven asset classes BB&K monitors. BB&K increased its bond allocation to 29% for U.S. bonds. It has also added international bonds to its list and has allocated 7% to them. Kaiser likes zero-coupon issues best. Long-term bonds represent good values near the depressed levels seen in October 1987. Buy and hold through the inevitable corrections. The 1987 dip in bond prices is a correction in a long-term bull market in bonds.

Neumark thinks that the yields seen at the highs in 1987 are attractive. Pick your spots to buy, but on price drops bonds are a buy. When guaranteed rates on investment-grade issues are in the double-digits, he considers it a conservative approach to locking in above-average returns.

McCarthy allocates 25% to bonds. He likes the double-digit yields available on high-quality issues. The only danger is a resurgence of inflation. Lighten your positions on any hint of increased inflation.

Wilson is quite bullish on bonds. He expects interest rates to decline in the first or second quarter of 1988. The 1987 bond market crash was not justified by the evidence. There was a very wide gap between the expectation of inflation and its actual level. Buy long-term investment-grade and government issues. Stay away from the muni market—it's too risky.

Zabalaoui advises buying, but only AAA—rated insured or "insurable" munis. Yields available at year end 1987 will provide good, stable, long-term income. She expects to be a buyer at least through the first half of 1987.

Not everyone is a buyer, though. Claire Longden counsels against buying long-term bonds until interest rates stablize. She expects that to happen in the first six months of 1988. In the interim, she recommends buying short-term CDs and rolling them over. However, she does say that if you have certain objectives that must be funded in the future such as college education, she'd buy zero-coupon bonds to meet the objective.

Brandes thinks bonds offer an insufficient risk/reward ratio to justify buying. Interest rate volatility is simply too great, and that makes risk too high. He notes that over the long term, equities outperform bonds substantially.

Not surprisingly, Jeremy Black allocates only 8% to U.S. bonds. He doesn't expect interest rates to change much. If they do, there is greater risk of an increase than a decrease.

Real Estate

Black likes real estate prospects (or should we say, takes comfort in its past record!). He recommends you invest 35% of your portfolio spread over a diversified collection of real estate vehicles. Distribute your funds across leveraged, unleveraged, equity REITs and mortgage REITs. Investigate limited partnership deals carefully, and don't buy just leveraged deals.

Interestingly, almost all our respondents cautioned against highly leveraged positions. The major problems of the last few years for many limited partnerships are still overhanging this market. Avery Neumark is a strong believer in real estate. Buy, but not high-leverage positions.

McCarthy expects real estate to do well in the near term due to a fall-off in new developments in 1987. He says that the decline in construction also bodes well for current holders. McCarthy looks for a slight pickup in inflation, which will boost real estate out of the doldrums.

Philip Wilson believes real estate is a good place to invest in 1988. The low correlation with equities will provide your portfolio with a good hedge if the stock market sells off. Although many cities are troubled with excess office space, an increasing number of attractive deals are coming up. It's still possible to buy undervalued, conservatively financed projects. A good project will always be in demand.

Claire Longden believes that it is possible to get some good deals as a result of forced sales of many projects owned by limited partnerships that are not structured for the new tax law. Stay away from highly leveraged deals. Buy only those projects that make good economic sense. Avoid those with tax gimmick features. Be careful of problems that further tax law changes may cause.

Judith Zabalaoui warns you to buy real estate as you would a bond: Look at cash flow and the ability to hold value. Stay out of highly leveraged positions. Aim for 40% equity and 60% leverage.

Ron Kaiser notes that BB&K is still underweighting real estate with only a 12% allocation at present. That level compares to a norm of 25%. Real estate is still in a bear market. He cautions you that what happened in Texas can happen anywhere.

Charles Brandes doesn't consider real estate an appropriate investment for individuals. He prefers equities. He notes that while unleveraged real estate historically outperforms bonds, it doesn't compete well with equities.

International Securities

International securities are viewed most bearishly of all the asset categories. Brandes says that the Asian markets are grossly overvalued. Don't touch the Japanese market due to very high risk there. Korea is also overvalued. The closed-end Korea Fund was selling at 150% of net asset value when closed-end funds normally sell at a discount. Poor prospects overall.

Kaiser suggests a total allocation of 19% to be split 7% to bonds and 12% to equities. He's been trimming exposure to international equities over the past couple years. His work shows that inclusion of international bonds can serve to reduce risk in a well-diversified portfolio without lowering return.

Wilson agrees with Kaiser. He notes that while international equity markets have outperformed the U.S. market for the past few years, now is the time to lighten up. The U.S. market represents better value and less risk. His current allocaton would be only 15%, down from 25–30% a few years ago. Stay away from international fixed-income instruments due to problems with foreign currency volatility. As foreign governments stimulate their economies, that will push their interest rates higher, knocking down their bonds.

Neumark advocates only modest positions. He says you should have some international securities "for the sake of diversification." However, he is not enthusiastic about most foreign markets. Stick with the least volatile markets. The best approach is to buy international funds.

McCarthy allocated only 2.5% to the international market due to the high risk there. Longden and Zabalaoui have no recommendations in this field.

Precious Metals and Tangibles

Zabalaoui believes you should look into buying an ownership interest in domestic oil cooperations. She believes that 1988 is an excellent opportunity to be a contrary investor and buy into oil. She's working with a broker who matches pools of investors with producers who want to sell existing wells or new fields. The investors take actual control of the wells or a percentage of the fields. Investors conscious of long-term inflation should look to invest in oil.

Kaiser agrees that the place to be is in oil rather than gold. However, he recommends NYSE-listed oil company stocks. He has cut the allocation for gold to a low 5%. Even then, he says don't buy the mines, they are significantly overvalued. Buy bullion.

Longden also recommends buying oil and gas stocks. She says that stocks participate and respond to the market quickly and are far less complicated than direct ownership. She cautions her investors to stay away from direct ownership of oil through master limited partnerships, especially those geared to specific tax benefits. She thinks that tax laws in this area could change yet again in the near future, adversely affecting your investment. As for gold, she recommends you restrict your investment to North American gold-mining stocks. Stay away from South African stocks.

Neumark is very cautious. Do not invest in these areas on a large scale. The only way he'd participate would be through buying NYSE-listed oil or mining stocks.

McCarthy allocates 2.5% of his recommended portfolio to the metals. He notes that gold and coins have run up well in 1987 and could move higher in 1988. However, keep your position small.

Wilson doesn't leave much doubt about his position on gold and coins: "Avoid them completely." He believes the trial balloon of Secretary of theTreasury Baker regarding tying the dollar to gold or a basket of commodities is a very bearish sign for the metals. The markets would interpret such a move as anti-inflationary. The price of oil is subject to wild swings due to the political situation. He thinks the true market price is $18–$22. Any moves beyond that range may offer short-term opportunities. Be very careful, though—the oil market is subject to very sharp fluctuations.

Brandes is even more adamant: "Completely avoid them at all times." He says these markets are very difficult to predict. He doesn't recommend participation by anybody "interested in building wealth!"

THE CONSENSUS 1988 ECONOMIC FORECAST

The National Association of Business Economists regularly surveys its members to obtain a consensus forecast on the economy. Their expectations are that real (adjusted for inflation) gross national product will expand 2.7% in 1988. They believe that an accommodative Federal Reserve will stave off a recession in 1988, which is an election year. A major part of the the projected GNP growth will come from a reduction in the trade deficit.

This same group looks for inflation to check in at around 4.8%. They look for interest rates to follow inflation higher. They also predict that the dollar will fall an additional 10–30% over the next four years.

CHAPTER 20

IMPLEMENTING YOUR
FINANCIAL PLAN

A GLANCE AHEAD

In this chapter, you'll learn

- *Alternative steps to getting your financial plan off the ground*
- *How to choose and use financial advisors*
- *How to put your priority on financial needs*
- *How to keep your financial plan on track*

Harnessing Those Good Intentions

The years had been good to Nancy. She was a 45-year-old marketing executive with a major corporation, in good health, with a husband, two grown children, and a six-figure annual income. They were comfortable—and knew it. That's when Nancy and her husband Bob began to get the nagging feeling that things just might be "too good to be true." They decided to make that long-put-off visit to a financial planner to discuss how and when they could begin putting their detailed but unimplemented financial plan to work.

It was a sobering discussion. The planner pointed out that Nancy and Bob were wasting, or using nonproductively, most of the money they made. After all, their kids still needed occasional loans, help with co-signing for major purchases, and countless emergencies experienced by young families.

When a little extra cash was accumulated, it seemed there was always a pressing need for it—burst pipes, a roof leak, retiling the pool, car repairs, therapeutic weekend out of town—and similar contingencies that are part of our hectic, modern, affluent society.

How could they "pay themselves first"—that all-important 10% of every dollar that came in the door—as their financial planner had so strongly advised them to do, when everything else took priority? Did net worth building mean a substantial reduction in their quality of life—the very thing they were working for?

By the end of the meeting, Nancy and Bob had learned that balance sheets, budgets, retirement goals, and all the rest were only so much paper unless *the plan* they represented was implemented with the same resolve and enthusiasm with which Bob and Nancy made and spent their money.

IMPLEMENTATION MEANS
TAKING ACTION!

When an individual or family settles on a financial plan or strategy that requires implementation, the time has come to *act*! It does not matter if the action required is simple or complex—the important point is to *do it!*

Almost everyone struggles with a certain amount of procrastination in his or her life. We have limited time and infinite choices for

The Nation's Largest Discount Brokerage Firms, 1987

1. Brown and Company Securities Corporation
2. Discount Brokerage Corporation of America
3. Fidelity Brokerage Services of America
4. Ovest Financial Services
5. Pacific Brokerage Services
6. Quick & Reilly, Inc.
7. Rose & Company Investment Brokers
8. Charles Schwab and Company
9. Muriel Siebert and Company
10. Spear Securities

fail to act. This is a good time to assess your current situation and to get a handle on where you would like to go. Do the things you hope for in life seem far beyond your grasp? Are you doubtful about your ability to sit down and make complete, rational sense of where you are and where you want to be in five years, ten years, or thirty years? Do you have a hard time thinking about these issues? Is it hard to discuss them with your mate?

 The emotional factors discussed in Chapter 2 make it very difficult to answer these money-related questions. Built-in biases and fears can keep us from really *doing* something about the things that matter most. Couples may find it especially difficult to come to agreement about financial goals: effective communication within a relationship is always a challenge. When the subject is money, the difficulty multiplies.

 Add a date and time to each of your implementation steps. Write down the specific things you have agreed to do in order to improve your financial life. Place specific target dates for completion immediately after each entry. Then pick a specific date each month to review your progress. Also specify the precise time of day for your review. Make an appointment with yourself (to include your spouse or other appropriate family member). You will be amazed at how a monthly review will help you continue forward toward your personal financial goals.

Figure 20-1 shows you an implementation list for a typical financial plan.

This illustration is only a sample; yours should be customized to fit your individual circumstances. The key points, however, should be clear:

1. Do *something* each and every month, even if only a review.
2. Consult with *everyone* who is appropriate. Include children.
3. If you notice a roadblock, write it down and give the *roadblock* its own date and time for resolution.
4. Year-end review should include an updated financial statement.

spending it. However, putting off the implementation of sound financial planning is one of the most expensive forms of procrastination we can indulge in. A financial plan is more than a household budget, a pension plan, an investment portfolio, or an estate plan—it's all of those and more. A plan is a road map to financial comfort and security—but you've got to put the vehicle in motion if you're ever going to get there. Household budgets, for example, don't just monitor and control expenses—they generate money that can be used to develop assets. Pension planning doesn't just create an asset base that compounds over time. It also helps you save taxes on the money you earn today so that even more can be put to work tomorrow. Insurance programs can help preserve your assets—and they give you or your heirs an important financial floor in the case of your death or disability. But policies must be purchased and updated regularly if they're to do their job. In short, an implemented financial plan delivers peace of mind. A *working* plan frees you to do more constructive things with your time and money than simply worry about the future; it makes that future happen.

 Start implementing your plan by reviewing Chapter 3. If you haven't set some goals for yourself, it's time to start. You have lots of new, useful knowledge and a wealth of good intentions that won't do a thing for you if you

Date and Time-Stamped List of Goals

as of January 31, 19__

Goal	Action Needed	Review Date and Time
Update will	Attorney visit	February 15, 19__
Establish trust	Attorney visit	February 15, 19__
Review taxes	Accountant visit	March 15, 19__
Place IRA	Planner/broker visit	April 1, 19__
Review stocks	Planner/broker visit	April 15, 19__
Review insurance	Planner/agent visit	May 15, 19__
Fund pension	Planner/broker visit	June 15, 19__
Mutual funds	Planner/broker review	July 15, 19__
Review bonds	Planner/broker review	August 15, 19__
Real estate	Planner/broker review	September 15, 19__
Annual budget	Set with family	October 15, 19__
Business review	Family advisors	November 15, 19__
Year end review	Family advisors	December 15, 19__

Figure 20-1 Implementation List for a Typical Financial Plan

5. Each month, ask yourself, "What can I improve?"
6. Each month, ask yourself, "Did I pay myself enough?"
7. Be organized. If you need help, hire it.

Sometimes—perhaps most of the time—the intervention of a third party is necessary. A good financial advisor can be your collaborator, validator, and motivator. Planners are futurists, they work in the gray area of the unknown. They rely on training and experience as their guideposts to help you implement your plan. Financial planners are trained to look at the whole picture.

WHERE YOU CAN GET HELP

As you learned in Chapter 5, a certified financial planner (CFP) is educated, trained, and experienced to care for the financial needs of individuals and families—just as a general practitioner is trained to care for health needs. Both professionals know when it's time to turn to a specialist.

Generally, a professional planner will be licensed to sell securities and may have an insurance license. Some states have credentialing requirements; you can check with the office of the state attorney general to determine the licensing and disclosure requirements imposed by the state on registered planners.

Beware of salespeople who call themselves planners. It's legitimate for a planner to specialize in real estate, insurance, or securities sales—but it's not appropriate for a sales representative to assume the mantle of planner unless he or she is licensed and registered to present you with a range of planning and product options.

The ideal probably falls somewhere between doing everything yourself and letting specialists do everything for you. There is much to learn from financial professionals, especially when a team approach is used. No single person can be expected to act as financial planner, attorney, and accountant simultaneously, Look for two to four professionals in the fields of most interest to you. Or find a lead advisor you trust, and ask for referrals to specialized expertise.

There is no such thing as a free lunch. All financial products—even good advice—cost money. Therefore, it is more important to focus more on *results* than on *fees*. Be cautious about selecting investments based upon the notion that it is a bargain because no "commission" is being paid. That may simply

Many Investors Meet with Frustration in

Last September, Gerald M. Kirschner started feeling that his investments were getting too big for him to handle.

So the Birmingham, Michigan, accountant gathered up his portfolio of roughly $250,000 and began searching for a money manager. It took him nearly a year to find one.

"I thought I had plenty of money to give someone," Mr. Kirschner says. "But the managers who have the right history and the right track record all want more money."

Mr. Kirschner is one of many investors with portfolios of under $500,000 who thought their search for a money manager would be simple—but who have been increasingly frustrated trying to find one who is trustworthy, experienced and willing to take on relatively small accounts.

Limited Backgrounds

"You can find guys who haven't been in business for five years and who don't have a good client list," says James P. Owen, managing director of NWQ Investment Management Co., a Los Angeles-based money-management firm. "But it's very, very difficult today for investors who are demanding in their criteria."

The bull market of the past five years has swelled the ranks of investors looking for private portfolio management. Moreover, the wave of corporate restructurings and takeovers has resulted in lump-sum payments to droves of upper and middle executives unaccustomed to managing their own retirement money. As a result, established investment firms can set high minimum amounts for clients and still get all the customers they can handle.

And while the number of investment advisors registered with the Securities and Exchange Commission has nearly tripled in the past five years to 12,0000, the best of the newer advisors usually aren't available to smaller investors for long. Money managers typically start out with smaller accounts, finding portfolio money where they can. But as their businesses grow the accounts increase in both size and number, the managers raise their minimums.

Balestra Capital, a New York money manager with about $45 million under management from 25 clients, recently doubled its minimum portfolio to $500,000. "We just can't go one taking small accounts," says James Melcher, a principal in the firm."It takes as much manpower, time effort, computer power, etc. to handle a small account as a larger account. If I'm spending time on the phone with the guy who has $250,000, I'm not spending time with the guy with 5 million."

Most money managers base their fees on a percentage of assets in an account—generally 1 to 2% of a client's total portfolio annually. (Transaction costs for trades are extra.) For a client with a $250,000 portfolio, a money manager charging a 2% fee would earn $5,000 a year; for a $1 million client, a manager might charge 1.5% and earn $15,000.

The manager's workload, however, would be roughly the same in both cases. In fact, many managers argue that the $250,000 client needs more handholding, which takes valuable time.

Unlike certified financial planners, who advise clients on overall financial strategy, money managers specialize in specific investment decisions for a client's portfolio. For example, a client might hand over $500,000 to a manager, who will then buy and sell stocks, options, bonds and other investments in line with a specific investment goal. Those actions often are taken without the client's preapproval because the overall investment goal has been established. Investors, in turn,

Kevin G. Salwen, *Wall Street Journal*, August 13, 1987. Reprinted with permission

Search for Established Money Manager

receive periodic statements of the account's status.

But the search for a manager can be frustrating. Andrea Wilcox Case, a La Jolla, California, housewife, began looking for a money manager about nine months ago, after inheriting $350,000.

Mrs. Case, 37 years old, contacted Thomas J. Hummer, a San Diego money management consultant, who arranged meetings with several advisors who shared Mrs. Case's investment concept: long-term growth that could provide some money for her three children.

After several weeks of studying her options, Mrs. Case selected a manager. The firm had a "fairly good record, and I liked the gentleman I was dealing with," she says. But a few days later, the president of the money management firm, which Mrs. case declines to identify, informed her that the firm had a $1 million minimum, and that her portfolio was too small.

"I was very disappointed," Mrs. Case recalls. After several weeks, she went back to the consultant and renewed her search; she has since found a manager.

Jack C. Collins of Rockville, Maryland, ran into similar problems when he left a small computer company in January and received a retirement fund payout of about $200,000. Since he needed to roll the money over into a individual retirement account and didn't feel he could manage the funds himself, he sought out a portfolio manager.

For six months, Mr. Collins, 53, researched and interviewed prospective managers, while his money languished in a money market account. He grew increasingly frustrated as manager after manager who would accept his account failed to meet his standards.

Finally, Mr. Collins found an E. F. Hutton & Co. program to which he was willing to entrust $130,000; he invested the rest of his funds in real estate.

Many banks and brokerages, though, offer only limited or costly assistance. Some banks set huge minimums. U.S. Trust Co., for example, requires $2 million for new accounts. Manufacturers Hanover Trust Co. doesn't set a minimum portfolio size but requires a minimum annual fee of %5,000/

New Options

In some sectors, though intriguing options are springing up. Investment consultants, many of whom work for major brokerages, screen money managers for potential clients. Several have created limited partnerships that pool the money of investors with similar investment goals. those partnerships are then managed by individual portfolio managers. Annual fees for such accounts, however, often run as high as 3#, including transaction costs.

E. F. Hutton, the New York-based brokerage, has created a unit, Hutton Select Management, that handles many administrative chores for money managers. Those managers, in turn, agree to accept investors with at least $100,000. Mr. Collins put his $130,000 in this program.

B. Hauptman & Associates, a Fairfield, Iowa-based investment consultant, will soon begin a program for investors with as little as $50,000. Each client will have a separate account, but the money will be pooled and then sent to a money manager who none of the clients could have hired individually. The firm says the program should begin next Monday.

Of course, an investor can try to beat the odds in shopping for an advisor from among the newer, less established firms. "If the investor with $250,000 does his homework, it's possible to come up with the one firm in 20 that is both hungry and very successful," says NWQ's Mr. Owen. "But it's a window that doesn't stay open very long."

mean the company producing the product is keeping more of your dollar "in house" and is reluctant to share with outside providers who may be more "client-driven."

Financial products change constantly. If you are not in the business of evaluating such products on an ongoing basis, you do not have the time to learn as much about such products as someone who is steeped in them full-time as a professional. Don't waste time "reinventing the wheel." You should be the architect of your own financial future, but don't be afraid to pay for the "expert builders" you may need to make those plans a reality.

BEGIN AT THE BEGINNING

When people begin to implement their financial plans, they sometimes expect things to happen fast, but structuring and implementing a financial plan in a hurry is like trying to "build Rome in a day." You have to start somewhere, but those dream castles won't rise overnight. It is helpful to compartmentalize your thinking by breaking tasks down into manageable steps.

The steps in establishing a financial plan follow a necessary and logical process. The first is to give some tangible shape to your dreams. In Chapter 3 you established your short-term, intermediate, and long-term goals—a procedure that translated your hopes and expectations into dollars and dates: the education fund for your children, the trips you want to make, or the future requirements for your retirement fund. You imagined where you really wanted to be in five, ten, twenty years and more. You took control, in short, over your financial future and began to give it shape.

Now, to produce results, you must put that plan into action.

REVIEWING ACTION ALTERNATIVES

What are your choices for implementing a financial plan? They are many—and, once your goals are set, most begin with selecting financial products and services.

The following are *eight easily understood action steps to make your plan happen*:

1. Review a category of financial products or investments yourself.
2. With a financial advisor, review the products you favor.
3. Make a rough draft of your will, trusts, and any estate transfer entities your plan requires.
4. Review the items listed in Step 3 with the appropriate advisors.
5. Create a home filing system to store the elements of your plan as it is implemented (see Figure 20-2).
6. Complete a personal balance sheet annually. Ask yourself, "Has my net worth increased?"
7. If the answer to the preceding question is no, identify the area of your plan that is costing you wealth.
8. Go back to Step 1 and work through the action steps.

Update Your Will

Eight action steps also apply to that most important of all wealth-preserving tools—your will:

1. Review your current will, if you have one.
2. Discuss your plans with family members, as appropriate.
3. Call your attorney, tax advisor, and/or financial planner as needed.
4. Instruct your attorney to draft and arrange for a witness to your will.
5. Go into your attorney's office and sign the will(s).
6. Determine location of original (signed) and copies (unsigned) and place them.
7. Inform affected family members of the location of original and copies as well as content, as appropriate.
8. Check "Update will" off your list of plan implementation goals.

Establish a Home Filing System

Many organizational aids are available to help you in your battle against procrastination.

Home Filing System

Filing sequence

1 Banking
- Financial statements
- Loan and liability records
- Credit card statements
- Checking account statements
- Savings account statements
- Money market fund statements
- Commercial and treasury bill records
- Other receivables records

2 Budget records
Worksheets

3 Business agreements
- Partnership(s)
- Leases
- Buy adfdfBuy and sell
- Stock option(s)
- Employment contract(s)
- Miscellaneous

4 Certificates
Licenses, etc.

5 Communications
Accountant
- AgendAgendas
- Billings for BilBillings for services
- Memos/correspondence
- IRS correspondence

6 Communications
Attorney
- AgendAgendas
- Billings for services
- Memos
- Correspondencea

7 Communications
Banker
- Agendas
- Billings for services
- Memos
- Correspondence

8 Communications
Financial planner
- Agendas
- Billings for services
- Financial plans/strategies
- Memos/correspondence

9 Employment Benefits
- Individual retirement account (IRA)
- Keogh (HR-10)
  Pension and profit sharing and ESOP
- Fringe benefit package

10 Estate directives
- Wills and trusts (copies)
- Powers of attorney (copies)
- Pre and post mortem letters (copies)
- Other special instructions

11 Insurance policies
Claims
- Medical
- Disability
- Life
- Annuity
- Auto coverage
- Real estate coverage
- Personal and professional liability
- Insurance agents' correspondence

12 Limited partnerships
Alphabetical order

13 Real estate
- Residence records
- Trust deeds (copies)
- Investment property records
- Property tax records
- Utilities
- Expenditures records

14 Receipts
Warranties, etc.

15 Records
Education, etc.

16 Securities
- Stock brokerage statements
- Mutual fund statements
- Other securities transactions
- Stock certificates (copies)

17 Taxes
Current year's
- Employment income records
- Investment income records
- Tax deduction records
- IRS forms/schedules
- Expense logs and diaries
- IRS audit correspondence

18 Taxes
Past 3 years
- Tax return
- Documentary evidence

19 Miscellaneous

_____

_____

_____

Figure 20-2 Home Filing system

Perhaps the best is to write down what got done. The form is less important. The critical point is to *face* your own personal "batting average" of accomplishing step-by-step goals and consistently make efforts to improve that average.

Each month, do something to improve your filing system and the quality of your files. Label them more clearly. Request copies of birth certificates and marriage license in writing. File and label them when they arrive. Tell your children where they are and when they might need them. The following is a home filing system that has worked well for many people seeking to implement and control a comprehensive financial plan.

1. Basic organizational aids you will need
   a. 20 hanging file folders (and tab inserts)
   b. 50 or more file folders and labels
   c. File box or file drawer
2. What to keep and what to throw away
   a. Be disciplined when looking for outdated or unnecessary papers to throw out.
   b. Separate documents by main category headings:
      • Proof of identification (all family members)
      • Proof of ownership
      • Proof of valuation
      • Proof of relationship (business and personal)
      • Important correspondence and memorandums
      • Journals, agendas, and meeting notes
   c. Select the appropriate subcategory folders in which to file your papers. File chronologically, with the most recent entries in front.
3. Additional filing suggestions
   a. Working papers file (portable expandable type.) Most people have an intermediate file system to handle monthly
      • Bills to be paid
      • Premium notices
      • Bank statements
      • Receipts

   b. Permanent file extensions (backup files to store)
      • IRS records (beyond three years from filing data)
      • Investment records (after the year of sale)
      • Any paper that, due to quantity or other reasons, you wish to file separately.
4. How long and where to keep
   a. With regard to how long you should keep any particular paper, you know best, and when in doubt, ask the appropriate professional advisor.
   b. The important documents locator will pinpoint where your original documents should be kept and to whom you might provide copies.
   c. When you don't have the time to file a new item properly, place it in a "to be filed" folder, in the front section of the home filing system.

Cover All the Bases of Your Financial Life

Whether you work with an advisor or on your own, the steps to implementing a financial plan will remain the same. In one form or another, you will need to accomplish the following:

Establish a household budget, such as a 10/20/70 budget, to

1. Stabilize monthly cash flow
2. Create more cash for current expenditures
3. Build and maintain an adequate emergency reserve
4. Reduce debt
5. Free money for savings and investing

Select investments that

1. Allocate funds over a wide variety of asset categories
2. Control risk while meeting your growth and income needs
3. Anticipate future risk
4. Are sufficiently liquid to take advantage of new investment opportunities

Pay and shelter tax dollars in such a way that

1. Current taxes are reduced
2. Year-end tax liability is accurately determined
3. Leftover tax issues from past years are disposed of

Purchase insurance benefits that

1. Provide adequate cash payout in case of death
2. Cover medical and disability contingencies
3. Protect you against property and liabiliy losses that could erode or eliminate net worth
4. Provide income in case of permanent disability

Create an estate transfer structure that

1. Includes a will
2. Transfers assets to others now, if necessary
3. Reduces potential estate settlement costs
4. Provides for others after your death
5. Takes into consideration your charitable or philanthropic concerns

Administer the mechanics of a financial plan that:

1. Keeps financial records straight
2. Simplifies your financial transactions
3. Keeps your advisors informed
4. Coordinates the efforts of planner, accountant, attorney, and other financial advisors
5. Establishes a review process to periodically assess your progress and replan and reimplement when necessary

In the beginning, your financial plan may be little more than a financial first aid program. If you are struggling, you must first concern yourself with making each paycheck work responsibly. You will need to compartmentalize your thoughts about money and direct the first 10% of your income to your "put-and-keep" account. Soon these skills will be like second nature as you regularly set aside money to replenish an emergency fund or contribute to retirement accounts. In the beginning stages, your new portfolio will probably consist of growth-oriented mutual funds. At first, it may seem that the money you are putting away is negligible, but don't forget the magic of compounding and dollar-cost-averaging. In time, even the smallest deposits can produce significant wealth.

Some people choose to begin the planning process where the most obvious needs exist. If your wills and insurance are in order but you regularly leave large chunks of cash in a checking or savings account, you should begin to direct some of that money to a retirement program or investment portfolio. Perhaps you have a great long-term strategy, but lack sufficient liquid assets to manage an emergency. Many self-employed people overlook liability income, one of the most important safeguards available, and some people are simply unaware of the value of an IRA or Keogh.

By and large, you should buy products and services that address defensive needs first. Although there are exceptions, tax and pension planning and insurance strategies should be developed before sophisticated investment strategies can take shape. You may not yet have a large estate to protect, but you should have a will to transfer what you *do* have in an orderly, efficient way regardless of your circumstances.

Obviously, it may take weeks, months, or even longer to put your entire plan in place; once it's implemented, though, a well-orchestrated plan is a thing of beauty.

As you implement your plan, you should become good friends with either your local librarian or your local computer database club (or subscription service) because you will need a great deal of information to evaluate available financial products and services. Assuming you have a reliable advisor, think of that person as the "star quarterback" on your personal financial planning team.

GETTING THE MOST FROM YOUR PERSONAL FINANCIAL PLANNING TEAM

There are three key ingredients to implementing a successful financial plan:

1. Knowing what to do
2. Knowing when to do it

INVESTING/ John C. Boland

Why Brokers May Not Give Good Tips

**They often must choose
stocks only from
approved lists.
Customers may be
getting stale advice.**

When a stockbroker offers a client an investment idea the selection may have little to do with the broker's own judgment. At many large firms, brokers are severely restricted in picking their own stocks. They must toe the "party line"—if the firm's research department

has not approved a stock, the shares most likely will be off-limits to the retail broker.

These restraints, which vary from firm to firm, are aimed at avoiding liability for a broker's ill-considered ideas. "The whole purpose is to give comfort that the broker does indeed have a reasonable basis for recommending the stock," said O. Ray Vass, head of compliance at Merrill Lynch, whose 12,000 "financial consultants" are kept on a short research tether.

But the price to investor, according to a number of long-time brokers, may be exposure to shopworn ideas, while better opportunities—perhaps local companies not followed by New York-based analysts—slip away. They argue that a good local broker who takes the time to do his or her own research may find some stock gems whose sparkle does not reach the home office.

One broker said research departments had become too powerful. "They would like nothing better than to control all the sales" he stated.

A Dean Witter broker, who like others spoke on this sensitive subject on the condition he not be identified, said that he must provide his firm's compliance department with detailed explanations whenever he seeks to accumulate shares of obscure companies. To buy stocks under $2, he said, his clients must sign a form acknowledging that the firm disavows its broker's selection. Typically, stocks that sell so cheaply lack the capitalization of more established issues. Moreover, such "penny" stocks usually cannot be bought on margin.

"We can't solicit orders for stocks under $2," confirmed a Dean Witter broker in another East Coast city. He said that last year one of the firm's oil analysts got in hot water by recommending "a nice company at F(7,8)." The broker went on: "The firm flipped out. They pulled the recommendation, and there was a systemwide memo."

The recommended issue, Weatherford International, was trading last week at 1 F(5,8) on Amex.

While both employees praised Dean Witter's intentions—"our compliance department is stronger than marketing," one said—such restrictions may not always serve customer's interests.

"There are brokers who make a lot of money for their clients not sticking to the recommended list," said a broker at A.G. Edwards Inc.

The "recommended list" draws scorn both from stock-picking brokers and from clients who complain about old familiar faces. "Why buy Raytheon or Texas Instruments?" asked a Bostonian who has worked at a number of firms.

The "list," which can contain hundreds of better known stocks, is particularly unhelpful to a contrarian-type investor, noted a West Coast money manager. "Since brokerage houses are sales firms, not investment firms, a research idea has to be something that will be bought," he said. "It must be benign, and as the market goes higher, good values usually aren't benign."

Stocks that are not on the list, of course, tend to be riskier. "Some brokers feel that using only research-recommended stocks gets the monkey off their back," said a Dean Witter executive. "I can't say that that's a stupid argument."

The constraints on offering personal research are complex enough at some firms to discourage any but the most determined stock picker. Merrill Lynch has one of the most "cumbersome" systems, according to a broker there who has worked at a number of other houses.

At Drexel Burnham Lamber, a broker needs only "a reasonable basis" for recommending a stock, he recalled, which in practice meant that "if you're asked about it you must have a file" on the company. He said he preferred that system and "felt it was in my client's best interest; but it's easier to do a 'no brainer' and just regurgitate the recommended list." Indeed, he has completed the lengthy justification requirement by Merrill Lynch for stocks

not favored by the research department "only once or twice, years ago."

Mr. Vass, Merrill's compliance chief, defended his firm's system. He said that getting approval of independent research ideas generally takes only "three to four days." But he added, "if somebody comes in with an obscure company or a small company, they might take a longer time." And compliance people in general argue that such delays are a small price to pay to protect customers from risky stock plays.

According to some of those interviewed, the defensive research approach reflects a shift in emphasis among the large brokerage houses in recent years away from old-fashioned stock sales to so-called asset accumulation.

"All they want you to do is get out and sell the packaged product, the tax shelters and funds," said a broker with a major firm. "The brokers are strictly salesman, that's what they are taught. New guys come back from training and they don't even know how to write a stock ticket. That's no exaggeration." The in-house mutual funds, in particular, offer brokers higher initial payouts than stock commissions and bring in what the firms view as captive money, which will pay management fees for years. For brokers trained in that school, stock selection may indeed be foreign ground. "Knowing what I know about brokers in general," said a Merrill executive, "if I were taught management at a brokerage firm I would want to have restrictions."

3. Knowing who will do it with you—or for you

Building a personal financial planning team is like building a major league sports organization. You must have enough interpersonal skills to hire the best players you can afford and be adept at directing their subsequent contributions.

For example, when you invest in a product or vehicle directly (by yourself), you should certainly know the following:

1. What is the investment's asset category and general characteristics?
2. What is the legal name of the investment?
3. What is the minimum required amount of investment?
4. What is the projected yield?
5. What is the projected term?
6. How liquid is this investment?
7. What are the potential risks?
8. Have I received at least one other opinion recommending this investment?

Investing Through Brokerage Firms

Several different types of brokerage firms are available to the consumer. Most traditional stock and bond houses emphasize the stock market and current investment decisions. Most avoid comprehensive and long-term financial planning. However, a few do make a serious attempt, or at least retain a few competent planning practitioners. Nevertheless, the best service usually goes to the clients with the largest accounts. There is no substitute for a face-to-face (or at least voice-to-voice) interview to determine if there is basic compatibility with the planner or broker who will be relied on to implement any portion of your financial plan.

Other brokerage firms emphasize financial planning as well as traditional brokerage (security trading) services. These firms tend to be newer and smaller, and as a result, they may have more emphasis on the analytical and planning aspects of the process, with less emphasis on current research for specific securities. There is no reason not to use more than one firm when you feel it is appropriate. There is no law against using a full-service

house one day, and a smaller, boutique-type specialty firm the next, and a discount broker the day after that. It makes sense, especially starting out, to keep an open mind and check out the competition.

Dealing with Attorneys

We have all heard jokes about greedy or contentious, litigation-oriented attorneys—but when your life's assets are at stake, a good lawyer is indispensable.

The first thing to find out from an attorney is whether or not he or she will be comfortable working with you as a part of a "team." That means the attorney you use should be willing to work closely with your financial planner, insurance agent, accountant, and/or whoever else you decide to hire for your personal financial planning team. If the attorney seems negative about the idea, then look up someone else. Once attitude has been cleared as a hurdle, discuss the attorney's expertise. If your biggest concern is taxation, don't pick an attorney who specializes in divorce. However, most legal general practitioners should be competent to care for a beginning financial plan: simple wills, trusts, or a review of the legal ramifications of special investment opportunities—such as closely held businesses or limited partnerships.

Finally, as with all of your "team" members, be clear and forward in asking about compensation at the beginning of the interview. There is no point going further if the money is going to present an insoluble problem from the outset.

Dealing with Accountants

If you need bookkeeping services, you may not necessarily need a certified public accountant (CPA). However, if you are a businessperson with several different accounting entities and requirements for tax and business planning during the year (and several tax returns to file), then by all means find yourself a good CPA. Again, you should focus on the *compatibility* and the *money*. If you leap over both hurdles easily, then you have found yourself another team member.

Dealing with Insurance Agents

Here again, the caveat is to use the specialists you need. Perhaps you have one agent who is great for property and casualty policies (home, auto, and so on), but doesn't know much about or deal much with life and disability products. If so, you will need two agents or brokers to obtain the protection you need. Just be certain that your agent reflects your own attitudes about money and understands your goals. Independent agents are normally the best place to get a "sense of the market," but certain one-company agents may actually come up with either the best rates or best service in certain or specialized areas. Therefore, the best idea is to keep an open mind and shop for benefits instead of "one size fits all" off-the-rack insurance products.

How to Use Management Consultants

If you are an entrepreneur or executive for a large corporation, don't forget to check into the many management consulting firms that have existed for many years or may be servicing your firm in other fields. While their services may not all be appropriate, many offer personal financial advice to senior executives of client firms. These resources can be especially valuable in optimizing the links between your money-earning (salary and profit-sharing plans) and your personal wealth-building goals.

Using Financial Underwriters

If you have a business interest that involves the potential for public or private offerings either now or in the future, check with one or more underwriters (typically broker dealers or investment bankers) who are active in your field or industry. They may be helpful in the financial planning process if a strategy of "taking your company public" is a possibility or in gaining access to the initial public offerings (IPOs) of other firms.

DON'T FORGET TO REVIEW AND REVISE YOUR PLAN

Change is the one constant in the financial world. Every investment decision you make today may be invalidated by economic development tomorrow. Keeping your mind open to new ideas and new economic realities is a modern survival skill. Computers and their software are advancing at an ever faster pace and can be powerful financial planning tools. Information on all financial products is becoming more complete, more time-sensitive, and more complex to understand, so the skills of self-education are as important to your plan's success as your initial implementation steps. Take financial management and investment courses, read financial periodicals, check your statements from investment sponsors, and read their annual reports. In short, learn more every year about your own money and supervise actively the wealth-building team you've created.

The planning process is ongoing. There is no end to it—simply transitions between successes and setbacks—all leading to steadily increasing financial muscle.

CHAPTER 21

PUTTING IT ALL TOGETHER: ASSET ALLOCATION STRATEGIES

A GLANCE AHEAD

Investment markets have undergone dramatic changes over the past decade and even more changes will come as a result of the stock market collapse of October, 1987. Investors have to deal with unprecedented high volatility in traditional markets such as stocks and bonds. At the same time they are bombarded with sales pitches for numerous new, supposedly "better," and certainly more complex investment vehicles.

In this chapter you'll explore the methodology that many professional investment advisors and money managers have used to achieve above-average returns in a wide variety of economic environments. You'll learn

* *Why risk considerations are just as important as profit potential*
* *The power of diversification over many asset categories in delivering higher, more consistent total returns*
* *The difference between adding value with diversification and merely holding different assets*
* *How to design a "low-involvement" portfolio that fits your investor personality*

* *The strengths and weaknesses of market timing*
* *Why asset category selection is far more important than individual security selection*

A CHANGING INVESTMENT ENVIRONMENT

The 1970s and 1980s will be remembered in years to come as an important transition period in investment history. Although stock and bond markets have gone through phases of high volatility before in the twentieth century (notably 1929 through 1933 and the late 1960s), the Wall Street "Crash of '87" has shown it is now an accepted fact of investment life. In the long run, all markets are volatile.

Even before the crash, the stock market in 1986 and 1987 was subject to huge daily swings despite a background of generally slow but steady economic growth. This fluctuation would be easier to understand if the markets were continously being jolted by surprises. But beyond the crash itself, the only real surprise has been the accuracy of the consensus economic forecasts of slow but steady growth for the past three years. Historically, consensus forecasts have been notoriously wrong.

Just when high inflation and high interest rates seemed to be facts of economic life, the tide turned. Throughout the 1980s, disinflation and declining interest rates (until mid-1987) defined the economic environment. This decline resulted in a booming (and ultimately over-valued) stock market dating from the dramatic bottom in the summer of 1982. Adjusting for real inflation, the stock market had made little progress for the previous 16 years, dating from the major peak in 1966.

Even real estate, the best investment for many Americans in the tumultuous 1970s, fell on hard times in the 1980s. Office space was grossly overbuilt. Office vacancy rates went over 20% nationwide, with some areas suffering over 50% vacancy rates! Even housing fell on hard times as rents actually declined in many parts of the country. Some areas were devastated. In Houston, over 14,000 apartment units were bulldozed!

Tax law changes have steadily stripped away many of the comparative advantages of owning real estate in recent years. Many limited partnerships have gone bankrupt that were organized around highly leveraged real estate projects to take advantage of tax preferences. In 1987, Equity Programs Investment Corporation was forced into placing 356 real estate limited partnerships into bankruptcy!

The United States' role as world economic leader is being challenged. Of the 10 largest banks in the world, 5 are now Japanese. Foreign companies have made major inroads in industries formerly dominated by U.S. companies. The two largest food companies in the world are Unilever of the United Kingdom and Nestlé of Switzerland. U.S. Steel has lagged behind IRI of Italy as the largest metal manufacturing corporation in the world. Only two of the largest four oil companies are U.S. companies.

Even more perplexing has been the demise of tried and true economic relationships. The current economic expansion has already set a peacetime longevity record. By October 1987 the economic upturn was in its fifty-ninth month—two times longer than the average. Yet despite this favorable background, the stock market tumbled, business failures are near historical peaks, and bank and thrift failures are at levels not seen since the Great Depression.

Individual consumers have not been spared. Consumer installment loan and mortgage delinquencies are near all-time highs despite the lowest unemployment rate in eight years! Consumers are heavily burdened with debt. Debt service requirements constitute a record proportion of income.

Even formerly accepted economic relationships seem out of kilter. In the 1970s high money supply growth was blamed for the high inflation rates. In the 1980s we've seen growth rates as high or even higher while inflation declined!

The 1986 Tax Reform Act has thrown yet another wrench into the works. It has literally changed not only many long-held investment practices but also how you should manage your business and your personal financial affairs.

Meanwhile investment alternatives have exploded. The first step in the deregulation of the banking industry began in the 1970s with the rise of money market funds. Things have developed rapidly since then. Now you can speculate on interest rates or the stock market itself with futures, options, or options on futures. You can even speculate on stock market rises and falls through CDs!

Today is indeed the "age of information." High technology has ushered in a flood of information. As a result it's easy to "drown" under the onslaught of available material. The problem is no longer one of obtaining information, but rather is one of winnowing out the useful nuggets of data. Today, anyone can readily access a mountain of details. Understanding and making practical use of the data are the real challenges.

Never have there been more and greater opportunities for your investments. Unfortunately, the very growth in the variety of investment alternatives carries with it grave risks for the unprepared. Later in this chapter we outline an investment approach that will help you minimize risk while still yielding above-average returns.

Building Your Portfolio: The Beginning Steps

As we've discussed in previous chapters, it is important to know where you are before you can plan where you want to go. You'll need to know how much much you are worth now. Calculate your net worth by adding up what you own (your assets) and subtracting what you owe (your liabilities). Far from being a tedious exercise in dumping numbers, it is an important and recurring step in building and keeping a higher net worth.

After you've accomplished the preliminary financial planning described in Part II of this book, you'll know how much you'll be able to invest on a regular basis to achieve your goals. Remember, even a savings account is an investment. How much are you able to save, and how will that money be best deployed?

Allocating Multiple Assets to Achieve Your Goals

We'd all like to get rich (or richer, anyway!) with our investments. If you read the junk mail investment solicitations or just the ads in many investment publications, you know that many people are out there offering systems or advice to make you rich. If it were that easy to get rich, we'd all be millionaires.

Robert Nurock, a panelist on *Wall Street Week*, advertises his investment advisory newsletter with the slogan "Get rich slowly!" Sound advice. Sure, getting rick quick certainly sounds more fun. But one indisputable fact of investment life is that no one *knows* the future with certainty. Your investment approach must be designed to minimize losses from the inevitable surprises that will occur.

In this chapter we emphasize the necessity of keeping your losses small, as the single most important factor in long-term investment success. Consider: if you lose 50% of your capital on a single investment fling, you need a 100% gain to get back to even! If you are able to limit your losses to 5%, it only takes a a 5.3% gain to recoup your principal.

In defining your investment strategy, you must deal with the element of risk. No matter how smart you or your advisor may be, mistakes will be made. A typical strategy in pursuit of personal financial goals would include

1. Preserving your capital; never taking a risk so large that it would devastate your municipal investment.

2. Achieving positive net returns after inflation and taxes.
3. Earning returns competitive with an objective measuring stick such as the S&P 500.

Your personal strategy may be more or less aggressive. It is most important to focus on the risk you're willing, financially able, and psychologically prepared to take.

The third element is not just a restatement of the first. Many people think they are grand speculators. Often, though, these same people get very tense or worried over minor adverse price movements. An old Wall Street saw says, "Sell down to the sleeping point"—the price that allows you to sleep at night. If your investment positions keep you in a continual state of stress, you have not designed the correct system for you.

Professional investors are usually calm because they know their complete trading plan in advance. They know how much they are willing to risk on each investment. More importantly, they are able to follow the discipline necessary to ensure that a manageable loss does not turn into a disaster.

The Multiple-asset Allocation Concept

There are two basic ways to approach your investments. You can concentrate on one particular asset category, or you can assemble a portfolio of different asset types. Some advisors advocate the first approach, saying, "Put all your eggs in the basket you know, and watch that basket closely!"

Every investment cycle has its outstanding performers. During the late 1970s tangible assets, particularly gold and silver, were the best-performing investments. Bonds were the place to be from 1982 through 1984. In the past few years, the stock market has drawn most of the attention at least until the October crash.

Since people generally want to earn the highest returns, we have a natural tendency to buy what is doing the best. Unfortunately, because of the cyclic nature of asset prices, risk increases with every advance in price. Gold at $500 was riskier than when it was $200. The stock market at 2,700 on the Dow was a higher-risk investment than when it was 700—as many investors found out on "Black Monday!"

For single-asset investments, greater risk inevitably accompanies higher potential returns. In the late 1970s, many people felt that the U.S. economic system was on the verge of collapse and that gold and silver offered the only salvation. Many people bought the precious metals all the way up even though risk became much greater as prices soared. That was fine as long as their paper profits built up. But then most speculators saw it all turn to dust (albeit "gold" dust!) in a matter of weeks. The fall came so unexpectedly, so swiftly that even billionaires were caught holding a rather sizeable—and empty—bag!

Of course,that incident was not so isolated. The stock market was just as liable to speculative excesses as precious metals or real estate. By August 1987, the stock market had posted a 40% gain for the year. Many investors and advisors didn't recognize the added risk inherent in the much higher prices. They had become so complacent that they greeted a record 91-point drop on October 6 with yawns. The market continued its plunge that week to finish down a record 158 points. It then plunged an additional 235 points the following week, including two more record single-day drops of 95 and 108 points—only to climax in the disastrous "Black Monday" collapse of over 500 points. Analysts and investors were stunned by the magnitude of the reverse. A market that had not set back more than 10% for three years suddenly was down over 20% in a single day.

The moral of the story is simple: prepare for the unexpected. When everyone is confident about the prospects for a particular investment, look out!

The multiple-asset allocation concept is designed to minimize risk in any one asset class, while still enabling you to earn good returns through a wider range of opportunities. This concept is quite different, however, from merely diversifying over a number of stocks or bonds.

Jeremy Black of InterFinancial Corporation in Denver notes that there are three main determinants of pension fund portfolio returns: timing, asset policy, and individual selection.

Moreover, he says, studies have shown that over 90% of the net return comes from the asset policy decisions. This pattern was illustrated very well by the performance of university endowment funds as detailed in *Fortune* magazine, October 26, 1987. The seven largest funds returned an average of over 16% for the preceding three years. This performance contrasts with that of the New York University endowment fund. In 1981 the NYU trustees decided to abandon multiple assets and to buy bonds. Despite having highly qualified trustees, including CBS chief executive Laurence Tisch and the chairman of Bear Stearns, Alan C. Greenberg, the NYU performance ranked near the bottom for the 10-year period ended June 1986.

No one knows for sure how the future will develop. By adopting a diversified portfolio incorporating slightly correlated assets, you can reduce risk without harming return. Different asset categories perform better in certain environments.

Bailard, Biehl, & Kaiser, a money management firm located in San Mateo, California, has done in-depth research on the multiple-asset approach. Using five major asset classes—domestic stock, domestic bonds, real estate, cash and equivalents, and foreign securities—they put together the BB&K Diversified Portfolio Index. This index assumes that a portfolio is divided evenly among the five major asset classes. Every quarter year, the portfolio is realigned to 20% for each category.

Over the 20-year period from 1966 through 1985, the BB&K Index showed an annual return of 10.2%. The S&P 500 earned a 9.4% annual return in the comparable period. Most significantly, though, the BB&K Index clearly demonstrates the chief value of multiple-asset diversification: lower risk. Risk, as measured by the standard deviation of annual returns in that time period, was only 50% that of the S&P.

Many investors make the mistake of thinking they have diversified their portfolio when they've simply purchased a variety of individual stocks. Yet study after study shows that the most important factor in stock price movement is the overall market's direction. That's where the concept of correlation comes into play. If all the asset classes in your portfolio are closely correlated—that is, if they move in the same general direction under the same conditions—you haven't really diversified. In an inflationary environment, gold and real estate will be performance leaders. Stocks provide a hedge in the early stages of an inflation. Bonds, however, would be hurt as higher interest rates accompany inflation. Cash and equivalents will provide some measure of purchasing power protection as interest rates rise, but little appreciation potential.

In a disinflationary environment such as the period since 1982, bonds and stocks will be leading performers. Gold and real estate will lag. International securities have been sterling performers. This merry-go-round effect cushions your portfolio from adverse price movements.

STRUCTURING YOUR PORTFOLIO

You can take two different approaches to the multiple-asset portfolio, depending on your investor personality, time available for money management, and investment vehicles you choose.

Permanent Portfolios

A permanent or fixed-mix approach is most suitable for those investors who do not have the time or inclination to devote to close tracking of their investments. In this approach, you merely divide your investment monies equally between the asset categories you have selected. For example, if you have decided on domestic stocks, bonds, foreign securities, gold, cash and its equivalents, and real estate, divide your investment funds into six equal parcels.

At regular intervals, you will need to readjust your portfolio to bring all asset categories back to an equal percentage. Some investors review their portfolios annually, while others prefer to do so quarterly.

The permanent portfolio approach has a number of advantages:

- Minimum time is required.

- By distancing yourself from daily market "noise," you can avoid emotional decision making.
- Maximizes the return of long-term reliable trends, because you are always investing on an average down basis when you readjust your portfolio.
- Transaction fees are kept to a minimum.

Of course, there are some disadvantages, too:

- Involvement and sense of satisfaction are minimal.
- You settle for "median" returns.
- The potential for greater profits is sacrificed to achieving greater safety.
- You can't take advantage of short-term timing signals.
- Your flexibility is limited.

Dynamic Portfolios

Markets go through cycles. According to a study done by Saloman Brothers, gold, oil, and real estate all posted double-digit annual returns during the inflationary 1970s. Yet during the first five years of the 1980s both oil and gold showed negative annual returns! Meanwhile, T-bills, bonds, and stocks, which had lagged behind in the 1970s, all posted healthy double-digit annual returns.

The very fact of uncertainty about the future ensures there will always be business cycles. If we all had perfect knowledge of the future—such as what amount of what product would be demanded, at what time, and for what price—business cycles would disappear. Socialist "planned economies" have proven poor at filling minimum consumer needs, to say nothing of eliminating business cycles. Individual human beings, not committees, still make the millions of daily economic decisions necessary to keep modern markets on the move.

Precise timing is impossible, despite the many claims you may hear. However, it is possible to identify long-term trends. By studying how various assets perform under different economic environments, you can weight your portfolio toward assets that have the greatest likelihood of performing well in the future.

For example, Bailard, Biehl, & Kaiser's staff have developed a number of valuation models they use for each asset class. Their asset allocation approach involves a detailed look at possible economic scenarios. They then calculate the potential returns for each asset under each potential environment. They calculate the probabilities of each scenarios and then weight the potential returns.

When they identify an undervalued asset, they increase their portfolio's allocation in that asset class. When assets they hold appreciate and move to overvalued status in comparison to their models, they sell into strength and take their profits. For example, in the early 1980s their models identified stocks as being undervalued. They increased their allocation levels for stocks and decreased it for real estate. In March 1987, they began to lighten stock positions (even though they felt the market had further to go to the upside), because the risk was increased and other assets began to look undervalued. The key to their success has been the ability to profit from long-term trends and not get bogged down with short-term trading.

Jeremy Black of InterFinancial Corporation takes a different approach. His firm's staff have compiled a detailed performance record for the various asset categories they follow. They calculate the returns that each asset has earned over time. They also figure in risk (as measured by standard deviation). They then look at how each asset correlates to the others.

Their program, called RAMCAP (Risk Adjusted Multiple Capital Asset Program), is then used to evaluate portfolios or to design portfolios to meet specific return and risk parameters. Rather than doing any economic projection, the program is based on the average reward and risk based on historical performance. By using the correlation coefficients of the various assets, they can design portfolios to stay within specified risk parameters.

For example, their work has shown that managed futures accounts have a *negative* correlation to stocks and bonds. That means that inclusion of managed futures as one asset category can significantly reduce your portfolio's overall variability. If stocks and bonds

fall, managed futures should appreciate. before this work was done, it was thought that gold provided the best countercyclical hedge for stocks. But both stocks and gold benefit in the early stages of inflation. Managed futures appears to be an even better pure hedge.

Black believes that the value of the multiple-asset approach rests in its distance from "timing." He cites studies showing that timing may actually have a negative effect on portfolio returns. He does concede, however, that it is not wise to plunge into all your positions at once, even in a diversified portfolio. For example, if RAMCAP calls for a particular client to have 40% invested position in stocks, the firm does not go out and buy the full allotment immediately.

Dynamic multiple-asset allocation offers some distinct advantages:

- Good timing can yield above-average results.
- Diversification still reduces overall risk.
- The client gains "hands on" involvement and sense of accomplishment.
- Greater flexibility allows investors to take advantage of short-term developments.

But we've yet to find the perfect approach for all investors. Some problems with the dynamic approach are that

- It is time consuming.
- Transaction costs are higher.
- Poor timing may result in greater losses.

CONSIDERATIONS IN IMPLEMENTING DYNAMIC MULTIPLE-ASSET ALLOCATIONS

Dynamic portfolio asset allocation should be done only with consistent objective guidelines. "Gut feel" is simply not good enough. You can develop your own guidelines or follow the advice of a professional manager. Whichever you decide, do it consistently!

 You may want to put together a "panel of experts" of your own. Take a stock market advisor who has a good record. When his or her position is "buy," increase your allocation. Sell down (though not out!) when he or she signals "sell." Use the same tactic for each asset class you've selected. Quantify the percentages you intend to use with which signals before embarking on the program. Remember, the whole process will be useless if you don't have an objective way to implement the signals.

When you select an advisor, it is important to find one who makes sense to you. There are many successful approaches (and many losing ways, too). You will find it difficult to follow the necessary discipline if you're not in tune with your advisor. Investment advisory letters advertise widely. Try a number of sample subscriptions.

If you prefer to meet with an advisor or planner in person, be prepared with a list of questions that are important to you. You would be mighty lucky if you found the ideal person the first time. Be prepared to spend time and effort in locating the right people to work with you. A good effort at the beginning will save much aggravation later.

 Some people (including many high-priced analysts) use simple moving averages to signal purchases and sales. When the S&P 500 rises above its rising 30-week moving average, you could increase your position. When the 30-week average turns down, sell a portion. When the S&P penetrates the average, sell to your minimum position. The same method could be used with similar indexes for most asset categories.

Remember what we've said earlier: 90% of successful investing is portfolio allocation. Only 10% of your return over time will be the result of timing and investment selection. Yet 95% of the information and advice that is so aggressively marketed is directed to market timing or stock selection. Don't be misled by extravagant claims. If it sounds too good to be true, it probably is!

James Arnold, editor of the stock market advisory letter, *The Primary Trend* (700 North Water Street, Milwaukee, Wisconsin 53202) summed up the key to successful investing: "The secret of successful investing is so simple, it is derided by those who claim to have all the answers . . . the secret is to avoid disasters." The multiple-asset allocation concept is the single best method for ensuring that you avoid the disasters in your own portfolio.

Conservative Permanent Portfolio

1. 20% U.S. stocks
2. 20% international stocks
3. 20% long bonds (10-year or longer Treasuries)
4. 20% money market funds
5. 10% gold (mutual funds diversified into North American mines and bullion)
6. 10% real estate

Aggressive Permanent Portfolio

1. 20% U.S. stocks
2. 20% U.S. bonds (Treasuries or municipals for high tax bracket)
3. 10% money market (funds or instruments directly)
4. 10% real estate investment trusts (REITs)
5. 20% international securities
6. 10% managed futures account
7. 10% gold (mutual funds diversified into North American mines and bullion)

Conservative 1988 Dynamic Portfolio

1. 15% money market funds
2. 20% U.S. stocks
3. 20% International securities (stocks and bonds)
4. 15% real estate (REITS or RELPs)
5. 10% gold (mutual funds diversified into North American mines and bullion)
6. 20% U.S. bonds

Aggressive 1988 Dynamic Portfolio

1. 10% money market funds
2. 25% U.S. stocks
3. 25% U.S. bonds
4. 15% international securities (stocks and bonds)
5. 5% real estate (REITs or RELPs)
6. 10% gold (mutual funds diversified into North American mines and/or bullion)
7. 10% managed futures account

Top-performing Stock Advisories

1. *Prudent Speculator*
2. *The Dines Letter*
3. *Value Line Investment Survey*
4. *The Zweig Forecast*
5. *Market Logic*
6. *The Professional Investor*
7. *Dow Jones Forecasts*
8. *The Chartist*
9. *Telephone Switch Newsletter*
10. *S&P Outlook*

CHAPTER 22

THE CRASH OF 1987

On Friday, October 16, 1987, the stock market capped off a disastrous week with a record-breaking 108.35-point drop on the Dow Jones Industrial Average. Analysts and investors alike were very worried by the huge record-setting volume of 338,480,000, which was over 36 million shares more than the previous record volume day January 23, 1987 (an up day). For the week, the market was down 235.47 points, setting yet another record.

Investor sentiment, which had been steadfastly bullish for the past three years, was finally shaken. Friday's precipitous collapse in the last hours of trading left even experienced professionals stunned. In the midst of the hectic trading, one stock index options floor trader on the American Options Exchange shrieked, "It's the end of the world." For the first time in years, the bull market seemed mortally wounded.

Friday's collapse followed closely on the heels of the previous single-day drop record: a 95.46 points only two days earlier, on October 14. And the 57.61 point-drop on the intervening day, October 15, the sixth largest single day plunge up that time. The latest and worst in a series of "October Massacres" really began with yet another record-breaking fall of 91.55 points on October 6.

BLACK MONDAY

On Friday, bullish investor enthusiasm was seriously shaken for the first time in years. But many observers were still blithely dismissing the chance of a 1929-like crash. After all, they pointed out, even after the two worst weekly point drops in history the market had only lost 15.01%—well within the definition of a "correction." The market had risen over 40% in 1987 alone, without a single setback of even 10%.

As trading opened Monday, October 19, 1987, few traders, analysts, or observers had any idea of the history that would be made that day. Apprehension gripped even the most experienced traders as the market began to slide, while volume increased. Then the collapse began in earnest: down 200 points, down 250 points in a matter of minutes. Even the normal din of the hustle and bustle on the New York Stock Exchange was silenced as the tape inexorably spelled out the unimaginable: down 300, down 400, and finally down 508 on the close!

In a mere 6 1/2 hours of trading, $500 billion was lost. Volume surged to 604,330,000 shares, nearly double Friday's record volume. Few were spared. Losing stocks outnumbered gainers 49 to 1, one of the most lopsided ratios in market history. Volume measures told an even worse story: the downside volume outnumbered the upside 533 to 1!

All 30 stocks in the Dow Jones Industrial Average—representative of the biggest and best that America can offer—were clobbered. Merck, one of the hottest stocks of the year, fell 33 points, an 18% drop. IBM—the most visible computer company in a world increasingly dependent on computers—also dropped 33 points, a 24% fall. Eastman Kodak dropped 25 1/2 points, a 30% plunge.

Other major corporations were pummeled as well. CBS fell 42 1/8, a 22% fall. Teledyne was down 49 3/4, Digital Equipment down 41 1/2, Litton Industries off 24 1/2. These were only a few of the thousands of stocks affected in the collapse.

Foreign companies fared no better. Matsushita Electric slid 37. Honda was down 18 7/8. Hitachi got hammered down 15 5/8 points.

Not surprisingly, the only group to avoid the carnage was gold. Newmont Gold Mining actually climbed 3 3/4, while Callahan Mining posted a 2 1/4 gain.

Worse Than 1929

Before Monday, October 19, investors had comforted themselves by remarking that the large daily point swings of early October were not really records when viewed as a percentage of the total Dow. Their equanimity, however, was shattered by Black Monday's plunge. The market fell 22.6%, easily surpassing the 12.8% drop of Black Tuesday, October 28, 1929, when the market fell 12.8%.

In fact, the only greater percentage fall was in the market's infancy when it fell 17.42 points on December 12, 1914, for a 24.39% decline. October's collapse was by far the largest drop for the mature stock market.

The combined decline for two days, Friday (October 16) and Monday (October 19), totalled 30%. This compares to a 23.6% fall for the comparable period on October 28 and 29, 1929.

By the close of Monday, the market as measured by the DJIA had given back the whole spectacular gain of the previous nine months and was actually showing an 8.3% loss. From the August 25 high of 2,722.42, the market had contracted 36.1%.

Some analysts were quick to point out that the 36.1% drop was already sufficient to qualify as a bear market. One pundit even observed that technology of automated buying and selling had enabled the financial marketplace to compress a two-year bear market into 2-months.

The days after the collapse were very volatile. Investors struggled to come to grips with a whole new environment. On Tuesday, October 20, the market opened 200 points higher, only to fall during the day to a negative trough, and then rallied to finish up a record 108 points! Previously unheard-of 100-point swings became commonplace over the next two weeks.

THE OTHER INVESTMENT MARKETS

In March 1987, after almost 5 years of rising prices as interest rates declined, the bull bond market came to an abrupt halt. Although there were the inevitable wide swinging gyrations that have become characteristic of today's financial scene, prices in general tended to fall. Hardest hit were the long-term bonds, as inflation fears increased over the year.

First, the heightened tension in the Middle East pushed oil prices higher. In 1968 the Consumer Price Index rose a mere 1.1% due to the sharp collapse in oil prices. When it became clear that the bottom had already been reached in these crucial prices, worried investors moved out of long-term bonds.

After anemic growth throughout 1986, the CPI posted sharply higher rates for the first quarter of 1987, climbing at a 6.2% rate. Other indicators also pointed to higher inflation, which inevitably brings higher interest rates. The Producer Price Index jumped sharply higher, too. The climb climaxed in April, with a 0.7% increase for that month alone.

Commodity prices edged higher, as shown by the Commodity Research Bureau's Index of Commodity Prices, which rose to 12-month highs early in the year. Gold, the classic inflation indicator, climbed steadily higher. While gold bullion was posting 15% gains, gold stocks soared sharply higher. Gains as much as 60–80% were common.

By the close of the third quarter, gold mutual funds were the leading industry group by a wide margin. Nine of the top ten performers for 1987 were gold funds:

1. Keystone Precious Metals
2. IDS Precious Metals

3. Shearson Precious Metals
4. USAA Gold
5. Van Eck Gold/Resources
6. Franklin Gold
7. Midas Gold Shares
8. United Gold & Government
9. G. T. Global Growth—Japan (the only nongold fund)
10. Fidelity Select—American Gold

There is a highly reliable *inverse* correlation between bond prices and the price of gold. When gold moves higher, bonds drop. In the face of these ominous inflationary signs, combined with the weak U.S. dollar, bond prices finally broke and moved sharply lower.

Before the climb began, 30-year Treasury bond yields had dropped to 7.5%. In what proved to be one of the worst bond market collapses of all time, yields on 30-year Treasuries moved to 10.4% on Friday, October 16. The consensus in the bond pits was very bearish. In September, the *Wall Street Journal* had even headlined a story "Debt-Securities Prices May Slide for Years, Many Analysts Think."

Bond prices sank across the board, with bond mutual funds leading the way. The phenomenal growth of the mutual fund industry since 1982 has been largely led by growth in bond funds, accounting for almost 65% of the increase. By mid-1987, though, rising interest rates and falling bond prices had discouraged bond fund investors. Heavy redemptions were being made as investors were lured by the promise of greater returns in the stock market.

Municipal bonds were particularly hard hit. By the end of September, most municipal bond funds had posted negative total returns (price change and reinvested income) ranging from a minus (2.1%) to a minus (8.0%).

Bonds and Cash on Black Monday

The bond markets opened lower on Monday, October 19, as they had been doing for weeks. The pervasive bearish sentiment was still very evident. However, as the stock market crash began in earnest, bonds began to strengthen. As the day progressed, money

flows began to switch as investors fled the stock market. Dividend yields on the Dow Jones Industrial stock were below 2%, and Treasury bonds were yielding over 10%. These two factors, plus the safety of government guarantee, quickly attracted investor money.

The bond market rally, which began amid much uncertainty, suddenly exploded. The "flight to quality" overwhelmed even the most bearish of bond investors. Bonds finished sharply higher on Monday. They continued to be the strongest factor in the financial markets for weeks thereafter.

The sudden change in investor sentiment from bearish to bullish for bonds, and vice versa for stocks, has little historical precedent. Investors simply scurried to find a safe haven until the dust settled.

The change was dramatic. Yields on the benchmark 30-year Treasury bonds plunged from 10.4% to below 10% on Black Monday and in the days following. By early November, the yields on 30-year Treasuries had dropped below 9%.

It wasn't easy going though. On Tuesday, October 21, 1987 the bond market traded in one of the most chaotic sessions ever. The 30-year bond prices jumped all over the map—at one point, they were up over 7 points! They finished up a still strong 2 3/4 points. Each 1-point move equals $10 per $1,000 face value bond. One analyst couldn't believe the wide-swinging trading: "We've seen a super interest rate cycle in one day."

People who didn't buy bonds immediately rushed into money market instruments. Money market funds had been growing steadily since the beginning of the bond market break in April 1987. The bond market rout accelerated, with Treasury yields going to double digits. Money fund assets climbed to new record highs in nearly every week leading up to Black Monday.

Short-term interest rates also dropped sharply as the Federal Reserve pumped additional reserves into the monetary system. The benchmark federal funds rate (the rate at which banks loan money to each other for meeting reserve requirements) dropped to 6.15% on October 21, from 7.07% on the 20th, and 7.61% on October 19.

The International Markets

In the weeks leading up to Black Monday, the international security markets were trading strongly higher. Japan's stock market was highly volatile, though the uptrend was intact. New highs were being reached despite P/E ratios that averaged over 60!

London was also strong, after the re-election of Margaret Thatcher and moves to lower interest rates. Other European markets were sedate, with little remarkable activity.

The Pacific Rim countries had featured the strongest markets for the past few years. Singapore remained strong. Hong Kong's highly speculative market had recently embarked on another upthrust to new highs.

The only worrisome signs in the international markets were the climbing interest rates in Japan and Germany just before the crash. Japan's rates had climbed significantly in the months before the crash, much to the chagrin of U.S. authorities.

International Markets on Black Monday

The response of markets around the world to the record-breaking collapse on Wall Street was swift. London's important market plunged steeply. The Financial Times 30-share Index fell 183.7 points to 1,629.2, a 10.1% drop.

Other European markets also fell dramatically. Frankfurt was off 43.85 points, to 569.85, a 7.14% tumble. Zurich's market fell 71.3 points to 558.2, an 11.3% fall. Brussels' stock index was off 504.4 to 4,303.42, a 10.5% drop.

The Pacific Rim markets were not spared. Hong Kong fell 420.81 points to 3,362.39. That's an 11.1% decline. Singapore fell 169.14 points to 1,223.28, a 12.2% reduction in value. The Malaysian market also fell over 11%. All three markets registered single-day point loss records.

Only Tokyo was able to hold up fairly well the first day, dropping 620.18 to 25,746.56, a mere 2.53%. However, by the following day selling moved into high gear and Tokyo's market posted the largest single-day percentage loss of its history: *minus* 14.9%.

Subsequent trading action in the international markets proved as volatile as U.S. trading. By Wednesday London's Financial Times 30-share Index surged 88.1 points to 1,527.3, for a new record single-day point gain! Tokyo also surged back on Wednesday, posting a 9.3% gain. Other European markets joined the upmove. Frankfurt climbed 6.8%, and Zurich jumped 4.9%.

By the time the dust settled, though, volatility—not particular price levels—was the main feature in all markets. It is interesting to note the net changes for key markets for the time period from October 16 to October 28:

Tokyo	−14%
London	−29%
Frankfurt	−20%
Paris	−25%

International bond markets, which had been drifting lower, also sharply appreciated as the respective governments stepped in to push rates lower. The following table shows the change in yield for 10-year government bonds for the major foreign markets.

Country	Rate 10/16	10/28
Japan	6.4%	5.7%
Britain	10.4	9.5
West Germany	7.2	6.7
France	11.0	10.2

Only Hong Kong, among major international stock markets, dropped more than London. The Hong Kong market was closed soon after the New York crash; when it reopened, the breakdown made up for lost time. By the beginning of November, the market was down 37.4%.

In Europe, only Zurich's markets posted a comparable decline, falling 23% as measured by the Credit Suisse Index. Combined losses in foreign markets during the October 16 to 28 period have been estimated at close to the $1 trillion that was lost in the U.S. markets in October.

Gold and Commodities

Gold is generally thought to be the single best inflation indicator and hedge. Some analysts, however, note that gold's role extends beyond that of inflation only. Harry Browne, noted analyst and author, makes the case that gold is the classic chaos hedge—more than merely an inflation hedge. In times of uncertainty and turmoil, investors turn to gold for an important sense of security.

There could be *nothing* more chaotic than a 508-point 600-million-share down day in the stock market. As noted earlier, the only stocks that bucked the devastating downdraft on October 19 were gold shares. Gold bullion, which had been trading in a narrow price range in the preceding weeks, also rallied, strongly soaring $10.10 on that day. That was the highest level in over four years.

However, even then the price action belied what was to follow. At one time in the day of October 19, gold was over $20 higher, only to close up $10. Traders were caught in a dilemma between buying gold to hedge against the stock market turmoil, and at the same time recognizing the stock selloff as a potentially deflationary sign.

Gold's price surge proved short-lived, however. The following day the dollar strengthened, and gold fell $18.50 to close at $463.20 for current delivery contract on the New York Commodity Exchange. This price action sent strong signals that the inflationary fears that so dominated the bond markets in early 1987 were probably overdone.

Other commodity prices—agriculture and base metals—finished sharply lower on October 19. The Commodity Research Bureau's futures price index of twenty-one raw material prices dropped 3.25 points to 229.43—an unusually large single-day move for the index.

Another key commodity, oil, also had an interesting day. After surging sharply higher at the opening as a result of the U.S. bombing of an Iran oil platform, prices reversed and plunged lower by the day's end. On the New York Mercantile Exchange, crude oil contracts for November delivery traded as high as $20.5 and closed at $19.80. That marked a 42-cent decline for the day. Traders decided that the potential for recession outweighed OPEC's saber-rattling. Oil prices drifted lower over the next few weeks of trading, much to the surprise of many observers who expected prices to stabilize at the $20 level.

HOW DID OTHER FINANCIAL SECTORS HANDLE THE CRASH?

Mutual funds are sold to investors who seek professional management of their stock and bond portfolios. Just how well did these highly touted managers do in the crash? According to Lipper Analytical Services, which monitors mutual fund performance regularly, diversified general equity funds did no worse than the market itself, dropping about 17% for the week ended October.

However, there were certainly losers among individual equity funds. The week ending October 23 provided an ideal test of how well managers were able to contain risk. Broad diversification, even within a single asset class, proved a valuable strategy. Of the ten worst-performing funds for that week, seven were sector funds concentrating on a single industry:

Worst-performing Funds	Down
1. 44 Wall St. Equity	36%
2. Fidelity Select (automation)	36
3. Valsearch Total Return	33
4. Fidelity Select (capital goods)	33
5. Fidelity Select (electronic)	32
6. Fidelity Select (industrial materials)	32
7. New England Zenith (capital growth)	32
8. Financial Portfolio (technology)	32
9. Fidelity Select (computers)	31
10. Hartwell Emerging Growth	31

Standard & Poor 500   17%

Many investors lose sight of the fact that a major consideration in selecting a fund should be how well it does in down markets. Some equity funds significantly outperformed the S&P. The top ten funds include

1. Rightime Blue Chip	+ 0.76%
2. Rightime	− 0.40
3. Paine Webber Asset Allocation	− 1.88
4. Santa Barbara	− 3.27
5. Valley Forge	− 5.17
6. Rea-Graham	− 5.68
7. Dreyfus Capital Value	− 6.03

8. Freedom Gold & Government
  Trust   – 6.09
9. Wellesley Income   – 7.96
10. ABT Utility Income   – 8.06

Unfortunately, the protection normally afforded by international diversification did not pan out immediately, although some foreign markets, particularly Japan, have outperformed the U.S. market since Black Monday. The average international fund was down 16% for the week.

Equities were obviously not the place to be. If you had been following the diversified asset allocation approach we've delineated in these pages, you'd have seen that the silver lining to the collapse was the performance of the fixed-income funds which had been devastated earlier in the year when stocks were reaching new highs. The average fixed-income fund gained 2.3%.

Measured from the stock market peak on August 27 through October 22, were the best-performing fixed income funds

Best-performing fixed-income Funds Up

1. Strong Government Securities   7.10%
2. Govaars Government   4.5
3. Industrial—Bond   4.28
4. RXR Dynamic Government   4.23
5. Treasury First   3.50
6. Dreyfus GNMA   3.43
7. Carnegie High Yield
   Government   2.46
8. Paine Webber Master Global   2.29
9. Principal Preservation
   Government   2.27
10. T. Rowe Price International
    Bond   2.01

After performance, the next question for mutual funds was how well they were able to handle customer orders during those hectic days. There were no problems handling redemptions which may have been aided by the fact that most investors merely switched money from equity funds into money market or fixed-income funds rather than withdrawing it.

Some fund groups did invoke the right to extend payouts for the allowable seven days. Fidelity Investments extended payouts on all its equity funds for redemptions registered after Friday, October 16.

A major problem did develop in the over-the-counter (OTC) market. Rather than executing orders in an open outcry auction system such as exists for listed stocks, OTC stocks are bought and sold through various firms that act as "market makers." The lower liquidity of OTC issues was proven clearly during the October debacle. Many market makers simply refused to answer their phones for fear of having to sell more stock and lose even more money.

For the month of October, the Dow Jones Industrial Average fell 24%. The NASDAQ Composite Index—which is made up of the larger capitalization OTC issues, fell 27% in October. Even worse was the performance of small and medium sized OTC issues which do not have the institutional sponsorship that larger capitalization issues have. By one estimate these smaller issues fell an average of 38% in October.

WHAT CAUSED THE CRASH OF 1987?

No one single profound event triggered the 1987 selloff. Most analysts agree that a series of concerns over time led to a loss of confidence which accelerated once stocks started their plunge. The dive was further exacerbated by computerized or program trading that triggered huge selling programs by institutional investors.

A number of factors have been cited as contributing causes. Chief among them were the continued problems with the trade deficit. Investors' expectations of improving trade figures were dashed yet again with the anemic change seen in the August data (released in October). Even though the August trade deficit narrowed to $15.7 billion, breaking the four-month trend of rising numbers, most analysts had expected much greater improvement. For the first eight months of 1987, the trade deficit was increasing at the far-too-large annual rate of $171.8 billion.

Even U.S. Commerce Secretary Bruce Smart was visibly disappointed: "While we are encouraged by the continuing favorable trend in real terms, it is apparent that our trade deficit continues on an unacceptably high plateau." The weak dollar policy, which saw a 40% depreciation of the dollar over the past 2 years, obviously was not working. The trade picture was not susceptible to simple solutions.

The primary concern of the marketplace (bonds and stocks both declined when the August trade figures were released) was that the persistence of the trade deficit would force the dollar even lower. A lower dollar meant higher inflation and higher interest rates. The inability of the Reagan Administration's weak dollar policy and "jawboning" of our major trading partners were seen as a sign of weakness at a crucial time.

Closely tied to the trade deficit problem was the fear that international cooperation over a united monetary policy was breaking up. On the weekend before the break, Secretary of the Treasury Baker was grousing about West Germany's decision to boost interest rates. His threat to let the U.S. dollar fall below levels agreed on by the Group of Seven (industrialized countries) was viewed as the Reagan Adminstration's last-ditch attempt to force German cooperation. Central banks had poured over $30 billion into the dollar stabilization effort since the Louvre agreement, and the market interpreted the infighting as destructive of all that effort.

West Germany was not the only international culprit. In the weeks before the crash, Japan had also nudged interest higher, putting additional pressure on the U.S.dollar.

Some analysts pointed to the increasing reliance on foreign investors to fund U.S. deficits through purchases of Treasury debt securities. In addition to helping to fund the budget deficit, foreign buying was playing an increasingly important role in driving the stock market higher. In 1986, net foreign purchases of U.S. stocks were $18.9 billion, more than triple the previous record set in 1981. In 1987, that record was surpassed in the first six months!

The argument is that overreliance can be disastrous if foreign investors decide the weak dollar made U.S. investing too expensive. Japanese buyers alone accounted for up to 35% of Treasury debt securities. A pullout therefore could cause substantive changes in the U.S. economy. Our U.S. status as a debtor nation—only a few short years after being the largest creditor nation in the world—has dire implications. These analysts warn that our new status places our economic future in the hands of foreign investors.

All these troubles were aggravated by a general loss of confidence in the Reagan Adminstration itself. Hamstrung by the Iran-Nicaragua controversy, locked in a losing battle over the nomination of Judge Bork, the administration was presenting a leadership vacuum just when the country needed a firm hand on the tiller. True, market psychology is impossible to quantify, but it is nonetheless a key factor. The stock market had been rallying in the face of these problems when the confidence level was high, but subtle changes over time added up to disaster.

And there were other confidence problems, as well. The Federal Reserve, with its crucial role in the fate of the economy, had only recently changed its leadership. Alan Greenspan had replaced the highly respected Paul Volcker. Volcker was credited with steering the economy out of steep inflation into a slow-growth, low-inflation, declining interest rate environment. That environment built the foundation for the greatest stock bull market of all time.

With the election year coming up, the question was widely asked whether Greenspan might prove more susceptible to political pressure than his predecessor. Despite Greenspan's move to raise the discount rate shortly after taking over, many Wall Streeters viewed him as an unknown quantity, and possibly soft on inflation. Greenspan himself had given conflicting signals. First he raised the discount rate, but then in speeches he repeated his view that inflation was not an immediate problem.

Of course, it only took a 508-point drop in the stock market to turn Wall Street itself around. No longer were they clamoring for a tighter monetary policy to ward off inflation. Rather, they almost unanimously applauded Greenspan's decision to pump money into the economy post haste.

Other analysts cited the persistence of the huge budget deficits as the central cause of the crash. Normally in previous expansions, budget deficits shrank dramatically; surpluses even appeared. This time, the longest peacetime expansion in history has been accompanied by huge budget deficits. Even the sharp improvement seen in 1987, caused by an unexpected surge in tax receipts, still left the country with a deficit of over $150 billion!

If the economy slowed down, the budget deficit could explode, draining funds from the private sector and stifling economic progress for years to come. The failure to seriously deal with the problem is causing real concern among foreign as well as domestic investors.

But all these things had been in existence for months. What triggered the fall on that particular day? The answer to that question will never be known with certainty. Market observers point to two primary "timing"-related developments.

Interest rates had risen sharply since March. The rates on long-term Treasury issues has climbed from 7.5 to 10.4%. The cross into double-digit territory had fueled the sharp decline just prior to Black Monday.

At first, long-term rates had moved sharply higher, without much confirmation from short-term rates. However, by late August short-term rates rose steeply. The federal funds and three-month Treasury bill rates jumped over a hundred basis points (1%) in less than eight weeks. A growing economy needs liquidity to fuel its growth. But rising rates made marginal projects unprofitable. The increasing cost of doing business negatively affected the whole economy.

Many analysts had argued for months that the stock market itself was overvalued by most traditional value measures. For example, most analysts use P/E ratios (price divided by earnings) as a method for evaluating the relative value of stocks. By the August peak, the P/E ratio for the S&P Index was over 20. Whenever that level had been seen in the past, it had indicated that stocks were fully valued. The last time those levels had been seen was in the late 1960s just before the long fall experienced by most stocks. That level was also seen in 1929!

Some analysts had argued that traditional valuation methods were not appropriate to this market. Yet they seemed right for a long time. However, even the most bullish advisor must have been struck by the wide divergence between the dividend yield on stocks (lees than 2%) and the yield on bonds (over

10%). You'd have to have very bullish expectations of capital growth in the stock to justify buying it. The yield disparity was brought into sharp focus when bond yields climbed over 10% for the first time in years.

Monetary Policy

Strangely absent in the early analyses of possible causes was any mention of monetary policy. Only a few short years before, virtually every slight market nuance was interpreted in the light of monetary policy. But the monetarists had lost favor after they erroneously predicted that "profligate" monetary policies in the early 1980s would bring back inflation.

Overly simple monetarist analysis has in fact failed to explain or forecast the economy and investment markets in recent years. However, it would be premature to dismiss a whole school of thought that has certainly helped develop intelligent economic analysis.

A look at recent monetary policy offers some clues to the causes of the market crash. It is also true that the empirical evidence provides a more satisfying explanation than the various "loss of confidence" arguments that are so popular.

Since February 1987, M2 (the most closely watched money supply measure of the Fed's) growth has been *below* the lower end of the Fed's announced growth targets. The Federal Reserve is required by law to publish its growth targets for the various monetary aggregates in advance. The Fed chairperson explains policy in a special session of Congress.

Despite its announced intention to ignore the monetary aggregates and to key off other indicators such as interest rates and economic statistics, targets are still published. Even M3, an even wider money aggregate than M2, has been growing at a rate *below* the lower target range. The Fed's lower growth target growth range for both M2 and M3 was 5.5%.

When those growth figures are adjusted for about 4% inflation we can see that there was no real growth for the seven months before the crash. That leaves precious little room for fueling economic growth. The stock market "looks ahead," anticipating the strength of the economy. Did the slow monetary growth, and its dire implications for economic growth, trigger the crash?

It is instructive to look at the economic statistics that were being released as the market began its slide in October. Housing for the first eight months of the year was down conspicuously. New home sales were lagging 9.1% behind sales for the previous year.

Retail sales figures for August and September 1987 were misleading about the strength of consumer buying. When we adjust them for the auto sales incentives, we can see that retail sales were flat for months.

The U.S. Commerce Department's Leading Economic Indicators Index posted its seventh consecutive monthly increase in August (released in late September). Although August certainly gained, a close look at the makeup of the increase shows that the whole gain was due to jumps in only two of the nine indicators: stock prices and a drop in new claims for unemployment insurance. Without these the index would have declined. By September, the index was posting its first decline.

Most analysts grant that Federal Reserve policy will play a pivotal role in how the economy and investment markets survive the crash period. Too few have examined the contribution of inept policy *before* the crash.

Program Trading

No discussion of the Crash of 1987 would be complete without examining the role played by "program trading." SEC Chairman Ruder and many others argued that program trading played a crucial role in the extent and rapidity of the crash.

Program trading encompasses a wide range of computerized trading techniques. The two factors most closely associated with Crash Monday are (1) portfolio insurance and (2) index arbitrage. We suggest you read the section on stock index futures in Chapter 15 to get a fuller understanding of the tools employed.

Portfolio insurance is a concept that has gained wide acceptance in recent years as the stock index options and futures market has grown in sophistication and liquidity. The idea is that a portfolio manager is willing to pay "premiums"—in the form of put option premiums or the cost of futures hedging to protect against dramatic falls in the value of his or her managed portfolio.

If the portfolio falls by a preset amount, the manager sells futures contracts in sufficient value to protect the portfolio. In other words, if the market continues to go down, the money made from shorting the index futures will balance out the losses of the cash stock portfolio.

Sounds simple, doesn't it? The problem is, there is no sure way to know when the stock market will continue to go down. If the trigger point on a portfolio is a 3% fall, what if the market then turns up without falling further? Then the "hedge" or insurance will prevent any gain from the subsequent appreciation until the hedge is lifted.

The concept is clear: money lost on the stock positions is made on the futures positions. Unfortunately, most managers admit that rather than just employing the index futures for "insurance," they have been speculating with these futures. However, that was not the main problem on Crash Monday.

On that day, the market fell too fast for managers to be able to sell their insurance positions. At some points in the day, the futures index was selling at a huge discount to the cash index, rendering the insurance useless.

"Index arbitragers" contributed more to the speed and extent of the fall than did portfolio insurance. An index arbitrager monitors the cash S&P index and the futures index carefully. When one or the other index gets out of line, the arbitrager makes a play. For example, if the futures index goes to premium over the cash (after figuring the carrying and transaction costs) the arbitrager will short the futures while buying an equivalent position in cash stocks. Because the two indexes must eventually come together (the futures settle at the cash price on settlement day), the arbitrager stands to make money when the indexes come back into line.

There are two ways that balance can be achieved. If the futures index falls, the arbitrager makes money on the short side. If the cash index rises to the futures index level, he or she will make money on the cash position. This concept is similar to portfolio insurance, except that this whole trade is motivated by the idea that the arbitrager can execute it with only nominal risk.

On Crash Monday, due to an imbalance of orders, the stock index futures opened before many stocks were able to open. The futures went immediately to a sharp discount. Arbitragers bought the futures index and sold an equivalent basket of stocks, thinking that the two indexes would come back into line and they could pocket the profit. Unfortunately for many arbitragers, the tremendous crash resulted in the futures index going to unprecedented discounts to cash. In other words, once the huge volume of theoretically "riskless" transactions was consummated, the futures index refused to cooperate.

The futures index continued to fall to even deeper discounts to the cash. Arbitragers were losing money on the futures index much faster than the other side of their hedge was making money. Many arbitragers attempted to recoup by buying even more futures and selling even more stock. These frantic attempts to recover accounts for some of the selling pressure seen that day.

However, the attempt to blame the collapse on computer traders, whether insurance or arbitragers, smacks of a desire more to find a scapegoat than to explain fundamental causes. Some of the very largest losses in the debacle were taken by options traders and futures arbitragers. They were caught by their own programs, much as other investors were caught by the extent of the fall.

HOW CLOSELY DOES THE 1987 CRASH MIRROR 1929?

Naturally, analysts compare the Crash of 1987 with that of 1929. In 1929 the stock market fell 12.8% on Black Tuesday, October 28, signaling the beginning of the Great Depression.

Looking first at the stock market, there were amazing similarities between the two crashes. On the days following the 1987 crash, the Dow closely mirrored the stock price action in 1929. In 1929, the market peaked on September 3, fell 15% in 31 days, rallied 8.5% over the next 6 days, then fell 35% below the September high. That occurred over 19 days, climaxed by a 2-day crash. It followed the crash with a 2-day rally of 19%.

In 1987, the market peaked on August 25. It fell 8.5% over a 36-day period. It then rallied almost 6% in 11 days. Its 17-day fall was capped by a 2-day crash of almost 30%. It finished down 36% from the August high.

Fortunately, the parallels end there. In 1929, the market fell another 27% in the next 13 days. In 1987, the market swung wildly but didn't tack on another downleg immediately.

After the 1929 collapse, the market moved strongly higher for six months until April 1930 (posting a 48% gain). That proved to be the final peak. Then it slid for two years dropping 86% in value to the bottom on July 8, 1932.

Obviously, there is no certainty of an equivalent follow-through in 1988. We are merely outlining the previous experience to provide a frame of reference. Things are far different now from conditions in 1929. And although history often repeats itself, rarely does it do so exactly.

Even more significant is the fact that on other occasions chart patterns started out the same as the 1929 experience only to yield very different episodes. The most frequently cited example is 1962, when a similar bearish pattern was followed by a sustained rally.

ECONOMIC PARALLELS

There has been much hand-wringing over the many similarities between 1929 and 1987. However, while it is important to examine similarities, it is equally important not to ignore the many disparities. A direct extrapolation of past events into the future ignores the most important feature of human progress: knowledge that each generation adds. Of course, we don't now have perfect knowledge as a result of studying history. However, 1929 and the Great Depression have been two (or one) of the most widely studied phenomena of all time. Have we learned any lessons from that experience? If so, then it would be foolish to expect a mimicking of the 1929 experience.

Many economists attribute much of the severity and length of the Great Depression to inept monetary policy. The nation's money supply peaked in early 1929, then flattened out for 12 months before turning sharply lower.

In 1987, the money supply as measured by M2 had been growing quite rapidly on a historical basis since 1980. However, beginning in early 1986 the money supply growth rate slowed significantly. By early 1987, the rate had started to flatten out.

In 1929 there was no Federal Depositors Insurance Corporation (FDIC) nor was there a Federal Savings & Loan Insurance Corporation (FSLIC) that insured depositor's balances. Today, federally chartered savings institutions carry insurance on up to $100,000 per account.

In 1929, when there was no such coverage, the monetary contraction was exacerbated as banks failed. Money supply was wiped out. Since the money supply was already being tightened, these failures resulted in a "waterfall" decline. As money became scarcer (liquidity in the system basically dried up), the economy began a decline, slow at first, that rapidly picked up pace.

Even with the slowdown since 1986, M2 has not shown actual negative growth, such as that seen by late 1929. This area will be crucial to watch. Even after Black Monday some analysts were calling for a tighter money supply, to shore up the falling dollar. The Federal Reserve is essentially caught in the position of trying to fend off a recession or worse without allowing the dollar to collapse.

On the one hand, antirecession policy would dictate an easier money policy. However, no one wants to live through another high-inflation experience such as the late 1970s. To prevent that, money policy must be sufficiently firm to prevent a wholesale collapse in the dollar. The Federal Reserve will have to walk the tightrope throughout 1988.

To monitor just how well the Fed is doing, you can follow the weekly credit market reports in the Friday *Wall Street Journal* or *Investor's Daily*. The Fed releases weekly money supply figures on Thursday. A declining growth rate in the face of dropping investment markets would have ominous implications. However, this time the Fed does have extensive experience to rely on.

Initial indications are that the Fed will not make the same mistake as was made in 1929. Federal Reserve Chairman Greenspan made it clear on the day following the crash: "The Federal Reserve, consistent with its responsibilities as the nation's central bank, affirmed today its readiness to serve as a source of liquidity to support the economic and financial system."

Currency Exchange Rates

Much debate rages over the value and costs incurred by the "floating exchange rate" system that exists today. Some analysts have argued that the uncertainty caused by the often wide daily fluctuations has negatively affected international trade. They argue that the major industrial countries should once again settle on a fixed exchange system such as prevailed before the collapse of the Bretton Woods agreement.

However, history does not support that notion. In 1929 the exchange rate between currencies was largely fixed. Some economists have argued that this artificial fixed-rate system was a chief contributor to the length and severity of the international depression. In fact, economic growth was more likely to appear in those countries that could no longer support their currencies at "official" rates. When they let their currencies fall, that correction stimulated growth.

The chief economic power at that time was Britain. The pound was backed by Britain's pledge to exchange it for gold on demand. In 1931, after years of losing gold through the fixed rate, Britain finally suspended payment at a set price. The British let the pound float. Shortly thereafter, their industrial production index slowed its decline and then actually turned upward for the first time since 1924.

Today, the U.S. dollar is still the world's major trading currency. Oil, for example, is priced and traded in U.S. dollars. And the world economy is more interdependent today than in 1929. Economic problems in the U.S. quickly permeate the whole world. The growth of export-oriented countries such as Japan, Taiwan, and Korea are the result of the vibrant U.S. market.

It will be very important to monitor the status of the dollar. Within weeks after the October Crash, the U.S. dollar was once again under pressure. It dropped to new lows against the yen. Observers speculated that Japan, Germany, and the United States had agreed to let the dollar trade at a slightly lower level than they had previously agreed in the February Louvre agreement. The Louvre agrement had guided dollar policy for most of 1987 as the dollar traded in its narrowest range in five years.

A sharply lower dollar could be counterproductive, though. Not only would it aggravate inflation domestically as import prices shot higher, but it would also aggravate our trading partners. Those trading partner nations have already threatened protectionist legislation to protect their home industries from "unfair" U.S. competition.

Even in the United States, sweeping protectionist legislation is being considered as this book is being written. One thing is sure: passage of the protectionist Smoot-Hawley Tariff Act in 1930 certainly aggravated an already worsening situation. It is difficult to believe that legislators could forget such a clear historical lesson. The passage of protectionist legislation should be viewed as a very negative development. In the 1930s countries declared economic war, raising tariffs and otherwise impeding the flow of goods and services. A repeat of that sad experience would mean a very deep recession— at best.

The Status of the Consumer

There has been much teeth-gnashing over just how well the consumer is situated in 1987. The economic expansion set a record for peacetime longevity in October 1987. The recovery was largely fueled by consumer spending. Critics had been warning virtually from the beginning, in 1982, that consumers were overextended and would be unable to continue their profligate ways.

This argument rests on two factors (1) consumer debt is now near all-time highs, and (2) the savings rate has steadily dropped throughout the recovery, to historically low levels. Combining these factors with nearly zero real income growth, many analysts have contended that only the steadily increasing net worth has supported increased spending. That net worth growth was in large part due to the booming stock market. By some estimates, the stock market from the summer of 1982 to the peak in August 1987 added $3 trillion to Americans' net worth.

The October collapse in the stock market wiped out $1 trillion, by many estimates. Given the equivalent loss of $1 trillion in foreign markets, this prop to continued spending is certainly weakened.

On the plus side has been the strong improvement in employment in all sectors of the economy. More people employed means more money for potential purchases. There are also signs that consumer conversion of much consumer debt to home equity debt to retain the tax deduction has not gotten out of hand. Consumers do not appear ready to risk their home equity in the headlong rush to consume even more.

In 1929 savings had dropped below 4%. That is somewhat above the levels seen in 1987, when the rate dropped below 3%. In 1929 only about 1% of all citizens owned stock. That number is now about 20% direct owners. Through pension plans and other programs, about 60% of the population is tied to stock today.

Although stock ownership is significantly more widespread today (remember, the wealth of the country is substantially greater today), some differences show up in the effect of that ownership on national income. For example, in 1929 stock dividends accounted for nearly 7% of all personal income. Today that figure is less than 3%.

Much has been made of the shift in industry from manufacturing to services. The argument has been made, though hardly proven, that the switch to service jobs carries with it lower pay and therefore is deleterious to the economy. The statistics certainly do not bear out that argument, but some people like to think that if an argument is repeated often enough it becomes true!

In 1929, consumer spending accounted for about 66% of total GNP. That ratio is approximately the same today. About 30% of expenditures went to services, much the same as today. On the positive side, services are generally considered less vulnerable to economic contractions. Today a far larger proportion of workers are employed in the service sector. That percentage is growing quite steadily.

The Trade Deficit

As we noted earlier, many analysts believe that the trade deficit is the major cause of the stock market crash. They consider the deteriorating trade picture as an important concern for the health of the economy. Observers from economists to congresspeople have argued that it must be a top priority of the Reagan Adminstration to pare that deficit or face steadily worsening economic consequences.

Not surprisingly, an examination of the data for 1929 does not support that conclusion. In 1929, trade actually showed a surplus! Trade was in surplus throughout the 1920s and even into the 1930s, though at lower levels.

It takes some strange logic to conclude that paring the deficit would stave off a depression. The connection between the trade deficit and a depression seems to be exactly the opposite. A trade surplus in 1929 obviously proved of no value in stemming an economic collapse. In fact, the evidence suggests that policies designed to artificially narrow the deficit may very well be counterproductive.

As we mentioned, the widely hailed protectionist legislation making the round in Congress in late 1987 holds a very real danger to the continued growth of the U.S. economy. Passage of any such legislation should be viewed as a strong negative. Retaliatory moves by our chief trading partners could create havoc quickly. If such legislation is passed, move to a defensive posture in all your investments. Emphasize liquidity.

The Budget Deficit

Following the Crash on October 19, Congressional leaders and President Reagan agreed to meet to negotiate a compromise on their disparate plans for reducing the budget deficit. Reagan even announced that he would be willing to consider selected tax increases (previously he had been adamantly opposed to any tax increase).

The Gramm-Rudman bill mandates a $23 billion cut in the budget deficit for 1988. If Congress and the President are unable to suggest voluntary cuts, the Gramm-Rudman legislation includes automatic implementation tools that would pare that amount from the budget by making equal cuts in defense and in social spending.

This debate over strengthening the resolve to cut the budget deficit comes at a strange time. Reductions of government expenditures now—at a time when the economy may already be turning to recession—could very well aggravate and worsen the downturn. Government spending stimulates the economy.

One of the most startling and worrisome trends in the current economic recovery has been the persistence of huge budget deficits throughout the expansion. Typically during times of expansion, the drain on government resources lessens as the private sector provides increased revenues from enhanced activities. The budget deficit normally shrinks and goes to a surplus. Not this time. The budget deficit actually expanded substantially in the first few years of the expansion and even in 1987, the fifth year of recovery, was still well over $100 billion.

In 1929 the federal budget had a surplus. Government spending accounted for a far smaller percentage of the total economy than it does now. In 1929 government debt was declining. You can't find a more glaring difference with recent experience! Government debt declined throughout the decade of the 1920s. It didn't rise again until well into the depths of the Depression in the 1930s, when government programs expanded rapidly.

Just as with the trade deficit, the lesson from 1929 is just the opposite of what is being widely bandied about as revealed wisdom today. Cuts in the budget and trade deficits may be the correct economic policy, but equivalent data in 1929 certainly do not support the argument that such cuts prevent economic depression!

International Debt Problems

The slowdown in economic growth around the world has hurt the trade balances of less developed countries (LDCs). These countries—including Brazil, Mexico, and Argentina—need to run substantial surpluses to pay off the huge debts they have run up with money center banks. All countries except

Mexico reported deep drops in their surpluses for 1987.

It has been a few years since these debt problems have been front-page news. However, it is still very real and very dangerous. In fact, of all the parallels with 1929, the third world debt problem appears the most ominous. In 1929, just as today, third world countries were deeply into debt, with little real hope of ever being able to pay their obligations. Finally, several South American countries simply quit paying.

The primary difference today is simply that many more independent countries face similar problems. Even though major money center banks, led by Citibank, have taken on huge loan loss reserves for their third world loans, this area could provide more unpleasant surprises. If the trend to lower surpluses by LDCs continues into 1988, expect the international debt problem to hit the front pages again.

If third world countries do quit paying, that would create major liquidity problems. A lack of liquidity could snowball into a severe depression if the Federal Reserve and the federal government.did not respond promptly. Mark this area *worrisome!*

CONCLUSION

Circumstances existing in 1929 differ significantly from those that exist now. Government "safety net" programs such as depositor's insurance, Social Security, and unemployment insurance provide a layer of protection that simply did not exist in the earlier period.

Regulatory changes have also meant that the banking and brokerage businesses are not tied so closely together. In 1929, when stock prices began to crash, many banks were caught by rapidly shrinking collateral and by the inability of many investors to repay their loans. Such pyramiding of financial resources does not exist today.

The stock market crash of October 19, 1987, was in every respect far greater than that of October 28, 1929. However, its impact on the economy as a whole is far less severe, due to fundamental changes both in the financial system and in the regulatory environment. And remember, even with the severe collapse, most long-term investors are still ahead. A good illustration of this fact is the performance of the Magellan Fund, one of the largest and most closely watched funds in the country. The fund lost over 30% during the disastrous week ending October 22. But when viewed in light of the fund's 340% gain over the past five years, the loss takes on much less significance!

The stock market crash in 1929 did not cause the Great Depression. The crash of October 1987 will not cause another depression. The Great Depression developed as a result of inept government policies. Although the intervening years hardly prove that government policy makers have become smarter, the well-studied, well-documented policies of 1929 serve as a guide of what *not* to do.

Of course, it is perfectly possible—one might almost say probable—that today's government policymakers could come up with totally new mistakes. However, if that happens the new mistakes could lead to a whole new series of events. So 1929 would not then serve as much of a guide.

In 1929 the Federal Reserve did not act promptly or strongly enough to protect the banking system. In the four years after 1929, 40% of the nation's 25,000 banks failed. This collapse resulted in a snowballing deflationary effect as business loans were called in. Businesses were forced to liquidate inventory and lay off workers in an attempt to raise cash as quickly as possible. With credit collapsing, unemployment rose.

The Federal Reserve has already demonstrated that it will be acting first and foremost to stave off recession. The Fed entered the money markets aggressively shortly after the market crash, to pump up reserves. To monitor the Fed's actions, follow the daily federal funds rate. Much of the Fed's daily market transactions are designed around targeting the Fed funds rate. If the trend in this rate turns higher, you can bet that the Fed's policy has turned tighter. If that trend persists for a long period of time, expect

1. A rise in interest rate for other instruments
2. A slowdown in economic growth as the economy is starved for capital

In recent years, the Fed has acted aggressively to prevent major bank failures. In 1984 billions of dollars were expended to rescue Continental Illinois Bank. The banking system today, unlike the bank system of 1929, is much safer than the securities industry.

Even in the securities industry, substantive differences are obvious between 1929 and 1987. The Federal Reserve Board's margin rules govern the amounts that can be borrowed to buy stock. In 1929, margin buyers could borrow up to 78% of the value of their stocks to buy more stock. In 1929 some 40% of all traders were buying on margin. Today the margin requirement is a much stiffer 50%.

As mentioned earlier, one of the more ominous parallels with 1929 concerns trade. In 1930 Congress passed the Smoot-Hawley Tariff Act, which sharply increased duties on imported goods. This legislation ignited an international trade war of retaliatory trade barriers and competitive devaluations. World trade quickly shrank to about 30% of its 1929 level.

Even after the 1987 Crash, some Congresspeople called for quick passage of a sweeping trade legislation package. Although the terms do not seem as onerous as the Smoot-Hawley Act, the idea that limiting of free trade will somehow enhance the prospects for the U.S. economy flies in the face of all the evidence. In fact, even in the normally widely divided economics profession there is near universal agreement that free trade should not be hindered.

Implications for the Economy

The stock market is one of the most reliable leading indicators of the economy. It is included in the Commerce Department's Index of Leading Economic Indicators, the government's chief economic forecasting tool. However, it is not infallible. Many economists like to joke that the stock market has predicted nine of the last five recessions!

However, it is instructive to see just how reliable it has been. In the period after World War II, we have had eight recessions. The stock market turned down an average of eight months before the beginning of each of those recessions.

The biggest danger the stock market crash presents to the economy is the effect on consumer confidence. If consumers retrench and refuse to buy, the economy will be in trouble. Remember, consumer spending accounts for 66% of the GNP. If protectionist sentiment gains ground internationally and domestic buying is cut back, a recession won't be far behind.

It is difficult to say just how much the loss of $1 trillion in net worth will affect the economy. Some economists estimate that each dollar of wealth created through stock market appreciation creates 3 to 6 cents of consumer spending. In 1987, it was estimated that the rising stock market (through April) would add about $90 billion to consumer spending. That would account for about 45% of the increase in consumption.

Using those same figures, the October massacre could contract spending by about $45 billion over the next six to nine months. That contraction could trigger a recession, because consumer spending is such a major component of the the GNP.

Obviously, the biggest variable effect of the stock crash is its effect on confidence. If consumer and business confidence is not shaken, then you should expect more of the same ups and downs for 1988. Watch these reports for clues:

- Consumer confidence is measured monthly by the Conference Board through polls. These data are reported regularly in the financial press.
- Retail sales give you a direct look at how consumers are spending.
- Capital goods expenditures by business gives you a direct insight into how business is feeling. Increasing expenditures indicate growing optimism.
- "Help wanted" advertising is a good lead indicator of employment prospects.
- Federal Reserve policy will be crucial. The best simple indicator of Fed intentions is the trend of the Fed funds rate. This rate trend is reported daily in the financial media. A downward trend indicates an easier policy.

What You Should Learn From the Debacle

When we were writing this book, we certainly did not want an experience like the 508-point crash on October 19, 1987, to definitively prove the value of our diversification approach. However, that event did occur during the writing process, and it gives an excellent illustration of how valuable diversification can be.

We have already mentioned the performance of mutual funds as a proxy for diversification. Diversified funds performed significantly better than sector funds. Bond funds actually rallied when equity funds were collapsing. Gold rallied on Crash Day.

In Chapter 19 we mentioned the broadly diversified approach adopted by Bailard, Biehl, & Kaiser, the San Mateo-based money manager. BB&K diversifies its portfolios over seven asset classes: cash and equivalents, common stocks, bonds, international equities, international bonds, real estate, and gold.

On October 19, when the Dow Jones Industrial Average dropped 22%, BB&K's portfolio fell a mere 2.3%! In line with its long-term value-oriented approach to investing BB&K had steadily cut back its allocation to the stock market from the 30% it held in September 1986, to the 13% it held on the day of the crash.

As described, the bond market literally exploded to the upside by that day's end, and subsequently moved even higher. Bailard, Biehl, & Kaiser had allocated 33% for bonds before the crash. Even though the stock market devastated many portfolios of equity money managers, this diversification helped BB&K minimize its losses.

The BB&K portfolio was hurt by the drop in U.S. stocks and international issues by a total of 3.7% on that fateful day. But their sizeable bond position posted a 1.3% gain. Precious metals added another 0.1%.

This acid test of the asset allocation approach merely confirmed what Bailard, Biehl, & Kaiser knew from the past ten years of experience. BB&K's portfolio management over that time period yielded a 12% average annual return after taxes. That compares to the S&P's average annual yield of 13.8%. Perhaps most significant is that over that time period, when the diversified portfolio was yielding returns close to that earned by the S&P, the diversified risk—as measured by volatility—was only 50% as much!

The Bailard, Biehl, & Kaiser experience was confirmed by other mutual funds that also practice a diversified approach. The Blanchard Permanent Portfolio Fund and the Paine Webber Asset Allocation funds were both in the top 20 performers when measured from the market's peak in August through the week ending October 28.

The wildly swinging investment markets make risk control an even more important concern than in more staid times. Research and experience have demonstrated the value of adopting a broadly diversified approach to your investment portfolio. Black Monday—October 19, 1987—may be the day America's investors learned that diversification is just about as good as gold!

APPENDICES

MONEY MANAGEMENT ATTITUDES QUESTIONNAIRE

MONEY MANAGEMENT ATTITUDES

FINANCIAL PLANNING and personal money management are not exact sciences. Not only must you make decisions based upon your understanding of the economy and how it affects your financial situation, but these decisions are made within a framework composed of your attitudes toward and experiences in managing your money. The following questionnaire will help identify your financial attitudes, needs, and goals. Complete the following pages quickly. Write down your immediate reactions, not your well-thought-out reasonable answers.

MONEY MANAGEMENT CONCERNS

Indicate the degree of your interest or the importance to you of each of the following: Use a scale of 1 to 5, with 5 being the most important.

_____ INFLATION—How concerned are you about having your money and asset values keep pace with inflation?

_____ TAX PROTECTION—How concerned are you about getting all of the tax relief to which you are legally entitled?

_____ SAFETY—How concerned are you about the risk of losing all or some of your money when making an investment?

_____ LIQUIDITY—How important is it that you be able to cash out your investments quickly and easily?

_____ DIVERSIFICATION—How important is it not to have "all your eggs in one basket"?

_____ PROFESSIONAL MANAGEMENT—How important is it that you be free from the day-to-day and technical decisions concerning your investments?

_____ INCOME—How important is it to be able to see or receive interest and dividends on your investments today and every day, as opposed to having them grow in value for tomorrow?

_____ GROWTH—How important is it that the value of your assets grow over time, as opposed to receiving dividends or interest today?

_____ RECESSION PROTECTION—How important is it that your assets not be exposed to the risk of loss in a recession?

_____ INCOME REPLACEMENT—How important is it that, regardless of how well you have been able to save and invest, your spouse and family be able to replace the income lost in the event of your death, or that your estate isn't substantially reduced by taxes and estate settlement costs?

RISK/REWARD OPINION

There is supposed to be a relationship between the potential for reward and the degree of risk. Oftentimes your experience, or the experience of others you know, has been such that your opinion about the potential for reward and risk differs from what the textbook may say. Your opinions are more inportant than the textbook.

Below are listed ten categories of investments Indicate the degree of risk or reward you feel is associated with each. Use 5 to indicate the highest degree of risk or reward, and 1 to indicate the lowest. Assign a different number to each item.

| | | Degree of | |
Category	Risk		Reward
Mutual Funds	_____		_____
Stocks	_____		_____
Savings Accounts	_____		_____
Corporate Bonds	_____		_____
U.S. Bonds	_____		_____
Your Own Business	_____		_____
Real Estate	_____		_____
Oil and Gas	_____		_____
Annuities	_____		_____
Gold	_____		_____

MONEY MANAGEMENT ATTITUDES AND EXPERIENCE

1. Everyone should keep the equivalent of _____ months income in a savings account for emergencies.

2. People buy life insurance for the following reasons:
   - _____ To save money.
   - _____ To replace the breadwinner's income.
   - _____ Other reasons:
   _____
   _____
   _____
   _____

3. My biggest financial worry is: _____
   _____
   _____
   _____

4. The best investment I ever made was: _____
   _____
   _____
   _____

5. The worst investment I ever made was: _____
   _____
   _____
   _____

6. Five years ago I wish I had invested in: _____
   _____
   _____
   _____

7. My attitude about my current tax situation is: _____
   _____
   _____
   _____

8. I consider myself to be (answer yes or no):
   - _____ A good money manager.
   - _____ A conservative investor.
   - _____ Aware about what tomorrow might bring.
   - _____ Prepared for tomorrow.
   - _____ A risk taker.
   - _____ Financially successful.
   - _____ Able to recover from financial losses.
   - _____ In control of my financial affairs.
   - _____ Controlled by my financial affairs.
   - _____ Happy with my accumulation of assets relative to the income I've earned during the last ten years.

FINANCIAL PLANNING GOALS

"The Whole World Steps Aside for the People Who Know Where They Are Going." What about your goals? Do you know where you are going? This is the most important step in the entire financial planning process. You must know all of your goals—hopes, dreams, commitments and obligations.

The next few pages will give you a chance to think through and write down exactly what your goals are and when you want to achieve them. Give yourself adequate time to think them through and discuss them with everyone concerned with their achievement.

Retirement

1. At what age do you plan to retire?_____

2. How much spendable monthly income do you want at retirement in today's dollars?

_____

Financial   Growth   Expectations

1. Based on the investment risk you are willing to assume, what is a reasonable rate of growth to expect for your investments?_____ %

2. Over the next 10 years, what do you expect the rate of inflation to be?_____ %

3. If you had to live off the earnings from your savings and investments without undue risk, what rate of return would you expect?_____ %

Income   Replacement

1. How much monthly income does it take for family maintenance currently? $_____
2. Does anyone in the family have any special needs that are of a continuing nature? How much monthly? $_____

3. Do you have the care of or contribute to the support of parents or others?_____ How much monthly? $_____

4. Is anyone in the family the beneficiary of any trusts or expect any inheritances?_____ If so how much and when? $_____

5. In the event of death or disablilty of the primary "breadwinner," will the surviving spouse work?_____
   If so, in what type of occupation?_____
   How much income potential? $_____monthly.
   Will there be any retraining or education needed? _____

Education

1. Do you plan to contribute to or pay the entire cost (circle one) of higher education for any family members?_____ .
   If yes, list famly members by name, number of support years, and expected amount of annual support.

NAME   YEARS $ AMOUNT

_____

_____

_____

_____

_____

_____

Short Term Goals

Goal   Dollars needed for each year (non-budget items only)

	1	2	3	4	5	BEYOND
Vacations						
Second Home						
New Autos						
Home Repairs						
Redecorating						
Recreational Vehicle						
Education Costs						
Totals						

   In order to accumulate funds for your short-term and long-term goals, are you in a position to devote any more of your current income to savings or investments? _____.
If yes, how much more on a monthly basis? _____.

Estate Preservation Goals

1. How important is it to you to preserve for the surviving spouse the value and income producing ability of your estate at death?_____

2. How important is it to you to preserve for your children or other heirs the value of your estate at the death of the surviving spouse?_____

3. How concerned are you about avoiding or reducing:
   Probate costs?_____
   Estate taxes? _____

4. Do you have any charitable interests you want to benefit from your last estate? If so, which charities?_____

   _____
   _____
   _____

APPENDIX B

PLANNING REVIEW CHECKLIST

PLANNING REVIEW CHECKLIST

	APPLICABLE YES/NO	COMPLETED YES/NO

A. INVESTMENT PLANNING
    1. Are you working within the budget?
    2. Are you on target with your savings and investment program?
    3. Is all action required to implement your investment program complete?

B. TAX PLANNING—1988 Financial Checkup
    1. Do you have an updated financial statement?
    2. Have you determined your 1988 tax projections?
       Note: TARGET DATE IS JUNE 30, 1988 or before!

C. RETIREMENT PLANNING
    Personal
    1. Have you a 1988 IRA in place now? Does your spouse?
       Note: Your 1988 IRA must be completed by April 15, 1988.
    Work-Related
    1. Are you covered under a pension or profit sharing plan?
    2. Are you covered under a tax sheltered annuity plan?
    3. Have you a deferred compensation plan?

D. ESTATE PLANNING
    1. Do you have a will? Does your spouse?
    2. Have you and your spouse established a trust?
    3. Do you need an attorney?
    4. Have you accomplished estate planning?

E. DISABILITY PLANNING
    1. Do you have disability insurance coverage?
    2. Do you have basic medical insurance coverage?
    3. Do you have major insurance coverage?

F. INSURANCE PLANNING
    1. How much insurance do you carry on your life?
    2. How much do you carry on your spouse's life?
    3. Are you satisfied with your insurance planning to date?

G. EDUCATIONAL FUNDING
    1. Have you accomplished your objectives regarding your children's college plans? Will you have adequate funds?
    2. Do you need help planning for education?

H. BANKING RELATIONSHIPS
    1. Is your line of credit established?   Personal line
                                             Business line
    2. Is it adequate?
    3. Do you need banking services information?
    4. Do you need refinancing for your home?
       Other?_____

APPENDIX C

FINANCIAL PLANNING CALENDAR

A YEAR AT A GLANCE

JANUARY

					1	2
3	4	5	6	7	8	9
10	11	12	13	14	15	16
17	18	19	20	21	22	23
24	25	26	27	28	29	30
31						

APRIL

					1	2
3	4	5	6	7	8	9
10	11	12	13	14	(15)	16
17	18	19	20	21	22	23
24	25	26	27	28	29	30

15 - File income tax return for 1988 and pay any tax due Pay quarterly taxes if you are not paying through withholding.

FEBRUARY

1	2	3	4	5	6
7	8	9	10	11	12	13
14	15	16	17	18	19	20
21	22	23	24	25	26	27
28	29					

MAY

1	2	3	4	5	6	7
8	9	10	11	12	13	14
15	16	17	18	19	20	21
22	23	24	25	26	27	28
29	30	31				

MARCH

		1	2	3	4	5
6	7	8	9	10	11	12
13	14	15	16	17	18	19
20	21	22	23	24	25	26
27	28	29	30	31		

JUNE

			1	2	3	4
5	6	7	8	9	10	11
12	13	14	(15)	16	17	18
19	20	21	22	23	24	25
26	27	28	29	30		

15 - Pay quarterly taxes if you are not paying through withholding.

1988

JULY

					1	2
3	4	5	6	7	8	9
10	11	12	13	14	15	16
17	18	19	20	21	22	23
24	25	26	27	28	29	30
31						

AUGUST

	1	2	3	4	5	6
7	8	9	10	11	12	13
14	15	16	17	18	19	20
21	22	23	24	25	26	27
28	29	30	31			

SEPTEMBER

				1	2	3
4	5	6	7	8	9	10
11	12	13	14	(15)	16	17
18	19	20	21	22	23	24
25	26	27	28	29	30	

15 - Pay quarterly taxes if you are not paying through withholding.

OCTOBER

						1
2	3	4	5	6	7	8
9	10	11	12	13	14	15
16	17	18	19	20	21	22
23	24	25	26	27	28	29
30	31					

NOVEMBER

	1	2	3	4	5	
6	7	8	9	10	11	12
13	14	15	16	17	18	19
20	21	22	23	24	25	26
27	28	29	30			

DECEMBER

				1	2	3
4	5	6	7	8	9	10
11	12	13	14	15	16	17
18	19	20	21	22	23	24
25	26	27	28	29	30	31

January 1988

To Do
• _____
• _____
• _____
• _____

1. _____

2/3. _____

4. _____

5. _____

6. _____

7. _____

8. _____

9/10. _____

11. _____

12. _____

13. _____

14. _____

15. _____

16/17. _____

18. _____

19. _____

20. _____

21. _____

22. _____

23/24. _____

25. _____

26. _____

27. _____

28. _____

29. _____

30/31. _____

February 1988

To Do
•
•
•
•

1. _____

2. _____

3. _____

4. _____

5. _____

6/7. _____

8. _____

9. _____

10. _____

11. _____

12. _____

13/14. _____

15. _____

16. _____

17. _____

18. _____

19. _____

20/21. _____

22. _____

23. _____

24. _____

25. _____

26. _____

27/28. _____

29. _____

March 1988

To Do
• _____
• _____
• _____
• _____

1. _____   16. _____

2. _____   17. _____

3. _____   18. _____

4. _____   19/20. _____

5/6. _____   21. _____

7. _____   22. _____

8. _____   23. _____

9. _____   24. _____

10. _____   25. _____

11. _____   26/27. _____

12/13. _____   28. _____

14. _____   29. _____

15. _____   30/31. _____

April 1988

To Do
•
•
•
•.

1. _____

2/3. _____

4. _____

5. _____

6. _____

7. _____

8. _____

9/10. _____

11. _____

12. _____

13. _____

14. _____

15. _____

16/17. _____

18. _____

19. _____

20. _____

21. _____

22. _____

23/24. _____

25. _____

26. _____

27. _____

28. _____

29. _____

30. _____

May 1988

To Do
•
•
•
•

1. _____

2. _____

3. _____

4. _____

5. _____

6. _____

7/8. _____

9. _____

10. _____

11. _____

12. _____

13. _____

14/15. _____

16. _____

17. _____

18. _____

19. _____

20. _____

21/22. _____

23. _____

24. _____

25. _____

26. _____

27. _____

28/29. _____

30. _____

June 1988

To Do
•
•
•
•

1.	17.
2.	18/19.
3.	20.
4/5.	21.
6.	22.
7.	23.
8.	24.
9.	25/26.
10.	27.
11/12.	28.
13.	29.
14.	30.
15.	31.
16.	

July 1988

To Do
•
•
•
•.

1. _____

2/3. _____

4. _____

5. _____

6. _____

7. _____

8. _____

9/10. _____

11. _____

12. _____

13. _____

14. _____

15. _____

16/17. _____

18. _____

19. _____

20. _____

21. _____

22. _____

23/24. _____

25. _____

26. _____

27. _____

28. _____

29. _____

30/31. _____

August 1988

	To Do
•	
•	
•	
•	

1.		17.	
2.		18.	
3.		19.	
4.		20.	
5.		21/22.	
6/7.		23.	
8.		24.	
9.		25.	
10.		26.	
11.		27/28.	
12.		29.	
13/14.		30.	
15.		31.	
16.			

September 1988

To Do
•
•
•
•

1. _____

2. _____

3/4. _____

5. _____

6. _____

7. _____

8. _____

9. _____

10/11. _____

12. _____

13. _____

14. _____

15. _____

16. _____

17/18. _____

19. _____

20. _____

21. _____

22. _____

23. _____

24/25. _____

26. _____

27. _____

28. _____

29. _____

30. _____

October 1988

To Do
•
•
•
•

1/2.	17.
3.	18.
4.	19.
5.	20.
6.	21.
7.	22/23.
8/9.	24.
10.	25.
11.	26.
12.	27.
13.	28.
14.	29/30.
15/16.	

November 1988

To Do
•
•
•
•

1. _____

2. _____

3. _____

4. _____

5/6. _____

7. _____

8. _____

9. _____

10. _____

11. _____

12/13. _____

14. _____

15. _____

16. _____

17. _____

18. _____

19/20. _____

21. _____

22. _____

23. _____

24. _____

25. _____

26/27. _____

28. _____

29. _____

30. _____

December 1988

To Do
• _____
• _____
• _____
• _____

1. _____   17/18. _____

2. _____   19. _____

3/4. _____   20. _____

5. _____   21. _____

6. _____   22. _____

7. _____   23. _____

8. _____   24/25. _____

9. _____   26. _____

10/11. _____   27. _____

12. _____   28. _____

13. _____   29. _____

14. _____   30. _____

15. _____   31. _____

16. _____

APPENDIX D

FINANCIAL PLANNING QUESTIONNAIRE

GENERAL INSTRUCTIONS

This questionnaire is designed to produce your financial plan. Include all your financial data. Round off values to the nearest dollar. You will need last year's tax data as well as your current records concerning your various checkbooks, savings accounts, loans, credit card balances, mortgage balance, etc. Your financial plan can only be as accurate as the information you provide for it.

These forms are designed to help you get a microscopic view of your financial plan by listing all of the elements that make up a major category. However, if you feel you don't need a microscopic view, just fill in the values for the major categories, leaving the descriptions blank.

For those of you who are using the microscopic approach, the majority of the forms have been laid out to enable you to cross out a major category (provided you don't have any of that category). You can then use the corresponding blanks for additional data for the category above the crossed out one. For example, let us assume that in the Net Worth-Assets section you have seven Short-Term Investments but no Notes Receivable. Cross out Notes Receivable and use two of the blanks for your additional short-term investments.

FAMILY INFORMATION

This section is self-explanatory with the exception of the education portion. Yearly costs should be the costs for one year of college stated in today's dollars. The Present Value of Funds should be the balance of any investment you have specifically made for the education of the child.

FAMILY INFORMATION

Your Name:_____   Job Title:_____
Birth Date: _____   Employer:_____
Social Security #:_____   Address: _____
Address: _____   _____

_____   Phone: _____

Spouse's Name:_____   Job Title:_____
Birth Date: _____   Employer:_____
Social Security #:_____   Address: _____
Address: _____   _____

_____   Phone: _____

CHILDREN

Name	BirthDate	SSN	Years Until College	Years In College	Yearly Costs	Present Value Funds

GRANDCHILDREN

Name	Birthdate	SSN

FAMILY TRUSTS AND PARTNERSHIPS

Name	Federal Identification Number

NET WORTH—ASSETS

Use this section of the questionnaire to record what you own. The first part of the form asks for a description of the asset, the owner code (C = Community, J = Joint, S = Spouse, Y = You), the current value of the asset, its current income, the date the asset was bought, its purchase price, and the reason that you have this asset. (G = Growth, I = Income, L = Liquidity). The second part asks for a subset of information. Don't include the cash value of your insurance here but list it under the life insurance policies section instead. This data will be used in assessing your net worth, an analysis of your investments, and establishing your gross estate. Please use an additional sheet of paper if necessary.

NET WORTH—ASSETS

	Description	Owner Code	Current Value	Current Income	Date Bought	Purchase Price	Objective
Cash							
Short-Term Investments							
Notes Receivable							
Marketable Securities							

	Description	Owner Code	Current Value	Current Income	Date Bought	Purchase Price	Objective
Real Estate							
Tax Incentive Investments							
Retirement Funds							
Other Investment Assets							
Residences							
Furnishings							
Vehicles							
Other Personal Assets							

NET WORTH—LIABILITIES

Use this section of the questionnaire to record what you owe. It is very similar to the previous section. Describe what you own, the ownership code, how much you owe, and the interest rate you are presently paying on the amount. Don't include any loans against insurance policies here. Instead, list them under life insurance policies. This information is used in assessing your net worth and your gross estate.

NET WORTH—LIABILITIES

	Description	Owner Code	Amount	Interest Rate
Consumer Credit Obligations				
Installment Loans				
Personal Loans				

	Description	Owner Code	Amount	Interest Rate
Accrued Income Taxes	_____	_____	_____	_____
	_____	_____	_____	_____
	_____	_____	_____	_____
	_____	_____	_____	_____
	_____	_____	_____	_____
	_____	_____	_____	_____
	_____	_____	_____	_____
Other Short-Term Obligations	_____	_____	_____	_____
	_____	_____	_____	_____
	_____	_____	_____	_____
	_____	_____	_____	_____
	_____	_____	_____	_____
	_____	_____	_____	_____
Loans for Investments	_____	_____	_____	_____
	_____	_____	_____	_____
	_____	_____	_____	_____
	_____	_____	_____	_____
	_____	_____	_____	_____
	_____	_____	_____	_____
	_____	_____	_____	_____
Loans for Personal Assets	_____	_____	_____	_____
	_____	_____	_____	_____
	_____	_____	_____	_____
	_____	_____	_____	_____
	_____	_____	_____	_____
	_____	_____	_____	_____
Mortgage on Residences	_____	_____	_____	_____
	_____	_____	_____	_____
	_____	_____	_____	_____
	_____	_____	_____	_____
	_____	_____	_____	_____
	_____	_____	_____	_____
	_____	_____	_____	_____
	_____	_____	_____	_____

INVESTMENTS SOLD

Use this section to record any investments you have sold this year. This information will be used to ascertain your realized capital gains or losses. Also, include any short or long term losses you can carry forward from last year as well as any capital gains distributions you may have or will receive.

INVESTMENTS SOLD

Description	Date Bought	Purchase Price	Date Sold	Sales Price

Short Term Loss Carryover _____

Other Long Term Gain _____

Long Term Loss Carryover _____

LIFE INSURANCE POLICIES

Use this section to record your current life insurance policies. List the company and policy number, the type of policy (term, group term, whole life, etc.), the face value of the policy, the cash surrender value of the policy, any loans on the policy, the owner of the policy, and the beneficiary. This information is used in assessing your net worth, an analysis of your life insurance, and your gross estate.

LIFE INSURANCE POLICIES

Company/Policy	Type of Policy	Face Value	Cash Surrender Value	Loan on Policy	Owner if Policy	Beneficiary
YOUR COVERAGE						
SPOUSE'S COVERAGE						

INCOME SOURCES

Use this section to record your current and projected expenditures. Indicate whether you or your spouse received the income. Use last year's tax return for the taxable items. Use your current records for the year-to-date, then estimate what the income will be for the rest of the year, and the following three years. This information will be used to analyze your current income/ expenditures, your current tax situation, and your income, expenditure and tax planning projections for the next three years.

INCOME SOURCES

	Description	Who	Last Year	Current Year to Date	Estimate for Rest of Year	Next Year	Second Year	Third Year
Wages								
Self-Employment Income								
Other Employment Income								
Taxable Interest Income								
Non-Taxable Interest Income								
Dividend Income								
Business Income								
Long Term Capital Gain								
Short Term Capital Gain								
Rent Income								
Partnership Income								
Other Income								

EXPENDITURES

Use this section to record your current and projected expenditures. This section is very similar to the last section on income except that it also asks for your estimate of expenses at retirement. For those items which are not taxable, you can put the entire year under the estimate for the rest of year.

EXPENDITURES

Description	Last Year	Current Year to Date	Estimate for Rest of Year	Next Year	Second Year	Third Year	Amount at Retirement

Housing

Transportation

Food

Clothing

Alimony Paid

EXPENDITURES (cont'd)

Description	Last Year	Current Year to Date	Estimate for Rest of Year	Next Year	Second Year	Third Year	Amount at Retire-ment
Medical							
Income Taxes							
Employment Taxes							
Other Taxes							
Other Basic Expenditures							
IRA Payments							
Keough Plan Payments							
Business Expenses							

EXPENDITURES (cont'd)

	Description	Last Year	Current Year to Date	Estimate for Rest of Year	Next Year	Second Year	Third Year	Amount at Retirement
Moving Expenses								
Other Adjustments								
Interest Paid								
Charitable Contributions								
Miscellaneous Deductions								
Other Discretionary Expenditures								

Indicate any casualty or theft losses you have suffered:

Indicate the number of exemptions:

Indicate your filing status for income tax purposes: _____

INSURANCE/ESTATE PLANNING

Use this section to record the different aspects needed to assess your insurance and your estate taxes. Begin by compiling an insurance policy information sheet.

INSURANCE POLICY INFORMATION SHEET

PROPERTY INSURANCE
Policy type:_____   Company _____
Agent's name:_____   Phone: (   )_____
Renewal Date:_____   Location of policy _____

LIFE INSURANCE
On Life of:_____
Policy type:_____   Company _____
Agent's name:_____   Phone: (   )_____
Renewal Date:_____   Location of policy _____

On Life of: _____
Policy type:_____   Company _____
Agent's name:_____   Phone: (   )_____
Renewal Date:_____   Location of policy _____

AUTO INSURANCE
Car #1:_____   Policy holder _____
Policy type:_____   Company _____
Agent's name:_____   Phone: (   )_____
Renewal Date:_____   Location of policy _____

Car #2:_____   Policy holder_____
Policy type:_____   Company _____
Agent's name:_____   Phone: (   )_____
Renewal Date:_____   Location of policy _____

HEALTH INSURANCE
Policy Holder #1:_____   Dependents covered: _____
Policy type:_____   Company _____
Agent's name:_____   Phone: (   )_____
Location of cards:_____   Location of policy _____

Policy Holder #2:_____   Dependents covered: _____
Policy type:_____   Company _____
Agent's name:_____   Phone: (   )_____
Location of cards:_____   Location of policy _____

INSURANCE/ESTATE PLANNING

	You	Spouse

Enter your estimate of the amount
   required, if any, for the following:

Funeral _____   _____

Administrative _____   _____

Current bills _____   _____

Emergency fund _____   _____

Mortgage (Does not need to be paid off.) _____   _____

Education _____   _____

Other expenses _____   _____

Enter estimated contributions and
   actual/estimated gifts and taxes:

Charitable Contributions from Estate _____   _____

Taxable Gifts Made after 1976 _____   _____

Gift Taxes Paid on Post 1978 Gifts _____   _____

Enter your estimate of the percent that current living expense will be reduced if you die:_____

Enter your estimate of the average tax bracket your spouse will be in:_____

Enter the amount of death benefits of retirement programs: _____

Enter the value of personal assets which your spouse could convert to cash:_____

Enter your estimate of your spouse's employment income if you should die _____

(Because of the situation, it may not be the same as the current employment income.):_____

Enter your estimate of any other income your spouse may receive:_____

LONG TERM OBJECTIVES

Use this section to record the amounts that you think you can set aside for your long-term objectives such as education, retirement, and investments. The remainder of the section asks you for input dealing with the different aspects of some of these objectives. This information will be used to complete your income and expenditure planning, and assess your financial independence, education, and retirement goals.

YEARLY EXPENDITURES FOR LONG TERM OBJECTIVES

	Description	Current Year	Next Year	Second Year	Third Year
Education					
Support of Dependents					
Retirement					
Investments (For Financial Security)					
Other					

LONG-TERM OBJECTIVES

What is your definition of financial security in terms of a desired annual income: _____

What annual earned income do you estimate you will be receiving when you achieve financial security? _____

In how many years would you like to reach financial security? _____

In how many years would you like to retire? _____

What is your estimate of the inflation rate between now and when you achieve financial security?

_____

What is your estimate of the inflation rate between now and when you retire? _____

Give your estimate of the income you will receive from the following when you retire:

_____

Social Security: _____

Company Retirement Plans: _____

Other Retirement Plans: _____

Estimate any lump sum distributions you will receive at retirement: _____

What is your estimate of the rate of return on your financial security investments? _____

What is your estimate of the rate of return on your education investments? _____

What is your estimate of the rate of return on your retirement funds? _____

Once you have achieved your goal, what is your estimate for the income producing rate of return

on your financial security investments? _____

on your retirement investments? _____

Estimate your average tax bracket when you retire: _____

FINANCIAL DOCUMENTS

Use this section to record your important documents and where they are located. This information becomes part of your financial plan and acts as the repository for this information. Please use a separate sheet of paper if necessary.

Where is your safe deposit box located? _____

Who has access to your safe deposit box? _____

In whose name is the safe deposit box registered? _____

Who has your durable power of attorney? _____

Description of Document:	Location:

FINANCIAL ADVISORS

Use this section to list your financial advisors such as your attorney, CPA, Financial Planner. Which one advisor would you consult first about a serious business problem or an important financial decision:

Advisor's title: _____
Name: _____   Address: _____
Firm: _____   _____
Phone: _____   _____

Advisor's title: _____
Name: _____   Address: _____
Firm: _____   _____
Phone: _____   _____

Advisor's title: _____
Name: _____   Address: _____
Firm: _____   _____
Phone: _____   _____

Advisor's title: _____
Name: _____   Address: _____
Firm: _____   _____
Phone: _____   _____

Advisor's title: _____
Name: _____   Address: _____
Firm: _____   _____
Phone: _____   _____

Advisor's title: _____
Name: _____   Address: _____
Firm: _____   _____
Phone: _____   _____

Advisor's title: _____
Name: _____   Address: _____
Firm: _____   _____
Phone: _____   _____

FINANCIAL PLAN ACTIONS

Use this section to put down on paper the actions you think you should take to achieve your objectives.

List specific steps you will take during the next year to implement your personal financial plan.

_____
_____
_____
_____
_____
_____
_____
_____
_____
_____
_____
_____
_____
_____
_____
_____
_____
_____
_____
_____
_____
_____
_____
_____
_____
_____
_____
_____
_____
_____
_____
_____

APPENDIX E

PERSONAL INFORMATION FILES

PERSONAL INFORMATION SHEET

Name _____

Spouse: _____

Date: _____

	Account Number	Institution
Checking accounts	_____	_____
	_____	_____
Savings Accounts	_____	_____
	_____	_____
Safety deposit box (Location of keys)	_____	_____
Brokerage account	_____	_____

Location of stock certificates_____

Location of deeds _____

Location of securities_____

Location of will _____

Name of executor(s) _____

Lawyer's name_____ Phone_____

  Address _____

Broker's name_____ Phone _____

  Address_____

Accountant's name_____ Phone _____

Address_____

Insurance agents, other brokers, etc._____

This sheet should be kept in your general file. Other members of your family should know where it is.

YOUR PERSONAL FILE SYSTEM

This system can help you to organize all your financial matters into one file box. Purchase a set of manila folders. Cut apart the various individual file information sheets and staple each to a separate manila folder. Place the required information in each file. Do not be afraid to weed out old information, policies, etc., as you replace them with new ones.

Contents and Operational Checklist
for Each File of Financial Records

Heading	Contents	Operational Checklist
General	Personal information sheet List of items in safety deposit box Letter of last instructions Copy of will (The original should be kept with an attorney or in a safety deposit box	Update personal information sheet to reflect any changes. Update safety deposit box list as new items are added or old ones eliminated.
Budgeting	List of goals Income statement Forecasts of income and expenses Forecasts for short-term and long-term goals	Review budget planning sheets. Revise goals, if necessary.
Housing	Purchase contract and receipt (deed in safety deposit box) Mortgage papers Title insurance policy Home improvement receipts (including landscaping expenses) Property tax receipts Termite inspection and policy Copy of lease or rental agreement	Keep records of all permanent home improvements so that you can establish an accurate cost basis if you ever sell your home.
Property Insurance	Details of property insurance coverage (Insurance policies should be kept *away* from the house in a safety deposit box. Personal property inventory (copy in safety deposit box) Pictures of highly valued items (negatives in safety deposit box)	Change insurance limits on policy annually to reflect changes in personal property holdings and/or changes in replacement costs of all structures. Update personal property inventory once a year: add new items; revalue old items; eliminate items sold or lost; take more pictures if necessary. Shop for rates. Get a minimum of three quotes before each renewal date.

Heading	Contents	Operational Checklist
Auto Insurance	Details of auto insurance coverage held (insurance policies in safety deposit box) Record of traffic violations and accidents Auto registration receipts (ownership certificates in safety deposit box.)	Update fact sheet annually by adding new cars, amending coverages, and increasing drivers' ages. Update traffic violation and accident records. Note which violations occurred over three years ago and stop including them in insurance applications. Shop for rates. Get a minimum of three rate quotes before each renewal date.
Health Insurance	Insurance policies or details of present health coverage, including employee plans Current medical history for each family member List of drugs to which each family member is allergic	Update health insurance fact sheet to reflect changes in limits, coverage, and so on. Update medical histories to reflect new ailments, diseases, and immunizations received.
Life Insurance	Details of insurance policies owned, including employee group plans (insurance policies in safety deposit box)	Recompute insurance needs every five years—sooner if new financial assets are acquired, or if family income or expenses change significantly. Update life insurance fact sheet to reflect changes in needs and coverage increases in employee policies. Shop for at least three rate quotes before each change in policy.
Investments— General	Goal planning sheet Annual balance sheets List of bank accounts	Replan your goals. Plot your progress using annual balance sheet.
Investments— Stock and Bonds	Records of purchase and sale (All stock certificates and bonds should be kept either with broker or in safety deposit box) Records of stock dividends and bond interest List of stock certificate numbers and dates of issue (if you keep certificates in safety deposit box rather than with broker) Transaction slips and monthly statement (in annual envelopes)	Update records to reflect purchases and sales evidenced by transaction slips. Add new stock numbers and dates of issue to list (if certificates are sent to you). Place each year's transaction and monthly statements in an envelope.

Heading	Contents	Operational Checklist
Investments—Mutual Funds	Records of purchase and sale of mutual funds (Keep mutual fund shares with broker, with the mutual fund transfer agent, or in safety deposit box.)	Use transaction slips and statements to update records of purchases and sales. Place each year's transaction slips and monthly statements in an envelope.
Tax	Purchase receipts, interest payment records, charitable gift confirmations, medical expense records, etc. Tax forms, schedules, and supporting data for past ten years Quarterly estimated tax forms W-2 forms, 1099 forms, and so on All cancelled checks for last seven years	File all receipts required to substantiate deductions. After your annual tax form is filed, place *all* receipts and other substantiating records in an envelope and file either here or in extra storage boxes.
Guarantees & Warranties	All warranties relating to appliances, tires, carpets, etc. Receipts Repair instructions	Add items to file as soon as purchased. Remove once per year all that have expired.
Employment Information	Employment contract, if any Employee handbook Fringe benefits information	Update file as necessary.
Personal Résumé	Details of previous education: years, major degree(s), major professors and advisors with addresses Employment record: job titles, dates, responsibilities, supervisors' names and addresses Residence record: dates and addresses	When you switch jobs, put information from employment file in here. Before you leave a school, update file with addresses you may need.
Credit Records	Papers showing resolution of prior debts Credit card number, names, and addresses	Update file as necessary.

Date_____

BALANCE SHEET

	Assets	Liabilities

MONETARY ASSETS _____
1. Cash
    On Hand _____
    Checking Account _____
    Savings Account _____
    TOTAL CASH _____

2. Money Loaned to others
    (repayment expected) _____

3. Investments
    Savings bonds _____
    Stocks and bonds _____
    Mutual Funds _____
    Cash Value of life
    insurance _____
    Cash value of
    annuities _____
    TOTAL INVESTMENTS _____

4. TOTAL MONETARY _____

FIXED ASSETS

5. Home and property _____

6. Other real estate
    investments _____

7. Automobiles _____

8. Ownership interests in
    small businesses _____

9. Personal Property _____

10. TOTAL FIXED ASSETS _____

11. TOTAL ASSETS OF _____

12. Unpaid Bills _____
    Taxes _____
    Insurance Premiums _____
    Rent _____
    Utilities _____
    Charge Accounts _____
    Other _____
    TOTAL UNPAID BILLS _____

13. Installment Loans (balance due)
    Automobile _____
    Other_____ _____

    TOTAL _____

14. Installment Loans (balance due)
    Bank _____
    Educational _____
    Other _____
    Accrued capital gain _____
    tax liability _____

    TOTAL _____

15. Mortgage loans (balance due)
    Home _____
    Other_____ _____

    TOTAL _____

16. TOTAL LIABILITIES _____

17. Net Worth of Family _____

For the Year Beginning January 1,_____ and ending December 31,____.

INCOME STATEMENT

1. Income
   - Wages or salary _____
     - Husband _____
     - Wife _____
   - Dividends and interest _____
   - Capital gains and losses (e.g.,sale of stock) _____
   - Rents, annuities, pensions, and such _____
   - Other _____
   - TOTAL INCOME _____
2. Taxes
   - Personal income taxes _____
   - Social Security and disability taxes _____
   - TOTAL TAXES _____
3. Amount remaining for living expenses
   and investments _____

4. Living expenses	Fixed	Variable
Housing		
Utilties	_____	_____
Repairs	_____	_____
Insurance	_____	_____
Taxes	_____	_____
Rent or mortgage payments	_____	_____
Other _____	_____	_____
Food	_____	_____
Clothing (including laundry, dry cleaning, repairs and personal effects)	_____	_____
Transportation		
Gas	_____	_____
Repairs	_____	_____
Licenses	_____	_____
Insurance	_____	_____
Auto payment or purchase	_____	_____
Recreation, entertainment and vacations	_____	_____
Medical,		
Doctor	_____	_____
Dentist	_____	_____
Medicines	_____	_____
Insurance	_____	_____
Personal	_____	_____
Life Insurance	_____	_____
Outlays for fixed assets	_____	_____
Other expenses_____	_____	_____
Subtotal		

TOTAL ANNUAL LIVING EXPENSES _____
5. Amount remaining for savings and investment _____
6. TOTAL OF 2, 4, and 5 _____

INDEX

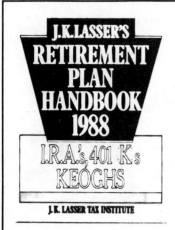

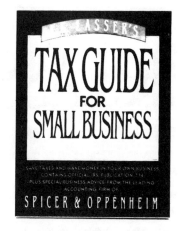
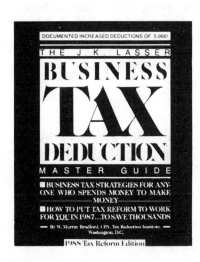

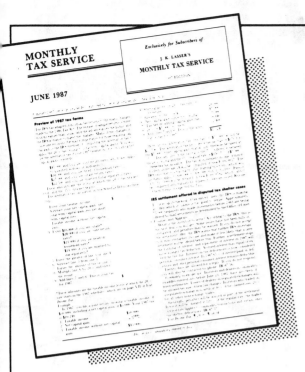

START SAVING ON NEXT YEAR'S TAXES... THIS YEAR

J.K. LASSER'S MONTHLY TAX SERVICE FOR 1987—88

STAY AHEAD OF THE CHANGING TAX LAWS!

Tax law changes require you to be alert to unprecedented opportunities to retain your money and lower your taxes...and to avoid tax traps you may be unaware of.

$24 COULD SAVE YOU $100!

At last there's a practical and economical way to keep on top of all these constantly-arising savings opportunities—for just $2 a month! It's J.K. Lasser's Monthly Tax Service, especially for users of YOUR INCOME TAX.

In brief newsletter form you get the essential facts culled from thousands of pages of tax data by the Lasser Institute Staff: a continuous flow of new tax-saving ideas and developments from IRS rulings, court decisions, and Congressional action —each and every month!

You also get a Monthly Question Box answering important problems raised by readers. So a few minutes' reading every month is all you need to be certain you don't miss a single chance to save on taxes!

Using a consultant for this same up-to-the-minute information could cost hundreds of dollars...maybe even more than you'd save. But with the special Monthly Tax Service, $24 (for 12 issues) is all you invest—and even that can be tax-deductible!

With the Monthly Tax Service, you can start saving immediately...money in your pocket you might normally have to wait a year to get back from the IRS. So start profiting now: just use the handy reply card located in the front of this book, or the coupon below. Satisfaction guaranteed or your money back!

67-60061 $24.00

MAIL TO:

J.K. LASSER TAX INSTITUTE

c/o Simon & Schuster
200 Old Tappan Road
Old Tappan, New Jersey 07675

☐ **YES**

☐ Enclosed is my check for $24.00 or charge my

☐ Master Card

☐ Visa

START MY SUBSCRIPTION TO J.K. LASSER'S MONTHLY TAX SERVICE 67-60061

Acct. # _____ Exp. Date ___ / ___ / ___

Signature _____

Name _____

Address _____

City _____ State _____ Zip _____